BASICs
for DOS

BASICs for DOS

Gary Cornell, Ph.D.

Windcrest®/McGraw-Hill

FIRST EDITION
FIRST PRINTING

© 1992 by **Windcrest Books**, an imprint of TAB Books.
TAB Books is a division of McGraw-Hill, Inc.
The name "Windcrest" is a registered trademark of TAB Books.

Library of Congress Cataloging-in-Publication Data

Cornell, Gary.
    Basics for DOS / by Gary Cornell.
       p.   cm.
    Includes index.
    ISBN 0-8306-2200-4   ISBN 0-8306-2199-7 (pbk.)
    1. BASIC (Computer program language) 2. QBasic (Computer program
language) I. Title.
QA76.73.B3C678   1991
005.26′2—dc20   91-30567
                                                                    CIP

TAB Books offers software for sale. For information and a catalog, please contact
TAB Software Department, Blue Ridge Summit, PA 17294-0850.

Acquisitions Editor: Brad Schepp
Book Editor: John C. Baker
Director of Production: Katherine G. Brown
Book Design: Jaclyn J. Boone
Cover: Sandra Blair Design and Brent Blair Photography, Harrisburg, PA   WT1

Contents

Acknowledgments

First off, I have to thank those people at Microsoft (whose names I unfortunately don't know) who created QuickBASIC 4.5. It's a great language. The people at Microsoft whose names I do know and whose help was vital to this book are Greg Lobdell, Lynn MacIntyre, and Kristy Gersich. Finally, I'd like to thank all those dedicated people at the TAB division of McGraw-Hill; without their dedication and patience this book would never have been possible.

Introduction

This book is a hands-on tutorial for BASIC on IBM PCs and compatibles. I place particular emphasis on QBasic, the version of BASIC included in DOS 5.0. This new version of BASIC is more powerful, faster, and generally much easier to program. BASIC still is the most popular language for programming. Besides making it more likely that BASIC will stay the most popular language, the advanced features in QBasic make almost any programming job easier. Nonetheless, I've tried not to slight users of the older versions of BASIC.

I hope this book can take a beginner to mastery and yet still be very useful to you if you already are experienced at programming in BASIC and want to move on to QBasic. I've tried hard to stress those features of QBasic that make it one of the best examples of a modern structured programming language: functional procedures, subprocedures, and user-defined types.

One way I've tried to keep your interest is to include many topics that usually are not covered in books at this level:

- An extensive treatment of recursion, including an introduction to fractals.
- Multiple methods of sorting and searching, including an introduction to binary trees.
- A treatment of elementary cryptography—keeping your files secret.

There also are over 150 programs. (Some of them are quite long. If you decide that you'd prefer not to enter them by hand, all of the programs are available on a convenient disk. See the back of the book for the coupon.)

Obviously, I'd like to hear from you, especially if you have any suggestions for improvements or corrections. You can reach me if you have a BIX account; my BIX account name is *gcornell*. You also can write to me at the address given on the order form for the convenience disk. I don't guarantee I'll respond, but I certainly will try.

Writing any book, especially one on microcomputers, is made easier by the tools those same microcomputers make possible. In my case, while programming in QuickBASIC, I made extensive use of two tools. The first, Inset by Inset Systems, is responsible for the many screen dumps in this book. The second, PC Tools Deluxe by Central Point Software, was both a useful add-on for manipulating files and an efficient way of keeping notes. The actual text of this book was done using WordPerfect.

1
CHAPTER

Getting started

This chapter is introductory. Most of it shows you how to use the integrated programming environment of QBasic. You'll see how to use the menus and the full-screen editor. There is not nearly as much to say about the more limited environment of the older interpreted BASIC that runs under MS-DOS or PC-DOS (GW-BASIC for clones, BASIC or BASICA for IBM PCs), so the one section at the end of this chapter tells you what you need to know.

I'm assuming that you are familiar enough with DOS to format and copy disks or to copy files. If you're new to DOS, then you'll need to learn how to do this before going on. (Some more advanced features of DOS are covered in chapter 16.)

First remarks

QBasic is included in the DOS 5.0 software package. It also is available in certain textbooks. The automated installation procedure for DOS 5.0 puts the program, QBASIC.EXE, in the \DOS subdirectory on your hard disk. For IBM PC compatibles, earlier versions of DOS come with a BASIC interpreter called GW-BASIC (GWBASIC.EXE). IBM PC users usually have three versions of BASIC. The most limited version, called cassette BASIC (CBASIC), is built into the ROM (read-only memory) of the PC. It might be a bit hard to believe, but the original IBM PC (from 1981) could be bought with only 16K of RAM (random access memory) and no disk drives. Lacking disk drives, they used ordinary cassettes as their storage medium.

Saving and loading a program to and from a cassette was a slow and error prone procedure, so IBM decided to build in a rudimentary version of BASIC. The second version of IBM BASIC was designed for machines that had a disk drive but had very limited memory—less than 64K. Today, the two earlier versions are pretty much irrelevant.

The final version, BASICA (A for advanced), is essentially equivalent to GW-BASIC. In this book, I'm assuming that you're using QBasic or one of the many equivalent forms of GW-BASIC. When I want to describe some feature common to all these BASICs, I will use the term *DOS BASIC*. I also will often use the term *GW-BASIC* as shorthand to include both GW-BASIC and BASICA.

QBasic, like many modern programs, can be used with a mouse. You can use the Microsoft mouse or a compatible mouse with QBasic for manipulating the menus and editing. (Mice are nice but, after a while, I suspect that you, like most experienced programmers, usually will end up preferring the various keyboard shortcuts of QBasic. See appendix C for a complete list of these shortcuts.) GW-BASIC can be programmed to recognize a mouse; however, in general, GW-BASIC neither knows nor cares if you have one attached.

If you want to use any of the graphics features of DOS BASIC, then you obviously must have a graphics adapter. QBasic can work with almost any kind of graphic card, from the Color Graphics adaptor (CGA) found on the earliest versions of the IBM PC to the VGA found on the PS2 series. QBasic also can work with the Hercules graphic card—more on how to do this later. Later versions of GW-BASIC (usually those numbered 3.2 or greater) can work with VGA cards as well.

In DOS 5.0, QBasic comes with online documentation and with a short description in the DOS 5.0 manual. On many machines, GW-BASIC came with a thick manual that describes the individual commands in detail. In neither case are you given much help on learning how to write programs. I hope this book can fill in this gap. I'll give you a fair warning, however, that I feel strongly that QBasic is a much better language for learning how to program, so I will spend much more time on it.

What exactly is DOS Basic?

A computer's native language, which usually is called *machine language*, is a seemingly endless series of 0s and 1s. Today, almost nobody has to know which of these sequences do what. This is because, early in the history of computing, people realized that machines could do some of the routine work. These people developed programs called *assemblers* that, at the very least, allowed you to use mnemonics for the basic operations: instead of saying 0001001, you could write ADD. Assembly language provides you with unsurpassed control over your machine, but at a price. Each computer has a different assembly language and all of them are cumbersome.

In the mid-1950s, the computer world recognized that it had to have computer languages other than the languages designed for specific machines. As long as a program for one type of machine was useless on another, progress was slow. Programs were less useful and programmers less versatile. This is not to say that programmers can escape assembly language completely. When a program needs a portion speeded up, rewriting that portion in assembly language is often the best way.

The first widespread solution to this problem was a scientific language, called FORTRAN (FORmula TRANslation). Programs written in FORTRAN could be run on any computer that had a special program, called a FORTRAN compiler, written for it. The compiler translated a FORTRAN program into the appropriate machine language instructions for that machine. FORTRAN had many features that were useful for scientific applications. It still is used widely on the CRAY supercomputers and for scientific applications in general. FORTRAN, however, was always unpleasant for beginners to learn, so, in 1964 at Dartmouth college, an offshoot of FORTRAN, called BASIC, was designed by John Kemeny and Thomas Kurtz. (BASIC supposedly stands for Beginner's All Purpose Symbolic Instruction Code, but the acronym might have come first.) BASIC now is the most widely known of all computer languages and among the most versatile. Almost all microcomputers come with a version of BASIC.

You need to understand the difference between compilers and interpreters—like the ones for DOS BASIC. First, they differ in how they translate, but not in what they translate. Both start with a series of instructions, usually called the source code, that make up your program. A BASIC interpreter—like the one supplied with most machines—translates the instructions in your source code one line at a time. Next, it processes the translation and then goes back for the next instruction until it's finished with your program.

A compiler, however, translates the whole program into machine language at once. With only a little extra work, the result, usually called object code, can be used independently and repeatedly. (Object code has to be linked with certain support routines to give an executable file. Linking usually is done by a separate program.)

Compilers have two main advantages over interpreters. Both advantages will give you programs that will run faster. The first is that you can save the translation. This way, if you need the program again, you don't have to have the machine retranslate it. In particular, you don't need to have a BASIC interpreter or compiler around any more. The linked object code will stand alone.

The second advantage deals with instructions that are used many times. An interpreter must retranslate the instruction each time it is encountered; a compiler translates it just once. If an instruction is repeated a few hundred times, then the time saved is considerable.

You might be wondering why people use interpreters at all. The main advantage is the immediacy that is possible with an interpreter. Type in a command and the computer processes it. Make a mistake and it's easy to change. With a compiler, on the other hand, if you make the slightest change, you have to do the whole translation again. Because the translation process can take a considerable amount of time, even for the simplest program, a simple typo might mean you wasted five minutes.

This problem occurs because a compiler usually gives you results that are impossible to relate back to the original program. Two different programs can have the same compiled version. Even an expert programmer would be hard pressed to translate compiled code back into your source code.

Microsoft changed all this with QuickBASIC 4.0. QuickBASIC 4.0 might be called an *interpiler*. Think of an interpiler as a combination compiler and interpreter. As you write your program, the QuickBASIC interpiler translates your program into an intermediate form. This intermediate form is called *threaded p-code*, but exactly what this code is a bit difficult to explain. The important point is that there's still a correspondence between the p-code and your original program. The compiler can go back and forth easily between the two forms, so you lose none of the immediacy possible with interpreters.

Also, once the program has been transformed into p-code, which happens as you enter each line, you can run the program much as you would with traditional interpreters, but the speed is close to that of a traditional compiler. Because you've lost little of the immediacy, you still can stop the program, make changes, and continue without having to recompile the program. Finally, once you're completely satisfied with the program, you can finish the process. Compile the program in the traditional way to make the fastest possible product.

QBasic is a stripped down version of QuickBASIC. It can't compile programs, lacks some of the sophisticated debugging features of QuickBASIC, and isn't designed for large programs. If you get serious about programming, plan to buy QuickBASIC. (For windows programming, there's a cousin of QuickBASIC called Visual BASIC.)

Microsoft made the GW-BASIC interpreter supplied with your machine obsolete for another reason: the company enhanced BASIC. QuickBASIC 4.0 (and QBasic) contained many new commands and improved versions of old commands.

Another related, and probably the more important, feature QBasic inherited from QuickBASIC is that you now can write programs in a more modern structured way. Structured programming is difficult to define precisely, but the problems it hopes to correct are real. As programs grow longer, the possibility for mistakes grows even faster. One of the complaints that professional programmers had about BASIC is that it encouraged bad programming habits.

Over the years, computer scientists have discovered ways to make large programming projects less painful, both in time and money. The key idea is that your program should be organized like the households of the very rich. The very rich don't often do housekeeping, run errands, or take care of similar chores. Instead, they have various subordinates who take care of these details. Programs are best written with the same type of organization. A powerful and flexible program should be made up of a few controlling statements together with many subordinate subprograms, which do the nitty-gritty work.

The problem with traditional BASICs (for example, GW-BASIC and BASICA) is that they lack the commands and features that make this structuring possible. One of the things I want to do in this book is to stress these new features of QBasic.

There are a number of advantages to using QBasic rather than a conventional BASIC interpreter. QBasic has mouse support, long integers, constants, and user-defined records (makes random access file programming easier). It allows structured programming through constructs, like SELECT CASE, the block IF-THEN, DO Statements, true subprograms, and multiple line functions. QBasic supports recursion. It has online help and a true windowing environment, including a smart full-screen editor. It also is faster and allows longer programs. It doesn't need line numbers and almost any program written in GW-BASIC will run in QBASIC.

Starting up QBasic

If you are using the DOS-Shell supplied with DOS 5.0, then you're opening screen will resemble the screen shown in Fig. 1-1. You now can double click on

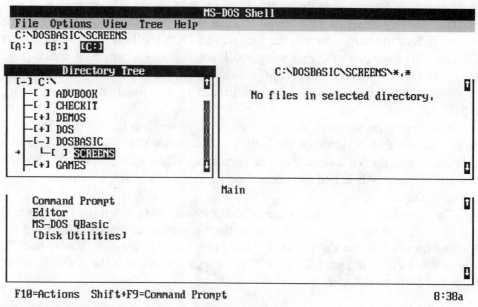

1-1 DOS Shell for QBasic.

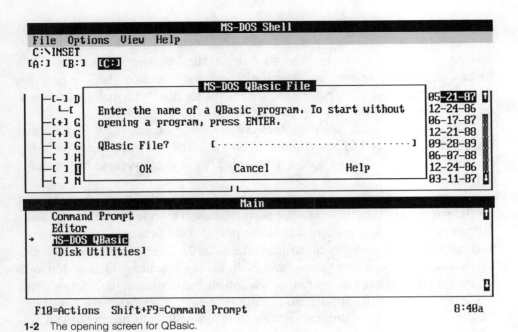

the line for QBasic to start it up. You'll see a screen that looks like Fig. 1-2. Hit the enter key to go into QBasic's opening screen.

You also can use the run option on the File menu in the DOS shell or start QBasic from the DOS prompt by entering QBASIC. You might want to make sure that your path command includes the location for QBasic. If you have a mono-chrome monitor attached to a graphics card, you should enter QBasic/B. (See appendix B or the help screen in the QBasic MS-DOS shell for other ways to start QBasic.) In either case, the first thing you'll see includes a copyright notice (Fig. 1-3). The QBasic survival guide (Fig. 1-4) mentioned here is a one-page summary of what to do. Hitting Esc will take you directly to the QBasic main screen (Fig. 1-5).

Notice how the screen is divided into one large window (called the View window) and one thin window on the bottom. The cursor (the blinking underscore character) is in the View window. The cursor marks the active window. The bottom (thin) window is called the Immediate window. You'll learn more about it in the next chapter.

To get started, try the following: simultaneously hold down the Ctrl key and the F10 function key (Ctrl−F10). Notice the View window has expanded and the Immediate window has disappeared. Now press Ctrl−F10 again. You're back to where you were at the start. Ctrl−F10 is a toggle. It switches the active window back and forth to full size.

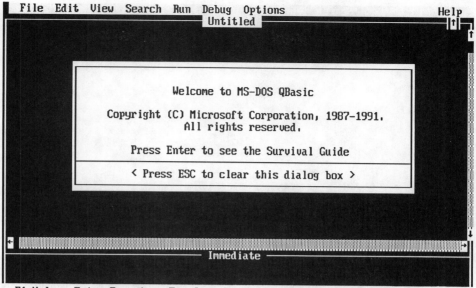

1-3 The copyright screen.

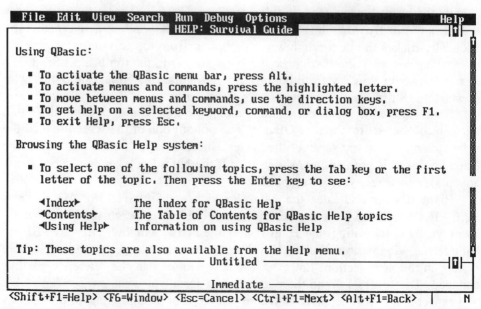

1-4 The survival guide.

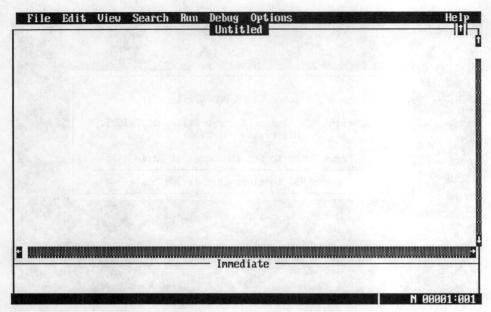

1-5 The QBasic main screen.

To change the active window, use F6. Try it now. Notice the cursor is now in the Immediate window, which is now the active window. Hit Ctrl−F10 again to expand the Immediate window to full size. Press Ctrl−F10 again to bring it back to normal. Finally, use Shift−F6 to make the View window active again. F6 cyclically makes the next window active, going from top to bottom. (Once the cursor reaches the bottom window, it wraps around to the top again.) Shift−F6 moves the active window from bottom to top to bottom. F6 makes the next window active; Shift−F6 makes the previous one active.

Next, notice the menu bar running along the top. The options on the menu bar control the environment of QBasic. The bottom line of the screen (called the *reference bar*) tells you some of the current shortcut keys. It also tells you if the Caps Lock key is pressed (a *C* shows up), if the Num Lock key is pressed (an *N* appears), and where you are in the file.

Right now, it indicates that you should press Shift−F1 for Help. Press Shift−F1. You'll see a screen like Fig. 1-6. Notice that the cursor is now in the Help window, indicating that Help is now the active window. Hit Ctrl−F10 to enlarge the window to full size. You'll see a lot more about the integrated help system in the next section; however, for now, notice that the reference bar has changed. The controls found there are context sensitive: what you see (and what you expect to control) depends on where you are. For example, one of the options now is <Esc = Cancel>. This means that pressing the Esc key closes the Help window. Press Esc to close this window. When you're working with QBasic, the Esc key will almost always bail you out of a situation. Press it a few times and you usually will end up back in the main screen with the ability to work with the options available on the menu bar.

More on Help

Go back and press Shift—F1 and expand the screen with Ctrl—F10. Now that the Help window is the active window, you can scroll through the information in it either with the arrow keys or with PgUp and PgDn.

The most important thing to know when using QBasic's online help is what a *hyperlink* is. These are words or phrases that are usually surrounded by highlighted or green (on a color monitor) angle brackets (< >). Think of these as gateways to new information. There are three hyperlinks in this initial Help on Help screen:

- Contents is the table of contents for the help files.
- Index lists all QBasic keywords. As you become more familiar with QBasic, you can use these keywords to find more information about specific commands. Although these are not surrounded by angle brackets, they are hyperlinks also.
- Back lets you move back up through the previous 20 screens.

When the cursor is within a hyperlink, pressing Enter sends you to the information contained at that link. You can move forward to the next hyperlink with the Tab key or back with Shift—Tab. You also could press the letter of the first word in the hyperlink. This quickly moves to the next hyperlink with that letter as its first character. (Pressing Shift plus a character moves the cursor to the previous hyperlink with that leading character.) For example, if you're in the screen indicated in Fig. 1-6, then pressing *I* moves the cursor to the hyperlink for the index. Once you're at a hyperlink, press F1, hit Enter, or click the right mouse button to access that information. (Alt—F1 moves to the previous help screen.) You also can print out any of the help screens (see the next section, "The main menu bar").

Although the information contained in it won't be terribly useful at this point, let's follow the Index hyperlink. Hit *I* or move via the Tab key and then hit F1. Enlarged to full size, the index looks like Fig. 1-7.

As I mentioned earlier, each command is also a hyperlink, so this Help screen is the gateway to information about all the commands in QBasic. Once you hyperlink to the information about a command, then you can get both details and examples about that command. The usefulness of this information can't be stressed enough. It makes the old-fashioned, thick reference manual obsolete.

To move within the index, you can use PgUp and PgDn or a shortcut: press a letter and the cursor moves to a command that begins with that letter (like with any other hyperlink). There is actually another kind of help: *environment help*. This feature shows up when you ask for help about dialog boxes, menus, and various errors.

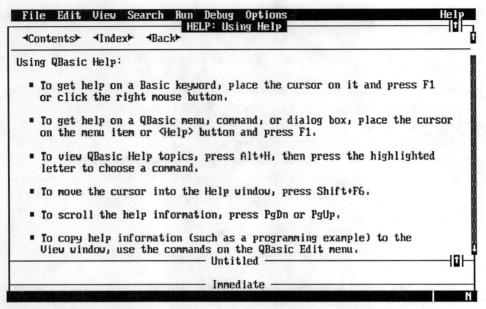

1-6 The initial help screen.

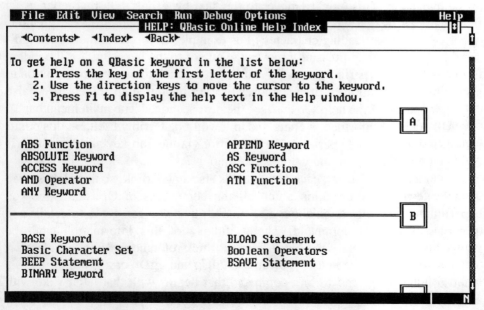

1-7 The index on the Help menu.

Here's a summary of the keys used to manipulate the help files:

Shift–F1	Gives Help on Using Help
Ctrl–F1	Goes to help on the next topic.
Shift–Ctrl–F1	Goes to the previous topic.
Alt–F1	Traces back through 20 previous hyperlinks.
Tab	Moves to the next hyperlink.
Shift–Tab	Moves to the previous hyperlink.
↑	Moves the cursor up one line, if possible.
↓	Moves the cursor down one line, if possible.
PgUp	Moves one screen up, if possible.
PgDn	Moves one screen down, if possible.
Any character	Moves to next hyperlink that begins with that character.
Shift–any character	Moves to previous hyperlink with that as its leading character.
Esc	Closes the help window.

If the Help window is active, then you also can use the Search menu to find a piece of information in it. (See the last section of this chapter, "What to do in GW-BASIC," for more on the features of the editor.)

Finally, as you become more familiar with QBasic, you'll want to study the help file on syntax conventions, which is a hyperlink available via the Contents screen. This file describes the conventions and abbreviations used by the help files when explaining commands.

The main menu bar

In this section, you'll see some of the power unleashed from the main menu bar. Press the Alt key for a moment. Notice that a bar in reverse video covers the File option and that one character on each entry in the menu bar is now highlighted. To open a menu, move that bar around with the arrow keys and hit Enter or press the highlighted letter. As a shortcut, you simultaneously can press the Alt key and the highlighted letter. For example, press Alt–F for the file menu, Alt–E for the Edit menu, etc. If a menu is open, then the left and right arrow keys close that menu and open the one to the right or left, respectively.

The File menu controls the saving, loading, and printing of files. It also is how you leave QBasic (X is the shortcut). Press Alt to make the menu bar active. Notice the File option is highlighted. Before hitting the Enter key to pull the File menu down, hit F1, the *Help on* key. Notice that a Help window opens with information about the menu bar (Fig. 1-8).

Although this particular screen isn't terribly informative, it is a good example of context sensitive help. Hit Enter or Esc to close this screen.

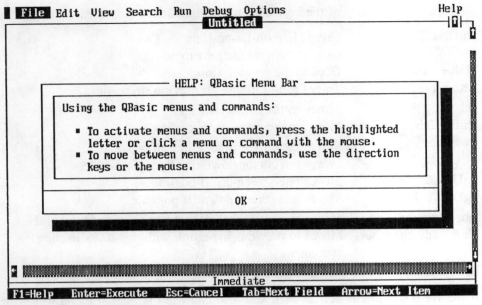

1-8 The help screen for the menu bar.

In general, when you press F1, QBasic will try to provide help about the choice, option, or symbol that the cursor is on.

When you open the file menu, you'll see the menu shown in Fig. 1-9 (the shortcut is Alt−F).

You choose options from a menu in one of three ways. The first is to move the highlighted bar around with the arrow keys. Once you're satisfied that you're at the place that you want to be, hitting Enter accepts that choice. Notice that each of the options in a menu has a highlighted letter. Pressing this letter is a shortcut to activate the option. If three dots follow an option (like the one for Print), this means that, if you choose this option (in our case by pressing a P), then you'll have a dialog box to deal with. You also can use the mouse and click on the left mouse button. Some menu choices have yet another way for you to select them—a super shortcut key that takes you directly from the View or Immediate window. For example, you already saw that Help on Help is available while in the View window through Shift−F1.

If you have a printer, it's easy to get a printed version of any help screen. To do this, use Print on the file menu. Hit Alt−F to open this menu and P for the Print option. The dialog box shown in Fig. 1-10 will pop up. Now, all you have to do is make sure that the help screen that you are interested in is the active window. Then, assuming your printer is online, hit Enter to get a hard copy. This only works if the bullet (•) is in the option marked active window. The arrow key moves the bullet. You also can select a portion of the information and print that

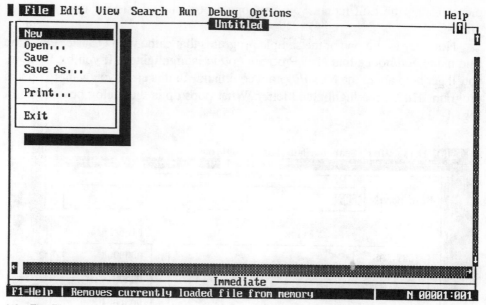

1-9 The File menu.

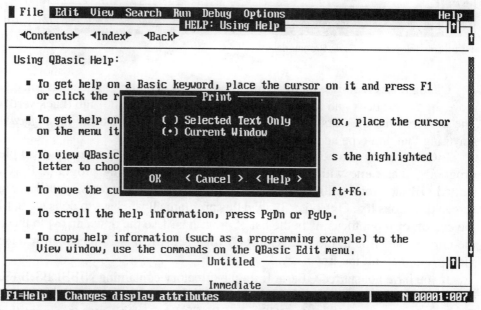

1-10 The print dialog box.

piece. Using the Edit menu, you can copy a portion and paste it into your programs.

Now, try to run one of the sample programs that came with QBasic. Open the File menu and notice that New Program option is highlighted. If you hit F1 now, you'll get help about the New Program command. In this case, you want to open a program. Hit O, the highlighted letter. What pops up is the dialog box shown in Fig. 1-11.

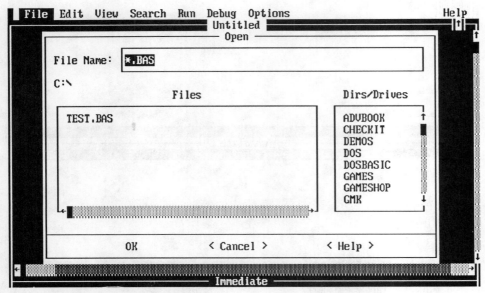

1-11 The dialog box for **Open Program**.

Dialog boxes require a bit of getting used to, but, for now, notice that you can move the cursor back and forth with the Tab (forward) or Shift−Tab (backward). The position that the cursor is at within a dialog box is called the *input focus*. Anything that you type appears there.

I want to show you how to open, or load, NIBBLES.BAS, one of the sample programs, that came with QBasic. This is a mildly amusing program. If you started QBasic from a directory containing the sample programs, you'll see a screen that looks like Fig. 1-12. To load this program all you have to do is tab until the cursor, or input focus, is in the list of programs. Use the down arrow to move the cursor until it is at the line listing NIBBLES.BAS (it will appear in reverse video) and then hit the Enter key.

If you have not started QBasic from the directory containing NIBBLES.BAS, make sure the cursor is in the box marked *File name* and type the full path name for this program (usually C: \ DOS \ NIBBLES.BAS). Hit Enter to accept this choice. The drive will whirl as QBasic loads the program.

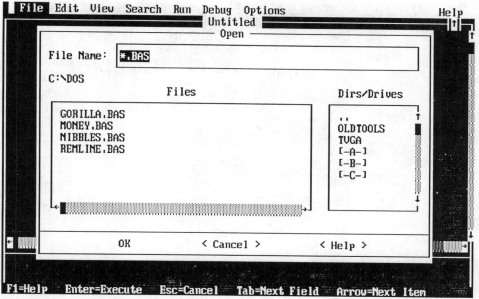

1-12 The screen for sample programs.

To run the program, press Shift−F5 and follow the directions. When you're tired of this, you can hit Ctrl−Break to see the source code for this program. At that point, you're back to the usual QBasic environment.

More on QBasic menus

Suppose now that you press Alt−O to open the options menu. If you try it, you'll see the options menu shown in Fig. 1-13.

Notice that the first option is called Display . . . This option lets you customize the display: what colors are used for highlighted text and so forth. The next option is called Help Path, which holds the paths where QBasic can find the file, QBASIC.HLP, which it needs. (QBasic always checks the current directory as well.) If you have a hard disk and used the setup program, then this information is already set.

Next, notice the last option, Syntax Checking. This option turns on or off the Smart Editor built into QBasic. When the editor is on, you'll see a bullet next to it. The bullet indicates that the editor (or any option) is toggled on. While you're learning the editor, you might want to turn Syntax Checking off. If there's a bullet there, then toggle Syntax Checking off by pressing S or by moving the highlighted bar to it and hitting Enter.

Turn Syntax Checking on and you've activated the Smart Editor. It (like many programming editors) knows some of the rules for QBasic and won't let you break them. Because some of the things, like batch files, that you might type when you

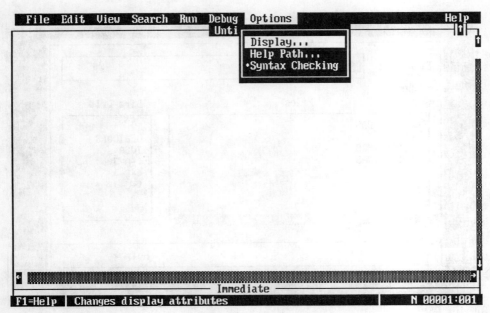

1-13 The Options menu.

practice using the editor surely will break QBasic's programming rules, for now, you're best off with Syntax Checking off. When you start programming (for example, by working through the next chapter), then you'll want what you type to be checked. When you've finished working through this chapter, I suggest turning Syntax Checking back on.

The anatomy of a QBasic dialog box

QBasic pops up a dialog box whenever it needs information to complete a choice. This situation usually is indicated by three dots on a menu option. The dialog box for Open Program demonstrates most of their features. First, it has a place to enter information, a text box. Next, there's a list of files and a list of directories or drives, two list boxes. Finally, there's a bunch of choices at the bottom. Each of these choices is surrounded by angle brackets ($<$ $>$). These choices are called *command buttons*. The command button surrounded by the highlighted angle brackets is the active button. If you press the Enter key, the dialog box closes and you've chosen that command. The command in turn uses whatever is listed at the moment in the various text boxes for its raw data. It is important to remember that you do not move around a dialog box by using the Enter key.

You already have seen two ways to move around the dialog box: use a mouse or with the Tab or Shift–Tab keys. Suppose you wanted to get to the command button for Cancel to close this box. You could hit Tab four times or Shift–Tab twice. You'll notice that the Cancel button is now active (it's surrounded by high-lighted angle brackets).

For moving to most places within a dialog box, there's a shortcut like the one for menus. Press the Alt key and you'll see that certain letters are now high-lighted. For example, pressing Alt−H moves the cursor directly to the Help button and makes it active. In general, you can reach most places in a dialog box by pressing Alt and a letter.

List boxes usually are used to display information needed to fill text boxes. For example, go back to the Open Program dialog box and hit Alt−F to quickly move the cursor to the Files list box. Move through this list box using the arrow keys. Pressing the down arrow highlights the first choice; subsequent presses move through the list of files. Notice that, as you move through the list, a choice is highlighted and automatically placed in the text box. Once you're satisfied with the choice in the text box, you can hit Enter to open that program. You don't have to do any typing at all, because the name of the program was transferred into the text box.

There's even a shortcut for moving within a list box. It works like the one for moving from hyperlink to hyperlink. Once the cursor is in a list box, if you press a letter, the highlighted bar immediately goes to the first item on the list beginning with that letter. If you hit Alt−F and then N, you'd be much closer to loading the NIBBLES.BAS file.

The Dirs/Drives gives you a list of possible drives and directories. If you make a choice here and hit Enter, the dialog box doesn't close. Instead, you'll be faced with a list of programs from the new directory (files with a .BAS extension) to choose from.

One final point about the Open Program box. Normally, it displays a list of files that have the .BAS extension. You can change this by moving the cursor to the box and typing whatever wild cards you want. For example, hit Alt−N and type *.*. You'll see a list of all the files in the current drive or directory.

The QBasic Edit and Search menus

QBasic comes with a full-screen editor that can insert, delete, find, and replace. It is essentially the same as the full-screen editor, called Edit, which is built into DOS 5.0. People who have used WordStar or any of Microsoft's word processors will find many of the commands familiar. In this section, I'll show you only the most important commands. A full list of editing keys is available online (follow the hyperlinks from the Contents to the hyperlink for Editing Keys or go to appendix C).

A full-screen programmers editor is used much like any word processor. The main differences are that a programming editor often lacks features like word wrap and print formatting. However, it should (and QBasic's Smart Editor does) have powerful features that make programming easier.

As with any editor, you have two choices when typing. You can either be in insert mode or typeover mode. When you are in insert mode (the default) any text you type pushes the text that follows it aside. In typeover mode, the text replaces the old text one character at a time. You switch between these modes by hitting the Ins key. When you are in typeover mode, the cursor looks like a solid rectangle. Also, in both modes, you have the usual two ways of deleting a single character: the backspace key deletes the character to the left of the cursor and the Del key deletes the character at the cursor.

As a way to become comfortable with the editor, I will lead you through a short example. I will assume that you will keep all your QBasic programs in a directory, which already has been created, called QBPROG and that you want to write a short batch file to start up QBasic after you switch to this directory. I also will be assuming that your path command includes the location of QBasic. Open the File menu and hit N (for new). Now, type C:, hit return, type CD C:\ QBPROG, and hit Enter. Finally, type QBasic. The screen will look like Fig. 1-14. (I've left the options menu down to show that syntax tracking is on.)

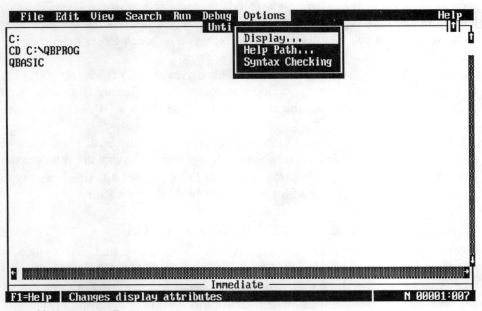

1-14 Making a batch file.

Open the file menu again and hit S (for save) or A (for the Save As command). Suppose you wanted to call this file BASICPRO.BAT, enter the full path name for where you want this file stored. (I keep all my batch files in a C:\ BAT directory included in my path, so I'd enter C:\ BAT\ BASICPRO.BAT.)

More on the editor

Suppose you want to study NIBBLES.BAS to learn how the program works. The first thing you want to do is to print this file. Open the File menu and hit P. A new dialog box will open. Make sure that a bullet is in the Entire Program option. Now, assuming that you have a printer attached to the first parallel port (LPT1:), hit Enter to print a copy of this file.

This file will print, but it won't be nicely formatted. It will lack top or bottom margins and too many lines appear on each page. There is no practical way to format the printout within QBasic; however, as a method to teach you the editor, I'll show you a truly horrible way to format the printout.

First, in the far right corner of the reference bar, notice the two counters which currently read:

00001:001

These counters mark the line and column. Because the file was just loaded, it is at line 1 and column 1. You will want to put a few blank lines for the top margin. Because the cursor is at the top left corner, hit Enter about four times. Notice that the text moves down four lines and the counter now reads 0005:001.

Hit the PgDn key and notice that you've moved to line 23. (PgUp and PgDn move the width of the window each time—19 lines in this case.) Hit PgDn twice more and press the down arrow key three times to move the cursor to line 60. Usually, each page on a printer is 66 lines, so you'll want to enter at least 10 carriage returns (six to end the page and four for the top of the next page). Continue this process and you have hand-formatted the text.

The point of this was to show you that you move through a file in the view window using the arrow keys, PgUp, and PgDn just as you did for the help files. Just as for help screens, you also can move to the top (Ctrl–Home) and the end (Ctrl–End) of a document. The Home and End keys move to the first character and the last character in a line, respectively.

There's another clumsy way to print this file that shows off something more useful: selecting text. When you want to do something with a block of text (move it, copy it, or print it), you first have to select it. This is done by moving the cursor to the start of the block and holding down the Shift key while using a mover key (like an arrow key, PgUp, or PgDn). As you do so, the text is highlighted. Be careful after you've selected text. When text is selected anything you type (even hitting the space bar) will replace the selected text. It's easy to do something disastrous when text is selected. If you select a page and hit the space bar by mistake, the entire page is gone, only to be replaced by a space. You must be careful to deselect text when you're finished doing whatever you wanted to do. You deselect the text by hitting any direction key when you are not pressing the Shift key. Always hit an arrow key to deselect, never the space bar or Enter key.

If you're careful, selecting text is extremely useful. One thing you can do with selected text is print it. For example, you could print a copy of the contents of the directions.

Search and replace

Rather than scroll until you find a specific item, you'll often want to use the Search menu. Hit Alt−S to open it and hit F for the Find option. A dialog box opens up that asks you various questions. One nice feature of QBasic's search facility is that, when the Help window is active, you can use it to browse through the help information. It's a nice complement to the built-in hyperlinks.

You also can use this menu to change text. For example, you could change all occurrences of QBasic to QB. The Change option opens a dialog box that has two text boxes. The first finds the text to be changed. In the second, you specify what you want the text changed to. If you leave this line blank, you can delete any occurrence of the text in the first box. Notice as well that one option is <Find and Verify>; the second says <Change All>. I almost always use the first, which, after each find, asks whether I want to change that occurrence. If you activate <Change all>, the changes can happen too fast, with no going back. Pressing the Esc key aborts a change and closes the dialog box but doesn't bring back the original version. However, there is one kind of undo that you can use. After you've made changes to a line and before you move the cursor off that line, hitting Alt−Backspace or Undo on the Edit menu brings the line back to its original state. This is useful, especially if you're prone to over-editing. Unfortunately, once you move the cursor off the line, you no longer can undo the changes.

Cutting and pasting

Cutting and pasting is done from the Edit menu and is always a two step process. First, you select the text you want to copy or move. Next, you open the Edit menu and choose whether you're cutting or copying. After you make the appropriate choice, QBasic copies the selected text into a temporary storage area, called the *clipboard*. Once information is in the clipboard, it can be pasted anywhere in your document. Move the cursor wherever you want and use Paste (the shortcut key is Shift—Insert). A copy of the text that was in the clipboard will appear at the cursor's location. Moreover, because the text remains in the clipboard until it is replaced by a new cut or copy, you can paste multiple copies of the same information.

There are many shortcut keys that you'll pick up over time. For example, cutting, copying, and pasting are Shift−Del, Ctrl−Ins, and Shift−Ins, respectively. To be honest, I usually just open the Edit menu. For example, I find it easier, less confusing, and not much slower to use Alt−E and press T (for cut). The one I find myself using is the cut a line to clipboard. If you hit Ctrl−Y, whatever line the cursor was on is moved to the clipboard. To get multiple copies of a line in the same place, I just use Paste a lot (Shift−Ins).

What to do in GW-BASIC and BASICA

If you are in the directory that contains your version of GW-BASIC or BASICA, you start them by entering GW-BASIC or BASICA. Another possibility is to use a batch file or set your path to tell DOS where to find the appropriate file. If you are using a SHELL program, then you should follow the directions for your shell.

After a short delay, you'll see a screen that looks something like Fig. 1-15. (For BASICA, the copyright notice will be from IBM.)

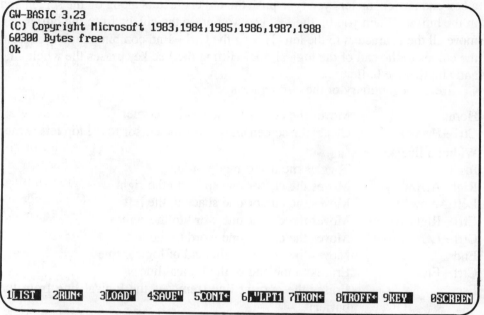

```
GW-BASIC 3.23
(C) Copyright Microsoft 1983,1984,1985,1986,1987,1988
60300 Bytes free
Ok
```

```
1LIST  2RUN←  3LOAD"  4SAVE"  5CONT←  6,"LPT1  7TRON←  8TROFF←  9KEY  0SCREEN
```

1-15 The opening screen for GW-BASIC.

The Ok is the GW-BASIC prompt. It means that the BASIC interpreter is ready to accept commands. The bottom line is for the *soft function keys*. These can be set by a program, but the defaults often are handy when writing programs. These function keys will be covered more in the next chapter.

GW-BASIC is fundamentally line oriented and so its editing facilities work one line at a time. The most important thing to remember is that the contents of a line are stored in a buffer until you hit the Enter key. Only at that point are they sent to the interpreter for processing.

Typing the Ctrl−Home combination clears the screen and moves the cursor to the top left corner. Pressing the Home key alone moves the cursor to the top without erasing the screen. You can use the up and down arrow keys to move the cursor around the screen, but you'll still be working one line at a time.

Within a given line, you can use the right and left arrow keys to move around. You can move the cursor one word to the right by using a combination of the Ctrl key and the right arrow key. To move one word to the left, press the Ctrl and left arrow combination.

When you type a character, it is stored and replaces the character in that position in the buffer. The buffer can store 255 characters, so a line (sometimes called a logical line) in GW-BASIC can be that long. When you hit the Enter key, you finish a logical line. Pressing the End key moves to the end of a logical line.

When you switch to insert mode by tapping the Ins key, the cursor changes to a box and any characters you type push the old characters along on the screen and in the buffer. When you hit the Del key, you erase the cursor from the buffer and move all the characters to the left. Hitting the Ctrl—End combination erases from the cursor to the end of the logical line. Hitting the Esc key erases the whole line and empties the buffer.

Here's a summary of the editing keys:

Home	Moves the cursor to the top left corner
Ctrl—Home	Clears the screen and moves the cursor to the top left corner
Within a line:	
Ins	Toggles the insert mode on/off
Right Arrow	Moves the cursor one space to the right
Left Arrow	Moves the cursor one space to the left
Ctrl—Right Arrow	Moves the cursor one word to the right
Ctrl—Left Arrow	Moves the cursor one word to the left
End	Moves the cursor to the end of logical line
Ctrl—End	Erases to the end of the logical line
Esc	Erases the current line (removes the logical line from the buffer)
Up Arrow	Moves the cursor up one line with no effect on the buffer.
Down Arrow	Moves the cursor down one line with no effect on the buffer.

2
CHAPTER

Statements in DOS BASIC: simple programs

This chapter will get you started writing simple programs. You'll see fundamental ways of getting information into and out of the computer. If you are using Q-Basic, you'll see how to begin to take advantage of its built-in Help system. At times you don't want to write a program; you need an immediate response. To do this, you'll see how to use the direct mode for GW-BASIC and the Immediate window in QBasic. (If you are using QBasic make sure that Syntax checking is now on.)

Getting started in QBasic

Now that you know something about the QBasic environment, it's time to start programming. A BASIC program consists of individual statements in what often seems like a pidgin English. Like any pidgin language, QBasic has its own rules of grammar and its own specialized vocabulary. As you will soon see, however, QBasic interprets many words (for example, PRINT or IF-THEN) in much the same way that you do.

I'll show you an example. Make the Edit window active (i.e., make sure the cursor is there) by selecting the New Program option on the File menu or by pressing F6, the window shifter key, enough times. Now, type in the program exactly as I've written it:

```
REM       CH2 \ P1.BAS
REM  a simple print/beep demo

CLS
  BEEP
  PRINT "HELLO WORLD!"

END
```

Hit the Return key after each line. Because the program is so short, there's no real need to enlarge the Edit window.

Let's go over this program statement by statement. First, notice that, unlike interpreted BASICs, such as BASICA or GW-BASIC (see the next section), line numbers are not needed in a QBasic program. You hit the Return key at least once to separate lines. Notice next that in my program each line is short. This is generally a good idea, but, strictly speaking, it's not necessary. The QBasic editor allows you to scroll horizontally. The end of a program line (sometimes called a logical line) comes only when you hit the Return key. QBasic allows you to have long logical lines—255 characters long, which is about four lines on a printed page. Extraordinarily long program lines make the inevitable editing/correcting process harder.

The first two lines are remark or REM statements. These are put into a program for the benefit of the programmer or anyone else who wants to read and understand the program. In this book, the first remark statement always contains a name for the program as a DOS (hierarchal) filename. Here, I'm explaining the first program in the CH2 subdirectory. (In addition to being a reasonable way to give cross references within this book, it also is how the programs are stored on the optional companion disk.) The .BAS extension fits QBasic's preconceptions that the source code for any QBasic program has this extension. (The Open option on the File menu first tries to list only those files having a .BAS extension, although you can override this.)

REM statements are not processed by the compiler and, therefore, do not take up any room in your compiled code. This situation is much superior to that of GW-BASIC where everything takes up space; there is a temptation to skimp on REM statements as a result. It's easy to question why REM statements are important until you try to modify (or even understand) a complicated program that you wrote months ago. Trying to change a complicated undocumented program (*documentation* is the explanation of a program, which is best contained in the source code) is usually a form of slow torture. To escape it, I've occasionally decided to rewrite a program from scratch.

Because REM statements are so useful, QBasic allows a shorthand for them; you can use just a single quote. This is usually found below the double quote mark, not the apostrophe that is found below the closing parenthesis:

```
' This is also a way to give a remark
```

Next, notice that I have inserted blank lines liberally within the program. Blank lines focus your attention on a program's structure. Inserting blank lines also makes the inevitable editing/correcting process easier. Unlike in GW-BASIC, blank lines are preserved when you save and reload a program. In this case, I've used two blank lines to separate the non-executable REM statements from the executable statements.

The CLS command clears the screen and moves the cursor to the top left corner of the screen. The BEEP command makes the speaker of the PC sound at 800 Hz for a quarter of a second.

The PRINT command (the shorthand is a simple question mark) is the fundamental way of getting information out of the machine and onto the screen. If what follows a PRINT command is enclosed by quotation marks, then QBasic will display exactly what appears inside the quotes. The casing of a command is irrelevant to QBasic typing print; Print or even PRinT work equally well. The Smart Editor automatically converts commands to uppercase. However, case is respected for what occurs inside quotation marks. PRINT "HELLO WORLD" and PRINT "hello world" would display differently. After processing a PRINT statement, QBasic moves the cursor to the beginning of the next line. If the cursor is already at the bottom of the display, then the top line disappears and the other lines move up (the display *scrolls*).

Processing in QBasic follows the ordinary flow from top to bottom. It is not affected by line numbers, should you choose to use them.

The END command is not, strictly speaking, necessary. When there are no more statements left to process, a program ends. Using the END command, however, is a good programming practice. Processing an END command stops the program, even if there are statements that follow it. Once a program that you are running from the QBasic environment ends, then you'll see the message, Press any key to continue, on the bottom line of the output screen. Hitting any key now gets you back to the development environment.

Because spaces within lines and carriage returns between lines are irrelevant to QBasic, I use them liberally. For example, in CH2 \ P1.BAS, besides blocking out the executable from the nonexecutable code, I slightly indented some of the lines. I feel that this makes the program more readable.

To get this program to work—to run it—use the Run option on the main menu bar. One way to do this is to hit the Alt−R combination to return to the Run main menu bar. Once you are there, hit S to run the program. Most programmers prefer using the Shift−F5 shortcut. As soon as you tell QBasic to run the sample program, you'll hear a beep and the message HELLO WORLD! will be displayed in the output screen.

Assuming you haven't made any typos, this program should have worked. It might be a good idea to save the finished version on a disk. As you saw in chapter 1, saving text is done from the File menu, so use Alt−F to make this menu drop down. Hit A to activate the Save As option or S for the Save option. Because Q-Basic doesn't know the name of this program yet, a dialog box pops up. There's a line for the name; enter a filename. You won't be able to use mine unless you have created a directory called CH2 first. You'll see a way to create directories from within QBasic in the section, "The Immediate window in QBasic," later in this chapter.

This program had no problems; it should run successfully. Let's see what happens if you had made a typo. Make the Edit window active and use the editing facilities of QBasic to force a typo. Instead of the correct command PRINT, make a mistake and have it read PRINTF. The changed program will look like this:

```
REM       CH2 \ P1a.BAS
REM       a simple typo

CLS
   BEEP
   PRINTF "HELLO WORLD!"

END
```

Now, try to run the program. Nothing happens in the output window and all you see is an error dialog box (Fig. 2-1).

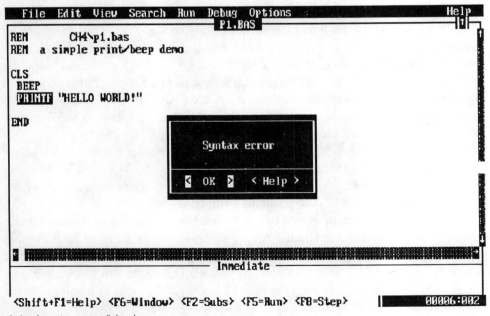

2-1 A syntax error dialog box.

Hit Return and QBasic will put the cursor on the line where the typo was. If you fix the error using the editing commands described in the last chapter and recompile the program, it will work again.

What you just saw was an example of a *compile time error*. This type of error means that your program contains a statement that QBasic can't translate into machine code. When this happens, QBasic stops compiling the program, tells you via a dialog box what it thinks happens, and, after you hit Return puts the cursor where it thinks the error occurred.

There are also *run-time errors*. These happen when your program is *syntactically correct*—conforms to the rules and has the right grammar for a QBasic program) but something forbidden happens while the program runs (for example, a program that tries to divide by 0).

Microsoft says that QBasic has a Smart Editor. What this means is that the editor seems to know certain facts about QBasic. For example, I mentioned that QBasic doesn't care if you enter Print, print or PRINT. As I said then, if you tried any forms of this command except the latter, you'd notice that after you hit Return this key word is transformed to PRINT. The Smart Editor automatically capitalizes all command words (key words). You can quickly find a typo by checking if what you thought was a key word becomes capitalized. If it doesn't end up in caps you've misspelled it. You'll see other features of the Smart Editor later.

To summarize: when you write a program from scratch, you usually use QBasic's integrated Smart Editor to enter these statements into the computer's memory. You also can load an existing program via the Open Program option on the File menu. This option lets you reuse, and usually speed up, most programs written in GW-BASIC.

Getting started in GW-BASIC

As you've seen, GW-BASIC doesn't use a windowing system and its editing facilities are primitive. For programming, the most important difference is that you now must have a line number before each program line.

For example, here's the program from the previous section rewritten for GW-BASIC:

```
10 REM            CH2 \ P1b.BAS
20 REM
30       CLS
40       BEEP
50       PRINT   "HELLO WORLD!"
60 END
```

Unlike QBasic, GW-BASIC doesn't allow blank lines. It does preserve space within a line. You type the line number, the statement, and then hit the Return key. GW-BASIC follows the numbering of your program lines, not the order in which you enter them. For example, this means you do not have to use the up or down arrow keys to insert a line numbered 15 in a given program. The following program works perfectly well:

```
10 REM              CH2 \ P1c.BAS
20 REM
30         CLS
40         BEEP
50         PRINT    "HELLO WORLD!"
60 END
15 REM     When you list the program these lines
16 REM     will occur in the proper order
```

Try this program and then use the LIST command to check that the new lines were inserted in the correct place. Use LLIST to get a copy from the printer, assuming one is attached appropriately.

You might have noticed that the left most entry on the soft function keys, which were mentioned in the previous chapter, looks like this:

```
1LIST
```

This indicates that if you press the F1 key, the interpreter puts the word LIST where the cursor was. Similarly, if you hit F2, the computer enters the word RUN for you. An arrow pointing to the left in a soft key indicates that a carriage return follows the word.

Most versions of GW-BASIC have other ways to abbreviate commands. These come from combination of the Alt key and various letters. For example, Alt−A gives the word AUTO. I find these shortcuts hard to remember, so I rarely use them. If you're interested in them, run through all the combinations and make yourself a list.

To make your programs more readable, I suggest inserting empty remark lines like:

```
21 '
```

to separate out key parts of your program. A consistent numbering scheme for programs helps as well.

To run this program, simply type RUN and hit the Return key or hit F2.

Now suppose you change line 50 to read:

```
50 PRINTF "Hello World"
```

To make this change, either retype the whole line or move the cursor with the up or down arrow keys to the original line 50. Toggle on insert mode and put the F in place. When you hit the Return key, this new line replaces the old line 50 in the memory of your computer. You can check this with the LIST command.

If you enter RUN, GW-BASIC replies with the statement, Syntax error in 50, and displays the offending line, with the cursor at the end of the line. You then can use the Del key to make the changes. After you hit the Return key, the corrected line replaces the incorrect one in the computer's memory.

There are two ways to save a program in GW-BASIC. The first is to save it in *tokenized form*. This form takes less space on the disk and loads somewhat faster for reuse. The disadvantage is that the program can't be read by any editor, including the one in QBasic.

To save the file in tokenized form use the SAVE command. For example:

```
SAVE "CH2 \ P1.BAS"
```

To save it in ordinary ASCII form add the ,a option as follows:

```
SAVE "CH2 \ P1.BAS" , a
```

Only programs saved in ASCII form can be reused by QBasic. (If you leave out the pathname, the file will be saved in the current directory.)

After you save a program, you can erase it from memory with the NEW command. Enter this command and whatever program was in memory disappears.

If you've saved your program, you can use the LOAD command to retrieve the file from a disk. If you don't use the full pathname, then the LOAD command retrieves the file from the current directory.

Some occasionally useful features in GW-BASIC

Some people like to have the computer generate the line numbers. This can be done with the AUTO command. Type AUTO and hit the Return key. The GW-BASIC interpreter will respond with a 10. Now, every time you hit the Return key, the interpreter will give you a new line number that is 10 more than the preceding one. To stop automatic line numbering, use the Ctrl−Break combination. The interpreter responds with an Ok after this.

The AUTO command is actually a bit more flexible. The command:

```
AUTO x,y (where x and y are positive integers)
```

numbers the first line as x and increases each subsequent line by an increment of y.

If you are guilty of inserting lines and want to clean up the numbering, the RENUM command is one way. For example, suppose you have loaded the program with the extra remarks statements numbered 15 and 16 from the previous section. Enter RENUM and the program in the computer's memory now will look like this:

```
10 REM              CH2 \ P1d.BAS
20 REM       When you list the program these lines
```

```
30 REM        will occur in the proper order
40 REM
50            CLS
60            BEEP
70            PRINT    "HELLO WORLD!"
80 END
```

The **RENUM** command gives three options. Its full form is:

RENUM x,y,z

The first line renumbered is determined by the y. The new numbers start with x and the increment is z. x had better be larger than y to avoid collisions. For example, if you have the previous program in memory and enter:

RENUM 100,50,20

the new program looks like this:

```
10 REM            CH2 \ P1e.BAS
20 REM            When you list the program these lines
30 REM            will occur in the proper order
40 REM
100           CLS
120           BEEP
140           PRINT    "HELLO WORLD!"
160 END
```

You can leave any of the x, y, or z line numbers out; however, you then must leave a comma as a placeholder. For example, the command

RENUM 100,,50

will renumber the whole program and increase the line numbers by 50 each time.

Next, you might want to list only part of a program. The forms of the LIST command are as follows:

LIST   Gives the whole program
LIST x-y   Lists all lines between x and y inclusive
LIST -z   List all lines up through z
LIST x-   List lines from x on.

You can use these variants with the LLIST command to get a hard copy of parts of your program.

Similarly, you can delete lines wholesale from your program:

DELETE   Works like the NEW command
DELETE x-y   Deletes all lines between x and y inclusive

```
DELETE -z      Deletes lines up through z
DELETE x-      Deletes lines from x on.
```

Calculations using DOS BASIC

Here are the symbols all the BASIC's recognizes for the five fundamental arithmetic operations:

+ addition
− subtraction
/ division
* multiplication (don't use an x)
^ exponentiation

Exponentiation means multiplying a number by itself a certain number of times. For example, 2^3 means multiply 2 by itself 3 times (2*2*2 = 8). For those who have need of them, you also can use negative or fractional exponents: 2^.5 is the square root of 2.

If you want to do more complicated calculations, I suggest using parentheses. Parentheses let you order mathematical operations. An equation like 4+(3*5) yields 19 because you would do the operation within the parentheses (3*5) first and only then add the 4. On the other hand, (4+3)*5 yields 35, because you add the 4 and the 3 to get 7 first and only then multiply 7 by 5.

When you use parentheses, you must work from the inside out; the innermost terms are evaluated first. I'll use the following equation as an example:

((4*6)+5)*3

The innermost parentheses yields 24. The second set tells you to add 5 to get 29. Finally, multiply 29 by 3 to get 87.

QBasic allows you to avoid parentheses, providing you carefully follow rules that determine precedence. For example, multiplication always has precedence over addition. This means that 3+4*5 equals 23, rather than 35. Because multiplication has higher precedence than addition, QBasic does the multiplication (4*5) first before doing the addition.

Here is the order, or hierarchy, of operations (which, at least for me, often are more trouble than they're worth):

1. Exponentiation
2. Multiplication and division
3. Addition and subtraction

Think of these as levels. Operations on the same level are performed from left to right. So, 36/6*2 is 12. Because division and multiplication are on the same level, the division is done first, yielding 6, and then the multiplication is performed. On the other hand, 36/3^2 is 4. The exponentiation, level one, is done first, yielding 9 and only then is the division performed.

To show you how complicated using the hierarchy of operations can be, try to figure out what DOS BASIC will do with:

$$4*2+16/8+2^3{}^4$$

First, the exponentials (level 1) are computed left to right: $2^3=8$ and $8^4=8*8*8*8=4096$. Now move to level 2 operations and work left to right. Multiply 4 by 2 to get 8 and divide 16 by 8 to get 2. Finally add (level 3) them all together to get 4106.

All in all, I hope I've convinced you that a judicious use of parentheses will make your life easier.

The Immediate window in QBasic

One way to do calculations in QBasic is to incorporate the mathematical symbols into a PRINT statement and use the Immediate window. Use F6 to make this window active (as always the cursor marks the active window). Among other things, the Immediate window allows you to have your computer imitate a $10 calculator. For example type PRINT 2 + 2 in the Immediate window. When you hit Return, you'll see a 4 in the output window.

More precisely, the Immediate window allows you to enter up to 10 lines. Any one of them can be executed by using the arrow keys to place the cursor on the line and hitting Return. For example, you might want to enter a CLS in the Immediate window and hit Return to clear the output screen.

Because you can use essentially any QBasic commands in the Immediate window, another use for the Immediate window is to give a quick way to make a directory, without leaving the QBasic environment. The command in QBasic also is MKDIR, only now the name of the directory is enclosed by quotes. So, MKDIR "C:\CH2" would make a directory on the C: drive called CH2. Similarly, there are commands to change a directory (CHDIR) and remove a directory (RMDIR). I'll have more to say about these types of commands in chapter 15.

Direct mode in GW-BASIC

The counterpart of the Immediate window in QBasic is the direct mode. If you type a statement in GW-BASIC without a line number, the interpreter tries to execute it directly. If you enter PRINT 2 + 2, you'll see a 4 followed by the Ok prompt. Similarly, you can use the MKDIR command in direct mode to create a new directory.

Variables

Computers get their power from their ability to automate. Suppose, for example, that you wanted to write a program that will compute the sales tax on an item. Because the price is probably different for each item, you want a way for the program to store a value for a time, use it in calculations, and yet allow it to change on demand. To do this, you need to set up the equivalent of a box in the computer's memory as well as a way to fill it. These boxes usually are called *variables*. The contents of the box is called the *value* of the variable. Look at the following program:

```
'       CH2 \ P2.BAS
'  A simple sales tax calculator

CLS
LET SalesTax = .0825
PRINT "At the ? mark, type the price and hit the RETURN key"
INPUT PRICE
PRINT
PRINT "The sales tax is";
PRINT SalesTax*PRICE

END
```

The first two statements are, as usual, REM statements. Notice that I am using the single quote here—the variant form of the REM command mentioned previously.

After processing, the next statement, LET SalesTax = .0825, sets up a variable (box) in the computer's memory and places the number 0.0825 inside. (0.0825 is the *value* of the variable.) The name of this variable is SalesTax. At any point in the program, you can retrieve the value of the variable (the contents of the box) by using its name. One nice feature of the Smart Editor is that it will consistently capitalize your variables. Whatever pattern you establish in the last use of a variable is used by the Smart Editor for the rest of the program.

Unlike GW-BASIC, QBasic is quite flexible about variable names. They must begin with a letter; however, other than that requirement, they can contain any number of letters, digits, and periods. No other characters are allowed. 1BASE is an illegal variable name because it begins with a 1, but BASE1 is allowed. Because no special characters except the period are allowed, BASE#1 is forbidden, but BASE.1 is acceptable. The casing is irrelevant. *Price*, *price*, and *PRICE* name the same variable; however, as mentioned before, the Smart Editor mimics the last version you choose. Choosing meaningful variable names gives a kind of self-documentation to a program and are the best way to clarify the point of many program statements.

A LET statement, often called an *assignment statement*, is the primary method for setting up (defining) a variable. The first PRINT statement prompts the user for the information that the program expects. The key statement in this program is in the next line. When QBasic processes a line containing an INPUT statement it does two things:

- It sets up a place in its memory, which is given the same name as the variable that follows the word INPUT. In this case, the box is called *PRICE*.
- It prints a ? on the screen.

In other words, an INPUT sets up a variable with a value that is, for the moment, unspecified.

Now, the user must type a number and hit the Return key. After that, the computer fills the box it just named *PRICE* with the number just entered. Numbers in DOS BASIC cannot use commas. When entering a number (in response to an INPUT statement, etc.), use 9987, not 9,987. Also, if you hit the Return key without entering a number, then 0 becomes the value of the variable.

The next line is an empty PRINT statement. This statement prints a blank line on the screen. The next PRINT statement tells you what to expect out of the program. Notice the semicolon at the end of it. As you saw earlier, usually after processing a PRINT statement, DOS BASIC moves the cursor to the beginning of the next line; however, placing a semicolon at the end of a PRINT statement stops this. The cursor remains fixed on the same line after the last character displayed.

Next, the interpreter processes the last PRINT statement. QBasic always does any calculations within a PRINT statement before it displays the result. Because this PRINT statement involves a variable, QBasic first retrieves the value of the variable before doing the multiplication. Also, when displaying a positive number, QBasic automatically leaves a space in front of the number. That is why I didn't leave a space at the end of the previous PRINT statement within the quotes. Similarly, DOS BASIC always leaves a space after printing any number, positive or negative.

Finally, you can combine the last two PRINT statements in this program. It's probably simpler to say:

```
PRINT "The sales tax is";SalesTax*PRICE
```

Here, as before, the semicolon keeps the cursor from dropping down to the next line.

If you actually run this program the answers you get are likely to look strange—far too many decimal places for a sales tax calculation. You'll see how to cure this problem in the next chapter.

The INPUT command normally displays a question mark. The PRINT statement that I used before the INPUT statement was put there in order to prompt the user. Programs that just display a bare question mark with no explanation of what is expected are confusing and not much fun to deal with. Because prompts are so important, DOS BASIC allows you to combine a prompt (that might ordinarily come from a PRINT statement) and an INPUT statement. This is done by placing the message within quotes after the command INPUT. Using the command in this way, you could combine two lines of the above program by saying:

```
INPUT "At the ? mark type the price and hit return"; PRICE
```

The semicolon after the prompt message forces a question mark to appear. To suppress the question mark, use a comma instead of the semicolon. You might want to do this if you used a slightly different wording:

```
INPUT "Type the price of the item and hit return ___ ", PRICE
```

When you use a semicolon after an INPUT prompt, you get an automatic space after the question mark. When you use a comma, you don't get any extra spaces. Keep this in mind when you're deciding whether to place spaces at the end of the prompt message. Also, immediately after someone hits the Return key in response to an INPUT statement, DOS BASIC moves the cursor to the beginning of the next line. Sometimes this is awkward, so you can prevent it. Place a semicolon immediately after the key word INPUT.

Obviously you could jazz this program up. You could allow someone to change the sales tax rate. Even better would be a way to reuse the program without having to rerun it. In its present form, the program computes the sales tax on a single item and then ends. A $5 calculator can do the job better. An even slicker program would eliminate some of the possibility for error. For example, if you made a typo—hit a letter instead of a number—you would see ?Redo from start and you'd get another chance to enter the data.

Variables in GW-BASIC

Variables in GW-BASIC can be as long as will fit on a logical line, but only the first 40 characters count. For variable names longer than two characters, you use up proportionally more space. Still, when you list the program, all letters are converted to uppercase. As always, GW-BASIC programs require line numbers, but otherwise the discussion from the previous section remains valid.

More on variables and assignment statements

Assignment, or LET, statements are ones that you will use frequently. It's worth spending a bit more time on them. Some of its properties might be surprising.

Look at the following statement:

```
LET I = I+1
```

On the surface, this statement makes no sense. You can't make 0 equal to 1, nor 3 to 4. However, what this statement means has nothing to do with making things equal to each other. The right way to think about it is that it is about changing the contents of a box. The above statement means that the number inside the box named I will be replaced with the number that is one more than was stored there already. For this reason, a statement like LET I + 1 = I makes no sense to QBasic or GW-BASIC. There's no box named I + 1 inside the computer's memory, nor could there be since it's not a legal name for a variable.

Over the years, people have proposed many alternatives to this confusing notation. Changing the equal sign to something else is a popular proposed alternative. Sometimes, people say that you should read the word *LET* as meaning the word *assign* or *get*, but this kind of crutch is common only in beginning programming classes. After a while, you will get used to it and then you might even decide to adapt a shortcut. DOS Basic, following tradition, makes the use of the key word LET optional. A statement like I = I + 1 has exactly the same meaning as LET I = I + 1.

Here's another example to accustom you to the assignment statement. Suppose you want to interchange, or swap, the contents of two variables, your first instinct might be to try:

```
LET A = B
LET B = A
```

This procedure, however, doesn't work. The reason for its failure is instructive. The first statement replaces the contents of the box named A with the contents of the box named B and discards what was originally in the A box. This means that the second statement fills the contents of the B box with what is now in the A box, which was the value that was originally in B. The result is that both boxes contain the same thing—the original contents of the B box.

When you need to SWAP the contents of two variables (and this happens frequently), you use the SWAP command. So, you would say:

```
SWAP A,B
```

DOS Basic sets up a temporary storage place to allow the swap. In older BASIC's you had to set up the temporary storage place yourself. This meant you needed three statements:

```
LET TEMP = A
LET A = B
LET B = TEMP
```

Now, one statement suffices. Still, it's a good idea to think about why this method works and the one using two statements doesn't.

Learning to program is like learning anything else; you need to practice. In many ways, programming can be easier to learn than most other things. This statement might seem strange and you may not believe it, but remember this: any problem can be solved by breaking it down into a succession of simple steps, each of which is usually clear. ("A journey of a thousand miles begins with a single step.") To write a program that will solve your problem, think first about how you would solve a possibly simpler but similar problem on paper. Next, use this analogy to break up the solution to the original problem into simple steps. (It's a good idea to make an outline before you start programming.) Finally, translate each step into a group of QBasic statements.

This book has three purposes. First, you will learn the commands that the various DOS BASICs can understand. Next, you will see some methods that, over time, have proven successful for breaking up a problem into simpler problems. This facilitates the translation process. Finally, you will see how to do the translation.

Let me illustrate this by writing another short program. This one accepts two numbers and then displays the product. Here's an outline that gives the steps needed to solve this problem (they're pretty easy):

1. Get the two numbers.
2. Multiply the numbers together.
3. Show the product of the numbers.

A QBasic program to do this is:

```
' CH2 \ P3.BAS
' Multiply two numbers

CLS

PRINT "Type two numbers, separate them by a comma and hit RETURN"
INPUT FirstNumber,SecondNumber

LET Answer = FirstNumber*SecondNumber
PRINT "The product is ";Answer

END
```

A GW-BASIC program requires line numbers.

The translation of the outline starts with the INPUT command. Here I am using another feature of the INPUT command: the ability to enter more than one item at a time. You do this by separating the names of the items to be entered by a comma. Similarly, the person entering the data separates the values of the items by commas. When he or she hits the Return key, the values are assigned to the variables in the correct order.

Notice that I didn't really need the new variable I called Answer. I could have had the interpreter do the multiplication within a PRINT statement. I did it this way because I wanted to do the program as a literal translation of the outline as closely as possible. Finally, notice that the names I chose for my variables had something to do with their function within the program. As I mentioned before, meaningful variable names help to ensure that a program that you return to after it's been put aside a long time still is understandable.

Most programs have to mix both words and numbers. You can use LET statements to stuff variables with letters, words, or any group of characters. To do this, you add an identifier to the end of the variable's name. The identifier for characters, or words, is a dollar sign. For example:

```
LET IBM$ = "Big Blue" or
Blank$ = "      " or
PC$ = "PS/2"
```

The value of the variable named Blank$ consists only of spaces. You might use a variable like this to line up information, although there are better ways (see the beginning of the next chapter). The last variable is a good example to keep in mind in that it omits the optional LET and mixes letters, numerals, and special characters.

A mixture of characters usually is called a *string* and the dollar sign is called the string type identifier. A variable that can hold strings—one with a name ends with the $—is called, naturally enough, a *string variable*. One that holds numbers is called a *numeric variable*.

String variables are quite versatile. In QBasic, a single string variable can hold up to 32,767 characters. In GW-BASIC only 255 characters are allowed. (Although the QBasic limit—roughly 15 pages—is unlikely to be reached too often, GW-BASIC's 255-character limit is often a problem.) You can store numbers inside a string variable. In this case, a number is considered only as a group of digits, so PRINT "2" * "2" makes no sense and will give you a type mismatch run time error.

You can only use the SWAP command on variables of the same type.

Using a printer with DOS BASIC

The PRINT command sends information out of the computer and onto the screen. A similar command, LPRINT, sends information to a printer.

Here's a QBasic program that prints invitations to a party on a printer.

```
'       CH2 \ P4.BAS
'   An invitation letter

CLS
INPUT "Enter the invitee's name – ",GUEST$
INPUT "Enter the street address – ", ADRS$
LINE INPUT "Enter the city state and zip code and hit RETURN – ";CT$

LPRINT "Friday 6'th November 1987"
LPRINT:LPRINT
```

```
LPRINT GUEST$
LPRINT ADRS$
LPRINT CT$

LPRINT:LPRINT

LPRINT "Dear ";GUEST$
LPRINT:LPRINT
LPRINT "I'm having a party at my house on 1313 Mockingbird Lane."
LPRINT "It will be held, of course next friday."

END
```

Notice that this slightly longer program is written in blocks. (For GW-BASIC, besides adding the necessary line numbers, I suggest using empty REM lines to block out the program.) I've separated the information being entered from the information going out. Again, this is designed to help anyone who's reading a program's source code. There are two reasons for blocking out the parts of a program (the input block from the two parts that print out the letter). The first reason is that your eye immediately identifies the pieces of a program. They now are digestible, making it easier to correct any mistakes you make. A good rule of thumb is that the blocks that make up a program should never be more than a single screen (20 lines or so) long. Secondly, when outlining a program, you rarely outline everything. It is much more common, as you grow more experienced, that each step of your outline corresponds to an independent, 10 to 15 line block. I'll have more to say about this in chapter 9.

The first new feature in this program is the command LINE INPUT. This is a variant on the INPUT command that accepts a whole line of data at a time, including any commas or spaces that might appear. Without the LINE INPUT command, you would have a conflict between the commas that are used in addresses and QBasic's use of a comma or a space to separate items. Unlike the INPUT command, the LINE INPUT command does not display a question mark. This single LINE INPUT command replaces three lines:

```
INPUT "CITY";CT$
INPUT "STATE ";ST$
INPUT "Zip Code";ZIP$
```

Actually, you could have used the INPUT command. If a person surrounds his or her text with quotes then embedded commas are allowed.

Next notice the Shift between PRINT and LPRINT. As I mentioned before, the LPRINT command works like the PRINT command except that it sends the information to a printer. If you don't have a printer attached and online, you still can process a program containing an LPRINT statement. However, any attempt to RUN the program without a printer will give a run-time error. You also will get an error message if your printer is attached to a serial port and you haven't used the MODE command from DOS to redirect the COM port to be a printer port. (If you have a serial printer see your DOS manual for details on how to do this.)

Finally, DOS BASIC lets you combine two commands on a single line by placing a colon between them, as I did in the last program in the line with the two empty LPRINT statements. While this feature is often useful, I never put disparate statements on a single line. Doing this always makes my programs harder to read. For example:

```
LPRINT "Friday 6'th November1987":LPRINT:LPRINT:LPRINT GUEST$
LPRINT ADRS$:LPRINT CT$:LPRINT:LPRINT:LPRINT "Dear ";GUEST$
```

The first version that I write of a program that will use a printer usually does not use the printer at all. Instead, I write the first version using the PRINT command. Once I'm sure the program is working correctly, then I use the global search and replace feature of the QBasic editor to change the appropriate PRINT commands to LPRINT commands. (In GW-BASIC, you'd have to do it by hand.)

It's hard to imagine correcting a long program working directly from the screen. Like most people, I prefer to work with a *hard copy*, or a version on paper. You can get a hard copy of a program's source code whenever you're editing it. Make sure the printer is online and use the Print option on the File menu for QBasic or the command LLIST for GW-BASIC.

Variables and reserved words in DOS BASIC

In the interest of good programming practices, you normally should assign a value to a variable the first time it occurs in a program. (This step is called *initializing* the variable.) Otherwise, the first time a numeric variable is encountered in a program, it automatically is given the value 0, the default value of a numeric value. (The *default* is what happens automatically—the natural state of a variable.) To see this feature in effect, change the line in the sales tax program to read:

```
PRINT "Tax is ";SalesTx*price (instead of SalesTax*price)
```

Run the program again. Because BASIC has never encountered a variable named SalesTx before, it is given the default value of 0, so the result of the calculation is also 0. Having a calculation give a strange—often zero—result is a common consequence of failing to initialize variables. You'll see ways of checking on this in the sections on debugging in this chapter.

This example demonstrates something else. In QBasic, all the characters in a variable's name are significant. In GW-BASIC, only the first 40 characters are significant. In either case, ThisIsAVariable and ThisIsAVariableee are different variables. However, because case is not important, salestax and SalesTax are the same variable as far as DOS BASIC is concerned. (Most people find the second version easier to read. I use this way of mixing upper and lowercase in my source code.) On the other hand, A and A$ are different variable names. Because variable names can be as long as you want and you can combine letters, digits, and periods, you obviously still have lots of choices for the names of your variables. However, certain choices are forbidden, or at least a bad idea, because they are already used in DOS BASIC. For example, you cannot set up your own variable named PRINT or LET because these are command words. However, you can have reserved words embedded in your variable names. MyLET$ is a perfectly acceptable name for a string variable.

On the other hand, there are reserved words that are not commands but instead have special functions. A good example is the reserved word DATE$. This word is preset to be whatever date that DOS thinks it is. Similarly, TIME$ is reserved for whatever time DOS thinks it is. Although most of the reserved words are commands, some (like DATE$ and TIME$) can be thought of as special variables that already are initialized, so they have a preset value. You might find yourself often using them in your programs. For example, a program containing the statement PRINT "Today's date is ";DATE$ tells the computer to read today's date from DOS and then display it on the screen.

Occasionally, you might want to reset the system's date and time from within a program. This can be done by assigning a string of the correct form to the DATE$ or TIME$ variables. For DATE$, the string must look like:

"mm-dd-yy"   A two digit value for the month, the date, and the year, separated by a dash (-)
"mm/dd/yy"   The same separated by a slash
"mm-dd-yyyy"   A four digit year
"mm/dd/yyyy"   The same separated by a slash

You would say LET DATE$ = "07/08/53" to set today's date to July 8, 1953. If you use the DATE$ command in this way, when you return to DOS, the system date will have changed as well.

Similarly, TIME$ can change the time for DOS. Assign it to a string of the form:

"hh:mm:ss"

where *hh* stands for the hours, using a 24 hour clock (0−23)
    mm is the number of minutes
    ss is the seconds

The minutes and seconds are optional; they default to no minutes after the hour. Both DATE$ and TIME$ can be set from the immediate window.

As another example, consider the reserved numeric variable TIMER. Using the time given on the system clock, this variable determines the number of seconds since midnight. It is accurate to within about a tenth of a second. You often use it to time how long a program takes to run. For example:

```
'  CH2 \ P5.BAS
'  Timing a multiplication

CLS
PRINT "Enter two numbers separated by commas."
INPUT "Then hit the RETURN key"; N1, N2

StartTime = TIMER              :REM the time within 1/10 second
ANS = N1*N2
EndTime = TIMER                ' also within 1/10 of a second

PRINT
PRINT "The answer is";ANS
PRINT "That multiplication took";EndTime-StartTime;"seconds"

END
```

The assignment statement StartTime = TIMER makes the value of the variable StartTime equal to how many seconds have gone by since midnight. Then, as QBasic does the multiplication, another variable checks the time again. The difference of the two times is how long the multiplication took.

As the remark statements indicate, the TIMER function is accurate only to about a tenth of a second. The remarks within this program demonstrate one peculiarity of QBasic: placing a remark (REM) statement within a line requires the colon, but using a single quote does not.

Unfortunately, the answer this program gives is likely to be zero. A single multiplication is not going to take even one tenth of a second. To time this kind of operation, you'll need to repeat the operation many times (see chapter 5 to learn how to do this).

A complete list of DOS BASIC reserved words can be found in Appendix E. For QBasic, the list is available from the online help file. Use Alt−H to activate the Help facility and ask for the index (I). This gives you a list of keywords that you can hyperlink through. It's easy to get quick summaries of how a command works. If you are writing a program in QBasic and want to check the use of a keyword within the program, place the cursor anywhere in the word and hit F1. Provided that QBasic knows where the help files are located, a window pops up with a detailed description of how to use that command word. (As you saw in the last chapter, by making the Help window the active window, you can use the Print function on the file menu to get a hard copy of this information.)

Some general words on debugging a program

Now that you've had some experience programming, you might have found that programs don't always run the first time or, even if they do run, they don't do exactly what you want. Take heart. Rarely can anyone write a serious program that runs perfectly the first time. If nothing else, a simple typo can bomb a program. The reasons why a program bombs are mistakes, usually called *bugs*. The process of fixing a program is called *debugging*. Writing clear and well-documented programs is the best medicine. It helps prevent mistakes in the first place (what I like to call *bugproofing*).

Whenever you try to debug a program, you're best off having a hard copy of the source code. Check each statement carefully. Are all the variables the ones you want? Are any spelled incorrectly (leading to default values that foul up the results)? If you have a friend or colleague that knows QBasic, asking them to look over a program is often the best debugging technique. Too often, when I try to debug a program, I see what I expect to see and not what my fingers typed.

You might be interested in the story of the first computer bug. Early computers used vacuum tubes, which generated a lot of heat. For this reason, the windows in the room often were left open. When one of the earliest computers (the MARK II) was not working, a repairman found that a moth had wandered in and got caught in a relay, which caused a short circuit. Grace Hooper, one of the most important of the early computer scientists, remarked that the removal of the moth was the "first successful debugging." She taped the moth to the computer's log book.

Debugging in QBasic

QBasic has reasonably powerful debugging facilities that are available via the Debug menu. I'll be devoting a lot of time to these features in the chapters that follow. For now, however, I only want to show how to use *breakpoints*. A breakpoint is a place where the program stops for a moment. Hitting F5, which is the shortcut for the continue option on the Run menu, causes the program to resume.

Why is being able to temporarily stop a program useful? Imagine that you are concerned with why a variable seems not to have the value that you want it to have at the end of a program. Set a breakpoint at some earlier place. (Breakpoints are toggled via F9 or B on the debug menu.) When the program gets to the breakpoint, it stops. You now can do two things: examine the output window (via F4) or use the Immediate window to examine the value of any variable in the halted (or, in certain situation, finished) program. To do this, wait until the program stops when it hits the breakpoint (breakpoints are shown in reverse video or highlighted). Now, move to the Immediate window and use the PRINT command to display the value of the variable.

Debugging in GW-BASIC

GW-BASIC doesn't have breakpoints. Instead, you can insert them manually with the STOP command. When the interpreter encounters this command, it halts just like it did with the breakpoints in the previous discussion. You can examine the value of variables by using PRINT statements in direct mode. When you're done use the CONT command to resume the program.

Summary

In this chapter, you saw how to use the following commands:

REM	Remark statements are used to explain a program. The single quote serves as well.
CLS	Clears the screen.
BEEP	Sounds the speaker for $1/4$ of a second.
PRINT	Displays something on the screen.
LET	Assigns a value to a variable (opens a box and fills the box with a value).
INPUT	Sets up and names a location in memory. Your response to the INPUT request fills up this box.
LINE INPUT	Accepts a whole line of text, including any commas or spaces that would otherwise act as separators.
END	Tells QBasic to go no further.
TIMER	Tells the number of seconds since midnight.
TIME$	Has a string as its value. Gives the time that DOS thinks it is. It can be assigned to change the time.
DATE$	Has a string as its value. Gives the date that DOS thinks it is. It can be assigned to change this date.

You saw how commas, semicolons, and quotation marks control the way results are displayed as well as the hierarchy of the five basic arithmetic operations. You also saw how to use the Immediate window for instant gratification.

3
CHAPTER

Fine-tuning your output

So far, you've used PRINT and LPRINT statements to display information. This simple use hardly taps the power of DOS BASIC. Moreover, when a calculation uses only these commands to display the results, they might look bizarre—far too many decimal places to be usable. The last section of this chapter shows you how to fix this problem.

Although the main purpose of this chapter is to show you how to completely control the form of a programs's output, along the way, you also will learn about the different types of numbers and the accuracy with which DOS BASIC does calculations. (As usual QBasic is a bit richer than GW-BASIC.)

The commands covered in this chapter are:

STRING$	SPACE$	TAB
SPC	CHR$	WRITE
ASC	INPUT$()	LOCATE
KEY OFF	KEY ON	PRINT USING
LPRINT USING	VIEW PRINT	

Simple string manipulations

Frequently, you will want to build a new string by placing one string next to another. DOS BASIC looks at *concatenation*, which is joining together one or more strings, as a kind of addition, so it uses the plus sign for this operation. For example, if:

```
ST$ = "The queen of England is "
QUEEN$ = "Queen Elizabeth "
```

```
A$ = "I"
B$ = "II"
```

then setting OLD$ = ST$ +QUEEN$ + A$ gives OLD$ the value "The queen of England is Queen Elizabeth I". To make the value of a string variable, say NotOLD$, "The queen of England is Queen Elizabeth II", you can use:

```
NotOLD$ = ST$ + QUEEN$ + A$ + A$ or
NotOLD$ = ST$ + QUEEN$ + B$ or
NotOLD$ = OLD$ + A$
```

These possibilities all work because there were no spaces before or after the I or II in the definition of A$ and B$. The concatenation operator joins strings together, including any spaces that might occur, in exactly the order they appear. Unlike adding numbers together, order is important when concatenating strings.

You can't use the plus sign to mix strings and numbers together. A statement like PRINT 3 + "D" gives a compile time error message. PRINT "3" + "D" is perfectly acceptable, as is PRINT "2" + "3", which gives the string of numerals represented by a 23.

The analogue of zero is the *null string*. Concatenating with the null string is like adding zero to a number—it doesn't change the string. You can assign a string variable, say NULL$, to be the null string by saying NULL$ = "" (i.e., hitting two successive quotes, making sure there's no spaces between the quotes). You also get the null string if you hit the return key alone in response to an INPUT statement that asks for a string—just as you would get zero as the value of a numeric variable. Finally, the null string is the default value of an uninitialized string variable. (Again, it's poor programming practice to rely on default values.)

Suppose you want to set off a part of a display by a row of asterisks. One possibility is to set up a string variable whose value is 80 asterisks:

```
RowOfAster$ = "********************....
```

My not finishing the variable's definition already indicates the problem; it's hard to be sure that I've typed exactly 80 asterisks. You would expect that this kind of mindless, repetitive task should be done by the computer. DOS BASIC makes it easy. The command STRING$(*x,y$*) sets up a variable whose value consists of multiple copies of a single character. To get a row of asterisks use:

```
RowOfAster$ = STRING$(80,"*")
```

For a row of 40 dashes use:

```
SmallRowDash$ = STRING$(40,"-")
```

Combining the plus sign with the STRING$ command makes it easy to get displays like:

—————————********************************—————————

To get strings consisting of rows of blanks, you actually have two choices: STRING$(80," ") or a new command, SPACE$(80). The SPACE$ command seems to be the more common, mostly because it saves a little typing and is a bit more mnemonic. If you use the STRING$ version, you don't have to count the number of blank spaces between the quotes, because only the first character from the second position of the STRING$ command is repeated. STRING$(80,"aB") gives 80 as.

With either command, you can use a numeric expression (a number, variable, or calculation) to determine the number of characters. The value of the expression must be greater than zero and no more than 32,767 for QBasic or 255 for GW-BASIC (the limit on the number of characters in a string variable). If the value is not an integer, the rounded off value is used. STRING(3.7,"4") gives you a string of four 4s, not the number 4444.

Simple screen movements

On an ordinary typewriter, hitting a single key lets you move quickly to prespecified locations within a line. For DOS BASIC, these locations, usually called *print zones*, are fixed 14 columns apart; you can't change them. You move to different print zones by using commas in PRINT or LPRINT statements. For example, a line like:

```
PRINT a, b, c
```

tries to print the value of the variable a printed in the first column, the value of b in the fifteenth column, and the value of c in the 29th column. I said tries because, when printing a number or string requires DOS BASIC to move into an adjacent print zone, a comma forces DOS BASIC to print at the beginning of the next available, or completely fresh empty, print zone. To see this at work, try the following short QBasic program:

```
'  CH3 \ P1.BAS
'  print zone demo

CLS

PRINT − 1,"a ",' test",− 1
PRINT
PRINT 1,"a ",' test",1
PRINT
PRINT 1/3,"a ",' test",1/7
PRINT

END
```

After the usual remark statements identifying the program, the first PRINT statement shows the comma doing what it's supposed to. The number -1 is printed in the first two columns, the phrase is printed starting in the 15th column, and the number -1 is printed starting in the 29th column.

The second nonempty PRINT statement should work the same way, but it doesn't quite. This difference is because, as mentioned earlier, DOS BASIC has certain ways of displaying numbers that are not easily overruled. Numbers are followed by an automatic space and positive numbers always are preceded by a space. (This space is for an implied plus sign; a negative number uses this space for the minus sign.) The 1s that were destined for the 1st and 29th column actually show up in the 2nd and 30th column. The automatic space that DOS BASIC leaves can be awkward; occasionally it means a print zone is used up without anything appearing in it.

The third nonempty PRINT statement works similarly.

You can even use commas with nothing between them to move quickly to new print zone. For example, PRINT "a",,"b" displays a b at the beginning of the third print zone, as would PRINT ,,"b". Print zones for a printer also are set 14 positions apart; just use commas within LPRINT statements.

Using a comma in a PRINT statement gives you a quick and dirty method for lining up your output. However, there is a better way. For example, suppose you were preparing a form letter and still wanted to retain a personal touch. The date should not be flush left as on a business letter, rather it should be printed at approximately the 70th position. One way to do this is with the SPACE$ command from the last section. Use a fragment like:

```
LET D$ = SPACE$(70)
LPRINT D$;DATE$
```

I'm assuming that DOS knows the correct date, otherwise you would have to use an INPUT statement combined with the DATE$ statement from the last chapter to get the correct date.

The problem with this approach is that it's easy to fill up your program with a lot of specialized variables. In this example, what you really want to do is move the printhead or cursor to the 70th position and then start printing. The command in DOS BASIC that lets you do this is TAB. In the previous example you could say:

```
LPRINT TAB(70);DATE$
```

The TAB command can't make the cursor or printhead move backwards on a line. Instead the cursor moves to the corresponding position on the next line. If the cursor is currently at the 30th position and you say TAB(29), the cursor will move to the 29th position on the next line—one space diagonally to the left of where it was originally.

Just as you could with the STRING$ and SPACE$ commands, you can use a numeric expression (a number, variable, or calculation) inside the parentheses, as long as what's inside will have a value between 1 and 255.

The TAB command is most frequently used to line up data. For example, if we wanted to make and fill in this chart:

ITEM   NUMBER COST   TOTAL

_____

1.
2.

One block of the program should accept the name of the item, the number desired, and its cost. Another block should calculate the cost. The final part will print out a nicely formatted chart (*formatting* means to control the shape or form of a display). Here's the program written in QBasic format:

```
'  CH3 \ P2.BAS
'  setting up a table

CLS
PRINT "Please type the item's name, number and cost."
PRINT "Separate each by a comma and then hit RETURN."
INPUT ITEM1$,QUAN1,COST1
PRINT
PRINT "Now do the same for the second item."
INPUT ITEM2$,QUAN2,COST2

CLS
PRINT TAB(5);"ITEM";TAB(30);"NUMBER";TAB(45);"COST";TAB(60);
PRINT "TOTAL"
PRINT STRING$(75,"-")
PRINT
TOT1 = QUAN1*COST1
TOT2 = QUAN2*COST2

PRINT "1.";TAB(5);ITEM1$;TAB(25),QUAN1;TAB(45);COST1;TAB(60);TOT1
PRINT "2.";TAB(5);ITEM2$;TAB(25),QUAN2;TAB(45);COST2;TAB(60);TOT2

END
```

Notice that, because you will be mixing numbers and strings, you could not use the LINE INPUT command from the previous chapter. You will need to have the user enter the separator, the comma, between items.

The next block controls the output. Notice the use of the STRING$ command to give a row of 75 dashes. (I separated out the extra PRINT "TOTAL" to make the program easier to read; lines in QuickBASIC can be up to 256 characters long.)

This program is deficient in many ways. For example, it doesn't check that the name of the item will fit into the 20 columns that I've set aside. Similarly, the answers are likely to be displayed with too many digits. To correct the first problem you'll need to use the techniques that will be covered in chapter 6. The latter problem will be taken care of in the last section of this chapter.

The TAB command sends the cursor to a specified location. A similar command, SPC moves it a fixed number of spaces. SPC(12) always moves the cursor or printhead twelve units from its last position. As with TAB, SPC can be used with any numeric expression. It also has the same restrictions; what is inside the parentheses must have a value between 1 and 255.

ASCII codes

A computer doesn't have one kind of memory for letters and another kind of memory for numbers. Anything you enter into a computer is changed into numbers (actually, a pattern of on/off switches, but more on that later). The computer keeps track of whether the numbers in its memory are codes for letters or not. For example, the capitol letter N is stored with a code number 78. In certain commands, the code numbers for the letters can be used instead of the letter itself. This might seem pointless until, for example, you ask how to display a quotation mark. Unfortunately, the quotation mark in a PRINT statement has a special meaning. If you enter:

LPRINT ""The unspeakable in pursuit of the inedible""

in an attempt to print out this remark of Oscar Wilde (about fox-hunting) as a quotation, the compiler will not accept it.

DOS BASIC lets you display any character by sending its code to the screen or printer. The command needed to do this is CHR$. (Programmers often call this *character-dollar* or *character string*.) For example, you might use it in the form:

PRINT CHR$(78)

to display a capitol N. The codes used in DOS BASIC are those made standard by IBM. They are called the *extended ASCII codes*. (ASCII stands for the American Standard Code for Information Interchange. An *ASCII file* or *text file* is a file that uses ASCII codes for the data.) There are 256 possible codes, numbered from 0 to 255. A complete list of these codes is available via the online help facility in Q-Basic. Go to Contents on the Help menu and look for the ASCII Character codes. Table 3-1 gives the ASCII codes for the 95 characters that an ordinary typewriter might have.

As you can see, the ASCII code for a quotation mark is 34. The command LPRINT CHR$(34) tells the computer or printer to print the character whose code

Table 3-1
ASCII codes for the typewriter keys.

32	space	33	!	34	"
35	#	36	$	37	%
38	&	39	'	40	(
41	)	42	*	43	+
44	,	45	–	46	.
47	/	48	0	49	1
50	2	51	3	52	4
53	5	54	6	55	7
56	8	57	9	58	:
59	;	60	<	61	=
62	>	63	?	64	@
65	A	66	B	67	C
68	D	69	E	70	F
71	G	72	H	73	I
74	J	75	K	76	L
77	M	78	N	79	O
80	P	81	Q	82	R
83	S	84	T	85	U
86	V	87	W	88	X
89	Y	90	Z	91	[
92	\	93	]	94	^
95	_	96	`	97	a
98	b	99	c	100	d
101	e	102	f	103	g
104	h	105	i	106	j
107	k	108	l	109	m
110	n	111	o	112	p
113	q	114	r	115	s
116	t	117	u	118	v
119	w	120	x	121	y
122	z	123	{	124	|
125	}	126	~		

number is 34, so it prints a quotation mark. To print the Oscar Wilde quotation you would use:

LPRINT CHR$(34);"The unspeakable in pursuit of the inedible";CHR$(34)

You also can set up a variable, say QU$ = CHR$(34), and then rewrite this statement as:

LPRINT QU$;"The unspeakable in pursuit of the inedible";QU$

The CHR$ command is powerful, but sometimes it's overused. To write PRINT CHR$(73);CHR$(66);CHR$(77) rather than PRINT "IBM" is silly. However, if you wanted to put IBM's name in quotes, then you would likely use

```
PRINT CHR$(34);"IBM";CHR$(34)
```

I say likely because there is a little used variant on the PRINT command, the WRITE command, that actually sends information to the screen surrounded by quotes. A statement like WRITE "The unspeakable in pursuit of the inedible" would display the quotation as a quotation. WRITE doesn't work on a printer, however. The WRITE command has other peculiarities that make it useful for dealing with files, which is the situation in which it is most used and where you likely will find it useful. For this reason, you'll see more about this command in chapter 15.

You can use the ASCII codes for a character instead of the character itself in the STRING$ command. STRING$(40,78) is the same command as STRING$(40,"N"). If you wanted to get a string of 40 quotation marks, you would have to use STRING$(40,34) because, just as before, you cannot say STRING$(40,""""").

The command ASC is the opposite of the command CHR$. ASC takes a string and returns the ASCII code of the first character of the string. For example, ASC("#3") is 33, because the ASCII code for a pound sign is 33.

The codes below 32 are called the *ASCII control codes*. For example, CHR$(7) was used to control the bell on old teletype machines. Even now, PRINT CHR$(7) works like the BEEP command; LPRINT CHR$(7) also works like the BEEP command if your printer has a bell.

When used properly, these control codes will give you exceptionally fine control of a printer (see the next section, "Controlling a printer"). In addition, these codes can display some useful shapes on the screen and on any IBM graphics compatible printer. For example, PRINT CHR$(1) gives you a smiling face; PRINT CHR$(3) displays a heart. PRINT CHR$(4) gives a diamond, PRINT CHR$(5) gives a club, and PRINT CHR$(6) gives a spade symbol. These are useful if you write a program to play card games.)

The codes over 127 correspond to what usually is called the *extended character set*. These include certain foreign characters and some useful shapes that will let you make bar graphs and boxes.

You also can enter the codes directly for a character; unfortunately the method is a little clumsy. To see it work you need to learn one new command, the INPUT$(x) command. This command picks up characters from the keyboard without echoing them (i.e., without displaying them on the screen). The number or value of the numeric expression inside the parentheses determines the number of characters. INPUT$(1) picks up one character, INPUT$(10^2) picks up 100 characters, etc. You can pick up to 32,767 characters with a single INPUT$ command. It's no coincidence that this is the same as the limit on a string variable, because you only use the INPUT$ command together with an assignment (for example, FiveKeys$ = INPUT$(5)). Any attempt to use the INPUT$ without assigning it to a string variable gives an error message.

After processing an INPUT$ command, the computer stops and waits for the correct number of keystrokes. (Actually, this is a bit sloppy; combinations of keystrokes that involve the Ctrl or Alt keys count as a single keystroke and the Ctrl−Break combination interrupts the program.) You can use the built-in pause of the INPUT$ command to give a user a breather. A fragment like:

```
PRINT "Press any key when ready ..."
Hold$ = INPUT$(1)
```

stops any action until you press a key. For example, this is useful if, during program development, you want to keep the ubiquitous Press any key to continue from appearing on the output screen until you've finished examining what's there.

To see how to use the code for a character directly, run the following short QBasic test program:

```
' CH3 \ P3.BAS
' A keyboard poller

CLS
PRINT "Press any key to see its ASCII code"

KeyPressed$ = INPUT$(1)
PRINT
PRINT Keypressed$,"The ASCII code was";ASC(Keypressed$)

END
```

This program picks up a single keystroke. Because the INPUT$ command was used, the keystroke is not displayed on the screen. The keystroke is displayed only when the second PRINT statement is processed and is followed by the ASCII code for that keystroke. (The extra PRINT statement was stuck in to demonstrate this more clearly—the character shows up following a blank line.)

You can try any of the normal typewriter keys. They and their codes will be displayed. Getting the codes for the nontypewriter keys into the program is a bit more complex. First, turn off the cursor control keys and activate the numeric keypad by hitting the Num Lock key (if you are in the standard QBasic screen, an *N* should appear in the right corner of the status line, before the line and column indicators). Now, rerun the program. The computer is waiting for a key to be pressed. Suppose you wanted to get a smiling face (ASCII code 1). Hold down the Alt key and press the 1 on the numeric keypad. When you let go of the Alt key, the face will appear, followed by the statement saying that its ASCII code is 1. Similarly, to get a ¹/₂ (ASCII code 171) on the screen, rerun the program, only this time hold down the Alt key and type 171 on the keypad. Only the numeric keyboard lets you enter codes this way; the number keys on the top row won't work here.

Unfortunately, there are certain keys and key combinations that, when pressed, do not return ASCII codes. These include the arrow keys, the function keys, and the Alt combinations. If you press these keys while running the test program, a character with ASCII code 0 is assigned to the string variable. All these keys blend together as far as the INPUT$ command is concerned. The techniques for dealing with these keys are a bit more complicated; you'll see them in chapter 7.

I should mention that you also can use the Alt key and the numeric keypad to enter keystrokes when responding to an INPUT command, providing they have ASCII value greater than 31. For example, you'd use this method to enter a name that requires an é (ASCII code 130).

Controlling a printer

Modern dot matrix or laser printers are quite versatile. Even the cheapest can print tiny letters (17 or 20 characters per inch, or cpi) or enlarged letters (5 cpi). They usually can print in italics and underline text as well. Many can even beep if you send the LPRINT CHR$(7) command. It's quite possible to control where each dot is placed on a line and how wide the spaces between lines will be. All these powers are invoked by sending special codes to the printer. For example, you might want to have the printer automatically move to the top of the next page after its finished printing a document. This usually is called *forcing a form feed*. All it involves—on every printer that I've ever encountered—is sending a Ctrl−L (ASCII code 12) combination out. This is most easily done by the statement:

```
LPRINT CHR$(12)
```

This command would have been useful at the end of the invitation letter program, CH2 \ P4.BAS. Forcing a form feed would ensure a fresh piece of paper for each invitation.

The codes that control the more sophisticated features vary from printer to printer. However, the most common codes are those belonging to the family of Epson (IBM graphics) compatible printers. For example, on these printers you turn on the large (5 cpi) printing by sending a Ctrl−O, CHR$(15), combination to the printer. To turn it off, you send out a Ctrl−R, CHR$(18). Table 3-2 lists some of the more useful Epson-compatible control codes.

Note that modern printers distinguish between a line feed, a carriage return, and the combination of the two. A line feed moves the paper up one line but doesn't move the printhead. A carriage return moves the printhead to the left margin but doesn't move the paper. The carriage return, line feed combination, CHR$(10) + CHR$(13), is what some people mean when they talk informally of a carriage return.

The compressed mode usually gives you 132 characters per line. Compress mode is useful for displaying wide tables or spreadsheets, especially when you have a normal-sized printer. The double-width characters make nice headlines,

Table 3-2

Simple Epson control codes.

Beep	CHR$(7)
Backspace	CHR$(8)
Line feed	CHR$(10)
Form feed	CHR$(12)
Carriage return	CHR$(13)
Compressed on	CHR$(15)
Compressed off	CHR$(18)
Double width (5 CPI)	CHR$(14)
Double width off	CHR$(18)

but be aware that, unlike the compressed characters, the CHR$(14) command that turns the double-width characters on only works for the current line.

Another way to control a printer involves sending it more than one control code at a time. Most of these combination codes are preceded by a special code (ASCII 27) that the keyboard generates when the Esc key is pressed. For this reason, they usually are called *escape sequences*. Table 3-3 is a list of some of the more common escape sequences for Epson and Epson-compatible printers.

Older printers might not support proportional spacing. Proportional spacing means that letters like an *m* take up more space than letters like *i*. This spacing gives a cleaner, more typeset look. Some printers let you combine these features. For example, printing in proportionally spaced italics or compressed superscripts. Obviously, printers are different and the manual that came with your printer is the best guide.

Table 3-3   Some common Epson escape sequences.

Italics on	CHR$(27)+CHR$(52)
Italics off	CHR$(27)+CHR$(53)
Underline on	CHR$(27)+CHR$(45)+CHR$(1)
Underline off	CHR$(27)+CHR$(41)+CHR$(0)
Double strike on	CHR$(27)+CHR$(71)
Double strike off	CHR$(27)+CHR$(72)
Superscript on	CHR$(27)+CHR$(83)+CHR$(0)
Subscript on	CHR$(27)+CHR$(83)+CHR$(1)
Subscript/superscript off	CHR$(27)+CHR$(84)
Proportional space on	CHR$(27)+CHR$(112)+CHR$(1)
Proportional space off	CHR$(27)+CHR$(112)+CHR$(0)
Master reset (cancels all active features)	CHR$(27)+CHR$(64)

I've given you only a sample of the features. You can control each pin separately and, most likely, have very fine control of the spacing between lines as well.

Here's a QBasic demonstration program that uses the control codes to print the same string in different ways.

```
' CH3 \ P4.BAS
' some common features of Epson compatible printers

CLS
PRINT "This demonstrates some common features of an Epson"
PRINT "compatible printer."
PRINT
PRINT "Enter a sentence—no longer than 80 characters"
INPUT A$

LPRINT CHR$(12)                              ' New sheet of paper

LPRINT CHR$(27);CHR$(52);A$                  ' start italic
LPRINT CHR$(27);CHR$(53)                      ' cancel italic

LPRINT CHR$(27);CHR$(71);A$                  ' start double-strike
LPRINT CHR$(27);CHR$(72)                      ' end double-strike

LPRINT CHR$(27);CHR$(45);CHR$(1);A$          ' start underlining
LPRINT CHR$(27);CHR$(45);CHR$(2)             ' end underlining

LPRINT CHR$(27);CHR$(112);CHR$(1);A$         ' proportional space on
LPRINT CHR$(27);CHR$(112);CHR$(0)            ' proportional space off

LPRINT "Water!":LPRINT
LPRINT "H";CHR$(27);CHR$(83);CHR$(1);"2";    'subscript demo
LPRINT CHR$(27);CHR$(84);                     ' subscript off
LPRINT "O"
LPRINT

LPRINT "And finally—heavy water!":LPRINT
LPRINT "H";CHR$(27);CHR$(83);CHR$(1);"2";
LPRINT CHR$(8);                               'back space
LPRINT CHR$(27);CHR$(83);CHR$(0);"2";        'superscript
LPRINT CHR$(27);CHR$(84);
LPRINT "O"

LPRINT CHR$(27);CHR$(64)                      ' back to default
END
```

I suspect that this program is pretty clear. I simply sent the appropriate control code out before printing the phrase.

Printing the symbol for heavy water, $H_2^2O_2$, was a little more complicated.

Heavy water, or deuterium oxide, is water where ordinary hydrogen is replaced by deuterium. The symbol for deuterium is H^2. To get a superscript and subscript in essentially the same place, I use the backspace code, CHR$(8), to move the printhead back one space.

Even if this program is pretty clear, it also is written pretty stupidly. I've broken a cardinal rule: write programs so they are as easy as possible to correct. Here the lines are made up of multiple CHR$ commands; it's far too easy to make a mistake. A far better written program would begin by assigning variables to the printer features that I wanted to control:

```
FormFeed$ = CHR$(12)                ' New sheet of paper
ItalOn$ = CHR$(27) + CHR$(52)       ' italic
ItalOff$ = CHR$(27) + CHR$(53)      ' cancel italic
DoublStr$ = CHR$(27) + CHR$(71)     ' double-strike
DoubleOff$ = CHR$(27) + CHR$(72)    ' end double-strike
        .        .        .
        .        .        .
```

Now, I would use these variables. Instead of saying:

```
LPRINT CHR$(27);CHR$(52);A$
```

I would say:

```
PRINT ItalOn$;A$
```

Besides making the program easier to read and correct, using variables instead of codes often can make it easier to adapt a program to a new situation. In this case, to use the correctly written program for other printers, all I have to do is change a few assignment statements, which are displayed prominently at the beginning of the program. I won't need to search through many lines of text and make multiple changes. QBasic allows you to set up named constants for situations like this (more on them later).

The LOCATE command and character-oriented graphics

SPC and TAB are used in PRINT statements to move within essentially a single line on the screen. They are impractical for moving the cursor long distances. Long distance moves are best done with the command LOCATE. This command gives you complete control over the cursor's position. For example:

```
LOCATE 1,1       moves the cursor to the top left corner
LOCATE 12,40     moves the cursor to the center of the screen
```

In general, the first number gives the row and the second gives the column. You normally use only the first 24 rows, because the 25th row often is reserved for information. For example, the soft function keys in GW-BASIC or QBasic use this line to explain what certain function keys will do at any given movement when you're in the windowing environment. (Chapter 9 explains how you can do this in your programs). QBasic also uses the 25th line to remind you to press any key to leave the output screen.

To get access to this row, it's best to first use the command KEY OFF. To reserve this row for information again (see chapter 10), use the command KEY ON. Once this command is processed, the LOCATE command will no longer be able to access the 25th row. Moreover, a variant on the CLS command allows you to clear every line except the 25th line. The command is CLS 2.

However, I often find myself wanting to put more than one line of rarely changing information on the screen. To do this you need a way to put part of the screen off limits. QBasic has a command for this; GW-BASIC doesn't. The command that does this is VIEW PRINT. For example, VIEW PRINT 1 TO 20 gives your program a text window of twenty lines, as if the other five lines were frozen. Any scrolling would take place within this window. After this command, a CLS command would clear this window only, leaving the remaining five lines unchanged. Obviously then, the most effective way to use this command is to first write what you need in the bottom five lines, freeze them with the VIEW PRINT command, and continue.

More generally, VIEW PRINT needs to be told the top and bottom lines of the 'text window':

VIEW PRINT *topline* TO *bottomline*

To clear the entire screen after you've set up a window, you use a variant on the CLS command: CLS 0. To release the window completely issue VIEW PRINT alone.

The LOCATE command lets you display rather primitive graphics, even in computers that lack a color display card. The graphics is done by regarding the screen as being an 80×25 grid. Each of these 2000 blocks can have a different character placed in it by the LOCATE command. I find the best way to decide on the many LOCATE commands needed for this kind of graphics is to use a piece of graph paper, with an 80×25 grid already marked off. For example, Fig. 3-1 shows a diagram to display a giant *B*.

To translate this picture into a program just requires the appropriate number of LOCATE and PRINT statements. Here's the QBasic program:

```
'  CH3 \ P5.BAS
'  A giant B

CLS

LOCATE 6, 35: PRINT STRING$(10, "B") LOCATE 7, 35: PRINT "BB";
SPC(8); "BB"
```

```
LOCATE 8, 35: PRINT "BB"; SPC(9); "BB"
LOCATE 9, 35: PRINT "BB"; SPC(10); "BB"
LOCATE 10, 35: PRINT "BB"; SPC(9); "BBB"
LOCATE 11, 35: PRINT "BB"; SPC(6); "BBBB"
LOCATE 12, 35: PRINT "BB"; SPC(4); "BBBBB"
LOCATE 13, 35: PRINT "BB"; SPC(6); "BBBB"
LOCATE 14, 35: PRINT "BB"; SPC(9); "BBB"
LOCATE 15, 35: PRINT "BB"; SPC(10); "BB"
LOCATE 16, 35: PRINT "BB"; SPC(9); "BB"
LOCATE 17, 35: PRINT "BB"; SPC(8); "BB"
LOCATE 18, 35: PRINT STRING$(10, "B")

END
```

As you can see, the translation from a grid to a program is straightforward if a bit messy. I did take advantage of the STRING$ command whenever possible. The next chapter will show you some other techniques that also can shorten this type of program. However, programming character-oriented graphics is almost always tedious.

The LOCATE command actually has five different options. If you use one of these extra features, then you must separate it from the next by a comma. You've seen the first two. They control the cursor's location. The next option controls

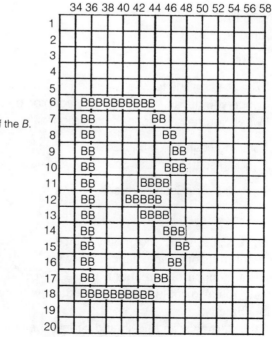

3-1 A graph of the B.

whether the cursor is visible or not. A command like LOCATE 1,1,0 moves the cursor to the top left corner, but the cursor is no longer visible. More generally, the command LOCATE ,,0 keeps the cursor fixed but turns it off. A fragment like:

```
CLS
LOCATE ,,0
I$ = INPUT$(1)
```

gives you a truly blank screen in QBasic, until you press a key. Then, in QBasic, the ubiquitous Press any key to continue pops up. Similarly, at any time while a program is running, the command LOCATE ,,1 makes the cursor visible at its current location.

Usually, the cursor is a fairly thin bar on the bottom of a line. You can widen or move it within a line by using the last two options for the LOCATE command. If you look closer at your monitor (perhaps with a magnifying glass), you can see that the image is made up of hundreds of lines of dots. Each of these lines is called a *scan line*. On a color display, there are seven scan lines per row of text (on a monochrome display there are 13). The normal cursor is made up of a single scan line on a color graphics display and the bottom two scan lines on a monochrome display. The fourth and fifth options control on which scan line the cursor should start and on which scan line it should end. For example, on a color graphics display, LOCATE ,,1,2,5 gives a cursor that takes up the middle of a text row. LOCATE ,,1,7,7 is the ordinary cursor shape for a CGA monitor. Try the following program:

```
'  CH3 \ P6.BAS
'  The Cursor's shape

CLS

PRINT "The Starting line for the cursor can be between 0-7"
PRINT "when you have a color graphics adaptor, between 0 and 13"
PRINT "when you have a monochrome monitor."

INPUT "Starting scan line"; StartScan
INPUT "Ending scan line";EndScan

LOCATE 12,40,1,StartScan,EndScan

END
```

Once you run this program, you might want to use the Immediate window to restore the cursor to its ordinary shape, otherwise it will remain in whatever form you left it. For a monochrome monitor, use LOCATE ,,0,7,7 to change the cursor back to normal. You also could use the Immediate window to experiment with the cursor's shape directly.

Usually, the starting scan line should be less than the ending scan line. However, if you experiment with the previous program, you'll see that this is not required. Making the starting scan line greater than the ending scan line gives a two part cursor made up of the scan lines greater than or equal to the starting scan line and less than or equal to the ending scan line (except, for some strange reason, when the cursor is on the first line).

To summarize, you have five possibilities, any of which can be left out as long as the comma is there as a placeholder:

LOCATE *row,col,on/off,startscan,endscan*

There are other features of your display that QBasic allows you to control. On a color monitor, for example, you can change the background color or the color of each character. On a monochrome monitor, you can control whether a character blinks or is highlighted. The end of the next chapter explains how to do this.

Numbers in DOS BASIC

Before you can control the way numbers are printed, you have to understand more about the various kinds of numbers that DOS BASIC can handle. The simplest numbers for DOS BASIC are ordinary integers. An *integer* is a whole number, like 0, 1, −1, 2, −2, and so on. You tell DOS BASIC that a variable will have only integer values by using a special identifier: the percent sign (%). For example:

LET A% = 3 or
I% = I% + 1

If a program tries to assign a number with a decimal part to an integer variable, the number is rounded off to the nearest integer. If the decimal part was exactly 0.5, for example 53.5, the number is rounded up to the nearest even (not odd) integer (in this case, to 54). If you say LET A%=3.4, A% will have the value 3. If you say LET A% = 52.5, A% will have the value 52 (the nearest even integer).

You must be aware that, although the whole numbers don't stop in nature, they do stop in DOS BASIC. Any attempt to assign a value greater than 32,767 or less than −32768 to an integer will result in an *overflow error*. Your program will either refuse to run or will behave erratically. Because of their limited size, programmers often refer to these type of integers as *short integers*.

Because short integer variables have an obvious disadvantage, why use them at all? The reason is that DOS BASIC handles arithmetic within the allowable range of integers very fast and completely accurately. They are so fast that using them as counters can measurably speed up your programs. Integer variables also take up the least amount of room in memory.

For situations where the range for integer variables is not sufficient, QBasic allows you to use another type of variable. This is the *long*, or large, *integer*. Arithmetic using these numbers, which are denoted by the ampersand (&) type identifier, also are very fast, although obviously not as fast as the short integer type. The range for long integers is quite large: $-2,147,483,648$ to $+2,147,483,647$ (roughly plus or minus two billion). Each long integer takes twice as much room in memory as a short integer. Within the allowable range, arithmetic for long integers is completely accurate. (Note that this type of integer is not available in GW-BASIC.)

For both types of integers, any calculation involving addition, multiplication, or subtraction is done rapidly and accurately. The main point to keep in mind in QBasic is what is usually called *intermediate overflow*. This is a fancy way of saying that, although the answer might be within the allowable range in the journey, you went beyond the boundary. For example, if $A\% = 12345$ and $B\% = 23456$, then $3*A\% - B\%$ generates an overflow error, although the answer, 13579, is well within the allowable range for short integers. You would need to use long integers to do this multiplication.

In high school, you might have spent some time on trying to understand what the teacher meant when he or she said $1/3$ was equal to 0.33333333. . . . This problem reoccurs when dealing with computers. They are finite machines and can't deal with numbers that go on forever. Computers have to stop and use approximations. The more accurate you want the approximation or the calculations to be, the longer the program usually will take to run. (I say usually because, if you have a math coprocessor chip for your machine, then this isn't true. The appropriate 87 chip for your machine calculates both extremely rapidly and to a high degree of accuracy. Having one can make it faster to calculate more accurately.)

The accuracy that DOS BASIC uses for its numbers is called the *precision* of the number. Because a calculation can be no more accurate than the numbers that go into it, the least precise number determines the accuracy of the calculation.

Single-precision numbers are DOS BASIC's stock-in-trade. Unless you specify otherwise, a variable automatically is defaulted to be a single-precision variable. They are accurate to only six or seven significant figures, although they can be displayed with 16 places. The word *significant* is best understood by means of an example: both 123,456 and 123,456,000 have six significant figures. The extra zeros are not relevant to the accuracy. On the other hand, a single-precision number cannot distinguish between 123,456,001 and 123,455,999 because both numbers now have nine significant figures (adding a one made the two zeros significant).

Perhaps the best way to think of what significant means is to think of the difference between 1 meter and 100 centimeters: there isn't any difference. Both are the same measurement. You wouldn't have any extra information if someone told you the water in your basement was 1 meter or 100 centimeters high. So, a zero is insignificant if you can change the units of measurement and not gain or lose information.

Significant figures measure the accuracy of a number, but the possibility of adding zeros—changing the units—measures the range. Single-precision variables have an enormous range. They can be as large as a 3.37 followed by 38 zeros.

Although DOS BASIC defaults variables to single precision, you're best off specifying this yourself. You specify a single-precision variable by adding a type identifier to it—much as the $, %, or & are used to distinguish strings, short integers, or long integers. To identify a single-precision variable, you use an exclamation point (programmers often refer to this as a *bang*). So, setting A! = ¹/3 gives A! a seven place approximation to ¹/3.

A double-precision variable is identified by a pound sign (#). Double-precision variables have a phenomenal range. They can have 308 decimal digits (a 4.19 followed by 308 zeros, roughly). They also are very accurate—to 16 (sometimes even 17) significant digits. The disadvantage to using them is that, unless you have the appropriate mathematical coprocessor, double-precision calculations take a lot longer.

More concretely, if the federal government used single-precision numbers in its calculations, it would not be able to distinguish between a deficit of 135,000,000,000 and 135,000,999,999. While this probably doesn't mean much, accuracy is nice, so I would suggest that calculations involving such large numbers use double-precision variables. Double-precision numbers can tell the difference between 135,000,999,999.01 and 135,000,999,999.99 and still have two places of accuracy left over. Because numbers like ¹/3 usually will be calculated in single-precision, you need a way to tell DOS BASIC to calculate more accurately. This is done by writing ¹/3#.

One problem with the different kinds of variables is that you might, by mistake, leave off the identifier. One way to avoid this problem is to use DOS BASIC's ability to specify that all variables beginning with a single letter or a range of letters will be used only for a single type of variable. This overrules DOS BASIC's default characterization of variables as single precision.

For example, to make all variables beginning with the letter *I* integer variables (so I, IZZY, and ICHABOD automatically would be integer variables), place the command DEFINT I in your program before you use any variables beginning with an *I*. Similarly, to make all variables whose names begin with *I*, *J*, or *K* integer variables, use DEFINT I-K. DEFINT A-Z makes all variables default to integer variables. In a sense then, the DEFINT A-Z command changes DOS BASIC's built-in default options.

However, just as for DOS BASIC's built-in defaults, you can always overrule this command by using the correct identifier. Even after a DEFINT A-Z, A# still is a double-precision variable. Here are the other definers:

DEFLNG   To define a long integer range (QBasic only)
DEFSNG   To define a single precision range
DEFDBL   To define a double precision range
DEFSTR   To define a string range

Just as for the DEFINT command, you can use the dash to define a range for variables of a fixed type. DEFDBL X-Z makes all variables beginning with *X*, *Y*, or *Z* double precision.

In general, most programmers use one of these definers only if most of the variables in the program are of a single type. DEFINT A-Z, for example, would be used if a programmer was convinced that he or she would be using mostly integers.

If you've tried any calculation involving very large numbers, you probably have found out that DOS BASIC often doesn't bother printing out large numbers of insignificant zeros. Instead, it uses a variant on scientific or exponential notation. For example, if you ask DOS BASIC to print a 1 followed by 30 zeros, what you end up with is 1E+030. If you are not familiar with this notation, then think of the E+ as meaning that you should move the decimal place to the right exactly the number places shown following the plus sign, adding zeros if necessary. When negative numbers follow the *E*, move the decimal point to the left. 1.7E−5 gives you 0.000017.

DOS BASIC starts using the E notation if the number requires more than 16 places to be displayed. However, you can enter a number using the E notation any time you find it easier to do so. DOS BASIC doesn't care whether you enter 1000, 1E3, or 1E+3. (To make the number double precision use *D* instead of the *E*.)

Finally, if you assign a single-precision variable to a double-precision variable, you do not suddenly increase its accuracy. The number might suddenly have more (or different digits) but only the first six or seven can be trusted.

Assigning a single-precision variable to a double-precision variable is an example of what programmers call *type conversion*. This means that DOS BASIC changes the type of a variable if it has to. If A% equals 3, then the assignment statement A# = A% would involve changing the 3 to a double-precision value for this statement to make sense.

When you use a constant in a program, DOS BASIC assumes that, if a number has:

- No decimal point and is in the range −32768 to 32767, it's an integer.
- No decimal point and is in the range for a long integer, it's a long integer.
- A decimal point and is in the range for a single-precision number, it's assumed to be single precision.

- A decimal point and its outside the range for a single-precision number, it's assumed to be double precision.

These assumptions occasionally lead to problems, because the realm in which an answer lives in QBasic is determined by where the questions lived. If you start with two integers, QBasic assumes the answer is an integer. For example, in a statement like PRINT 23456*12345, QBasic assumes that both 23456 and 12345 are integers. The answer also is assumed to be an integer, but it's too big. This statement would generate an overflow error. The cure is to add the double precision or long integer identifier to one of the numbers. Write PRINT 23456#*12345. This command forces QBasic to treat the 23456 and the answer as a double-precision number.

Another way to force a type conversion is to use special built-in functions. CINT would convert a small number to an integer by rounding. CLNG would convert it to a long integer by rounding. CSNG converts to single precision and CDBL to double precision. In any case, GW-BASIC users don't have to worry, the older interpreter actually is better at making implicit type conversions.

One final point worth keeping in mind is that you cannot use the SWAP command to interchange the contents of two variables of different types. SWAP Integer%, A& is impossible, even if the value of A& happened to be within the proper range for an integer.

Pretty printing

You already have seen a problem with calculations done by DOS BASIC: the answers to simple calculations look strange. You end up with 16 decimal digits when you really want an answer with only two decimal digits. You can overcome this problem with a variant on the PRINT and LPRINT commands called PRINT USING and LPRINT USING.

These commands work with *templates*, or *format strings*. For numbers, these templates usually consist of pound signs (#) with a decimal point followed by more pound signs. For example, a command like:

PRINT USING "###.##";438.37123456

yields 438.37. Moreover, if necessary, the compiler will round the number so that it fits into the template. If you ask it to:

PRINT USING "###.##";438.37649678

what you will see is 438.38, because this number is rounded up (the digit after the 7 is a 6) to fit into a template having only two decimal places.

Similarly, if you use the PRINT USING command and follow it with a calculation, the computer will do any rounding necessary to fit the result inside the template. For example, consider the following program fragment:

```
CLS
PRINT 1000/7
PRINT USING "###.##";1000/7
```

What you will see is:

```
142.8571428571429
142.86
```

Notice that the display is indented one space for the first calculation and flush left for the answer displayed using the PRINT USING command. This difference occurs because the PRINT USING command, unlike the PRINT command, does not leave room for an implied plus sign. If you want a plus or minus sign in front of a number, you must put it in front of the format string. For example:

```
PRINT USING " + ###.##";342.71
```

yields +342.71

The result of using a format strings can be complicated. Suppose you work through the following example without using the computer and that your template has five pound signs before the decimal place and three after it. The PRINT USING "#####.###" command tries to print any number using no more than five digits before the decimal point and three digits after. It will try to print any number in a nine space block. If there are fewer than three decimal digits after the decimal point, you will get trailing zeros. If there are fewer than five digits in front of the decimal point, you will get leading blanks. This means that printing more than one number with the same template always lines up the decimal points—extra spaces are placed to the right and left as needed.

What happens if you try to print a number with more than five digits in front of the decimal point? For example:

```
PRINT USING "#####.###";123456.123
```

DOS BASIC prints the entire number but precedes it by a percent sign to tell you that the format string didn't fit the number.

The leading blanks that the PRINT USING command leaves can be a problem. Suppose you were writing a program that will print out checks. You obviously don't won't to have any leading blanks; they are an invitation for someone to fill in a larger amount. Another kind of format string takes care of this problem. If you place two dollar signs in front of any format string, a dollar sign is placed flush with the beginning of the number—no leading spaces will show up. One of the two dollar signs stands for the dollar sign that is printed in front of the number, the other one plays a dual role. A statement like PRINT USING "###.##" allows numbers as large as 999.99; however, a statement like PRINT USING "$$###.##" allows dollar amounts as large as 9999.99.

Similarly, if you place two asterisks in front of a format string, all leading spaces are replaced by asterisks. Here, however, both asterisks count as digit positions, so:

PRINT USING "**###.##"

allows numbers as large as 99,999.99 (although, in printing a number as large as this, no asterisks would be used).

Finally, if you want to put commas after every three digits within your numbers, use a comma before the decimal point. For example:

PRINT USING "$$###,.##";9999.89

gives $9,999.89.

Occasionally, in accounting for example, you might want to print numbers like:

$4444.00+ or
$332.23−

This also can be done with the PRINT USING command; merely place a plus sign at the end of the format string. To display a minus sign and leave a blank (if the number was positive), use a trailing minus sign.

Scientists sometimes like numbers to be printed in exponential, or scientific, notation. They like 1E03 better than 1000. If you need to use scientific notation, place four (or five if you have too many digits in the exponent) exponential signs (^) after the template:

PRINT USING "#.##^^^^";1000

gives 1.00E03.

You can place a group of characters in the quotes along with the template; they will be reproduced exactly. For example:

PRINT USING "I will pay you $#######,.## if ..."; 1000000
gives:

I will pay you $1,000,000.00 if ...

Suppose you wanted to write a program that would convert numbers to percentages. At the key conversion step, you can't say:

PRINT Number*100;"%"

because the automatic space that DOS BASIC sticks on at the end of the calculation would force the percent sign over by a space. Instead, assuming you want only two decimal points, say:

PRINT USING "###.##%";Number*100

Another way to put a string at the end of a number is to follow the PRINT USING statement by a semicolon. This accomplishes the same thing as the previous example because the semicolon suppresses the automatic carriage return here as well.

Finally, let me end this section by pointing out that programs that use complicated format strings are as badly written as my original printer control program was and for much the same reason. The cure also is the same: use string variables for your format strings. (The STRING$ command combined with the plus sign concatenation operator makes setting up these variables easy.) Instead of saying:

PRINT USING "$$#######,.##"

use an extra statement:

LargeNumber$ = "$$" + STRING$(7,"#") + ",." + STRING$(2,"#")
PRINT USING LargeNumber$;

This might take up more room, but I'm sure you'll find that it is a lot easier to debug a program with the latter type of statements rather than the former.

The PRINT USING command is so important but the number of options and possibilities so large that I find myself frequently referring to the online help in QBasic for this command. Luckily, the online help includes a complete, detailed summary of PRINT USING's many variations. GW-BASIC users should consult the reference manual that came with their machines if they need more information.

Summary

This chapter showed you how to better control output to the screen and the printer using the following commands:

ASC	Is the opposite of CHR$ and gives the ASCII code of the first character inside the parentheses.
CHR$	Gives the character determined by the ASCII code inside the parentheses.
CLS	Clears the text view port (see VIEW PRINT).
CLS 0	Clears the whole screen, even if a VIEW PRINT is in effect
CLS 2	Clears all but the bottom line of the screen
INPUT$	Picks up keystrokes without echoing them on the screen (the number is determined by the value inside the parentheses).

KEY ON	Displays key information.
KEY OFF	Is the best way to prepare to make the 25th line usable.
LOCATE *row*, *col*	Sends the cursor directly to the row and column specified and has other options to control how (or whether) the cursor is visible.
LPRINT USING	Completely controls (using certain templates) the way a number is printed.
PRINT USING	Completely controls (using certain templates) the way a number is displayed on the screen.
SPACE$	Creates a string that consists of blanks.
SPC	Moves the cursor or printhead a specified number of spaces
STRING$(*x*,*y$*)	Creates a string consisting of multiple copies of the second entry.
TAB	Moves to a specified location within a line
VIEW PRINT *top* TO *bottom*	Makes part of the screen as "off limits" to scrolling and sets up a text window.
WRITE	A rare command used to display strings on the screen with quotation marks.

You saw the ASCII codes for the characters and the Alt key and numeric keypad method for entering the higher order ASCII codes.

4
CHAPTER

Doing things repeatedly

Computers excel at repetition; that's one of the main reasons they're so useful. Although you can't just say:

DO *instructions* 500 TIMES

in QBASIC, you can come close. (In GW-BASIC, you're more limited as usual.) This chapter shows you one way to program loops; chapter 5 will show you another way. In addition, you'll see how to use the higher ASCII codes, which were mentioned in chapter 3, to draw boxes and other useful shapes. Next, you'll see how to control the way text appears on the screen. For example, I'll show you how to change the color (for color graphics adaptors) or intensity (for monochrome adaptors) of the text. Finally, you'll learn some new debugging techniques.

The commands covered in this chapter are:

FOR-NEXT (with STEP)
COLOR
SLEEP

Getting started

The simplest way to repeat operations in DOS BASIC looks like this:

FOR
        statements in DOS BASIC to accomplish what you want
NEXT

FOR and NEXT are a pair of commands—they must always be used together. The part of the program starting with FOR and ending with NEXT is called a *FOR-NEXT loop*. The statements between the key words FOR and NEXT are called the *body* of the loop.

For example, remember the old-fashioned punishment of having to write "I will not be late" 500 times? If you had a teacher who believed in this sort of thing yet was open enough to new ideas to let you use a printer and QBasic to generate them, then you could use the following program:

```
'      CH4 \ P1.BAS
'     punishment (?)

FOR I = 1 TO 500
    LPRINT "I will not be late!"
NEXT I

END
```

Think of a FOR-NEXT loop as winding up a wheel inside the computer so that it will spin a fixed number of times. During each spin of the wheel the computer can be told things to do.

The command FOR sets up a counter variable (in the example above, it's the I, which has a starting value of 1). The computer first checks that the counter variable is less than the *test value*, which is given by the number following the key word TO. After this initial check, DOS BASIC processes all subsequent statements until the computer gets to the command NEXT. At that point, it adds one to the counter variable, returns to the top of the loop, and checks again. These cycles continue until the counter is greater than (not equal to) the test value. As soon as this happens, DOS BASIC jumps past the body of the loop to the first statement following the key word NEXT.

In the above program, a copy of the "I will not be late!" phrase is sent to the printer during each cycle. When the loop is finished, DOS BASIC jumps to the END statement, finishing the program.

It's a good idea to make sure that you understand why this program prints out 500 copies and not 499 or 501 copies before going any further. *Off-by-one errors* are the most common type of problems that you'll run into when using FOR-NEXT loops. There are three ways that I use to try to avoid these type of errors. First, I keep in mind that a loop terminates only when the counter exceeds (not equals) the test value. Next, I often check (by hand) how many times the loop will work using a much smaller test value. In this case, I probably would try to program the case FOR I = 1 TO 2 by hand. By doing this, I would discover that I would get two copies of the phrase. I'd be confident in extrapolating to the case where the test value was 500 or 1000. Finally, a more abstract alternative that I occasionally adopt is to say to myself that on each pass the variable I increases by 1, so it's going to take 500 tries to get it past 500.

To see the initial check that DOS BASIC does in a FOR-NEXT loop try this program:

```
'      CH4 \ P2.BAS
'      A nonexecuting FOR-NEXT loop

CLS

FOR I = 1 to 0
      PRINT "Will you see this?"
NEXT I

END
```

In this program, the counter already is greater than the test value, so the loop is never started. The answer to the question on the PRINT statement is that you won't see it.

You can use any type of numeric variable for the counter; however, when possible, choose an integer variable. Using an integer variable for your counters ensures that DOS BASIC spends as little time as possible on the arithmetic needed to change the counter. Some people like to restrict variables whose names begin with I for integer variables (like counter variables) because it reminds them both of the word *integer* and the word *index*, which is a fancier word for counter. If you choose this strategy, the DEFINT command from chapter 3 (in the form of an early DEFINT I) makes this easy.

After you outline a program, there is a good rule of thumb for determining if the program needs a FOR-NEXT loop. If you want to perform an operation a fixed number of times, you'll need a FOR-NEXT loop. If you just want the operation to repeat but aren't sure of the number of times, you'll need another type of loop. Other types of loops are explained in chapter 5.

Finally, you might have noticed that I indented the body of both of the FOR-NEXT loops in this section. As always, the spacing within a program is an attempt to make the program more readable and easier to debug. Indenting the body of a loop makes it clearer that there is a repeated operation at work. Because the designers of QBasic feel as strongly about the need to indent FOR-NEXT loops as I do, they've made it easy. The QBasic editor features an auto-indent option. What happens is that the Smart Editor remembers the indentation of the previous line. Every time you hit Enter, the cursor returns to a spot directly below where the line above began. If you get into the habit of using the Tab key to start each level of indentation, then you can undo the indentation pattern for a block by selecting the block and hitting Shift−Tab. In any case, to unindent a line when you're below an indented line, you always can use some combination of the Home key, backspace, left arrow, or Ctrl−S.

More on FOR-NEXT loops

Most often, you don't want to do the same thing time after time; something changes. You can use a counting variable to grab hold of that change. For example, to display the numbers from 1 to 100 on the screen in QBasic:

```
'  CH4 \ P3.BAS
'  using the counter in
'  a FOR-NEXT loop

CLS

FOR I% = 1 TO 100
    PRINT I%
NEXT I%

END
```

Notice that, in this program, the counter variable appears in the PRINT statement in the body of the loop. On each cycle of the loop, DOS BASIC uses the current value of the counter variable I in the PRINT statement. On the first pass through the loop, I has the value 1, so a 1 pops out. On the second cycle, it has the value 2 and a 2 pops out, and so on for 100 cycles.

In a FOR-NEXT loop, you easily can check that the counter really has changed. One way to check the counter is to add the line PRINT I% before the END statement in the previous program and run the modified program. Another way is to wait for the program to end, go to the Immediate window (or use direct mode), and enter PRINT I%. One debugging tool available in QuickBASIC (but not in QBasic) lets you monitor the value of a counter variable on each pass of a loop.

Notice as well that the counter I% was an integer variable. To figure out how much faster using an integer counter variable is than using a single-precision counter (which it would have been if I'd used a plain I as the counter), you need to use the TIMER command from chapter 3. You will recall that this command gives you the number of seconds that have passed since midnight. You need the value of the TIMER at the beginning and the end of each loop. Here's a program that does this:

```
'  CH4 \ P4.BAS
'  an integer counter in
'  a FOR-NEXT loop versus a
'  noninteger counter

CLS
Time0 = TIMER    'starting time

FOR I% = 1 TO 100
```

```
        PRINT I%
NEXT

Time1 = TIMER    'end of first loop

FOR I = 1 TO 100
    PRINT I
NEXT I

Time2 = TIMER    'end of second loop

FirstLoop = Time1 − Time0
SecondLoop = Time2 − Time1

PRINT "Total time elapsed integer loop is ";FirstLoop
PRINT
PRINT "Total time elapsed non-integer loop is";
PRINT SecondLoop;"seconds"
PRINT
PRINT "An integer counter saves";
PRINT SecondLoop − FirstLoop;"seconds or about ";
PRINT USING "##.###%";(SecondLoop − FirstLoop)/FirstLoop*100;
PRINT "faster."

END
```

If you run this program, you'll see that you save about four seconds on a basic PC, which really is quite a lot considering that almost all of DOS BASIC's time is spent printing the numbers, not changing the counters.

Notice that I used REM statements at the end of the lines to explain what the variables stood for. In this case, I wasn't convinced that the names I chose for the variables were sufficiently selfdocumenting. Finally, notice the PRINT USING statement, which gives you a nicely formatted percentage.

In GW-BASIC the customary way to speed up a FOR-NEXT loop was to say NEXT rather than NEXT I, leaving off the counter variable usually saved a little time.

Here's an example of a QBasic program that prints all the ASCII characters along with their code numbers.

```
' CH4 \ P5.BAS
' ASCII codes

CLS

FOR I% = 1 TO 255
    PRINT I%,CHR$(I%)
NEXT I%

END
```

Obviously, the display in this program goes by too fast; you need to slow the display down. There are various ways to do this. One way is the Ctrl−Num Lock combination. Holding down the Ctrl key and pressing the Num Lock key freezes the display. After the display is frozen, hitting any key restarts it. The problem with using this method is that it becomes a kind of super reflex tester—a battle to see whether you can hit the Ctrl−Num Lock combination at exactly the moment you want.

A much better way is to put an empty INPUT$ statement before the NEXT command. Here's a modified version of the previous program:

```
'  CH4 \ P5a.BAS
' ASCII codes revisited
CLS

FOR I% = 1 TO 255

    LOCATE 1,1
    PRINT "To see the next ASCII code press any key."
    KeyPress$ = INPUT$(1)
    LOCATE 12,30
    PRINT I%, CHR$(I%);

NEXT I%

END
```

The instructions are printed starting in the top left corner. The process is repeated on each pass through the loop. Normally, this would be poor programming; you waste a lot of time by rewriting the directions 255 times. Unfortunately, some of the ASCII control codes do strange things to your display. For example, PRINT CHR$(12) clears the screen as well as acting as a form feed for a printer. Without reprinting the directions each time, they would quickly disappear.

After the directions are displayed, DOS BASIC gets to the empty INPUT$ statement. As you saw in chapter 3, after processing an INPUT$ command, DOS BASIC suspends any further operations until you press a key. Once a key is pressed, DOS BASIC moves on to the next command: the cursor moves to the 30th position in the middle row. Next, the number of the ASCII character is printed. Then, DOS BASIC moves to the next print zone and the character itself is displayed. Finally, DOS BASIC goes back and repeats the process.

The technique of using an empty INPUT$ statement to control processing within a loop is quite common. This is because in chapter 5, you'll see how to continue or leave a loop, depending on what key was pressed.

While I'm on the subject of things going by too fast, you might have decided that, sometimes at least, it would be nice to have the computer slow down. The empty INPUT$ statement used in the above program is useful if you want to have the person at the keyboard control the action. Suppose, however, that you wanted to display a message on the screen for a few seconds, erase it, display another message, and so on. You can do this by using a trick that involves a FOR-NEXT loop. Recall that each time the machine encounters a FOR-NEXT loop, it must cycle as many times as you tell it. Each spin of this wheel takes a certain amount of time. For example, on my PC, the following program running in the QBasic environment takes about five seconds to run in the development environment.

```
' CH4 \ P6.BAS
' A five second EMPTY FOR-NEXT loop

FOR I = 1 TO 1883
NEXT I

END
```

More precisely, because I used the TIMER function to check it and it is accurate to only about a tenth of a second, it took somewhere between 4.9 and 5.1 seconds. To see a dramatic demonstration of how much faster an integer counter is than a single-precision counter, modify this program and add the appropriate TIMER statements to time this new empty FOR-NEXT loop.

The trouble with using these empty FOR-NEXT loops to delay a program is that they depend completely on the computer you're using (in computerese, they are *system dependent*) and whether you're running the program as a stand-alone. An AT-type machine easily can be 10 times faster than a basic 4.77 Hz PC. For this reason, QBasic has added a command, the SLEEP command, that suspends the program for a specified number of seconds. A statement like SLEEP 5 stops a program in its tracks for five seconds. SLEEP .1 should stop it for a tenth of a second, but unfortunately it doesn't. The SLEEP command currently rounds the value and always waits an integral number of seconds. The outline for a program that sets up a reading test is simple:

1. Ask how much time the test should take.
2. Print the passage.
3. Wait the right number of seconds.
4. Now erase the passage.

Here's the program, which will not work in GW-BASIC because it uses the SLEEP command:

```
' CH4 \ P7.BAS
' A reading test

CLS
PRINT "When the question mark appears, enter the number of"
```

```
PRINT "seconds you think you will need to read the first "
PRINT "amendment to the constitution of the United States."

INPUT TimeToWait
CLS

PRINT "Congress shall make no law respecting an establishment of"
PRINT "religion, or prohibiting the free exercise thereof; or "
PRINT "abridging the freedom of speech, or of the press; or the"
PRINT "right of the people peaceably to assemble, and to"
PRINT "petition the Government for a redress of grievances."

SLEEP TimeToWait
CLS
PRINT "If you haven't finished yet, you guessed too low!"

END
```

I used multiple PRINT statements to keep the display from being chopped up in weird ways. This program is a good test that you might want to try on some friends.

The SLEEP command has another use. SLEEP without any time specified suspends the program until you press a key. (SLEEP 0 works like a naked SLEEP command; SLEEP .1 works this way as well.) Using this variant and the TIMER statement, you can modify the previous program to measure how long the person took to read the amendment. This naked SLEEP command replaces the older method of writing:

```
PRINT "Press any key ...."
I$ = INPUT$(1)
```

that you already have seen. You also should keep in mind that a command like SLEEP 5 also would be overridden by a key press. If you want the program to wait five seconds without risking the SLEEP being interrupted, you'll need to use the techniques covered in chapter 5.

You can do almost anything in the body of a loop; switching between a printer and a screen is quite common. For example, suppose you wanted to print 100 personalized invitations. You easily could modify program CH2 \ P4.BAS by enclosing it in the appropriate FOR-NEXT loop.

It's not a good idea to change the counter variable within the body of the loop, although nothing in DOS BASIC prevents you from doing so. Consider the following program, but please don't run it yet.

```
' CH4 \ P8.DAN
' PLEASE DON'T RUN THIS YET!!

FOR I = 1 TO 10
```

```
     I = 1
     PRINT ych
NEXT I

END
```

This program will try to run forever. On each cycle of the loop, the counter is set back to the start—I goes back to 1. This is the first example of an *infinite loop*—a loop that never ends. Inadvertently setting up an infinite loop is a common problem, especially in the more complicated loops that you will soon be using. DOS BASIC has a way to break most any loop. Hit the Ctrl− Break combination. Fortunately, once you break a program, there usually still is a way to continue. For QBasic, just as with the breakpoints from chapter 3, hit F5 or select Continue on the Run menu. For GW-BASIC, use the CONT command.

With a FOR-NEXT loop, you can compute compound interest without ever knowing a formula. Common sense suffices. With compound interest, you get the interest added to your original amount to form the new base to compute the interest on next time. Now, you compute the interest on this new amount, add it, and keep going. This common sense description is close to a complete outline for a program:

1. Get the original amount.
2. Find out how many times to compound it.
3. Find the interest on the amount in each period.
4. Add the interest to the original amount.
5. Repeat step 3 as many times as you're doing the compounding.
6. When you're past step 5, print out the final amount.

You need to remember two more things when translating this outline into a program. The first is that people like to give a percentage without using decimals (for example, $12\% = 0.12$). The second is that, if you were getting 8% interest compounded quarterly, you would be getting 2% interest per quarter. Here's the Q-Basic program:

```
'  CH4 \ P9.BAS
' compound interest

CLS

INPUT "What is the original amount"; OrigAmount
INPUT "How many years should it be compounded"; Years
INPUT "Now the interest rate, ex. use 6 for 6%"; IntrstRate
INPUT "How often should it be compounded each year"; Compound

PERIODS = Years * Compound
    RealIntrst = (IntrstRate / 100) / Compound
```

```
    NewAmount = OrigAmount     'keep track of the original amount

    FOR I% = 1 TO PERIODS
      Interest = NewAmount * RealIntrst
      NewAmount = NewAmount + Interest

    NEXT I%

    PRINT USING "$$######,.## was the original amount"; OrigAmount
    PRINT USING "After compounding you have $$######,.##"; NewAmount

    END
```

Notice that this program computed both the number of periods and the interest rate per period before entering the loop. Obviously, you want to do as few calculations within a loop as necessary. If a number isn't going to change during a loop, do the calculation before entering the loop. Such numbers are called *loop invariants*.

Finally, notice the PRINT USING command. Here, as described at the very end of chapter 3, I'm combining a message with a formatting template. The first PRINT USING command tells DOS BASIC to print the number in the form defined by the template, followed by the string. In the second command, it prints the string followed by the number. The template I used allows amounts up to $9,999,999. Recall that one of the dollar signs in a PRINT USING "$$" command can give you an extra digit, if necessary.

This program is quite versatile. Adding just two lines lets you figure how much someone might have in an account (like an IRA) to which they add money frequently. For example, to allow new money to be added each time the interest is credited, change the body of the loop to read:

```
    INPUT "Any new money? Enter 0 or the amount – ",NewMoney
    Interest = NewAmount*RealIntrst
    NewAmount = NewAmount + Interest + NewMoney
```

Doing it by STEPs or backwards

Suppose you want to find the product of the numbers from 1 to 6. (If you are wondering why anyone would want to know this number, it's the number of different results a six-horse race can have.) The outline is clear: start with 1, multiply it by 2, multiply the result by 3, and so on. Here's the QBasic program:

```
    ' CH4 \ P10.BAS
    ' product of the numbers from 1 to 6

    DEFINT A-Z
    CLS
    Finishes = 1
```

```
FOR I = 1 TO 6
   Finishes = Finishes*I
NEXT I

PRINT "The number of possible finishes is";Finishes

END
```

Do you see why I had to initialize the variable Finishes at 1 before the loop starts? If you try the program without this statement, you'll see that the result is zero. As you have seen before, the first time a numeric variable is encountered, it's given the value zero, unless you do something about it. Without the right kind of initializing, the multiplication done within the loop is always by zero, which always gives zero.

The product of the number from 1 up to n often is needed in mathematics. It's used whenever you have to calculate the number of different ways various things can happen. It's called the *factorial*. The symbol is simply an exclamation point. What this program computed would be symbolized by 6!. If you try this program with another number then you'll see that factorials grow very quickly. The DEFINT A-Z command in this program would quickly lead to an overflow error. (Make it DEFINT I.) Factorials are good candidates for the long integer or double-precision variables described in chapter 3. However, even the enormous range of a double-precision variable can not handle 171!.

You might have noticed that, in the program to compute 6!, you really don't have to start the multiplication by multiplying by 1. You really want to start the process with I = 2. FOR-NEXT loops are quite versatile; you can start the counter variable anywhere you like:

```
'  CH4 \ P10a.BAS
' factorial done right

DEFINT A-Z
CLS
Finishes = 1

FOR I = 2 TO 6
   Finishes = Finishes*I
NEXT I

PRINT "The number of possible finishes is";Finishes

END
```

As another example of this, suppose you wanted a variable whose value was "ABCDEFGHIJKLMNOPQRSTUVWXYZ". Although you could set it up by typing, its easier to have DOS BASIC do it for you:

```
UpAlph$ = " "
FOR I% = 65 TO 90
   UpAlph$ = UpAlph$ + CHR$(I%)
NEXT I
```

Moreover, you can use variables for both the starting and test values. For example, suppose you wanted a table that would give you the conversion from Celsius (centigrade) degrees to Fahrenheit. The following QBasic program allows you to decide where to start and where to end.

```
'  CH4 \ P11.BAS
'  A Fahrenheit / Centigrade converter

CLS
DEFINT C
INPUT "Where should I start the conversion table";First
INPUT "Where should I end the table";Last
PRINT
PRINT "F", "C":PRINT                       'A

FOR CenTemp = First TO Last                'B

   F = (9/5*Centemp) +32                   'C
   PRINT CenTemp,;                         'D
   PRINT USING "###.##"; F                 'E

NEXT CenTemp

END
```

Notice that this program has a slightly different format. At the end of some of the lines is the single quote, which marks a remark statement, followed by a comment. As the programs in this book get longer and more complicated it becomes harder to comment on them in a free-form fashion. When necessary, I'll be using this method to indicate the lines that I want to discuss.

A The point of the space is to better align the table. Recall the extra space that DOS BASIC leaves in front of numbers.

B The starting point and ending point are determined from the previous INPUT statements.

C I prefer not to do calculations within PRINT statements. If you studied the hierarchy of operations described in chapter 2, you probably have realized that the parentheses aren't necessary here.

D The semicolon at the end of the PRINT statement keeps the cursor on the current line, in preparation for the PRINT USING statement.

E Two decimal places are enough.

You don't always count by ones. Sometimes it's easier to count by twos or threes or even backwards. You can do this in DOS BASIC by adding the STEP command to your FOR-NEXT loop. The STEP command tells the computer to change the counter by this new amount instead of by one, as was the case previously. For example:

```
' CH4 \ P12.BAS
' Doing it by steps
' the odd numbers

CLS
DEFINT I

FOR I = 1 TO 100 STEP 2
   PRINT I
NEXT I

END
```

Here, each time the NEXT command is processed, the counter increases by two. (Leaving off the STEP command is the same as saying STEP 1.)

You also can count backwards by using a negative STEP. For example, a space simulation program would not be complete without:

```
' CH4 \ P13.BAS
' negative steps
' BLASTOFF!

CLS
DEFINT I

FOR I = 10 TO 1 STEP −1
 PRINT "It's T minus";I;"and counting."
NEXT

PRINT
PRINT "Blastoff!"

END
```

When you use a negative STEP, a FOR-NEXT loop is bypassed completely if the starting value isn't more than the test value, which is exactly the opposite of what happens with a positive STEP.

Up to this point, I've used only integers for the steps and, for reasons of speed, even in the counter variables. Sometimes, however, you want to start at a fraction, move up by a fraction, or both. For example, mortgage tables often go up by $1/4\%$ amounts. Stepping by fractions is easy to do, but you do have to make sure that your variable is given the right identifier, single- or double-precision. Make sure that you don't force the issue with the DEFINT command.

As an example of stepping by fractions, here's a program that prints out a simple mortgage table. The formula for computing the amount of a mortgage can be found in many books. The required monthly payment is:

$$\text{Principal} * \frac{(\text{MInterest})}{1 - [1/(1+\text{MInterest})^\wedge \text{Years}*12]}$$

where MInterest is the monthly interest

A simple program that will give the mortgage amount for a single possible interest involves translating this formula. It might look like:

```
INPUT "The principal of your mortgage";Prin
INPUT "The yearly interest rate";YrInterest

MIntrst = (YrInterest/100)/12

Amount = Prin*MIntrst/(1 - (1/(1 + MIntrst))^Months)
PRINT USING "$####.##";Amount
```

However, at this point, you have the tools to do something much more useful. You could allow someone to enter an interest rate and have the program print out the mortgage amount for a range of interest rates around the one they entered. Here's the QBasic program:

```
'  CH4 \ P14.BAS
' A simple mortgage table
' using the formula
'

'   Principal *        (Interest)
'              ────────────────────────────
'              1 - [1/(1 + Interest)^Years*12]
'

CLS
DEFDBL A-Z

PRINT "Please enter the interest rate."
PRINT "Use 9 for 9%, 9.5 for 9 1/2 % etc."
INPUT "Interest rate"; NTRST
INTRST = (NTRST/100)
StartIntrst = INTRST - .005        ' Do 1/2% either        'A
EndIntrst = INTRST + .005          ' way.
TEP = 1/800                        ' 1/8 percent steps

PRINT
INPUT "Now enter the principal - no commas of course"; Prin
```

```
INPUT "Now enter the number of years ";Yrs
Months = Yrs*12
PRINT:PRINT

FOR I = StartIntrst TO EndIntrst STEP TEP                    'B

    MIntrst = I/12
    PRINT USING "##.###%";I*100;TAB(25);                     'C
    Amount = Prin*MIntrst/(1 – (1/(1 + MIntrst))^Months)
    PRINT USING "####.##";Amount

NEXT I

END
```

A   When you use a complicated formula, it's a good idea to include it in the remark section.

B   The program moves through a range of interests rates by $1/8$% steps.

C   All I've done is fold the previous fragment inside the appropriate FOR-NEXT loop. These lines convert the decimal back to a percent and use a string inside the PRINT USING command to place a percent sign flush with the interest rate. The TAB command aligns the table.

Nested FOR-NEXT loops

Suppose you want to print out a multiplication table for any one number. At this point, it shouldn't be hard. Here's a fragment that uses a FOR-NEXT loop to print out the first line of such a table. I'm assuming the table starts with the 2s.

```
FOR J = 2 TO 12
    PRINT 2*J;
NEXT J
```

Now, for a multiplication table, you want to use the same fragment with the 2 replaced by a 3, the 3 by a 4, and so on. Obviously, this calls for a FOR-NEXT loop as well. The program's outline might look like:

1. Start with 2
2. Do a line of the table
3. Now do it for 3
4. Continue on through 12

Think of the outer part as defining a large controlling loop and the inner loop as doing what the program has to, pretty much independently of the outer loop. Here's a fragment that translates this outline:

```
FOR Number = 2 TO 12
    FOR J = 2 TO 12
```

```
        PRINT Number*J;
        NEXT J
    NEXT Number
```

This fragment might look a little complicated the first time you see it. The way I prefer to think about this procedure is that the inner loop, just like in the outline, really does one thing. It's like a command in DOS BASIC that does something a bit more complicated than the usual commands. Here's what happens: the value of the variable Number starts at 2 and then the inner loop begins. When the inner loop finishes (J > 12), then DOS BASIC processes the NEXT Number command and so Number changes to 3. The value of Number remains the same for an entire course of the inner loop.

The display of this program isn't very nice looking. Here's a more polished QBasic version:

```
' CH4 \ P15.BAS
' a multiplication table
' demonstrating nested FOR-NEXT loops

CLS
DEFINT A-Z

FOR Row = 2 TO 12

    FOR Col = 2 TO 12
        LOCATE 1,5*Col: PRINT Col;                          'A
        LOCATE 2*Row,1: PRINT Row;                          'B
        LOCATE 2*Row,5*Col:PRINT USING "###";Row*Col;       'C
    NEXT Col                                                'D

NEXT Row

END
```

A   I decided to print the numbers in the first row of the table.

B   Ditto for the columns, except that I decided to leave a blank row between lines of the table. That's the point of the 2*ROW.

C   This line prints the table, separating each entry from the next by five spaces and using the PRINT USING command to make sure that everything lines up.

D   When nesting FOR-NEXT loops, it's a good idea to leave blank lines separating the inner loop from the outer loop. Finally, I should point out that the semicolons at the end of each PRINT statement are there to prevent inadvertent scrolling.

Nested FOR-NEXT loops have a bad reputation. They are supposed to be hard to program and even harder to understand. The reputation is undeserved. If you are careful about your outlines, they won't be hard to program. If you are careful about your indentation, they won't be hard to understand either.

The rule for nesting a FOR-NEXT loop is simple: the inner loop must be completed before the counter for the outer loop is changed.

As another example, you easily can modify the mortgage program to vary the interest rate and the principal. If you think of that program as defining a very complicated command in DOS BASIC, then the outline of the program is:

```
FOR Prin = StartPrint TO EndPrin STEP 1000
    The original mortgage program
NEXT Prin
```

Here's the program, slightly jazzed up to make the display more appealing:

```
'  CH4 \ P16.BAS

CLS
KEY OFF                                                    'A
DEFDBL A-Z

PRINT "Please enter the interest rate."
PRINT "Use 9 for 9%, 9.5 for 9 1/2 % etc."
INPUT "Interest rate"; NTRST
Intrst = (NTRST / 100)
StartIntrst = Intrst − .00375   ' Do 3/8% either           'B
EndIntrst = Intrst + .00375   ' way.
TEP = 1 / 800                   ' 1/8 percent steps

PRINT
INPUT "Now enter the principal − no commas of course"; Principle
StartPrin = Principle − 5000
EndPrin = Principle + 5000
PRINT

INPUT "Now enter the number of years "; Yrs
Months = Yrs * 12

CLS
Row = 5
Col = 10

LOCATE 1, 1
PRINT "Principle"; TAB(34); "INTEREST RATE";

FOR Prin = StartPrin TO EndPrin STEP 1000
```

```
        LOCATE Row,1                                                   'C
        PRINT USING "######,"; Prin;                                   'D

        FOR I = StartIntrst TO EndIntrst STEP TEP

            MIntrst = I / 12
            LOCATE 3, Col: PRINT USING "###.###"; I * 100;             'E
            Amount = Prin * MIntrst / (1 − (1 / (1 + MIntrst)) ^ Months)
            LOCATE Row, Col                                            'F
            PRINT USING "####.##"; Amount;                             'G
            Col = Col + 10                                             'H

        NEXT I

            Row = Row + 2                                              'I
            Col = 10                                                   'J

    NEXT Prin

    LOCATE 2, 25                                                       'K
    PRINT "(Press any key when finished.)";
    I$ = INPUT$(1)

    END
```

A   The program needs all 25 lines of the display.

B   Unfortunately, there wasn't room for a $1/2$% spread.

C   As you've seen, nicely formatting a program's output requires frequent use of **LOCATE** and **PRINT USING** commands. I displayed the current value of Prin on the current row.

D   Allows amounts up to $999,999. Because of the comma in the **PRINT USING** command, the number is displayed with a comma.

E   As in the first version, these lines convert the decimal back to a percent and use a string inside the **PRINT USING** command to place a percent sign flush with the rate.

F   The amount is printed in the current row and column.

G   Prints payments up to $9999.99. Notice that this format string has seven characters, as does the template in E. Matching up template size is the key to aligning tables.

H   Because the numbers will use up seven positions, spacing them 10 columns apart seems reasonable.

I   This line increases the value of Row by 2 in preparation for recalculating the mortgage amount for the next value of Prin.

J   The value of column must be reset back to the start to begin a new row.

K   This block prevents the bottom line from scrolling and leaves the information on the screen as long as needed.

To send this information to a printer, use the Shift−PrtSc combination to take a snapshot of the screen. I've arranged the display so that it takes exactly one screen. On the other hand, it's a good exercise to rewrite this program so that it will work equally well on the screen as on the printer. (You would have to replace the LOCATE command by SPC and TAB commands as well as print the heading first.) Finally, if you need to figure out how much principal you're going to pay back each month, subtract the interest on the current principal from the monthly payment.

FOR-NEXT loops and the graphic characters

FOR-NEXT loops sometimes simplify the character-oriented graphics discussed in chapter 3. Suppose, for example, you wanted a giant X, as shown in Fig. 4-1.

```
    22 24 26 28 30 32 34 36 38 40 42 44 46 48 50 52 54 56 58
 1
 2          XXX                       XXX
 3           XXX                     XXX
 4            XXX                   XXX
 5             XXX                 XXX
 6              XXX               XXX
 7               XXX             XXX
 8                XXX           XXX
 9                 XXX         XXX
10                  XXXXXX
11                    XXX
12                   XXXXX
13                  XXX XXX
14                 XXX     XXX
15                XXX       XXX
16               XXX         XXX
17              XXX           XXX
18             XXX             XXX
19            XXX               XXX
20           XXX                 XXX
21          XXX                   XXX
22          XXX                     XXX
23         XXX                       XXX
24        XXX                         XXX
25
```

4-1 The giant X.

This picture is made up of two different ramps; they happen to coincide in the middle. On each pass through a loop, you need to use the LOCATE to move forward and backward by 1, starting at the 28th and 52nd positions on the first pass. Here's the QBasic program:

```
' CH4 \ P17.BAS
' An X of X's

KEY OFF
CLS

FOR R = 2 TO 24

    LOCATE R,27 + R
    PRINT "XXX";
    LOCATE R,53 - R
    PRINT "XXX";

NEXT R

END
```

The only subtle point is the two semicolons that follow the PRINT statements. Without these, the screen would scroll at the end of the loop, ruining the picture.

Suppose you wanted to make the *X* blink five times. The program that follows again uses the idea of considering the loop in this program as a specialized command in QBasic. (This program won't work in GW-BASIC because of the SLEEP command). You would make this specialized command the inner loop in a program using a nested loop.

```
' CH4 \ P17a.BAS
' A blinking X of Xs

KEY OFF

FOR J = 1 TO 5
CLS

    FOR R = 2 TO 24
        LOCATE R,27 + R
        PRINT "XXX";
        LOCATE R,53 - R
        PRINT "XXX";
    NEXT R
SLEEP 1

NEXT J

END
```

Single-line box characters

218	⌐
196	—
191	¬
179	│
192	L
217	⌐

Single line with tick marks

194	┬
195	├
197	┼
180	┤
193	┴

Table 4-1 Some useful higher order ASCII characters

Double line

201	╔
205	=
187	╗
186	║
200	╚
188	╝

Double lines with tick marks

203	╦
204	╠
206	╬
185	╣
202	╩

In the last chapter, I mentioned that some of the higher order ASCII codes (those above 127) would be useful for drawing boxes and other useful shapes. FOR-NEXT loops make this task a bit easier. Table 4-1 summarizes the most important of these shapes.

Suppose you want to write a program to draw a rectangle on the screen. You need to have the size of each of the sides and the location of one of the corners. After that, it's just a matter of using a FOR-NEXT loop for the vertical lines. The horizontal lines can use the STRING$ command along with the plus sign (concatenation operator). Here's the QBasic program:

```
' CH4 \ P18.BAS
' A rectangle drawer

CLS

INPUT "Please enter the row that the box should start on";RW
```

```
INPUT "Now the column";Col
INPUT "The horizontal size 2-78";HSize
INPUT "Now the vertical size 2-24";VSize

TopLftCor$ = CHR$(218)                                              'A
TopRtCor$ = CHR$(191)

BotLfCor$ = CHR$(192)
BotRtCor$ = CHR$(217)

HorizLine$ = STRING$(HSize − 2,196)
VertLine$ = CHR$(179)

Top$ = TopLftCor$ + HorizLine$ + TopRtCor$
Bot$ = BotlfCor$ + HorizLine$ + BotRtCor$

CLS

LOCATE RW,Col
PRINT Top$;

Start = RW + 1                                                     'B
VertFinish = RW + VSize − 2
EndCol = Col + HSize − 1

FOR I = Start TO VertFinish

    LOCATE I,Col
    PRINT VertLine$;
    LOCATE I,EndCol
    PRINT VertLine$;

NEXT I

LOCATE VertFinish + 1,Col
PRINT Bot$;

END
```

A   The purpose of using variables is to make it easier to adapt this program.
    To draw a double-line rectangle, all you have to do is change the variables.

B   As I've mentioned before, any calculation that leads to loop invariants
    should be done once before the loop is started. Notice as well that a box
    with a vertical size of 10 rows has 8 rows of vertical segments. A similar
    situation holds for the number of horizontal segments in the top and bot-
    tom rows.

I should point out that this program is incomplete. Ideally, it should check that the
values entered for the various sizes are permitted.

219	■
178	▦
177	▩
176	⠿
32	blank

Table 4-2   ASCII codes for bar graph fillers.

Some of the other useful shapes are the various kinds of space fillers. Table 4-2 shows these fillers from darkest to lightest. You can use these characters to draw bar graphs. A *bar graph* compares the sizes of things by piling up blocks. The piles show the relative sizes.

If you had 20 computer programs and your friend had only 5, you might represent your total by piling up 20 blocks and he or she would pile up only 5. Figure 4-2 shows what this bar graph might look like.

The left edge and bottom are called the *axes*. The horizontal edge usually is called the *x-axis*; the vertical edge is the *y-axis*. A program to draw this kind of graph could use the tick mark characters to draw the axis. One subtlety in writing a program that draws bar graphs is that the bars start at the bottom and go up. For example, suppose that you wanted to represent a 5-unit block as in Fig. 4-2. Because you are starting at row 23 and moving up, you would pile blocks until you got to row 19 before you would stop.

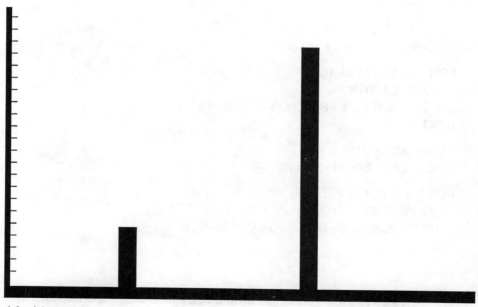

4-2   A bar graph.

Here's the QBasic program:

```
'  CH4 \ P19.BAS
' A bar graph program

CLS

PRINT "This program draw a two-bar bar graph. The maximum height"
PRINT "is 23 units. Press any key to continue."
I$ = INPUT$(1)
CLS

INPUT "How high is the first bar – 23 is the limit";HowHigh1
INPUT "How high is the second bar – 23 is the limit";HowHigh2

CLS

' Draw axes                                                       'A
TickMark$ = CHR$(95)
BoxChar$ = CHR$(219)

FOR I = 1 TO 22
   LOCATE I,1
   PRINT BoxChar$ + TickMark$;
NEXT I

LOCATE 23,1: PRINT BoxChar$; LOCATE 24,1: PRINT STRING$
(78,BoxChar$);

' Draw first bar
TopOfBar1 = 24 – HowHigh1                                         'B

FOR I = TopOfBar1 TO 23                                           'C
   LOCATE I,20
   PRINT BoxChar$ + BoxChar$ + BoxChar$;
NEXT I

' Draw second bar
TopOfBar2 = 24 – HowHigh2

FOR I = TopOfBar2 TO 23
   LOCATE I,50
   PRINT BoxChar$ + BoxChar$ + BoxChar$;
NEXT I

END
```

A   I decided to use an underline for the tick marks after experimenting with
     various combinations. Basically, what I wanted is for the bars to touch

the tick mark. This rules out any characters, like CHR$(195), which have the tick in the middle. Similarly, I eliminated corner pieces as well.

B   I figured this out by trying various special cases. For example, because the top row is row number 1, a bar that is 23 blocks high should go to there. Similarly, a bar one unit high should give a 23 in this formula.

C   This loop starts drawing the bar at the top and works its way down. This method makes it easier to modify the program for a printer.

Character attributes

When you mark blocks in DOS BASIC's editor, the block is either highlighted (if you have a monochrome monitor) or the background color changes (for color monitors). You can control these features in your own programs using the COLOR command. For example, COLOR 1 sets the character color to blue (or underlines the text on a monochrome monitor). More precisely, the color command usually works with two pieces of information:

COLOR x, y

The first entry controls the *foreground color*, which is the color the text will appear in. The second entry controls the background color. There are eight possible background colors. Here's a QBasic program that displays a test phrase in blue against the different possible background colors:

```
'  CH4 \ P20.BAS
' Color test I

DEFINT A-Z
CLS
PRINT "To see background color 0 press any key."
H$ = INPUT$(1)
CLS

FOR BkGrnd = 0 TO 7
   COLOR 1,BkGrnd
   LOCATE 12,32
   PRINT Background color;BkGrnd
   LOCATE 13,20
   PRINT "Press any key to see background color";BkGrnd + 1
   H$ = INPUT$(1)
NEXT BkGrnd
CLS

END
```

If you have a color monitor on hand, then running this program is the best explanation. If not, here's what happens: the color of the text is determined by the first position of the COLOR command. In this program, it stays fixed at blue (color 1). The background color of the text changes according to the value of the counter variable I. (When I=1, the background and foreground are the same, so the characters are invisible).

The most interesting feature happens at the final clear screen command. The CLS command works differently when a COLOR command is in effect. It clears the screen and changes the entire background to the color specified in the COLOR command. If you wanted to see the text displayed with the background completely changed, place a CLS command after the COLOR command. (Use the Immediate window to change the output screen back by issuing another COLOR and CLS combination.)

Table 4-3 summarizes the possible colors for characters (the foreground color). On some monitors, the colors might show up a bit differently.

You can make a character blink by adding 16 to the color codes given in Table 4-3. For example, COLOR 18,5 gives blinking green characters on a magenta background.

Table 4-3 Possible foreground colors.

0	Black	1	Blue
2	Green	3	Cyan
4	Red	5	Magenta
6	Brown	7	White
8	Gray	9	Light blue
10	Light green	11	Light cyan
12	Light red	13	Light magenta
14	Yellow	15	High intensity white

You can display all these features by using a nested FOR-NEXT loop. You have to wrap the previous program inside another loop that control the foreground color. Here's how to do it:

```
' CH4 \ P20a.BAS

CLS
PRINT "Press any key to start"
I$ = INPUT$(1)

FOR ForGrnd = 0 TO 31

    FOR BkGrnd = 0 TO 7

        COLOR ForGrnd, BkGrnd
        CLS                                              'A
```

```
        LOCATE 11, 30
        PRINT "The Background color is"; BkGrnd
        LOCATE 12, 20
        PRINT "and this text appears in Foreground color"; ForGrnd

        LOCATE 24, 20                                                     'B
        COLOR 1, 2
        PRINT "Press any key to see background color"; BkGrnd + 1;
        H$ = INPUT$(1)

    NEXT BkGrnd

  NEXT ForGrnd

  END
```

A   As mentioned above, putting the CLS command here changes the entire background to the background color given in the previous statement.

B   The purpose of this block is to ensure that the directions are never lost when the color changes.

In summary, the first entry can range from 0 to 31, with numbers after 16 forcing the text to blink. The background colors can range from 0 to 7.

What happens with a monochrome monitor (which in spite of their name are actually two colors, usually black and some other color) depends on what kind of adaptor you have. If you have a monochrome adaptor, the effects of the COLOR command are summarized in Table 4-4. (I called the other color white; however, it could be green or amber. I've even seen a bright yellow monitor once.) Background colors 0 through 6 give a black background; 7 through 15 give a white background.

Table 4-4 Effects of the
COLOR command on a monochrome adapter.

0	Black
1	Underline
2-7	White
8	Black
9	High intensity underline
10-15	High intensity white
16	Black
18-23	Blink
24	Black
25	High intensity underline and blink
26-31	High intensity blink

If you have a monochrome monitor attached to a color graphics adaptor, what you see will be close to the list in Table 4-4. It's best to run the previous program, which shows all the possible combinations for all possible monitors, to be sure what colors you will get.

Summary

This chapter showed you how to repeat operations a fixed number of times. You also saw how to control the color or intensity of a monitor.

The commands covered in this chapter were:

FOR *instructions* NEXT [STEP]	Sets up a loop with a counter variable. The optional step is added to the counter each time the NEXT command is processed. The loop ends when the test value is exceeded.
COLOR *frgrnd,bkgrnd*	Controls the attributes of a display. On a color monitor, COLOR changes the color; on a monochrome monitor, COLOR controls intensity, underlining, etc.
SLEEP *TimeToWait*	Put the program on hold for the specified number of seconds or until a key is pressed. Used without a time, it suspends execution of the next statement until a key is pressed. *TimeToWait* is rounded to be an integer. (QBasic only)

5
CHAPTER

Indeterminate loops

Suppose, you add $2000 a year to a retirement account that is earning 9% interest. How long will it be until you have $100,000? In chapter 4, you saw how to write a program that could figure the balance in this type of account for any fixed number of years. With the programming tools you have at this point, all you can do is randomly try different ending values for the needed loops. If you found one value that worked, you still would not be done; you need to find the smallest value that works. Obviously, this method is a pretty silly way to proceed. You need a way to decide whether to keep on repeating an operation or not, depending on the results of calculations within the loop. You need commands that say:

DO *a bunch of DOS BASIC statements* UNTIL *something happens*

The purpose of this chapter is to show you the many ways that QBasic lets you do this kind of loop. Unfortunately, GW-BASIC is much more restricted. In GW-BASIC, there is only one way to do this kind of loop and it's more cumbersome. You'll see it in the last section. Nonetheless, I recommend that GW-BASIC users read through this chapter. Using indeterminate loops correctly requires a different mind set than that needed for FOR-NEXT loops. The more sophisticated programming tools in QBasic make it easier to acquire this mind set.

Getting started with QBasic

Suppose you wanted to start a program with a form of *password protection*. You want to prevent anyone from using a program until they enter the correct password. An outline for this kind of fragment might be:

1. Enter PASSWORD
2. If PASSWORD isn't right reenter PASSWORD

This outline describes a repetitive operation—a loop—of a special sort. It's of indeterminate length. (After you start using these types of loops, you must be especially careful that you haven't inadvertently set up an infinite loop.) The commands in QBasic needed for this kind of loop are quite close to English. Assuming the password was my name, a fragment to do this is:

```
DO
    INPUT "Password please" ;Password$
LOOP UNTIL Password$ = "Gary Cornell"
```

The command DO starts an indeterminate loop. QBasic works its way through the statements that follow the keyword DO until it reaches the keywords LOOP UNTIL. These key words are followed by something QBasic can test. In this example, the test is whether the password entered via the INPUT statement is indeed my name. If it is, then QBasic ends the loop and moves on. If not, it goes back to the first statement following the keyword DO and repeats the process. Just like a FOR-NEXT loop, the statements that repeat are called the *body* of this loop. This kind of loop usually is called a *DO UNTIL loop* or simply a *DO loop*.

Often you don't want the password to appear on the screen. To do this change the INPUT to an INPUT$(12) and put the prompt inside a PRINT statement.

A stand-alone, or EXE, version of this program gives you a reasonably secure form of password protection. However, it's only reasonably secure because an expert programmer could break the protection and find the password by carefully examining the EXE file. (You'll see many more secure methods in later chapters.)

It's important to remember that the test for equality is strict. Entering GARY CORNELL would not work, nor would Gary cornell. Another thing to keep in mind is that the check is done only at the end of the loop. For example, if you change the fragment to read:

```
DO

    Password$ = "Gary Cornell"
    INPUT "Password please";Password$

LOOP UNTIL Password$ = "Gary Cornell"
```

Then, whether this loop ends still depends on the response to the INPUT statement. Initializing the variable Password$ to the correct value is irrelevant.

Obviously, something within the body of a DO LOOP that bears on the test had better change, otherwise the test will always fail and you will be stuck in an infinite loop.

The relational operators

For more sophisticated programs, you need ways to check for something besides equality. This test is done by means of the *relational operators*. They are:

< >	Not equal
<	Less than
< =	Less than or equal
>	Greater than
> =	Greater than or equal

For strings, these operators test for ASCII order. This means that *A* comes before *B*, but *B* comes before *a*. A space comes before any typewriter character. The string *aBCD* comes after the string *CDE* because uppercase letters come before lowercase letters.

For example, suppose you wanted to prevent a divide by zero error (DOS BASIC is no better at dividing by zero than you are). A QBasic fragment might look like:

```
DO
    INPUT "Number to divide by"; Number
LOOP UNTIL Number < > 0
```

Similarly, to test that a number being entered was strictly greater than zero, in QBasic you can say:

```
DO
    INPUT "Only positive numbers allowed"; Number
LOOP UNTIL Number > 0
```

To allow the number to be greater than or equal to zero, change the last line to read LOOP UNTIL Number > = 0. For GW-BASIC, you need a WHILE/WEND loop (see the last section of this chapter).

You could use the following fragment to test that the first character of a string is not a space or a control code:

```
DO
    INPUT "text to work with";Text$
LOOP UNTIL Text$ > CHR$(32)
```

LOOP UNTIL Text$ > "" also works; however, for me, it is a bit harder to decipher.

These kind of loops stop the user from entering the wrong kind of data. Testing INPUT data is one way to begin to bulletproof a program, or make it more robust. A large part of bulletproofing programs requires making them tolerant of INPUT errors. Instead of blowing up because of a typo, they check that the data entered is usable. The more robust a program is, the less likely it is to behave strangely for a naive user.

Moving on with indeterminate loops in QBasic

You now can write the program mentioned at the beginning of this chapter. Add $2000 yearly to an account earning 9% interest. You will keep track of the total and the number of years. Here's a QBasic program:

```
' CH5 \ P1.BAS
' A retirement program

CLS
Total = 0
YearCount = 0
InterestRate = .09
YearlyDeposit = 2000

DO
    NewAmount = YearlyDeposit + InterestRate * Total
    Total = Total + NewAmount
    YearCount = YearCount + 1
LOOP UNTIL Total > = 100000

PRINT "After"; YearCount; "years you will have";
PRINT USING "$$######.##"; Total

END
```

First, notice that the interest rate and yearly deposit are set up as variables outside the loop. This makes it easy to experiment using different interest rates or yearly deposits. The body of the loop is much like the one in the compound interest program from chapter 3. Figure the yearly change and add it to the previous total to get a new total. This time, however, you have to set up your own counter, Year-Count, to keep track of the number of years. Finally, the loop continues as long as the value of the variable Total is less than 100,000. The moment the total is equal to or exceeds the target, the loop ends and QBasic processes the final PRINT statements and reports the results.

Let me end this section by warning you about a frequently occurring problem with these new kind of loops. Consider the following QBasic program:

```
' CH5 \ P2.BAS
' a warning

Total = 0
PassNumber = 0
```

```
DO
    TOTAL = TOTAL + .1
    PassNumber = PassNumber + 1
    PRINT PassNumber,Total
LOOP UNTIL TOTAL = 1
```

You might think this program would end after 10 passes through the loop. It doesn't. This fragment gives you an infinite loop and you'll need the Ctrl−Break combination to stop it. The reason that this program fell into an infinite loop is subtle but important. In this program, all the numbers are values of single-precision variables. As you now know, these numbers are only approximations. Q-Basic's internal characterization of 0.1 is off by a little in, say, the seventh place. As you add 0.1 to the total, tiny errors accumulate and the resulting total, while it gets awfully close to 1, never equals exactly 1. The moral of this program is to never test single- or double-precision variables for equality. Rewrite the program to allow for a tiny error:

```
'  CH5 \ P2a.BAS
'  a warning
'revisited and corrected

Total = 0
PassNumber = 0

DO
    TOTAL = TOTAL + .1
    PassNumber = PassNumber + 1
    PRINT PassNumber,Total
LOOP UNTIL TOTAL > .99999999

END
```

Now, the program will stop after 10 passes through the loop. Among the various types of numbers you'll use in QBasic programs, only test integers and long integers for equality. Single- and double-precision variables can be checked only to see if they are close. By the way, another possibility is to change the test line to read LOOP UNTIL Total > = 1.

Suppose you want to add up the number of different types of insects that occur in North America. You take out your dictionary and you observe that this list has to end with the *zyzzyva*. This makes your job easy:

```
'  CH5 \ P3.BAS

CLS
InsectCount = 0
```

```
DO
    INPUT "The next insect name";InsectName$
    InsectCount = InsectCount + 1
LOOP UNTIL InsectName$ = "zyzzyva"

PRINT "The number of different types of insects is";InsectCount

END
```

This program seems like a prototype for many kinds of programs—ones that read in a list of names until the last one is encountered, keeping count all the while. On the other hand, it's a bit of a coincidence that the last word in my dictionary is an American insect.

Suppose that you wanted to count the number of names on a long list. To use an indeterminate loop to keep count, you need an ending name to test for. In general, you won't know the last entry, so you're likely to use a group of strange characters, like ZZZ, to act as a *flag*. Instead of testing for the zyzzyva you test for a flag.

It's easy to modify CH5 \ P3.BAS to test for a flag. Here's a program that does this:

```
' CH5 \ P4.BAS
' trying to count the names in a list

CLS
NameCount = 0

DO
    INPUT "Name – enter ZZZ when done";Entry$
    NameCount = NameCount + 1
LOOP UNTIL Entry$ = "ZZZ"

PRINT "The total number of names is";NameCount

END
```

The problem with this program is that it suffers from an off-by-one error. Imagine that the list consists of only one name other than the flag. What happens? Work through this program by hand: You enter the first name; the count increases to 1. Next, you enter ZZZ. However, because the test is done only at the end of the loop, the count increases to 2 before the test is done. When the loop ends the count is 2 when it ought to be 1. One possible cure is to subtract one from the count once the loop ends. The trouble with this type of ad-hoc solution, or *kludge*, is that you end up having to constantly figure out how far off the results of your loops are when they finish.

Moving backwards is a bit silly when QBasic makes the cure for this problem so easy—move the test to the top. Consider the following program:

```
'CH5 \ P4a.BAS
'  A counting program revisited

CLS
NameCount = 0
INPUT "Name – ZZZ to end";Entry$

DO UNTIL Entry$ = "ZZZ"
   NameCount = NameCount + 1
   INPUT "Name – ZZZ to end";Entry$
LOOP

PRINT "The total number of names is";NameCount

END
```

Now, the user enters the first name before the loop starts. Once the first name is entered, the computer does an initial test. Only if this test fails do you enter the loop and start adding 1 to the counter. Notice that this kind of loop also works if there is nothing in the list except the flag.

Here's another example. Suppose you wanted to total a list of numbers. Use an enormous number, say 1E30, as the flag. Here's the program:

```
'  CH5 \ P5.BAS
'  A program to total a list of numbers
'  and count them as well

NumberOfNumbers = 0
Total = 0
CLS
INPUT "Enter the next number, 1E30 to end"; Number

DO UNTIL Number = 1E + 30
   NumberOfNumbers = NumberOfNumbers + 1
   Total = Total + Number
   INPUT "Enter the next number"; Number
LOOP

PRINT "The number of numbers is"; NumberOfNumbers
PRINT "The total is"; Total

END
```

Notice that the program assumes that all the numbers entered fit into the range for single-precision variables. A fully bulletproof program would check this.

A good rule of thumb is that, if you are going to use a flag, put the test at the end, otherwise put it at the beginning. More precisely, with the test at the end, the loop always is executed at least once; with the test at the beginning, the loop might not be executed at all. Also, remember that, when the test is at the top, you obviously have to have something to test; therefore, when the test is done at the beginning, initialize all variables before the loop starts. Finally, don't forget that you usually have to have two INPUT statements when the test is at the top. The first comes before the test; the second is inside the loop.

You can use a DO loop with the test at the beginning to replace the FOR-NEXT loop. Doing this is a good way to test your mastery of the DO loop.

Nesting loops

I mentioned in chapter 4 that on my basic PC the empty FOR-NEXT loop:

```
FOR I = 1 TO 1883
NEXT I
```

took about 5 seconds to run. I obviously didn't pull a number like 1883 out of my hat. What I did was write a little test program that combined a FOR-NEXT loop with a DO loop that followed the following outline:

1. Try a FOR-NEXT loop with a counter
2. Test the time it took
3. Change the ending value for the loop
4. Repeat until it takes 5 seconds

Here's the QBasic program:

```
' CH5 \ P6.BAS
'   How long for a 5 second
' FOR-NEXT loop?

CLS
Count = 0

DO
   Count = Count + 1
   StartTime = TIMER

      FOR I = 1 TO Count
      NEXT I

   EndTime = TIMER
   PRINT "Using"; Count; "as the ending value for a FOR-NEXT loop"
   PRINT "took"; EndTime - StartTime; "seconds."
LOOP UNTIL EndTime - StartTime > = 5

END
```

First off, I don't suggest running this program yet, at least not with the counter, Count, starting at 0. The program would take over an hour to finish. One way around this is to use Ctrl−Break to stop the program after its been running for a while. Then, use the Immediate window or direct mode to initialize Count at a reasonable level. Note that the timer keeps ticking while you're making this change; therefore, when you continue the program, the first timing will be off; you must reset the variable EndTime back to 0 from the Immediate window as well. Notice that, because, in a sense, I'm going to use the final test value (via the value of Count), I placed the test at the end. Next, notice that I find the value of EndTime before the PRINT statements. After all, PRINT statements take time to process as well.

Finally, notice the indentation pattern. The FOR-NEXT loop is indented from the timing and PRINT statements, which are indented away from the boundaries of the DO LOOP. This kind of indentation pattern is useful, especially if there were many statements within the FOR-NEXT loop. Compare the above program to the following:

```
'  CH5 \ P6a.BAS
'  How long for a 5 second
'  FOR-NEXT loop? (revisited)
Count = 0
DO
StartTime = Timer
Count = Count + 1
FOR I = 1 TO COUNT
NEXT I
EndTime = TIMER
PRINT "Using";Count; "as the ending value for a FOR-NEXT loop"
PRINT "took";Endtime − StartTime;"seconds."
LOOP UNTIL EndTime − StartTime > =5
END
```

Writing a program this way makes the inevitable editing/debugging/correcting process a nightmare.

You must follow similar rules when nesting a DO loop with a FOR-NEXT loop or with each other as you follow for nesting FOR-NEXT loops alone. Inner loops must be finished before the outer loops are tested. Choose a reasonable indenting pattern and you will not have any problems.

As another example, if you ran the compound interest program from the first section, you discovered it took 20 years to accumulate a little more than $100,000. What happens with other rates of interest? Here's a modified QBasic program that tries different rates of interest:

```
'  CH5 \ P7.BAS
'  A retirement program
```

```
'  revisited
CLS
FOR InterestRate = .05 TO .15 STEP .005     '1/2% steps
   Total = 0                                                              'A
   YearCount = 0
   YearlyDeposit = 2000

      DO
         NewAmount = YearlyDeposit + InterestRate * Total
         Total = Total + NewAmount
         YearCount = YearCount + 1
      LOOP UNTIL Total > = 100000

   PerCent = 100 * InterestRate                                           'B
   PRINT USING "With an interest rate of ##.##%"; PerCent;               'C
   PRINT "after"; YearCount; "years you will have: ";
   PRINT USING "$$######.##"; Total
NEXT InterestRate
END
```

A   For each different interest rate, I need to reinitialize the various variables.

B   Multiplying by 100 changes decimals to percents.

C   As usual, the string inside a PRINT USING command is mirrored in the display. This gives a flush percent sign.

Most of the modifications were straightforward. Essentially, I again thought of the original compound interest program as a single command—one that I could use inside the body of a FOR-NEXT loop. Notice how the indentation pattern clearly shows that the FOR-NEXT loop controls all the action. Notice as well that the initialization and the various PRINT statements are not indented in as far as the DO-LOOP.

The INKEY$ command and Boolean operators

Often, programs begin by displaying directions, then the person presses a key to clear the screen and continue. As you have seen, one way to do this is with an empty INPUT$ command:

```
PRINT "Press any key to continue."
KeyPress$ = INPUT$(1)
CLS
```

or the naked SLEEP command, which is not available in GW-BASIC. The problem with this approach is that the INPUT$ command stops the computer from using the time—it just sits and waits. Often, you want to program something whose outline looks like:

1. Do things until a key is pressed
2. Clear the screen

To convert this outline into QBasic, you need a way to test for a key press that doesn't stop the computer in its tracks. In DOS BASIC, it's the command INKEY$. INKEY$ is a special variable. Its value remains as the null string until a key is pressed, then it picks up the key. The translation of the above outline into QBasic is:

```
DO
   KeyPress$ = INKEY$
   ' here's where you do the 'things'
LOOP UNTIL Keypress$ < > ""
```

Another advantage of the INKEY$ command over the INPUT$ command is that it is sensitive enough to differentiate among the non-ASCII keys, such as the arrow keys. (Recall INPUT$(1) mushes all these keys into a CHR$(0) code.)

One point worth keeping in mind is that DOS BASIC always is asking a TRUE-FALSE question in an indeterminate loop; it's just hidden sometimes. To understand what really is going on in this kind of loop, you have to know that ultimately computers deal only with numbers. This means that DOS BASIC needs a way to understand true and false statements in terms of numbers. To DOS BASIC, *TRUE* is represented by the number -1 (or any nonzero number) and *FALSE* by the number 0. As an example of how QBasic deals with true and false, enter PRINT 2=2 in the Immediate window. What you'll see is a -1 on the output screen. Ultimately, a relational operator, like the equals sign, asks a question, then gives either 0 or -1 as the answer.

Luckily, all arithmetic operators have a higher precedence then the relational operators. QBasic has no trouble interpreting:

```
LOOP UNTIL Number*5 > 10
```

as meaning do the calculation first, then do the test. (This command is a complicated way to test if Number > 2.)

In computer science, anything that tests for true or false is called a *Boolean operator*, after the pioneering English logician George Boole. Any variable that has only two possible values is called a *Boolean variable*. So, you might see the relational operators referred to as *Boolean operators*.

Using DO loops with AND, OR, and NOT and the DO WHILE loop in QBasic

QBasic has other kinds of loops, these loops consist of replacing the keyword UNTIL with the keyword WHILE. This new loop might seem superfluous; you always can change a DO UNTIL into a DO WHILE by reversing the relational operator:

```
DO
UNTIL INKEY$ < > " "
```

is the same as:

```
DO
WHILE INKEY$ = " "
```

and

```
DO UNTIL Number > 5
```

is the same as:

```
DO WHILE Number < = 5
```

Given this, why bother learning to use the DO WHILE loop? There are two reasons why I don't think the WHILE command is superfluous. The first is that, as much as possible, I want to write a program conforming to the way my mind works. Sometimes I think of an operation as going on until something happens, while other times I think of it as continuing while the status is quo. The richness of QBasic makes the fit between my internal thought patterns and the computer program I'm trying to write better.

Psychologists have found that tests with positive conditions are easier to understand. DO UNTIL Number = 0 is easier to process than its counterpart DO WHILE Number < > 0. Similarly, DO WHILE INKEY$ = " " is easier to process than DO UNTIL INKEY$ < > " ".

This reason is only a minor point in favor of the four possibilities and not enough to tip the balance. The best reason comes when you have to combine conditions, which is done most commonly with the keywords OR and AND. These two key words work just like in English. You can continue a process as long as both conditions are true or stop it when one turns false. For example, suppose you want to continue a program as long as the user presses a Y or a y at a key point. You can use the keyword OR in the loop:

```
DO
   Continue$ = INKEY$
LOOP WHILE Continue$ = "Y" OR Continue$ = "y"
```

Now, it's possible to translate this test so that it works in an UNTIL loop, but it's certainly unnatural. The translation would be:

```
LOOP UNTIL Continue$ < > "Y" AND Continue$ < > "y"
```

For another example, recall for a moment the frame building program, CH4 \ P18.BAS. Suppose you want to start bulletproofing the input. First off, you might want to make sure that the row number is between 1 and 24. To check the row value, you need to check two conditions at once. One way to do this is done with the keyword OR. You can replace the simple INPUT command with:

```
DO
    INPUT "Enter the row number 1 - 24";RW
LOOP WHILE RW < 1 OR RW > 24
```

Again, a translation into an UNTIL test is possible; however, I feel it is slightly less natural:

```
LOOP UNTIL (RW > 1) AND (RW < = 24)
```

Obviously you should choose for yourself the indeterminate loop that meshes best with your way of thinking. The advantage of QBasic over some other programing languages is that you are not forced to conform to the way someone else thinks.

Here's the frame program after being made much more robust:

```
'  CH5 \ P8.BAS
'  A rectangle drawer
'  revisited and improved
CLS

DO
    PRINT "Allowable rows are 1 to 23"
    INPUT "Please enter the row that the box should start on"; Rw
LOOP UNTIL Rw > = 1 AND Rw < = 23

O.K.Vert = 25 - Rw                           ' Determines the # of rows
PRINT "The vertical size can be between 2 AND "; O.K.Vert

DO
    INPUT "What vertical size"; VSize
LOOP UNTIL VSize > = 2 AND VSize < = O.K.Vert

DO
    INPUT "Now the column 1-79"; Col
LOOP UNTIL Col > = 1 AND Col < = 79

O.K.Horiz = 80 - Col              'The column determines the permitted size

    PRINT "The horizontal size can be between; 2 AND "; O.K.Horiz;

DO
    INPUT "What horizontal size"; Hsize
```

```
LOOP UNTIL Hsize > = 2 AND Hsize < = O.K.Horiz

TopLftCor$  =  CHR$(218)
TopRtCor$  =  CHR$(191)
BotlfCor$  =  CHR$(192)
BotRtCor$  =  CHR$(217)
HorizLine$  =   STRING$(Hsize − 2, 196)
VertLine$  =  CHR$(179)
Top$  =  TopLftCor$ + HorizLine$ + TopRtCor$
Bot$  =  BotlfCor$ + HorizLine$ + BotRtCor$

CLS

LOCATE Rw, Col
PRINT Top$;

Start  =  Rw + 1
VertFinish  =  Rw + VSize − 2
EndCol  =  Col + Hsize − 1

FOR I  =  Start TO VertFinish
    LOCATE I, Col
    PRINT VertLine$;
    LOCATE I, EndCol
    PRINT VertLine$;
NEXT I

LOCATE VertFinish + 1, Col
PRINT Bot$;

END
```

As you can see, bulletproof programs, like bulletproof clothing, are bulkier. This program, like any protective garment, isn't completely bulletproof. It's hard to stop every sort of mistake from penetrating your programs. The more protection you put in, the longer the program gets. Luckily, a modern programming language like QBasic has ways of preserving the balance.

What to do in GW-BASIC

GW-BASIC has only one form of an indeterminate loop, which is available in QBasic as well. It's called the WHILE/WEND loop. It is a variation of the DO WHILE loop. Instead of saying:

```
DO WHILE X = 0
LOOP
```

you can say:

```
WHILE X = 0
WEND
```

Because the test always is done at the top of the WHILE/WEND loop, you must be careful. Remember to initialize the variable to be tested appropriately. Because you do not have the option of testing the condition at the end of the loop, you might need to do some mental contortions. For example, you often will need to change the relational operator (for example, use the NOT or replace an AND with an OR) to cook up the appropriate test.

For example, the divide by zero test needs to be rewritten:

```
100 Number = 37
110   WHILE Number < > 0
120     INPUT "Number to divide by";Number
130   WEND
```

Another good example of this is the counting program, CH5 \ P4a. Here's a version of the counting program written for GW-BASIC:

```
10  'CH5 \ P4b.BAS
11  ' A counting program revisited
12  ' this time for GW-BASIC
20  CLS
30  NameCount = 0
40  INPUT "Name – ZZZ to end";Entry$
98  '
99  '
100  While Entry$ < > "ZZZ"                                   'A
110    NameCount = NameCount + 1
120    INPUT "Name – ZZZ to end";Entry$
130  WEND
138  '
139  '
140  PRINT "The total number of names is";NameCount
150  END
```

A   Notice that I had to change the test from equal to not equal.

6
CHAPTER

Making decisions

At this point, all your programs can do is to decide whether to repeat a group of statements or not. As yet, you can't change which statements are processed depending on what the program has already done or what it has just encountered. This chapter takes care of this shortcoming. It shows you how to make decisions within a program. You'll see how a program can process one set of statements because one thing happened and a completely different set if something else should occur.

All the commands in this chapter, in one way or another, deal with turning into DOS BASIC an outline containing a phrase like:

IF *thing* THEN DO *something otherwise* DO *something else*

Simple IF-THENs

You need a command that can translate the conditional in English—sentences like *If I get an A, then I'm happy*. Luckily, DOS BASIC uses the IF-THEN in much the same way as you do in normal English. Here's an example in QBasic:

```
'  CH6 \ P1.BAS
'  A simple IF-Then

CLS
PRINT "What's the name of the company that though it had the"
PRINT "machine for the 'rest of us'?"
```

```
Company$ = "APPLE"
IF Company$ = "APPLE" THEN PRINT "Ah yes, Granny Smith's company"

END
```

DOS BASIC processes the line containing the IF-THEN by determining whether the contents of the variable Company$ contains the word *APPLE*. Because Company$ does contain this word, the program immediately processes the command following the keyword THEN. It therefore prints:

Ah yes, Granny Smith's company

More generally, when DOS BASIC encounters an IF-THEN statement, it checks the first clause (called the *IF clause*) and checks whether it's true. If that clause is true, the computer does whatever follows (called the *THEN clause*). If the test fails, then processing skips to the next statement. For example:

```
'  CH6 \ P2.BAS
'  A FALSE 'IF-CLAUSE'

CLS
SuperHero$ = "Clark Kent"
IF SuperHero$ = "Superman" THEN PRINT "from Krypton?"

END
```

If you run the program, you'll see that nothing happens on the output screen. The variable named Superhero$ did not contain the string Superman, so the THEN clause was not processed.

Just as in the loops from chapter 5, you can use the IF-THEN to compare numbers or strings. For example, statements like:

```
IF A$ < B$ THEN PRINT A$;" comes before ";B$;
```

test for (ASCII) order or

```
IF A < = B THEN PRINT A; " is no more than "; B
```

tests for numerical order.

Using these ideas, it's easy to write a program to find the smallest number on a list or the word that alphabetically would come first. An outline for this program is simple:

1. Set up a place for the first name
2. While there are names on the list
   - Get the next word
   - Keep on comparing
   - Each time something is smaller, throw it into the box that held the previous smallest word
3. Continue until there are no more words.

The following program uses *ZZZZ* for the flag:

```
' CH6 \ P3.BAS
' Finding the first word on a list

CLS
PRINT "Enter the names on the list one by one."
PRINT "Enter 'ZZZZ' to end"

INPUT "The first word"; Word$
Smallest$ = Word$

   DO UNTIL Word$ = "ZZZZ"
      INPUT "The next word?";Word$
      IF Word$ < Smallest$ THEN Smallest$ = Word$
   LOOP

PRINT "The first (alphabetically) word is ";Smallest$
IF Smallest$ = "ZZZZ" THEN PRINT "Wasting time aren't you?"

END
```

Again, as usual, because the test was done at the top, I initialized the variables before the loop began. (For GW-BASIC you'll have to use a WHILE loop and change the equal to not equal.) As you enter each word, the program compares it to the word that's currently first. If it precedes the current champion in ASCII order, the program makes it the new value of the variable Smallest$.

The final IF-THEN might seem superfluous, but I stuck it in to point out a problem with this program. Suppose you enter all the words in lowercase. Because the ASCII code for any lowercase letter is greater than that of a capitol *Z* (90 versus 97 to 126), *ZZZZ* would end up as the smallest word on the list. The cure for this problem is the command UCASE$(*string*) or its sibling, LCASE$ (*string*), which are available only in QBasic. (For GW-BASIC you would have to write a subroutine. See chapter 9.) These commands switch the case of any letters in the string or the value of the string expression inside the parentheses. For example, if A$ = UCASE$("Hello"), then A$ = "HELLO". Similarly, if B$ = LCASE-$("Hello"), then B$ = "hello".

Using, say, the UCASE$ command, it's easy to prevent the problem described above. Change the IF-THEN statement within the loop to read:

```
IF UCASE$(Word$) < UCASE$(Smallest$) THEN Smallest$ = Word$
```

Not all the problems with this program are gone yet. If someone would mistakenly hit the Return key alone, then the null string would be assigned to Word$. The null string comes before any string. To prevent this problem, you could put a DO loop inside this loop—one that would ensure that only non-null strings are assigned to Word$. The main difficulty in bulletproofing a program is figuring out the silly mistakes people can make.

You also can use the keywords AND, OR, and NOT in an IF-THEN. These key words let you check two conditions at once. For example, some new cars have microprocessors checking that the number of revolutions of the motor is within some critical range. You can mimic this check with source code like:

```
INPUT RevNumber        'this comes from a sensor
IF RevNumber > 1500 AND RevNumber <4000 THEN PRINT "Engine o.k."
```

Another place the AND would have proved useful was in the program that finds the smallest name on a list. It would have been better to change the crucial line to read:

```
IF Word$ < Smallest$ AND Word$ < > "ZZZZ" THEN Smallest$ = Word$
```

A teacher might write a program to compute final grades based on the average of four grades. Here's a QBasic version:

```
'  CH6 \ P4.BAS
'  A simple grade book

CLS

PRINT "This program calculates the average of four grades."
PRINT "Enter a negative number for the first grade to end."
INPUT "First exam grade";Grade1

DO WHILE Grade1 > =0

    INPUT "Second exam grade";Grade2
    INPUT "Third exam grade";Grade3
    INPUT "Fourth exam grade";Grade4

    Average = (Grade1 + Grade2 + Grade3 + Grade4)/4

    IF Average > = 90 THEN PRINT "Grade is A"
    IF Average > = 80 AND Average < 90 Then PRINT "Grade is B."
    IF Average > = 70 AND Average < 80 Then PRINT "Grade is C."
    IF Average > = 60 AND Average < 70 Then PRINT "Grade is D."
    IF Average < 60 Then PRINT "Sorry you fail."

    INPUT "First exam grade a negative number to end ";Grade1

LOOP

END
```

As usual, because you are doing the test at the top, you need to initialize the variable and redo the input section inside the loop. (Notice that you can use a DO

UNTIL instead and change the test to read DO UNTIL Grade1 < 0.) In GW-BASIC, you could have the loop read WHILE Grade1 > = 0.

This program needed a trick to avoid awkwardness, because you don't want to wait until all four grades are entered before stopping. As it's constructed, the program accepts the remaining three grades only if the first grade is positive. After that, it's pretty straightforward. It computes the average and checks its range. If it's 90 or more, the person gets an A. Scores between 80 and 89 get a B, and so on.

If all the ANDs together with the conditions that follow them are removed, anyone whose average was, say, 97 would see:

```
Your grade is an A
Your grade is a B
Your grade is a C
.
.
```

Without using the AND, an average like 97 would satisfy all the IF conditions, so DOS BASIC would activate all the THEN clauses.

Finally, in QBasic, there are other ways to write this program that are more straightforward. What you really want to do is to leave the loop immediately when a negative number is entered, whether it's the first or the fourth score. You'll see the tools to do this shortly.

I hope the ways of using AND are pretty clear, but one word of caution. In both speaking and writing, people sometimes say, "If my average is greater than 80 and less than 90, then . . . ." Translating this sentence construction directly won't work in DOS BASIC. You must repeat the variable each time you want to test something. To do the translation from English to DOS BASIC, you need to say, "If my average is greater than 80 and my average is less than 90, then . . . ."

You do not have to use the same variable when using AND. A statement like:

```
IF (Grade4 > Grade3) AND Average > 60 THEN PRINT "Improving I see"
```

is a perfectly good DOS BASIC statement. (The parentheses are there only to improve readability; they are not needed. DOS BASIC calculates relational operators before worrying about the logical connectors, like AND.)

Using the keyword OR in an IF-THEN is similar. The test is successful if any of the conditions are true:

```
INPUT "Two numbers - at least one non-zero number";A,B
IF A < > 0 OR B < > 0 THEN PRINT "Input successful"
```

As another example, suppose you wanted to allow a person to end a program if they type yes or YES but not if they mixed uppercase and lowercase. (You might want to do this on the grounds that someone who can't get that straight probably doesn't really want to end the program.) The UCASE$ or LCASE$ commands are out, because they change the case of all the letters. Instead, use the OR:

```
INPUT "Enter YES or yes to END";Ans$
IF Ans$ = "YES" OR Ans$ = "yes" THEN END
```

There are other, less common ways of combining tests. For example, there's the XOR (exclusive OR), which corresponds to the English: *If A or B but not both.*

Similarly, there's the NOT whose use depends a lot on personal taste—a lot like the DO WHILE versus DO UNTIL distinction. I usually find it easier just to change the relational operators. For example:

```
IF NOT (A$ = "Big Blue")
```

is harder to write than:

```
IF A$ < > "BIG Blue"
```

Similarly:

```
IF (NOT A>50)
```

is exactly the same as:

```
IF A < = 50
```

If you prefer to use the NOT, then you'll need parentheses. Without them, your program is apt to be unreadable.

Eureka loops: combining the IF-THEN with DO or WHILE loops

Suppose you wanted to program a reading test so that it would clear the screen if either the time was up or if the person taking it indicated that they were finished (for example, by striking a key). You easily could modify program CH4 \ P7.BAS to do this. All you need to do is eliminate the SLEEP command and replace it with:

```
StartTime = TIMER
DO UNTIL (EndTime − StartTime) > = DelyTime OR KeyPress < > ""
   EndTime = TIMER
   KeyPress$ = INKEY$
LOOP
```

This DO loop ends if either of two things happen: too much time has elapsed (much like the SLEEP command with a time interval would do) or someone presses a key (as the SLEEP command always does). You probably are wondering why you would want to bother with this construct; a SLEEP DelyTime statement would do it faster. (Note that the DO loop allows more precision in the timing.) Suppose, however, that you needed to know exactly what happened—exactly why the loop ended. This situation is tailor-made for an IF-THEN. Merely add the following lines after the loop ends:

```
IF KeyPress$ < > "" THEN PRINT "Guessed too high!"
IF (EndTime – StartTime) > = DelyTime THEN PRINT "Guessed too low!"
```

Remember that you can't test a single-precision variable for equality.

These kind of loops are so common they have a special name, *eureka loops* (after Archimedes' famous bathtub experience). You set up a loop to end if either one of two things happens. Then, you follow it by testing to determine which one actually happened.

A version of this loop written with a WHILE loop is a much more contorted:

```
WHILE (EndTime – StartTime) < DelyTime AND KeyPress$ = ""
```

This statement is equivalent to the DO loop because an AND statement fails when either one of the clauses fails. So, you would finish the loop either when the time is up or when someone presses a key, which is exactly what the DO loop did.

QBasic provides another way to combine the IF-THEN with a loop (what I used to regard as the holy grail of loop writing): a clean, clear way to write a loop that tests in the middle. To do this type of loop, you need to combine the IF-THEN with a command that is new to QBasic: the EXIT DO. For example, consider this rewritten version of part of the grade book program:

```
DO

    INPUT "First exam grade - negative number to end";Grade1
    IF Grade1 < 0 THEN EXIT DO

    INPUT "Second exam grade";Grade2
    INPUT "Third exam grade";Grade3
    INPUT "Fourth exam grade";Grade4

    IF Average > = 90 THEN PRINT "Grade is A"
    IF Average > = 80 AND Average < 90 Then PRINT "Grade is B."
    IF Average > = 70 AND Average < 80 Then PRINT "Grade is C."
    IF Average > = 60 AND Average < 70 Then PRINT "Grade is D."
    IF Average < 60 Then PRINT "Sorry you fail."

LOOP

END
```

Notice that in this fragment there is neither a test at the top or bottom. The only test occurs in the form of an IF-THEN after the first grade is entered. It determines whether the first grade is less than zero. If it is, then QBasic processes the THEN clause. In this case, it's the statement EXIT DO. What this command does is pop you out of the loop; QBasic jumps to the statement following the keyword

LOOP, which, because it's an END statement, stops the program as well. (Although the original program did the same thing, this program seems to be more natural.)

More generally, QBasic allows you to set up a potentially infinite loop at any time: just leave off the tests in a DO loop (an unadorned DO at the top and an equally unadorned LOOP at the bottom). Once you've done this, the loop will end only when QBasic processes an EXIT DO statement (or Ctrl−Break).

You can use the EXIT command to leave a FOR-NEXT loop in QBasic as well. In this case, it takes the form EXIT FOR. For example, suppose you want a FOR-NEXT loop to end abruptly—say when someone presses the Ctrl−C combination (ASCII code 3). This loop would take the form:

```
FOR counter = starting value TO test value

    IF INKEY$ = CHR$(3) THEN EXIT FOR
    .
    .
    .
NEXT counter
```

I must confess that I've gotten so used to the way that DO WHILE/UNTIL loops test either at the top or at the bottom that I rarely use the EXIT command to end a loop in the middle. Also, the trouble with ending a loop in the middle is that you easily can lose the sense of what the loop is all about. Many people's minds seem to work best with loops that end either at the top or at the bottom. As usual, you must be the judge of what fits your way of thinking.

I must say one word of caution, however. QBasic places no restrictions on the number of IF-THEN statements that lead to an EXIT DO statement. It's all too easy to find yourself writing a loop that has 47 different ways to EXIT. It's awfully hard to figure out what this kind of loop is really doing. It also is a nightmare to debug. For this reason, some computer scientists advocate that all loops be *single-entry single-exit* (one way in and only one way out). This would mean using no more than one EXIT DO command and only if you hadn't placed a test at the top or bottom. Like most academic rules, this one goes to far. Rather than have a eureka loop with 10 conditions:

```
DO UNTIL A = 3 OR B = 4 OR C = 5 OR D$ = "DOG"....
```

I probably would use multiple EXIT-LOOP commands. Similarly, you often have to have two ways out of the loop. The first way is the natural way (the way you expected the loop to end); the second way is for unnatural activities (perhaps to bulletproof the loop). Readability and clarity should be the goal, not obeying some abstract rule.

Finally, once in a while, you don't want to exit the loop; you want to end the program prematurely. For example, suppose you want to give someone three tries to enter a password:

```
' CH6 \ P5.BAS
' ending a program prematurely

Tries = 0
DO
    IF Tries = 3 THEN END
    PRINT "Password please"
    Password$ = INPUT$(12)
    Tries = Tries + 1
LOOP UNTIL Password$ = "Gary Cornell"
```

Now, if someone gives three incorrect passwords, then the program ends. Do you see why this fragment gives a person three chances and not two or four?

IF-THEN-ELSE

Suppose you want to write a program that accepts two numbers and then prints them out in numerical order. Your first instinct might be to write something like:

```
INPUT A,B
IF A > = B THEN PRINT B,A,
PRINT A,B
```

This fragment seems to work. Suppose A is less than B. The test is unsuccessful and the THEN clause (the PRINT statement) is disregarded. The program will print A first, then B, just as it's supposed to. The problem occurs because the second line, PRINT A,B, always is processed. In this situation, you really want to mimic the English construction: "IF A is greater than B, THEN print B followed by A, ELSE (otherwise) print A then B". This important variant of the IF-THEN exists in DOS BASIC and is called the *IF-THEN-ELSE*. The fragment should read:

```
INPUT A,B
IF A > = B THEN PRINT B,A ELSE PRINT A,B
```

When DOS BASIC processes an IF-THEN-ELSE, it does the test. If the test succeeds, it processes the command that follows the keyword THEN (the THEN clause). If the test fails, it processes the statement that follows the keyword ELSE (the ELSE clause.)

Here's another example. Some credit cards charge you 18% interest if your balance is less than $2000, otherwise (ELSE) they charge you 15%. This would translate into:

```
IF Balance < 2000 THEN IntRate = .18 ELSE IntRate = .15
```

As a final example, consider the test that you'll do at the end of a eureka loop (for example, the one in the reading test). Almost always, this test calls for an IF-

THEN-ELSE, rather than two IF-THENs. The IF-THEN-ELSE construction makes a program clearer; it shows that the program always will choose one of two alternatives.

When you start using the IF-THEN-ELSE, you quickly run past the limits of an 80 column line. There are various ways around this limitation. In GW-BASIC, you usually end up having to extend the line, possibly using colons to add multiple statements. Another possibility is to use a subroutine (see chapter 9). In QBasic, you have a better choice.

The block IF-THEN in QBasic

If you use the 255-character limit on a logical line in QBasic, you give up the ability to see what's going on. (Your printouts will look horrible as well.) A better choice is to use the more powerful form of the IF-THEN command available in QBasic. It's called the block IF-THEN. This command lets you process as many statements as you like in response to a true condition:

```
IF I win the lottery THEN
    I'm happy,
    my family is happy,
    and the tax man is happy.
```

Here, I have three statements in response to something being true. The way Q-Basic translates this construction, the block IF-THEN-ELSE, has a slightly different format then the usual IF-THEN. It looks like:

```
IF thing to test THEN
    lots of statements
ELSE
    more statements
END IF
```

You do not put anything on the line following the keyword THEN. This bare THEN is how QBasic knows it's beginning a block. The word ELSE is optional, putting it there (again, alone on a line) means that another block will follow, to be processed only if the IF clause is false. However, whether the ELSE is there or not, the block IF must end with the keywords END IF.

For an example of this feature, consider the problem of calculating social security taxes for a non-self-employed person. The way these taxes worked (in 1989) is that, if your salary was less than $48,000, then you paid 7.51% of it in social security taxes. After that, whether you make $48,001 or $1,000,000, you still pay only on the first $48,000. This amount works out to $3604.80 for anyone whose salary is above the magic number. Here's a fragment that calculates the social security tax:

```
MagicNumber = 48000

INPUT "What is your salary";Salary

IF Salary < MagicNumber THEN
    PRINT "Tax is" .0751*Salary
ELSE
    PRINT "Exceeded maximum - tax is";MagicNumber*.0751
END IF
```

Here's another example. Suppose that you work for a company and that the bonus you get for selling widgets (and the discount the customer gets) depends on the number of widgets the customer buys. If you sell at least 1000 widgets, then they get a 40% discount and you get a $500 bonus. Otherwise, they get a 35% discount and you get a $100 bonus. Here's a fragment for this:

```
INPUT "How many widgets did you sell";WidgetCount

IF WidgetCount > = 1000 THEN
    Discount = .4
    BONUS = 500
ELSE
    Discount = .35
    BONUS = 100
END IF
```

As usual, the indentation is there to make the program more readable; QBasic doesn't care.

Another place where the block IF could come in handy is in the simple grade book program. Suppose the teacher wanted to print out the name of the student followed by the grade. Modify that program as follows:

```
'  CH6 \ P6.BAS
'  A simple grade book revisited

CLS
PRINT "This program calculates the average of four grades"

DO
    INPUT "The student's name - ZZ to end"; StuName$
    IF StuName$ = "ZZ" THEN EXIT DO
    PRINT "Enter the four grades, separate them by commas and";
    PRINT " hit RETURN."
    INPUT Grade1, Grade2, Grade3, Grade4

    Average = (Grade1 + Grade2 + Grade3 + Grade4) / 4
```

```
        PRINT StuName$; " your grades were: ";
        PRINT Grade1; Grade2; Grade3; Grade4
        PRINT "Your average was"; Average

        IF Average > = 90 THEN
            PRINT "Grade earned is A."
            PRINT "Congratulations!"
        END IF

        IF Average > = 80 AND Average < 90 THEN
            PRINT "Grade is B."
            PRINT "Not bad."
        END IF

        IF Average > = 70 AND Average < 80 THEN
            PRINT "Grade is C."
            PRINT "Not working hard enough."
        END IF

        IF Average > = 60 AND Average < 70 THEN
            PRINT "Grade is D."
            PRINT "Obviously you could do better"
        END IF

        IF Average < 60 THEN
            PRINT "Sorry you fail."
            PRINT "Please make an appointment to see me."
        END IF

        PRINT

    LOOP

    END
```

Although, in certain cases, there was room to combine the PRINT statements on one line, the program probably would be harder to read. As it is, it's getting near the limits of readability. To improve it further you need one more kind of statement that makes decisions: the SELECT CASE statement. This statement is the subject of the next section and, unfortunately, is not available in GW-BASIC.

SELECT CASE

The previous program dealt with a quite common situation: a road with many branches—a program with many possibilities. When this happens, you always can use multiple IF-THENs to eliminate all but one of the possibilities. (In GW-BASIC, you really don't have much choice.) However, most programmers feel that the IF-THEN-ELSE should be reserved for a program fork—a place where you have 2 choices, not 14.

For times when you have multiple branches, QBasic has the SELECT command. To use this command, you start with something you want to test. For example, suppose you want to test if a character is a vowel. You could write:

```
IF UCASE$(CHAR$) = "A" THEN PRINT "Vowel"
IF UCASE$(CHAR$) = "I" THEN PRINT "Vowel"

      .            .
      .            .
```

Using this new command you write:

```
SELECT CASE UCASE$(CHAR$)

   CASE "A"
      PRINT "Vowel"

   CASE "E"
      PRINT "Vowel"

   CASE "I"
      PRINT "Vowel"

   CASE "O"
      PRINT "Vowel"

   CASE "U"
      PRINT "Vowel"

   CASE "Y"
      PRINT "Y is a problem - sorry"

END SELECT
```

The SELECT CASE command makes it clear that a program has reached a point with many branches; multiple IF-THENs do not. The clearer a program is the easier it is to debug.

What follows the keyword SELECT CASE is a variable or expression. What QBasic is going to do depends on the value of the variable or expression. The keyword CASE is shorthand for *in the case that the variable (expression) is*, which usually is followed by a relational operator. For example, to begin to check that the value of the variable CHAR$ is a letter, you can add the case:

```
CASE IS < "A"
   PRINT "Character is not a letter."
   PRINT "Meaningless question"
```

To eliminate all possible non-letter values, you have to eliminate those characters with ASCII codes that are between 91 and 95 (consult the ASCII chart via the HELP menu or look in appendix E). This refinement is done as follows:

```
CASE CHR$(91) TO CHR$(95)
    PRINT "Character is not a letter."
    PRINT "Meaningless question"
```

Here the keyword TO allows you to give a range of values. So, this statement is shorthand for *in the case that the variable is in the range from CHR$(91) to CHR$(95) inclusive*. Finally, having eliminated the case when the character was not a letter, you want to print out the message that it is a consonant. This is done with the CASE ELSE, which is shorthand for *do this case if none of the other situations hold*. Here's a more polished version of the program that incorporates all these conditions:

```
'  CH6 \ P7.BAS
'  A vowel tester revisited

CLS
PRINT "Press any key and I'll tell you if it's a consonant"
Char$ = INPUT$(1)
Char$ = UCASE$(Char$)                                        'A

SELECT CASE (Char$)
CASE "A", "E", "I", "O", "U"                                 'B
    PRINT "Vowel"

CASE "Y"
    PRINT "Y is a problem - sorry"

CASE IS < "A"
    PRINT "Character is not a letter."
    PRINT "Meaningless question."

CASE IS > "Z"
    PRINT "Character is not a letter."
    PRINT "Meaningless question."

CASE ELSE                                                    'C
    PRINT "Consonant"

END SELECT

END
```

A   I feel more comfortable doing the conversion outside of the SELECT CASE statements. This method makes it easier to make any changes needed to make this program part of some larger program.

B   QBasic allows you to combine many tests for a single case, just separate the tests by a comma. Think of the comma as an OR. This line replaces 10 or so lines of the original version and makes the program more readable.

C   Here's the ELSE case, which is done in any remaining situations.

Similarly, you can use the SELECT CASE to replace the body of the loop in the grade program by testing the numeric variable Average. Here's how:

```
SELECT CASE Average

   CASE > = 90
      PRINT "Grade earned is A."
      PRINT "Congratulations!"

   CASE 80 TO 89
      PRINT "Grade is B."
      PRINT "Not bad."

   CASE 70 TO 79
      PRINT "Grade is C."
      PRINT "Not working hard enough."

   CASE 60 TO 69
      PRINT "Grade is D."
      PRINT "Obviously you could do better"

   CASE ELSE
      PRINT "Sorry you fail."

END SELECT
```

I think this fragment is much cleaner and easier to understand than the original program. In particular, notice how the keyword TO fits the English very well. Notice, as well, that I could replace the CASE ELSE with CASE IS < 60.

Although I don't like doing it, you could replace the CASE 80 TO 89 with CASE > 80. This can be done because QBasic executes one CASE—the first one it finds to be true—at the most. If someone has a grade of 90, the compiler would activate the first clause but then skip past the remaining ones.

Finally, let me end this section with a program that lets you move the cursor around, much like the QBasic editor does. This kind of fragment is frequently needed. Because you haven't yet seen how to read the arrow keys, I'll just mimic how the editor reads the control keys.

An outline is:

1. Initialize
   • Make the cursor large
   • Move it to the top left corner

2. Read a keystroke

Ctrl−D (ASCII 4)	Move right one column
Ctrl−S (ASCII 19)	Move left one column
Ctrl−E (ASCII 5)	Move up one row
Ctrl−X (ASCII 24)	Move down one row
Ctrl−R (ASCII 18)	Page up (In this program, move to the top row of the same column)
Ctrl−C (ASCII 3)	Page down (In this program, move to the bottom row of the same column)

3. Stop when an *X* is hit.

Whenever your outlines have this form (lots of different CASEs), you probably will use the SELECT CASE statement in the translation.

Here's the program:

```
'  CH6 \ P8.BAS
'  A cursor mover

CLS
PRINT "This demonstrates the WordStar key movements. Ctrl + ";
PRINT " S, D, E, R and C and X "

PRINT "will move a large cursor around."
PRINT
PRINT "Press any key to start. A capital 'X' ends."

KeyStroke$ = INKEY$
IF KeyStroke$ < > "X" THEN
   CLS
   KEY OFF
      LOCATE 1, 1, 1, 0, 7                          ' make the cursor large
      Row = 1:Col = 1
END IF

DO UNTIL KeyStroke$ = "X"

   DO
                                   'A
      KeyStroke$ = INKEY$
   LOOP WHILE KeyStroke$ = ""

   SELECT CASE KeyStroke$

      CASE CHR$(4)                     'Ctrl − D              'B
         IF Col < = 79 THEN Col = Col + 1
      CASE CHR$(19)                    'Ctrl − S
```

```
        IF Col > 1 THEN Col = Col − 1
      CASE CHR$(5)                            'Ctrl − E
        IF Row > 1 THEN Row = Row − 1
      CASE CHR$(24)                           'Ctrl − X
        IF Row < 25 THEN Row = Row + 1
      CASE CHR$(18)                           'Ctrl − R
        Row = 1
      CASE CHR$(3)                            'Ctrl − C
        Row = 25
      CASE ELSE                                          'C
          IF KeyStroke$ < > "X" THEN BEEP                'D

  END SELECT

  LOCATE Row, Col

  LOOP

END
```

A   Waits until a key is pressed.

B   This line is the first of the many CASEs needed to implement the outline. Obviously, there are many of them, but they all should be straightforward.

C   I could have eliminated the small DO loop at the top by writing:

```
IF KeyPress$ < > "" AND KeyPress$ < > "X" THEN BEEP
```

however, I'm sure you will agree that this negative test is confusing. So confusing that when this kind of double negative test does come up, I sometimes prefer to waste a statement and write something like:

```
IF KeyPress$ = "" OR KeyPress$ = "X" THEN
    'DO NOTHING
ELSE
    BEEP
END IF
```

I personally find this much clearer. If the IF clause is true, then I want to do nothing (as the remark statement indicates). The ELSE clause is the translation of the complicated IF KeyPress$ < > "" AND ... statement.

D   The program ends when a capital *X* is pressed. In chapter 8, you'll see how to read the arrow keys.

You might want to add the appropriate LOCATE command before the END command to reset the cursor back to normal. You also could use the Immediate window to do so.

Odds and ends of QBasic's IF-THEN: the ELSEIF

The SELECT case can test only one expression—one number or string. Suppose you have two numbers (A, B) and your outline looks like this:

IF $A = B$ DO ....
IF $A > B$ DO ....
IF $A < B$ DO ....

One way to program this outline is to set up a variable:

Difference = A − B

Then, SELECT on whether the value of Difference was zero (A equals B), greater than zero (A is greater than B), or less than zero (A is less than B). This method probably is the way I would do it.

Now, suppose someone throws in one or two extra conditions:

IF A > B AND A<2∗B
IF A > 2∗B

It's no longer obvious how to use the SELECT CASE command. You could write four block IF-THENs corresponding to each of the different conditions in the outline. Most of the time this wouldn't cause any problems; however, problems might happen if you have to do something to A or B in one of the blocks. From that point on, you're in trouble. All further tests are off. More precisely, suppose the outline was:

Do one of the following:

1. If $A = B$, then print A
2. If $A < B$, then print A and add two to A
3. If $A > B$, then print B and add two to B

Here's a translation of this outline:

```
' CH6 \ P9.BAS
' A demo

INPUT "Two numbers please"; A, B

IF A = B THEN PRINT A

IF A < B THEN
   PRINT A
   A = A + 2
END IF
```

```
IF A > B THEN
   PRINT B
   B = B + 2
END IF

END
```

Suppose the value of A was 4 and the value of B was 5. Then, the second option is taken and the program prints out 4 and changes the value of A to 6. Now, the third option is activated, contrary to the outline, which says to do only one of the possibilities.

The situation is a bit like the one right before I introduced the ELSE. You need to continue testing within the confines of the original IF-THEN. This testing is done with the command:

```
ELSEIF ... THEN ....
```

Here's the correct translation of the IF-THEN in the previous program:

```
IF A = B THEN
   PRINT A
ELSEIF A < B THEN
   PRINT A
   A = A + 2
ELSEIF A > B THEN
   PRINT B
   B = B + 2
END IF
```

Now, everything is tied together. Just like in the IF-THEN-ELSE or the SELECT command, QBasic activates one clause at the most. In particular, if A is less than B, then QBasic processes only the second clause. When QBasic is done doing that, it bypasses any other ELSEIFs that might be contained in the block. It goes immediately to the statement following the END IF (in this program, it's the END command that finishes the program). You could replace the final ELSEIF with a simple ELSE; you've eliminated all the other possibilities.

A block IF-THEN can have as many ELSEIFs as you like, but the block can have only one ELSE (as the last clause). The limits are determined by how much you can process, rather than by what QBasic can do. (That's why I prefer to use the SELECT CASE if I can. Although any SELECT CASE can be transformed into an IF-THEN-ELSEIF, I find the latter much harder to read and to debug.)

The final point I want to mention is that the block IF-THEN is extremely flexible. You can put any QBasic statement following the keyword THEN. In particular, you could place another IF-THEN-ELSE after the THEN. Consider the following:

```
IF Grade4 < 65 THEN
    PRINT "You failed the final exam."
    IF Average > 70 THEN
        PRINT "You pass because your average is sufficiently"
        PRINT "high to blot out failing the final exam."
    ELSE
        PRINT "I'm sorry failing the final and a marginal ";
        PRINT " passing average means failing the course"
    END IF
END IF
```

Is it clear that the ELSE belongs to the inner IF-THEN? The way to see this is to play computer. For the ELSE to belong to the outer IF-THEN, the inner IF-THEN already must have finished. However, it hasn't because, to that point, no END IF has shown up. The first END IF finishes the inner IF-THEN; the second finishes the outer one. So, the ELSE must belong to the inner IF-THEN.

Named constants and more on debugging

As you might expect, QBasic ultimately deals with IF-THENs by converting the relational operators to numbers—just like it does for the DO WHILE/UNTIL commands. For example, in a statement like:

```
IF Done THEN PRINT "I'm done!"
```

then you'll see the message if and only if the value of the variable Done was non-zero, true. An extension of this idea lets you make all your loops single-entry single-exit. Suppose, for example, that you wanted to write a program or fragment that would accept a single word. (In this example, a word is any sequence of characters ending with either a space, a comma, a semicolon, a colon, a period, a question mark, an exclamation point, or a carriage return, which are examples of *delimiters*.) At this point, such a program shouldn't be hard. You select on the basis of the character. The key lines might be:

```
CASE " " , "," ,";" , ":","?","!",CHR$(13)
    EXIT DO
```

The trouble with this method is that all the commas make the command close to unreadable. Instead, I probably would use the method shown in the following program:

```
' CH6 \ P10.BAS
' A super INPUT - for a single word
```

```
CLS
PRINT "This program accepts a single 'word' and then echoes it."
Word$ = ""

DO
  Char$ = INPUT$(1)

  SELECT CASE Char$
    CASE " "
      EXIT DO
    CASE ","
      EXIT DO
    CASE ";"
      EXIT DO
    CASE ":"
      EXIT DO
    CASE "."
      EXIT DO
    CASE "!"
      EXIT DO
    CASE "?"
      EXIT DO
    CASE CHR$(13)
      EXIT DO
    CASE ELSE
      PRINT Char$;
      Word$ = Word$ + Char$
  END SELECT
LOOP

PRINT
PRINT "Here is your word again stripped of any punctuation ";
PRINT Word$

END
```

As I mentioned before, however, some people don't like the idea of having eight different ways to leave a loop. They prefer to set up a flag variable. They might rewrite the program as:

```
'  CH6 \ P10a.BAS
'  A super INPUT - for a single word
'  Revisited

Word$ = ""
Done% = 0
```

```
DO

    Char$ = INPUT$(1)
    Word$ = Word$ + Char$

    SELECT CASE CHAR$

        CASE " "
            Done% = -1
        CASE ","
            Done% = -1
        CASE ";"
            Done% = -1
        CASE ":"
            Done% = -1
        CASE "."
            Done% = -1
        CASE "!"
            Done% = -1
        CASE "?"
            Done% = -1
        CASE CHR$(13)
            Done% = -1
        CASE ELSE
            PRINT Char$;
            Word$ = Word$ + Char$

    END SELECT

LOOP UNTIL DONE%

PRINT
PRINT "Here is your word again stripped of any punctuation ";
PRINT Word$

END
```

Here the loop ends when the variable Done% flips from 0 (false) to −1 (true). This switch happens when the user enters one of the delimiters. By rewriting the loop this way, it now has only one way out: when the variable Done% demands it. This technique is especially useful once you learn about user-defined functions (see chapter 8).

If you end up preferring single-entry single-exit loops, then I suggest you combine them with QBasic's named constant feature. This feature lets you give mnemonic names to constants. For example:

```
CONST TRUE = -1
CONST FALSE = 0
CONST FALSE = NOT TRUE
```

Now, instead of saying Done% = -1, you can say Done = TRUE, which certainly looks better to my eye.

A named constant consists of the keyword CONST followed by any legal QBasic name. You can set up a named constant only once. You might have constants of any type. For example:

```
CONST ErrorMessage = "Bad Mistake!"
```

would set up a string constant. You can add the dollar sign type identifier if you want, but it's not needed.

```
CONST Pi = 3.141592635
```

would give pi to 10 decimal places.

Programs that do a lot of Boolean operations almost always start out with the two named constants TRUE and FALSE, given as shown previously. Failing to do so often makes the program a morass of -1s and 0s.

Named constants can make your programs more readable in other ways. They prevent the *MEGO* (my eyes glaze over) syndrome common when reading programs that have lots of mysterious numbers sprinkled about. For example, if you were writing a program that worked with a printer, you might set up a named constant:

```
CONST PaperSize = 66
```

rather than use a variable PaperSize% that you assign the value 66 to. One advantage of using a named constant over a variable is that you can't change it, even by mistake. Stand-alone programs with named constants also run a bit faster.

In any case, use one or the other. As you've seen, programs that say:

```
DO UNTIL Count = 66
```

are a lot less clear than ones that say:

```
DO UNTIL Count = PaperSize)
```

(In GW-BASIC, I recommend setting up variables where you would use constants in QBasic.)

Suppose you have to debug a program that uses an IF-THEN. Obviously, it would be helpful not only to watch the value of a variable, but also to watch if a relation is true or false. In QuickBASIC, you have tools available on the debugging menu for this. In QBasic and GW-BASIC, you have to improvise. Judicious use of PRINT statements, combined with breakpoints (for QBasic) or the STOP command (for DOS BASIC), can partially take the place of the more sophisticated tools available in QuickBASIC.

For example, suppose you didn't read the discussion from chapter 5 and were concerned with why the following program seemed to run forever:

```
Total = 0
PassNumber = 0

DO
   TOTAL = TOTAL + .1
   PassNumber = PassNumber + 1
   PRINT PassNumber,Total
LOOP UNTIL TOTAL = 1
```

To debug this program, I would add a few lines:

```
Total = 0
PassNumber = 0

DO
   TOTAL = TOTAL + .1
   PassNumber = PassNumber + 1
   PRINT PassNumber,Total
   PRINT "Boolean Relation", (Total = 1)          'A
   A$ = INPUT$(1)                                 'B
LOOP UNTIL TOTAL > .99999999

END
```

A   This line reminds me that I'm testing a Boolean relation. The statement (Total = 1) will be 0 when it's false and −1 when (and if) it became true.

B   This line often is more practical than a breakpoint or a STOP command.

Think about this type of debugging procedure if one of the branches of an IF-THEN never seems to be chosen or if it's chosen too often.

7
CHAPTER

The built-in functions

This chapter covers DOS BASIC's built-in functions. These are the commands—the tools—that transform raw data into the form you need. For example, there are functions that take strings apart as well as ones that put them together. You even can manipulate individual characters within a string. You also will see how the pseudo-random number generator lets you build an element of indeterminacy into your programs, which is a necessary tool for programming games of chance.

Finally, don't be surprised if, at many times in this chapter, you need to check the online help about a specific function. The examples given there complement the ones given in this chapter. Similarly, if you are using GW-BASIC, you might want to check the documentation that came with the program.

Simple string functions

Suppose you wanted to center a message on the screen. You can use the LOCATE command to move the cursor, but where exactly should you move it to? For example, suppose you had a message like HELLO WORLD! This message is 12 characters long (counting the space). To center it on a line, you have to move back six positions from the midpoint of a line and then start printing. To do this, you need a command that finds the length of a string. In DOS BASIC it is: LEN(*string*), where the parentheses hold a string expression. Here's a QBasic program to center a message on the screen.

```
' CH7 \ P1.BAS
' centering a message on the screen
```

```
CLS

PRINT "Enter a string to center on the screen. Press return"
PRINT " when done."
LINE INPUT "?"; Message$                                          'A
LenMessage = LEN(Message$)

IF LenMessage > 80 THEN                                           'B
   PRINT "TOO LONG!"
   BEEP
ELSE
   CLS
   LOCATE 12, 40 – (LenMessage / 2)                               'C
   PRINT Message$
END IF

END
```

A   I use the LINE INPUT command in case there's a comma within the message. The question mark is there because the LINE INPUT command doesn't display one.

B   Notice the block IF-THEN-ELSE. In GW-BASIC, you would need to use a fairly long and ugly line. If the message is too long, QBasic so indicates, with some audio reinforcement. Otherwise, it processes the ELSE block that centers the message.

C   If the message has an odd length then taking half of its length gives a fraction. However, as you might expect, because the LOCATE command expects an integer, it rounds off any fraction.

The plus sign lets you join two strings together to form a new string. Because the limit on a single string in QBasic is 32,767 characters, you usually can combine strings to your heart's content. GW-BASIC's 255-character limit is more restrictive.

However, you're more likely to turn to the commands in DOS BASIC that cut up strings. These commands let you pull individual letters or larger chunks out of a string. The most important of these functions is $MID\$(x\$, y, z)$. The first entry holds the string (or string expression) that you want to cut up. Next comes the starting position of the characters that you want cut out of the string. The last position specifies the number of characters that you want to pull out. For example:

```
MID$("Quick BASIC",1,5) = "Quick"
MID$("Quick BASIC",1,6) = "Quick "
MID$("Quick BASIC",7,5) = "BASIC"
MID$("Quick BASIC",6,5) = " BASI"
MID$("Quick BASIC",6,6) = " BASIC"
```

Notice the blank spaces in the second, fourth, and fifth lines.

If you leave out the last entry (the one that tells DOS BASIC how many letters to pull out), then DOS BASIC retrieves the rest of the string, starting from the position determined by the second entry. So:

```
MID$("QuickBASIC",7,5)
```

equals

```
MID$("QuickBASIC",7)
```

equals

```
"BASIC"
```

You also get the rest of the string if the third entry is greater than the number of characters remaining. MID$ is a function of three (or occasionally two) *arguments*. (Argument is a term borrowed from mathematics. Think of it as meaning *things to play with* or *pieces of information to be manipulated*.) The MID$ usually uses three pieces of information: a string in the first position and two integers in the remaining two positions.

Suppose you want to explode a word by printing it vertically instead of horizontally. The program must grab a letter from the word, print it, then move on to the next letter in the word. Obviously, this calls for a FOR-NEXT loop. Here's the QBasic program:

```
'  CH7 \ P2.BAS
'  exploding a word

DEFINT I
CLS

INPUT "Enter a string to explode"; Message$
LenMessage = LEN(Message$)                                    'A

FOR I = 1 TO LenMessage
   PRINT MID$(Message$, I, 1)                                 'B
NEXT I

END
```

A   Because the limit for the FOR-NEXT loop doesn't change (it's a *loop invariant*), it should be computed once before the FOR-NEXT loop starts.

B   On each pass through the loop, the position—the value of I—where the MID$ command starts working increases. The number of characters pulled out remains constant at one.

If you change the MID$ command slightly, the program works quite differently.

For example, change the crucial line to read:

```
PRINT MID$(Message$,1,I)
```

Now, on each pass through the loop, the program pulls out more and more letters. (The third position controls the number of letters pulled out.) The result is a word ladder. If Message$ equals QuickBASIC, then you'll see:

```
Q
Qu
Qui
Quic
Quick
QuickB
QuickBA
QuickBAS
QuickBASI
QuickBASIC
```

Similarly, if you have the loop in the original program go backwards (FOR Len-Message TO 1 STEP − 1), then the program explodes the word backwards. Now, if you add a semicolon to the PRINT statement, then the program will print the word backwards.

You can use this idea to determine whether a phrase is a *palindrome*. (A palindrome reads the same backwards as forwards; spaces and punctuation are not counted. A strong palindrome is one where the spaces and punctuation do count. *Madam I'm Adam* is a weak palindrome, while *Able was I ere I saw Elba* is a strong palindrome.)

Writing a program to determine whether a phrase is a strong palindrome is easy using MID$. Here's a naive QBasic version (for GW-BASIC, you've seen how to work around the lack of a block IF-THEN):

```
' CH7 \ P3.BAS
' a 'strong' palindrome checker

DEFINT I
CLS

INPUT "Enter a string to check"; Message$
LenMessage = LEN(Message$)
Reverse$ = ""

FOR I = LenMessage TO 1 STEP − 1
   Reverse$ = Reverse$ + MID$(Message$, I, 1)          'A
NEXT I
```

```
IF Reverse$ = Message$ THEN
    PRINT "Success! "; Message$; " is a strong palindrome."
ELSE
    PRINT "No luck."
END IF

END
```

A A naive approach to solving a problem usually is a bit inefficient; this program is no exception. The inefficiency comes because the entire reversed phrase is built before determining whether it is a palindrome.

How can this program be made more efficient? How can it be modified to check for any kind of palindrome? As usual, efficiency requires a more complex program and the possibility for mistakes grows.

An outline for a more efficient program is:

1. Find the next character going forward
2. Find the next character going backward
3. If they are equal and there are characters left, repeat steps 1 and 2
4. If the loop stopped because two characters aren't equal, then the phrase isn't a strong palindrome.
5. If the loop stopped because there were no more characters, then the phrase is a strong palindrome.

One nice feature of this outline is that you easily can modify it to check for a weak palindrome. Change steps 1 and 2 to read:

1. Find the next alphabetic character going forward
2. Find the next alphabetic character going backward

More on strings

The MID$ command has two cousins that occasionally are useful: LEFT$ and RIGHT$. As the names suggest, LEFT$ picks out characters from the beginning of a word and RIGHT$ picks them out from the end. Of the two, RIGHT$ is the more common. It avoids a subtraction inside the MID$ command and will work a bit faster as a result. For example:

```
MID$(A$,LEN(A$) − 3,3)
MID$(A$,LEN(A$) − 3)
RIGHT$(A$,3)
```

all have the same effect.

LEFT$ works the same way, but it only saves you from putting a one in the second position of the MID$ function. If you want the first five characters in a string use either:

    MID$(A$,1,5) or
    LEFT$(A$,5)

(DOS BASIC has around 100 built-in functions. It shouldn't be surprising that many of them overlap in their powers.)

I mentioned earlier that, when you press a function or arrow key, the INPUT$(1) command only shows that some key was pressed, but you can't always use it to tell which one. To determine which one of these non-ASCII coded keys was pressed, you combine the INKEY$ command with the string manipulation functions you've just seen. Suppose you set KeyPress$ = INKEY$. If LEN(Key-Press$) equals 0, then no key was pressed. If LEN(KeyPress$) equals 1, then a key (or key combination) having an ASCII code was pressed.

If LEN(KeyPress$) equals 2, then a non-ASCII coded key was pressed. In this case, the first character has ASCII value 0. The ASCII code of the second character determines which key was pressed. Picking up this code is rather messy. Because the code given by the rightmost character is the one that matters, you need to use ASC(RIGHT$(KeyPress$,1)).

Table 7-1 tells you what the most common of these code numbers mean. A complete table of these scan codes is available via the online help facility in Q-Basic. For example, if someone presses the Ins key, then RIGHT$(KeyPress$,1) equals CHR$(82).

Table 7-1 Code numbers for common key combinations.

Code	Key pressed
16-25	Alt−Q to ALT−P (2nd row+Alt)
30-38	Alt−A to Alt−L (3rd row+Alt)
44-50	Alt−Z to Alt−M (4th row+Alt)
71	Home
72	Up arrow
73	PgUp
75	Left arrow
77	Right arrow
79	End
80	Down arrow
81	PgDn
82	Ins
83	Del

Now that you know these codes, its easy to modify the cursor mover program from chapter 6, CH6 \ P8.BAS. Here's the QBasic program:

```
'  CH7 \ P4.BAS
'  A cursor mover revisited
CLS
KEY OFF
LOCATE 1, 1, 1, 0, 7                         ' make the cursor large

Row = 1:Col = 1

DO
  LOCATE Row, Col

  DO
    KeyPress$ = INKEY$
    LOOP WHILE KeyPress$ = ""

  KeyStroke$ = RIGHT$(KeyPress$, 1)                              'A

  SELECT CASE KeyStroke$

    CASE CHR$(4), CHR$(77)          'Ctrl – D or Right Arrow         'B
      IF Col <= 79 THEN Col = Col + 1

    CASE CHR$(19), CHR$(75)         'Ctrl – S or Down Arrow
      IF Col > 1 THEN Col = Col – 1

    CASE CHR$(5), CHR$(72)          'Ctrl – E or Up Arrow
      IF Row > 1 THEN Row = Row – 1

    CASE CHR$(24), CHR$(80)         'Ctrl – X or Down Arrow
      IF Row < 25 THEN Row = Row + 1

    CASE CHR$(18), CHR$(73)         'Ctrl – R or PgUp
      Row = 1

    CASE CHR$(3), CHR$(81)          'Ctrl – C or PgDn
      Row = 25

    CASE CHR$(71)                   'Home                            'C
      Row = 1
      Col = 1

    CASE ELSE
      IF KeyStroke$ <> "X" THEN BEEP
  END SELECT

LOOP UNTIL KeyStroke$ = "X"

LOCATE 1, 1, 1, 7                         ' cursor back to normal
END
```

A   The RIGHT$ command works perfectly here. If the key pressed is a normal ASCII-coded key, then it has a length of one. RIGHT$(*string*, 1) is a fancy way of getting the key. If it has length two, then this gives the character whose code the program needs to check.

B   Notice how simple it is to modify the SELECT CASE statement from the previous program to this new situation. In each case, all I have to do is add a check for an extra character.

C   I added a home cursor option. I'll leave adding an end option to you.

The MID$ command has one other useful feature. It lets you make changes inside a string. For example, if

    BestBasic$ = "TurboBASIC"

then the statement:

    MID$(BestBASIC$,1,5) = "Quick"

gives BestBASIC$ the value "QuickBASIC". When you use MID$ this way, then the second position controls where the change will start and the third position controls how many letters to pull out from the string on the right side. These are the letters that will be switched into the original string. For example:

    MID$(BestBASIC$,1,5) = "QuickBASIC by MicroSoft"

gives the same result as before. If the right side has fewer characters than the entry in the third position of the left side demands, then DOS BASIC changes as many characters as occur on the right side. So:

    MID$(BestBASIC$,1,5) = "QB"

gives BestBASIC$ the value "QBrboBASIC".

The MID$ statement makes changes within a string but never changes the length of the original string. If the number in the third position is too large relative to the number in the second position—is greater than the remaining number of characters—then only the characters remaining can change. Finally, just as with the MID$ function, you can leave out the last position:

    MID$("In the beginning ",8) = "middle was"

changes the string to:

    "In the middle was"

In this case, there's just enough room to fit the string on the right side into the string on the left, starting at the eighth position.

If you want to change the size of a string, then the MID$ statement is of little use. This procedure requires brute force; it's a bit like splicing tape. For example, suppose you want to change the string:

"Turbo Pascal is the best programming language"

to read:

"QuickBASIC is the best programing language"

Because the string "Pascal" has 6 letters and the string "BASIC" has five, you cannot use the MID$ statement. Instead you must follow the splicing analogy:

1. Cut out the phrase "Turbo Pascal"
2. Hold the phrase "is the best programming language"
3. Splice in the phrase "QuickBASIC" and reassemble the string

Here's the fragment:

```
phrase$ = "Turbo Pascal is the best programming language"

Begin$ = "QuickBASIC"
EndPhrase$ = MID$(phrase$, 13)
phrase$ = Begin$ + EndPhrase$

PRINT phrase$
```

Programming this kind of change can be a bit painful if you always have to go in and count characters to find which position, for example, the word *Pascal* started and ended. As usual, this task is simplified by one of DOS BASIC's built-in functions: INSTR. Like the MID$ function, INSTR also works with three (and occasionally two) pieces of information. It's a function of three (occasionally two) arguments.

INSTR tells you whether a string is part of another string, or is a *substring* of that string and, if so, at what position the substring starts. Using the same variable, phrase$, then the value of INSTR(1, phrase$, "Pascal") is 6, because the string "Pascal" occurs in the phrase "Turbo Pascal is the best programming language" starting at the sixth position.

In this case, DOS BASIC searches the string starting from the first position, until it finds the substring. If it doesn't find the string, then it gives back a value of 0. So:

```
INSTR(1, phrase$, "pascal")
```

has a value of 0, because "pascal" isn't a substring of the phrase "Turbo Pascal is the best programming language". (Remember that case is important inside quotes, so the INSTR function is case sensitive.)

In this situation, the INSTR function essentially translates the following outline into a single command:

1. Pull out characters 1 through 6.
2. Determine whether they are the searched for substring. If so, then return a value of 1 and stop.

3. Now, do it for characters 2 through 7. If successful, return a value of 2 and stop.
4. Continue until there are no more substrings to check. If totally unsuccessful, return a value of 0.

You easily can translate this outline into a program that, using MID$, would work for any string (replace the number in the second position with LEN(*string*)). However, the program you end up with will take much longer to do what INSTR does.

The general form of the INSTR function is:

INSTR([*where to start,*] *string to search, string to find*)

Here, I am following the conventions in the DOS BASIC manual and the online help. Anything that is optional in the description of a command is enclosed by brackets. In this case, the optional first position specifies from what position to start the search. If you leave this entry out, the search automatically starts from the first position.

Notice as well that the comma is within the brackets. This means that, if you put something here, you need the comma. If the bracket fell before the comma, it would indicate that the comma always is needed. If you are using QBasic, it's worth getting comfortable with the notations used in the manual and the online help.

The deeper you go into DOS BASIC, the more benefit you'll derive from the manuals and, for QBasic, from the online help. In particular, as I mentioned in the introduction to this chapter, the examples in the DOS BASIC manual or available online can't help but complement the explanations I give here.

Another good example of how to use the INSTR command is a program that *parses*, or take apart, a string into its component parts. Suppose you had a string made up of individual words, each separated from the next by a single space. An outline to pull out the individual words is:

1. Find the first occurrence of a space. The stuff up to the first space is a word.
2. Find the second space. The stuff between these two spaces is a word.
3. Now, find the third space. The stuff between the second and third space is a word.
4. Continue until there are no more spaces.
5. The stuff between the last space and the end of the string is the last word.

Here's a QBasic program that implements this outline:

```
' CH7 \ P5.BAS
' This program uses INSTR to parse a phrase
' by searching for a space as the separator

CLS
```

```
DO                                                           'A
    INPUT "Please enter the phrase to parse"; Phrase$
    LenPhrase = LEN(Phrase$)
LOOP UNTIL LenPhrase > 0

Separate$ = CHR$(32)        'equals space

BeforeSpace = 0                                              'B
AfterSpace = INSTR(BeforeSpace + 1, Phrase$, Separate$)      'C

DO UNTIL AfterSpace = 0                                      'D

    SizeOfWord = AfterSpace − BeforeSpace − 1                'E
    NextWord$ = MID$(Phrase$, BeforeSpace + 1, SizeOfWord)   'F
    PRINT NextWord$
    BeforeSpace = AfterSpace                                 'G
    AfterSpace = INSTR(BeforeSpace + 1, Phrase$, Separate$)  'H

LOOP

PRINT MID$(Phrase$, BeforeSpace + 1)                         'I

END
```

A   It's hard to take apart the null string.

B   This initialization makes it easy to start the process. Without this line, the program would have to treat the first word separately.

C   The next space is found by starting one position in from the previous space—in this case, from the first position (see comment A).

D   The loop stops when no more spaces are encountered. By testing at the top, the program takes care of the case when there is only a single word (see comment I).

E   I figured this out by working an example through on paper. For example, if spaces were at the 5th and 9th positions, then the actual word took up positions 6, 7, and 8 (i.e., the word was three characters long).

F   Computing the size of the word in the previous step made this statement cleaner. There's rarely a need to combine many statements into one.

G   This line moves along to the position of the next space.

H   The program looks for the next space. If it finds it, the cycle continues; if not, the program moves to the line at comment I.

I   The program now knows there are no more spaces; the rest of the string must be a word.

One problem with this program is that it can't handle multiple spaces within the phrase. The problem stems from the outline. I assumed that a word is bounded by no more than one space. How can the program take care of the quite common possibility of a double space or even more? Changing the outline is simple. You only have to change the second step:

2. Find the second space. The stuff between these two spaces is a word.

to read:

2. Find the second space. The stuff between these two spaces is a word, if it is not empty space.

What really happens if there are two consecutive spaces? As always, an example helps. Suppose the phrase$ was:

"THIS   IS   A TEST"

In DOS BASIC:

"THIS" + SPACE(2) + "IS" + SPACE(3) + "A" + SPACE(1) + "TEST"

Now, it's time for you to play computer. Especially when dealing with loops, this technique often is best done by setting up a little chart detailing the value of the variables on each pass. Table 7-2 shows the results found by partially running through the program by hand. (You often use a table like this when you debug with the instant watch; however, watching is of little use unless you know what's supposed to happen).

Table 7-2 The results of running through part of CH7 \ P5.BAS by hand.

Before entering loop	BeforeSpace = 0
	AfterSpace = 5
Start of first loop	SizeOfWord = 4
End of first pass	BeforeSpace = 5
	AfterSpace = 6
Start of second pass	SizeOfWord = 0
End of second pass	BeforeSpace = 6
	AfterSpace = 9
Start of third pass	SizeOfWord = 2
End of third pass	BeforeSpace = 9
	AfterSpace = 10
Start of fourth loop	SizeOfWord = 0

As you can see, this little table seems to indicate that whenever there are two spaces together, the variable SizeOfWord has value zero. This will always be true. If you have two consecutive spaces, the value of AfterSpace always is one more than the value of BeforeSpace. So:

```
SizeOfWord = AfterSpace − BeforeSpace − 1 = 0
```

Knowing this fact makes it easy to modify the program. Change the PRINT statements to read:

```
IF SizeOfWord > 0 THEN ....
```

I'll leave the changes to you. A version of this program that takes this possibility into account and also checks for other word separators (like commas, periods, and question marks) can be found in chapter 8.

Although you need a bit of work to pull out extra spaces within a string, in QBasic, you don't have to do very much for spaces at the beginning or end of a string. QBasic comes with two built-in functions for stripping these spaces for you, LTRIM$(*string*) and RTRIM$(*string*). Neither of these functions occur in GW-BASIC. As the names suggest these function trim spaces from the left and right, respectively. For example, if:

```
A$ = "     This has too many spaces on the left"
```

then

```
LTRIM$(A$) = "This has too many spaces on the left"
```

Also, if

```
A$ = "This has too many spaces on the right     "
```

then

```
RTRIM$(A$) = "This has too many spaces on the right"
```

Manipulating numbers as strings

Because the string manipulation functions are so powerful, DOS BASIC gives you a way to change a number into a string of digits. The command STR$ does this. If:

```
X = 1234567890
```

then

```
STR$(X) = " 1234567890"
```

Notice the space in the string. DOS BASIC always adds an extra space at the beginning of the string representation of a positive number for the implied plus sign. Converted negative numbers keep the minus sign and have no space at the beginning.

For example, the following QBasic fragment would print a number without any spaces:

```
X$ = STR$(A)
PRINT LTRIM$(X$)
```

At first glance, the STR$ command does not seem very useful. For example, PRINT USING can do the same thing as the above fragment. Moreover, when you change a number into a string, you lose the ability to add, subtract, or multiply. However, what you gain in return is the ability to isolate each digit. After you isolate a digit, you can use another function, VAL, to change that digit back into a number.

Here's an example of why this process might be useful. One problem when using the PRINT USING command is deciding on the number of digits before the decimal point. If you are wrong, then you'll be stuck with the % flag in front of the number. This situation is easy to avoid if you combine the STR$ command with the INSTR command. Here's an outline:

1. Change the number to a string.
2. Find the decimal point using INSTR.
3. If the value from the previous step is zero, there's no decimal point and the number of digits is one less than the length of the converted number. Otherwise, the number of digits in front of the decimal point is two less than the value given by the INSTR function because of the extra space that STR$ sticks on and the decimal point.

Here's the QBasic fragment:

```
' find the number of digits

Number$ = STR$(Number)
Digits = INSTR(Number$,".")

IF Digits = 0 THEN
    NumOfDigits = LEN(Number$) – 1
ELSE
    NumOfDigits = Digits – 2
END IF
```

Now, I'll show another example of the power of STR$. Shipping companies often determine the charge for sending a package by looking at the first three digits of the zip code in the address where the package is to be sent. For example, they might use the information in Table 7-3 to determine the zone.

Once you isolate the first three digits of the zip code, you can use the VAL command to change it back into a number. Once it's a number again, you can use the SELECT CASE statement to check the range. Here's a QBasic program that does exactly this:

```
' CH7 \ P6.BAS
' A simple zip code check
' uses STR$ and VAL
```

Table 7-3 Assigning shipping codes according to the first three digits of the customer's zip code.

First 3 digits of Zip code	Zone
001 to 374	8
375 to 399	7
500 to 599	5
600 to 699	4
700 to 799	3
800 to 999	2

```
CLS
INPUT "Enter the zip code for the address"; ZipCode
ZipCode$ = STR$(ZipCode)                                        'A
Zone$ = MID$(ZipCode$, 2, 3)                                    'B
Zone = VAL(Zone$)                                               'C

LOCATE 12, 37
SELECT CASE Zone

    CASE 1 TO 374
        PRINT "Zone 8"

    CASE 375 TO 399
        PRINT "Zone 7"

    CASE 500 TO 599
        PRINT "Zone 5"

    CASE 600 TO 699
        PRINT "Zone 4"

    CASE 700 TO 799
        PRINT "Zone 3"

    CASE 800 TO 999
        PRINT "Zone 2"

    CASE ELSE
        PRINT "Not a zip code"

END SELECT

END
```

A Here, as before, the string command changes a zip code into a string of digits.

B Now, the program isolates the first three digits of the zip code. Notice that the program has to start at the second position because of the extra space that QBasic sticks on in a transformation using STR$.

C Now, change the zip code back into a number so that QBasic can check its range.

Notice that the VAL command disregards any spaces at the beginning of a string of digits. However, always keep in mind that, although the VAL command disregards any spaces in the front of a word, it reacts badly to other nonnumerals in the word. For example, if the leading character of a string isn't a numeral, VAL always gives 0. Moreover, if any intermediate character isn't a space, the conversion stops at that point. For example, VAL("12zx345") has a value of 12, but VAL("12 345") has a value of 123450.

Another use of VAL is to give you a super INPUT command. Suppose you want part of a program to accept a number, but you want it to disregard commas, extraneous decimal points, etc. The outline for this is:

1. Get a character.
2. If it's a digit, stick it on the right.
3. If it's the first decimal point accept that and also stick it on the right. Otherwise, disregard it.
4. Continue until the Return key is hit. Now, change the string into a number.

Here's a QBasic program that follows this outline:

```
'  CH7 \ P7.BAS
'  This program combines VAL
'  and INPUT$ to accept a number and only a number

CLS
PRINT "Type a number - commas allowed! Hit enter when done."

CONST TRUE = - 1          '  - 1 is true
CONST FALSE = 0

Numeral$ = " "
DecimalFlag% = TRUE                                          'A

DO
   KeyStroke$ = INPUT$(1)                                    'B

   SELECT CASE KeyStroke$

      CASE "0" TO "9"                                        'C
```

```
          Numeral$ = Numeral$ + KeyStroke$
          PRINT KeyStroke$;

       CASE "."
         IF DecimalFlag% THEN                                          'D
           Numeral$ = Numeral$ + KeyStroke$
           PRINT KeyStroke$;
           DecimalFlag% = FALSE
         ELSE
            BEEP                                                       'E
         END IF

       CASE ","
         PRINT KeyStroke$;

       CASE CHR$(13)
         PRINT KeyStroke$                                             'F

       CASE ELSE
          BEEP                                                        'G

     END SELECT

  LOOP UNTIL KeyStroke$ = CHR$(13)

  PRINT "The number was "; VAL(Numeral$)                             'H

  END
```

A   To make the program more readable, I've used the named constants
    that were introduced in chapter 6. GW-BASIC users might want to use
    variables.

B   A loop using INKEY$ would work as well. With both these com-
    mands, however, the character isn't displayed. The program has to dis-
    play the digits as they are entered, otherwise there's no feedback to the
    user. You've seen how to change this loop to a WHILE/WEND loop
    also. The SELECT CASE would have to be replaced by a long list of
    cumbersome IF-THENs.

C   This line is the key to this improved INPUT routine. If a character is in
    this range, then it's a digit. So, it is concatenated to the end of the
    string of numerals that the program eventually will transform into a
    number. Also, as mentioned previously, you need to display the num-
    ber to provide some visual feedback to the user.

D   This case accepts a single decimal point in the number; however, enter-
    ing a decimal point flips the flag to false.

E   If this case is selected after the variable DecimalFlag% is set to 0, then the ELSE clause is always processed and a beep follows.

F   Entering a carriage return lands the program in this case. This case is the one that ends the DO loop. Printing it here gives a blank line before the number is displayed in comment H. You also could have used the EXIT loop here and eliminated the test at the bottom.

G   Audio feedback is a good way to make programs more user friendly.

H   This statement displays the number. Obviously, if this program was part of a larger program, you probably would manipulate it in some other way at this point.

The RND function

There are programs that let you play blackjack, backgammon, or most any game of chance on a computer. In card games and most other games, the play is unpredictable. This unpredictability is exactly what is meant by a game of chance. On the other hand, computers are machines; the behavior of machines should be predictable. To write a program in DOS BASIC that allows you, for example, to simulate the throwing of a die, you need a command that makes the behavior of the computer seem random. This command is RND. For example, try the following QBasic program:

```
'  CH7 \ P8.BAS
'  10 pseudo-random numbers

CLS

FOR I = 1 TO 10
   PRINT RND(1)
NEXT I

END
```

After you compile and run this program, 10 numbers between 0 and 1 (usually having 16 digits) will roll down the screen. These numbers seem to follow no pattern; that's what usually is meant by random. They also will have many, but not all, of the sophisticated statistical properties that scientists expect of random numbers. Each time the computer processes a line containing the statement PRINT RND(1), a different number between 0 and 1 pops out. In theory, the number can be 0, but it can't ever be 1.

It's natural to wonder what a number with 16 decimal places is good for. Suppose, for example, you wanted to write a program that simulated a coin toss. There are three possibilities: it could be heads, it could be tales, or it could stand on edge. A QBasic program to simulate a coin toss might look like this:

```
'  CH7 \ P9.BAS
'  A coin toss simulator
CoinToss = RND

SELECT CASE CoinToss

    CASE IS < .5
        PRINT "Heads"
    CASE .5
        PRINT "Stood on edge!!!!"
    CASE ELSE
        PRINT "Tails"

END SELECT

END
```

Try the following variation, which keeps track of the number of different kinds of flips:

```
'  CH7 \ P10.BAS
'  A multiple coin toss simulator

DEFINT I-Z
CLS
INPUT "How many trials"; Trials

NumOfHeads = 0
NumOfTails = 0
Unbelievable = 0

FOR I = 1 TO Trials

    CoinToss = RND(1)

    SELECT CASE CoinToss

        CASE IS < .5
            NumOfHeads = NumOfHeads + 1
        CASE .5
            PRINT "Stood on edge!!!!"
            BEEP: BEEP
            Unbelievable = Unbelievable + 1
        CASE ELSE
            NumOfTails = NumOfTails + 1

    END SELECT

NEXT I
```

```
PRINT "Number of heads was"; NumOfHeads
PRINT "Number of tails was"; NumOfTails
IF Unbelievable > 0 THEN
    PRINT "The coin stood 'on edge'!"
END IF

END
```

Notice that, because of the DEFINT I-Z command, I could not choose a variable whose name began with a letter in this range. If I had called the variable Toss instead of CoinToss, it would always be an integer—it always would have a value of 0 or 1, depending on how it was rounded off. Because it's equally likely that the number would be rounded up as rounded down, I could have changed the program to determine the coin's position using this feature—if I didn't mind eliminating the standing on edge possibility, which, to be quite honest, has never happened, no matter how many trials I ran.

Try this program with different number of trials. You should get roughly the same number of heads as tails and no standing on edges. For a large number of trials, it would be very unlikely that you'd get equal numbers of heads and tails. Now, run this program using the same number of trials each time. If you do, you'll notice that you get exactly the same number of heads and tails. This result certainly would be unusual behavior for an honest coin.

The numbers you get using RND(1) are only *pseudo-random*. (Pseudo generally means false.) You've just seen one of the problems of pseudo-random numbers. Every time you start a program, you will get the same sequence of pseudo-random numbers. It's as if there is a book of these numbers in the computers memory and, after each program is over, the book gets turned back to page one. So, the deck always starts out in the same order and, therefore, the results are fixed. You need a way to shuffle the deck each time the program starts up. This shuffling can be done in many ways. A slow but sure way is to start your program with something like:

```
PRINT "Everyone who wants to play should press a number key."
PRINT "Then hit the return key."
INPUT Number%

FOR I% = 1 TO Number%
    X = RND(1)
NEXT I%
```

This fragment advances you to a place in the list that no one can tell before hand. The problem with this approach is that moving ahead in the list and generating all those pseudo-random numbers takes time; it's silly to wait. You can eliminate any wait by changing what you put inside the parentheses of the RND function, or slightly modifying it.

First off, suppose you issue an RND(0). You will get the last pseudo-random number generated. This is useful in trying to debug a program. RND(0) gives you the only way of checking what pseudo-random number the machine just used. Imagine trying to check a program if an important number changes each time you run it and you don't know what the number was.

(From this point on I'm going to be slightly imprecise and stop saying *pseudo-random* and speak of the numbers coming from the RND function as being *random*.)

Suppose next that there is a negative number inside the parentheses. Each time you give the command RND(*negative number*), you get the same random number. This feature is another important debugging tool. It lets you rerun a program keeping the random numbers temporarily stable. A good way to think about what a negative seed does is to imagine that there is a different list of random numbers, each one corresponding to a different negative seed.

The best way not to stack the cards is to use the exact time of the system clock to reseed the random number generator. Because the clock is accurate to around a tenth of a second, it's quite unlikely that a program will start at exactly the same moment each time it is run. This technique is done by combining the command RANDOMIZE with the TIMER command in the form of the following statement:

RANDOMIZE TIMER

You saw the TIMER command in chapter 2. Recall that it gives you the number of seconds since midnight, within a tenth of a second.

The RANDOMIZE command is a general shuffler. In this case, it takes the value of the TIMER function and uses it to reseed the random number generator. It also can be used in the form:

RANDOMIZE

whereupon the program stops and asks for a seed. So you can have a fragment like:

PRINT "At the ? enter a number."
RANDOMIZE

What a user will see is the message Random Number Seed?

Think of a seed as the number from which the random numbers grow. The numbers are calculated by transforming the seed through a rather complicated method called the *linear congruential method*.

The RANDOMIZE statement also can be a useful debugging tool, because you can use any numeric expression in the RANDOMIZE command (for example, RANDOMIZE Xexpress, RANDOMIZE Yexpress, etc.) and you get the same random numbers whenever Xexpress and Yexpress have the same value. In the current version of QBasic, it's best to use negative numbers as seeds if you want to take advantage of this feature.

With a little work, numbers between zero and one might be good for imitating a coin toss, but the method I used earlier would be cumbersome for, say, a dice simulation. The outline would be something like this:

1. If the random number is less than $1/6$, make it a 1
2. If less than $2/6$, make it a 2
3. If less than $3/6$, make it a 3

Thinking about this outline leads to a simple trick called *scaling*, which more or less automates this process. Suppose you take a number between 0 and 1 and multiply it by 6. If it was less than $1/6$ to start with, it will now be less than 1; if it was between $1/6$ and $2/6$, it now will be between 1 and 2; and so on. All you need to do is follow the following outline:

1. Multiply the number by 6 and move up to the next integer

In general, if the number was between 0 and 1, but never quite getting to 1, then the result of multiplying by 6 goes from 0 to not quite 6.

Unfortunately, there's no command in DOS BASIC to move up to the next integer. Instead, there's a command to throw away the decimal part of a number. It's called FIX. for example:

```
FIX(3.456) = 3
FIX(-7.9998) = -7
FIX(8) = 8
```

However, by adding one to the results of FIXing a positive number, you will have moved, in effect, to the next highest positive integer. Here's a QBasic program that shows this:

```
'  CH7 \ P11.BAS
'  A dice simulation using FIX

RANDOMIZE TIMER
CLS

DIE = FIX(6 * RND(1)) + 1                              'A
PRINT "I rolled a"; DIE

END
```

A   This line is the key to the program. The number inside the parentheses, (6*RND(1)), is always between 0 and 6, but it can't be 6, because RND(1) is never 1. Applying the FIX function yields an integer between 0 and 5 (i.e. 0, 1, 2, 3, 4, or 5). Now, you only have to add one to make it a proper looking die.

There's another function that works much the same way as FIX. It's called INT. INT gives the *floor* of a number—the first integer that's smaller than or equal to the number. Its technically called the *greatest integer function*. However, thinking of it as the floor function makes it easy to remember what happens for negative numbers. With negative numbers, you move down. For example:

```
INT(-3.5) = -4
INT(-4.1) = -5
```

So, FIX and INT work the same way for positive numbers but are different for negative ones. Using INT and adding one always moves to the next largest integer. Here's a rewritten version of the previous QBasic program using INT. It looks much the same:

```
'  CH7 \ P12.BAS
'  A dice simulation using INT

RANDOMIZE TIMER
CLS

DIE = INT(6 * RND(1)) + 1                'see the previous comment A
PRINT "I rolled a"; DIE

END
```

The INT and FIX functions have other uses. For example, the post office charges for first class mail are 29 cents for the first ounce and 23 cents for each additional ounce *or fraction thereof*. Suppose an item weighed 3.4 ounces, the cost would be 29 cents for the first ounce and 69 (3×23) for the additional ounces, counting the fraction. The cost is:

```
.29 + INT(3.4)*.23
```

In general, in QBasic it's:

```
IF INT(WeightOfObject) = WeightOfObject THEN
   COST = .29 + .23*(WeightOfObject - 1)
ELSE
   COST = .29 + .23*(WeightOfObject)
ENDIF
```

More on using the random number generator

Suppose you wanted to write a jumble program. This program would take a string and shuffle the letters around. It's a prototype for many other types of operations (for example, shuffling a deck of cards). Here's an outline for one way to do it:

1. Start at the first character
2. Swap it with a randomly chosen character
3. Do the same for the second character
4. Continue until there are no more characters left

The swapping can be done with the MID$ statement, because you are never changing the size of the string. Here's a QBasic program that implements this outline.

```
'  CH7 \ P13.BAS
'  a Jumble program
'  demonstrates MID$ as a statement
'  and the RND function

DEFINT A-Z

CLS
RANDOMIZE TIMER

PRINT "Enter the phrase to jumble."
LINE INPUT "?"; Phrase$
Jumble$ = Phrase$

LenPhrase = LEN(Phrase$)

FOR I = 1 TO LenPhrase

    INum = INT(LenPhrase * RND(1)) + 1          'A
    NewChar$ = MID$(Jumble$, INum, 1)           'B
    OldChar$ = MID$(Jumble$, I, 1)              'C

    MID$(Jumble$, I, 1) = NewChar$              'D
    MID$(Jumble$, INum, 1) = OldChar$           'E

NEXT I

CLS
PRINT Phrase$: PRINT
PRINT "In jumbled form: "; Jumble$
END
```

A   This line gives the random position within the string.

B   This line gives the character at the random position.

C   This variable contains the character that the program is going to swap with the character selected in comment B. It's determined by the counter in the FOR-NEXT loop.

D   The MID$ statement lets you replace a character within a string, but this statement must be combined with the next statement to preserve all the letters in the original string.

E   Because there is no statement like SWAP MID$(Jumble$,INum,1), MID-$(Jumble$,I,1), the statements in comments C, D, and E combine to form one.

To make this program into a card shuffler, all you need to do is give Phrase$ the right value. You can do this using the CHR$ command. I'll return to this program in chapter 9.

To this point, all the random integers that you've used have started from 0 or 1. Sometimes, it's convenient to have random integers that span a range. For example, take a random four-letter combination. How likely is it to be a word in English? To try this idea out, you need to generate four random letters and string them together. An obvious way to do this process is to apply the CHR$ command to a random integer between 65 and 90 (the range of ASCII codes for the upper-case alphabet). To get a random integer in this range, you would generate a random integer between 0 and 25 and add it to 65.

A translation of this is:

```
CharNum = INT(26*RND(1)) + 65
```

Here's a QBasic program that uses this line to generate random four-letter combinations:

```
' CH7 \ P14.BAS
' Random 4 letter 'words'
' demonstrates RND for a range

DEFINT A-Z
RANDOMIZE TIMER
CLS

PRINT "This program generates random 4 letter combinations. It"
PRINT "stops when you press any key."
PRINT "Press any key to start."
I$ = INPUT$(1)

DO
  WORD$ = ""
    FOR I = 1 TO 4
      CharNum = INT(26 * RND(1)) + 65                          'A
      WORD$ = WORD$ + CHR$(CharNum)
    NEXT I
  PRINT WORD$
```

```
LOOP UNTIL INKEY$ < > ""                                          'B
END
```

A   As explained in the outline, this statement gives a random integer in the right range. The next statement turns it into a random uppercase letter. As usual, these two statements could have been combined into one:

```
Word$ = Word$ + CHR$(INT(26*RND(1)) + 65)
```

However, this command clearly is less readable than the lines in the program.

B   I just got tired of saying LOOP WHILE INKEY$ = "".

As another example of using this technique to get a range of values, suppose you wanted to write a typing reflex tester. You generate a random typewriter key and display it on the screen. Then, use INPUT$(1) or INKEY$ to grab the key that someone pressed. To get a random typewriter ASCII code, you need a number between 32 and 126. However, the space bar doesn't show up too well on the screen, so the following QBasic program makes the range 33 to 126.

```
'  CH7 \ P15.BAS
'  a reflex tester

DEFINT I-N
RANDOMIZE TIMER

CLS
PRINT "I'm going to generate 10 different characters. When the"
PRINT "character appears press that key (using the Shift key if"
PRINT "necessary)."
PRINT
PRINT "The number correct will be listed at the end, followed by"
PRINT "the program's run time."
PRINT
PRINT "Press any key to start."

SLEEP

StartTime = TIMER
NumRight = 0

FOR I = 1 TO 10

   CLS
   N = INT(94 * RND(1)) + 33
   GuessKey$ = CHR$(N)
   LOCATE 12, 40: PRINT GuessKey$

   ANS$ = ""
```

```
        DO WHILE ANS$ = ""
           ANS$ = INKEY$
           IF ANS$ = GuessKey$ THEN NumRight = NumRight + 1
        LOOP

     NEXT I

     EndTime = TIMER

     LOCATE 24, 1
     PRINT "Your score was "; NumRight;
     PRINT " - total runtime was "; EndTime − StartTime; "seconds."

     END
```

I can't resist giving one last application of the RND function: abstract tiling. Recall that the CHR$(219) character is a solid block. If a COLOR command has changed the foreground, it's a colored block. The following QBasic program generates a random foreground color and paints the screen accordingly.

```
' CH7 \ P16.BAS
' Abstract designs

RANDOMIZE TIMER
CLS
PRINT "Press any key to see a random design. When the screen is"
PRINT "filled, press any key to erase it and end."

FOR Rw = 1 TO 24
   FOR Col = 1 TO 80
      COLOR INT(16 * RND(1))
      PRINT CHR$(219);
   NEXT Col
NEXT Rw

SLEEP
CLS
END
```

Some of the other built-in functions

I'm not going to bother going over all the built-in functions. Now is a good time to take out the manual or start working through some of the online examples. On the other hand, where I can think of something useful that is not mentioned or not sufficiently stressed in the manual or in the online help, I will point it out in the following sections.

The Screen functions

CSRLIN gives you the line that the cursor currently is on. Combine it with POS(1) function, which gives the column the cursor is on, gives you a way to restore the cursor to its previous position, no matter how far it's strayed:

```
OldColumn = POS(1)
OldRow = CSRLIN

LOCATE OldRow,OldColumn          'back to where it belongs
```

The SCREEN(*row*, *column*) function gives you the ASCII code of the character at location *row*, *column*. If that space is blank (for example, because of a CLS command), the value of SCREEN is 32, which is the ASCII for a space.

One of my favorite applications of the SCREEN function is to find the amount of free space that's on the disk, completely from within DOS BASIC. DOS BASIC has a command, FILES, that gives you a list of the files on the current directory. It works like a DIR/W command from DOS. To find the files on another directory, for example, on the directory C: \ QB \ Programs, say:

```
FILES "C: \ QB \ Programs"
```

You also can use standard DOS wild cards. FILES "A:*.BAS" would give all files on the A drive with the BAS extension. Figure 7-1 is an example of the information that the FILES command gives. Notice that the number of bytes is given on

```
C:\QB45
qb
C:\QB45

            .   <DIR>           ..  <DIR> DEMO1   .BAS     DEMO2   .BAS
DEMO3   .BAS         QB      .BI     QCARDS  .BAS     QCARDS  .DAT
REMLINE .BAS         SORTDEMO.BAS    TORUS   .BAS     EXAMPLES    <DIR>
QB      .EXE         QB      .INI    QB45QCK .HLP     BC      .EXE
BRUN45  .EXE         LIB     .EXE    LINK    .EXE     BQLB45  .LIB
BRUN45  .LIB         QB      .LIB    QB      .QLB     BCOM45  .LIB
MOUSE   .COM         MOEM    .OBJ    QB      .PIF     SMALLERR.OBJ
QB45EMER.HLP         QB45ADVR.HLP    ADVR_EX     <DIR> START      .1
SCREENS     <DIR>    INIT    .SCR    INIT1   .SCN     EDIT       .1
EDIT    .2          T       .BAS    TEST1   .BAS     T       .OBJ
P1      .OBJ         P1      .EXE    FRAG2   .BAS     TEST1   .OBJ
TEST1   .EXE         TEST2   .EXE    TEST3   .EXE     TEST4   .EXE
CH9F2   .BAS         TEST    .BAS    FIG3_4  .PIX     FIG3_5  .PIX
TESTCH5 .BAS         CH3P1   .BAS    APPEND  .1       A       .PIX
FIG2_5AA.PIX         FIG2_6  .PIX    FIG2_7  .PIX     TEST
TESTFIL .BAS         XYCOORD .BAS    COSINE  .BAS     CH13       .1
CH13        <DIR>    TE              EST              TEST34  .BAS
TEST57  .BAS         P2      .BAS    CLEAR   .OBJ     CLEAR   .EXE
FIG2_4  .PIX
     620544 Bytes free

Press any key to continue
```

7-1 Using the FILES command.

the last line. Now, imagine I clear the screen and issue the FILES command. To find out the number of free bytes all I have to do is:

1. Start out at the bottom line
2. Determine whether the second entry is blank
   - If it is, then this line contains the information you want
   - If it is not, move up a line and ask the question again

Here's a QBasic program that translates this outline:

```
'  CH7 \ P17.BAS
'  Finding free disk space
'  cute but inefficient

DEFINT A-Z
CONST SpaceCode = 32
Row = 25            'start from the last line

CLS

PRINT "Enter the drive identifier or pathname."
INPUT "For example A: for the A drive"; Drive$

CLS
FILES Drive$

TestChar = SCREEN(Row, 2)
DO WHILE TestChar = SpaceCode                          'A
   Row = Row - 1
   TestChar = SCREEN(Row, 2)
LOOP

Col = 2
TotalBytes$ = ""
DO                                                     'B
   Bytes = SCREEN(Row, Col)
   Bytes$ = CHR$(Bytes)
   TotalBytes$ = TotalBytes$ + Bytes$
   Col = Col + 1
LOOP UNTIL Bytes = SpaceCode

CLS
LOCATE 1, 1: PRINT "Total bytes free is"; VAL(TotalBytes$)

END
```

A This loop looks at the first character code in the second column in each row, starting from the bottom row. The loop ends when it picks up a code other than 32 (ASCII space).

B   This loop reads the digits of free space. When a space shows up the loop is done.

To be quite honest, this program is more a demonstration of the techniques that you've seen to this point than a good way to find out the amount of free space on a disk. Besides messing up the screen, it takes far too long. I hope Microsoft soon makes free disk space into a built-in function in QBasic. When and if you upgrade to QuickBASIC, you can use a DOS function call. It then will take only a few lines to find the free space on your disk and won't mess up your screen.

Some numeric functions

If you don't do a lot of scientific work, you'll be less likely to use this information. As it is, I'm describing only a handful of DOS BASIC's numeric functions.

ABS(*numeric expression*) gives the absolute value of whatever is inside the parentheses. All this function does is remove minus signs:

ABS(−1) = 1 = ABS(1)

One common use of this function is form of ABS(B − A), when it gives the distance between the numbers A and B. For example, suppose A = 3 and B = 4 then:

ABS(A − B) = ABS(B − A) = 1

because 3 and 4 are one unit apart. As another example:

ABS(ASC(A$) − ASC(B$))

gives the distance between the first two characters of the strings A$ and B$.

LOG(*numeric expression*) gives the natural logarithm of a number. To find the common log (log to base 10), use:

LOG10(*x*) = LOG(*x*)/LOG(10)

which gives the common logarithm of the value inside the parentheses, which must be positive. Once you see how to build in this function (see chapter 8), you'll learn another way to find the number of digits for a template.

IF X > 1 THEN Digits = INT(LOG10(X)) + 1

makes the value of the variable Digits equal to the number of digits after the decimal point. The idea is that, for example, LOG10(197) is between 2 and 3 because LOG10(100) is 2 and LOG10(1000) is 3.

Also, for those who need them, DOS BASIC has the built-in trigonometric functions SIN (sine), COS (cosine), and TAN (tangent). The only problem is that DOS BASIC expects the angle inside the parentheses to be in radian measure. To convert from degrees to radians, you need the value of pi. The conversion formula is:

radians $=$ degrees$*$pi$/180$

To get the value of pi, the easiest method is to set up, early on in your program, a variable, PI#, using the ATN (arctangent) function in the form of:

PI# $=$ 4$*$ATN(1)

(The arctangent of 1 is pi/4.) Sometimes, you might want this value to be the value of a named constant. You also can use the ATN function to get all the other inverse trigonometric functions.

DOS BASIC has two built-in functions that are useful for dealing with integers and long integers (available in QBasic). The first, *integer division*, is denoted by a backslash (the same character used as the DOS path separator). Some examples are:

$$7 \setminus 3 = 2 \quad 10 \setminus 3 = 3$$
$$12 \setminus 4 = 3 \quad 97 \setminus 11 = 8$$

Integer division disregards the remainder after dividing, so it always ends up with an integer. To find the remainder, you use the MOD function. (Mathematicians use the word *modulo* for remainder.) Some examples are:

$$7 \text{ MOD } 3 = 1 \quad 10 \text{ MOD } 3 = 1$$
$$12 \text{ MOD } 4 = 0 \quad 97 \text{ MOD } 11 = 9$$

For example, if you add two one-digit numbers, like 9 and 7, then the carry is $(9+7) \setminus 10$ and the ones digit is $(9+7)$ MOD 10. As simple as this idea is, it is the key to the infinite precision addition program in chapter 8. (Those who are familiar with the MOD function from mathematics should be aware that MOD does not work for negative numbers: -1 MOD 5 still is -1, not 4.)

Finally, as you saw in chapter 3, QBasic doesn't tolerate intermediate overflow very well. (Remember that an intermediate overflow is an operation that works with integers that along the way end up out of bounds.) The cure for this is the CDBL(*numeric expression*) or CLNG(*numeric expression*) functions mentioned earlier. These functions convert the numeric expression inside the parentheses to double precision or a long integer, respectively; overflow is no longer a problem. However, if A% $=$ 32000 and B% $=$ 32000, you can't just say:

Answer $=$ CDBL(A% + B%)

because the CDBL function only goes to work after the two numbers were added. Instead, say:

Answer $=$ CDBL(A%) + B%

This statement avoids the intermediate overflow. You also can convert numbers. CDBL(2345) works the same as saying 2345#. What goes on internally when you say CDBL is a bit tricky, but basically DOS BASIC converts its internal representation of the number to a new form. In particular, this conversion means that CDBL(X%) takes up more space than X% did.

If the number is small enough, you can convert to an integer (CINT), a long integer (CLNG), or a single-precision number (CSNG). When you do these conversions, the appropriate rounding takes place. Finally, let me emphasize that, when you use CDBL, you do not gain precision. Converting a single-precision variable might allow you more room or might give you more digits, but only the first six can be trusted. For example, try the following:

```
A  = 7.1
B# = 7.1
PRINT A
PRINT B#
PRINT CDBL(A)
```

What you'll see in QBasic is:

```
7.099999904632568
7.1
7.099999904632568
```

The point is that, when DOS BASIC stores a number like 7.1 as a single-precision number, because of the way its internal arithmetic works, DOS BASIC usually uses an approximation. Only a double-precision number usually would be accurate enough not to make any changes. Changing a number to double precision using CDBL doesn't magically make it more accurate.

8
CHAPTER

User-defined functions

In chapter 7, you saw how to use most of DOS BASIC's built-in functions. This chapter shows you how to create new functions—essentially to add new commands to DOS BASIC. To create these functions, you'll learn how to use the FUNCTION command for QBasic, as well as the older DEF FN (define function) command in DOS BASIC.

Getting started

Start thinking about defining your own functions when you use a complicated expression more than once in a program. For example, suppose you need a random integer between 1 and 10. You could write INT(10*RND(1)) + 1 each time you needed it; however, this repetition eventually might grow tiresome. Now, suppose the same program needs a random integer between 1 and 40, between 1 and 100, etc. The statements needed for these are so similar to the previous statement that one would hope there is a way to automate the process: have DOS BASIC do some of the work. What you do is add the statement:

    DEF FNRdInt%(X) = INT(X*RND(1) + 1

to your program before you need any random integers. Now, to print out a random integer between 1 and 10, the statement would be:

    PRINT FNRdInt%(10)

You've *called the function*. The DEF is supposed to remind you of the word *define*; the FN is to remind you of the word *function*. The name of the function (in this case, RdInt%) must follow the same rules as those for variables in DOS BASIC, which is why you can't have a variable whose name begins with FN because DOS BASIC thinks you're calling a user-defined function. Just as you could for variables, you can have a type identifier at the end of the name of a function. In this case, the percent sign shows the RdInt% function is an integer type. The type identifier determines the function's value.

The key to this function's smooth operation is the X. It's called a *formal parameter*, but you can think of it as a placeholder. To use, or *call*, this random integer function, you replace the formal parameter with a numeric expression (variable, number, or calculation). What DOS BASIC then does is replace all occurrences of the placeholder in the definition of the function by the value of the numeric expression. In particular, it does any calculations that are called for. So, if:

A = 3 and B = 2

then:

N% = FNRdInt%(A*B + 37)

has the same effect as:

N% = FNRdInt%(43)

which, in turn, is the same thing as saying:

N% = INT(43*RND(1)) + 1

The value you sent the function is sometimes called the *actual parameter*. You shouldn't expect to get too large of a random integer out of FNRdInt%, because FNRdInt%, like any integer expression, can't be larger than 32,767.

The X used as a parameter in the definition of the function has no independent existence. If you used an X as a variable somewhere earlier (for example, by setting X = 10), then this assignment never effects the value of the function.

FNRdInt% is passed, and works with, the value of one piece of information. In general, the values DOS BASIC passes to a function are determined by a type identifier at the end of a placeholder, or by any DEFINT (DEFLNG, DEFDBL, etc.) that happen to be in effect. In particular, I probably should have changed the definition of the function to be:

DEF FNRdInt%(X%) = INT(X%*RND(1)) + 1

Now, the values you can send to the function (what eventually replaces the integer placeholder X%) must be within the range of DOS BASIC short integers: −32,768 to 32,767. The value of any numeric expression within this range that you send to the function as a parameter will be rounded off.

The function, FNRdInt%, works with one piece of information; it's a function of one variable, or argument. You frequently want the value of a function to depend on more than one piece of information. For example, suppose you wanted a range of random integers between X and Y, then you can modify FNRdInt% as follows:

DEF FNRdIntRange%(X,Y) = INT((Y − X+ 1)*RND(1)) + X

This statement might seem a little tricky. If it does, try to see what happens with numbers like 5 and 37. Multiplying RND(1) by Y−X+1, or 33, gives a range between 0 and 32, or Y-X. Finally, add X to get the range wanted (5 to 37).

To get a range suitable for the ASCII typewriter codes program (CH7 \ P15.BAS), you can use:

FNRdIntRange%(33, 126)

When DOS BASIC processes this statement, it looks up the definition of the function and gives the placeholder X the value 33 and the placeholder Y the value 126. The result is that, any time you call this function, a random integer from 33 (ASCII code for the exclamation point) to 126 (ASCII code for the tilde) pops out. If you want to make sure that the function uses only integer values, rewrite it as:

DEF FNRdIntRange%(X%, Y%) = INT((Y%−X% + 1) *RND(1)) + Y%

Now, the placeholders can have only integer values. If you set:

Number% = IntRange%(2.7, 39.2)

then 2.7 is rounded up to 3 and 39.2 is rounded down to 39 when DOS BASIC substitutes their values into the function definition. If you said:

Number% = IntRange%(3, 300000)

then you'd get an overflow error.

Because the name of a function (i.e., what follows the letters *FN*) follows the same rules as the names of variables, choose meaningful function names. These certainly will make your program more readable, as well as easier to debug. The only thing to keep in mind is that, unless you give it an explicit type identifier, the type of the function is determined by a type identifier or any DEF-type statements that currently might be in effect.

One way to avoid any problems is to put the function definitions before any DEF-type statements. I think the best way, however, is to stick the appropriate type identifier at the end of every function name, overruling any DEF-type that might be in use.

If you are writing a program that needs one of the inverse trigonometric functions that are not built into DOS BASIC, make a user-defined function out of it. For example, to define the inverse sine (arcsine):

DEF FNArcSine#(Angle#) = ATN(Angle# − SQR(1 − Angle#*Angle#))

Just like the ATN function on which it is based, this function works with radians, which means you might have to do the conversion (with another function) from degrees to radians before calling this function.

Obviously, you need to check the information you send a function before you call the function. With the arcsine, in QBasic, you could do this with the following fragment:

```
IF(ABS(Value) < = 1 THEN
    PRINT FNArcSine(Value)
ELSE
    BEEP
    PRINT "Can't find an angle whose sine is greater than one!!!"
END IF
```

Check the values you send to functions before you call the function, otherwise you risk a fatal error.

There are no restrictions on where you define functions other than that you must define it before you use it. Obviously, a program is clearer if all the function definitions are grouped together.

You can define functions of as many as 16 variables, or *formal parameters*. For example, the volume of a box FNVolOfBox(L,W,H) = L*W*H has three formal parameters.

Here's a program that uses a three variable function to solve quadratic equations. For a quadratic equation like AX^2+BX+C, the formula is:

```
Answers = (-B + SQR(B*B - (4*A*C))/2*A
```

The A, B, and C are called the *coefficients of the equation*. The numeric expression inside the square root is called the *discriminant of the equation*. If the discriminant is less than zero, then the quadratic has imaginary roots (i.e., the answers involve the square root of -1, or i).

```
'CH8 \ P1.BAS
' A quadratic equation solver

DEFDBL A-Z                                                  'A
CLS
Tplate$ = " + #########,.#######"

DEF FNDisc(A,B,C) = B*B - (4*A*C)                           'B

INPUT "Enter three coefficients of the quadratic";A,B,C    'C

Discrim = SQR(ABS(FNDisc(A,B,C)))                          'D

IF FNDisc(A,B,C) < 0 THEN                                   'E
    PRINT "roots are imaginary"
    PRINT "First Root is "; -B/(2*A)
    PRINT USING Tplate$ + "i"; +Discrim)/(2*A)
```

```
        PRINT "Second Root is "; – B/(2*A)
        PRINT USING Tplate$ + "i";(– Discrim)/(2*A)
    ELSE
        PRINT "roots are real"
        PRINT "First Root is ";
        PRINT USING Tplate$;(– B + Discrim)/(2*A)
        PRINT "Second Root is ";
        PRINT USING Tplate$;(– B – Discrim)/(2*A)

    END IF

    END
```

A   This define-type command effects all the variables and functions that follow it.

B   As mentioned earlier, the discriminant is a function of the three coefficients. Here, they are all double-precision variables (see comment A).

C   Although it takes some getting used to, the A, B, C used in this statement have no relation to the A, B, C used as placeholders in the function's definition—at least until comments D and E.

D   This line sets up a variable whose value is closely related to the discriminant. It's only here to make the program more readable.

E   Now, the values of the variables A, B, C are sent to the function. Notice the PRINT USING command (with a string) that is used to print the *i* flush with the square root. I'm allowing nine digits before the decimal point and six digits after the decimal point. Moreover, I decided to print a plus or minus sign, as well as using commas, if needed. If you really want to cover all bases, you can use the INSTR (or LOG10) trick mentioned in chapter 7 to decide on the number of digits before and after the decimal point.

You can work with numbers to get strings or use numbers and strings to get numbers; all possible combinations are allowed.

First steps in multi-line functions using QBasic

GW-BASIC is limited to the kind of functions described in the previous section. As you can well imagine, there's a limit to what you can do in a single line. Q Basic, on the other hand, allows you to take as many steps as you want in defining a function. For example, to find the largest of two numbers use:

```
DEF FNLarge(X,Y)
    IF X < Y THEN FNLarge = Y ELSE FNLarge = X
END DEF
```

As this example indicates, you begin defining a multi-line function by using the key word *DEF* followed by the name of the function and the formal parameters that it's going to use. (Again, up to 16 placeholders are allowed.) However, unlike the situation with the simple one-line functions from the last section, you immediately hit the Return key and begin the statements that will define the function. Somewhere in what follows, you make an assignment that will determine the value of the function. In the previous example, which assignment is made depends on which of the two numbers was larger. As this example indicates, when you make the assignment that defines the function you don't say FNLarge(X,Y) = ..., you just use the function's full name:

```
FNLarge = ...
```

The statement END DEF marks the end of the definition. Just like with loops, the statements between the DEF and the END DEF are called the *body of the function*. If you make more than one assignment to the function within the body of the loop, only the last one counts.

A multi-line function can be useful if you need many PRINT USING templates. A function that sets up the number of decimal digits for any number might look like:

```
DEF FNTemplate$(Number,DecDigits)

    IF Number > 0 AND Number < 1 THEN
        FNTemplate$ = "#." + STRING$(DecDigits,"#")
    ELSE
        Digits = INT(FNLOG10(ABS(Number))) + 1
        FNTemplate$ = STRING$(Digits,"#") + "." + STRING$(DecDigits,"#")
    END IF

END DEF
```

where FNLOG10 is the QBasic function that you previously have defined following the outline from chapter 7. (By putting the absolute value inside the parentheses, you've taken care of negative numbers as well.)

Suppose you wanted to write a function that would allow you to chop out any substring. You saw how to do this in chapter 7: use INSTR to find out where the string was and then use RIGHT$, LEFT$ and MID$ to do the cutting. Here's one way to try to write the function (don't pay too much attention to it, you shortly will see a much cleaner definition):

```
DEF FNCutStr$(Big$, Small$)
    IF INSTR(Big$, Small$) = 0 THEN
        FNCutStr$ = Big$
    ELSE
        FNCutStr$ = LEFT$(Big$,INSTR(Big$,Small$) − 1) + MID$(Big$, INSTR
```

```
        (Big$, Small$) + LEN(Small$) + 1)
    END IF

  END DEF
```

To actually enter this function into QBasic, you'd have to go past the limits on a single line. It would be necessary to scroll horizontally, which puts this definition at the limits of readability. To make it more readable and to be in a position to fully exploit the power of user-defined functions, you need to use temporary variables within them. To do this properly you have to switch from the older DEF FN structure to a newer one called *FUNCTION procedures*.

FUNCTION procedures can do everything that DEF FN can do and more. Using this new construct, DOS BASIC allows you to set up variables, called *local variables*, that exist only within a function. Each time the function is called, they are reinitialized—they'll start over from scratch. Here's a much more readable version of the previous function (but hold off entering it and trying it out for a moment):

```
FUNCTION CutSmall$(Big$,Small$)

  Place = INSTR(Big$,Small$)
  Length = LEN(Small$)

  IF Place = 0 THEN
    CutSmall$ = Big$
  ELSE
    CutSmall$ = LEFT$(Big$,Place – 1) + MID$(Big$,Place + Length)
  END IF

END FUNCTION
```

The local variables named Place and Length have no effect on any other variables with the same name that might occur elsewhere within the program. I said that you shouldn't try it yet because something strange happens once you enter the function. Figure 8-1 shows what your screen looks like after you type the first line but before you hit return.

Now, hit return. Notice the screen has changed dramatically and now looks like Fig. 8-2. What has happened is that QBasic has opened a new window to edit your function. This change is indicated by the name. It's called:

```
Untitled:CutSmall
```

The colon separates the name of the subordinate function from the name of the program, or *main module*.

Type the function exactly as I've written it. When you're done typing and want to test this function, hit Shift−F5 and the program will run. However, nothing has been fed to the function, so nothing happens. You need to return to the

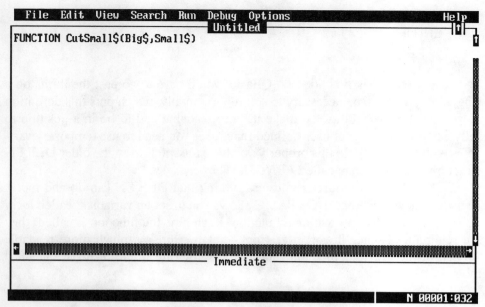

8-1 The screen before you hit Return.

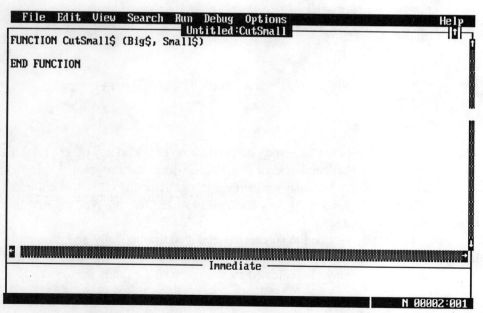

8-2 The screen after you hit Return.

main module to use this FUNCTION procedure. To return to the main module, hit Shift−F2. Notice that DOS BASIC has closed the previous window and returned you to the main module, or the *module-level code*. (In general, Shift−F2 cycles through the main module and the various subordinate functions that you've written.) Now, enter a line like:

```
PRINT CutSmall("This is not a test","not ")
```

and run the program. (Once you've finished a function, you also can use the Immediate window to test it. For example, you could have moved to the Immediate window and typed the line above.)

Assuming you haven't made any typos, this program should run. So, suppose you try to save it—give it a name and open the File menu to do the save. Notice that, after the save, QBasic has added a line:

```
DECLARE FUNCTION CutSmall$(Big$, Small$)
```

at the top of the program. DECLARE statements are used by the QBasic interpreter for bookkeeping. In this case, the interpreter is indicating that you are using a string function of two string variables. QBasic automatically adds the appropriate DECLARE statement whenever you save the program.

While developing your program within the QBasic environment, you rarely need a DECLARE statement. However, it's good programming practice to include it, because having DECLARE statements is essential in creating certain kinds of stand-alone programs if you move up to QuickBASIC.

As another example, suppose you wanted to write a QBasic function that counted the number of times a character appeared in a string. This command would be a function of two string variables and should return an integer. Lets call it CharCount%:

```
FUNCTION CharCount%(X$,Y$)

'This function counts the number of times
'the character Y$ is inside the string X$
'If Y$ is not a character or Y$ does not occur in
'X$ then this function returns zero
' Three local variables: I%, Count% and LenString

Count% = 0
LenString% = LEN(X$)

FOR I% = 1 TO LenString%
   IF MID$(X$, I%, 1) = Y$ THEN Count% = Count% + 1
NEXT I%

CharCount% = Count%

END FUNCTION
```

First, notice the extended remark section. In defining a complicated function, you're best off explaining what's supposed to happen. Explain what kind of information the function expects to deal with, what local variables it uses, and what it is supposed to send out. If you know what the function expects, then you're more likely to check what you send it before the program blows up in your face.

To this point, most of the example programs in this book have been sparsely commented—mostly because the surrounding text hopefully explained them. However, when I'm hired to write a program, I'd be expected to comment the program as I did in this last example. I probably would explain what the local variables were doing as well.

This function uses three local integer variables: Count%, I%, and LenString%. It's good programming practice to initialize the local variables before going on to the main business of the function. Being local variables, they have no connection with any variables that might share the same name elsewhere in the program. The advantages this feature gives over the older DEF FN can't be stressed enough. For example, a complicated string handling program might have 17 different functions with 17 different local variables named LenString% or Count%. You would not want their values contaminating each other.

Next, notice that I initialized the Count% variable to be 0. I did this step for the same reason that I'd initialize a variable in the main part of a program: relying on default values is sloppy and dangerous. LenString% doesn't change in the loop that follows. Because it is a loop invariant, I calculate it once before the loop starts to speed the function up.

The FOR-NEXT loop runs through the string, character by character, checking whether there is a match, adding one to Count% if there is a match. Finally, the value of the local variable Count% is the information this function will return. In this case, I ended the body of the function with the assignment that defines the function.

Using a variable, like Count%, to accumulate information as a function works is quite common. When your done, you use the accumulator in the final assignment that determines the value of the function.

As another example, return to the find-the-next-word program from chapter 7. Here it is:

```
'CH7 \ P5.BAS
'   This program uses INSTR to parse a phrase
'   by searching for a space as the separator

CLS

DO                                                    'A
    INPUT "Please enter the phrase to parse"; Phrase$
    LenPhrase = LEN(Phrase$)
LOOP UNTIL LenPhrase > 0

Separate$ = CHR$(32)           '= space
```

```
BeforeSpace = 0                                                        'B
AfterSpace = INSTR(BeforeSpace + 1, Phrase$, Separate$)                 'C

DO UNTIL AfterSpace = 0                                                 'D

   SizeOfWord = AfterSpace – BeforeSpace – 1                            'E
   NextWord$ = MID$(Phrase$, BeforeSpace + 1, SizeOfWord)              'F
   PRINT NextWord$
   BeforeSpace = AfterSpace                                             'G
   AfterSpace = INSTR(BeforeSpace + 1, Phrase$, Separate$)             'H

LOOP

PRINT MID$(Phrase$, BeforeSpace + 1)                                    'I

END
```

Suppose you want to modify this program so that it gives the next word, no matter what separator you use. Using a user-defined function makes this change almost trivial. All you have to do is replace the statement:

```
AfterSpace = INSTR(BeforeSpace + 1,Phrase$,Separate$)
```

with a function that finds the next separator. Before I show you an outline for this function, think about the information this function needs to massage, or manipulate. It will work much like INSTR, except that the separators will be built into the function. Once you convince yourself of this fact, then understanding the following outline for the function shouldn't be a problem.

1. The function works with a string and a position number.
2. It should search starting at the position after the position number.
3. It should look character by character until it finds a separator.
4. If successful, the function should return its position number.
5. If unsuccessful, it should return zero.

Here's a function definition that follows this outline:

```
FUNCTION FindSeparator%(Phrase$,Position%)

   AfterSpace% = Position% + 1                                         'A
   Answer% = 0                                                         'B
   LenString% = LEN(Phrase$)

   DO UNTIL Answer%< >0 OR AfterSpace% > LenString%                    'C

      NxtChar$ = MID$(Phrase$, AfterSpace%, 1)
      SELECT CASE NxtChar$

         CASE CHR$(32),"!","?"                                         'D
            Answer% = AfterSpace%
```

```
           CASE ".", ";", ":"
              Answer% = AfterSpace%
           CASE ","
              Answer% = AfterSpace%
           CASE ELSE                                              'E
              AfterSpace% + AfterSpace% + 1
        END SELECT

     LOOP

     FindSeparator% = Answer%                                     'F

END FUNCTION
```

A   The program starts looking from one position further along in the string.

B   This local variable plays a key role in what follows. As the program moves through the loop, this variable accumulates information, either by staying equal to zero (in which case, no separator was found) or by being made positive (the value would be where the separator is).

C   This kind of loop has to stop either if the accumulator says the hunt was successful or if there's no place else to look (the loop's finished searching all the characters in the string). Notice that instead of using a eureka loop, I could have used multiple EXIT LOOP commands.

D   I could have put all the tests done in the next three cases on one line, but the program would have looked awful. (If you can think of a separator I left out, add it on.)

E   If the character wasn't a separator, the program moves on to the next character.

F   The value of the accumulator variable Answer% will be zero if no separator was found, otherwise it will be the position of the separator.

I could have also written this as a function of three variables much like INSTR itself is.

Here's the revised find-word program (notice the DECLARE statement at the top):

```
DECLARE FUNCTION FindSeparator%(Phrase$, Position%)

' CH8 \ P2.BAS
' This program uses the function
' FNFindSeparator to parse a phrase
' by searching for the separators
' . , : ? ; ! and the space
```

```
' it finds all words contained in the
' phrase
CLS
DO
    PRINT "Please enter the phrase to parse."
    LINE INPUT "?"; Phrase$
    LenPhrase% = LEN(Phrase$)
LOOP UNTIL LenPhrase% > 0

BeforeSpace% = 0
AfterSpace% = FindSeparator%(Phrase$, BeforeSpace%)

DO UNTIL AfterSpace% = 0

    SizeOFWord% = AfterSpace% - BeforeSpace% - 1
    NextWord$ = MID$(Phrase$, BeforeSpace% + 1, SizeOFWord%)
    IF SizeOFWord% > 0 THEN PRINT NextWord$                      'A
    BeforeSpace% = AfterSpace%
    AfterSpace% = FindSeparator(Phrase$, BeforeSpace%)

LOOP

PRINT MID$(Phrase$, BeforeSpace% + 1)

END

FUNCTION FindSeparator% (Phrase$, Position%)

    AfterSpace% = Position% + 1
    Answer% = 0
    LenString% = LEN(Phrase$)

    DO UNTIL Answer% < > 0 OR AfterSpace% > LenString%

        NxtChar$ = MID$(Phrase$, AfterSpace%, 1)

        SELECT CASE NxtChar$

            CASE CHR$(32), "!", "?"
                Answer% = AfterSpace%
            CASE ".", ";", ":"
                Answer% = AfterSpace%
            CASE ","
                Answer% = AfterSpace%
            CASE ELSE
                AfterSpace% = AfterSpace% + 1

        END SELECT
```

```
    LOOP

    FindSeparator% = Answer%

END FUNCTION
```

A   As mentioned before, this statement takes care of two separators occurring together.

Let me end this section by pointing out that many of the example programs that you've seen to this point were really functions in disguise. A good example was the super input program, CH7 \ P5.BAS, that accepted numbers, disregarding commas and decimal points.

Nothing prevents a function from calling another function; you'll find yourself doing this frequently. A good exercise would be to change the find-all-words program to be a find-next-word function. It still will use the find-separator function somewhere. However, while QBasic allows you to call as many functions as you want from within a given function, you can't nest function definitions. Only one function can be defined at any one time.

Functions in QBasic can call themselves. This ability is called *recursion* and is so important and fascinating that the topic deserves, and gets, a chapter of its own (see chapter 13).

Shared and static variables in QBasic

The purpose of using local variables is to avoid inadvertent *side effects*. A side effect is when something you do in the function affects the rest of the program. For example, if you place a CLS command in a function, every time the function is called the screen will clear; clearly a side effect.

There's certainly nothing wrong with a controlled side effect; however, the key word is *controlled*. You must know exactly when they're going to happen and what the fall-out is for the rest of the program.

One way to avoid problems is to use what are called *shared variables*, or *global variables*. These variables are another way to communicate information between a program and a function, besides using parameters.

When you declare a variable as shared, it is visible to both the function and the main module. Any changes you make to this variable will persist in the main module. For example, if a program needs the value of pi in 20 different functions, it's a perfect candidate for a shared variable:

```
FUNCTION AreaOfCirc(R)
    SHARED Pi#
        AreaOfCirc = Pi#*R*R
END FUNCTION
```

This function assumes Pi# has been defined in the main module.

As another example, consider a program that will manipulate the same phrase in a 100 different ways, using a 100 different functions. It's quite likely that the length of the phrase will pop up repeatedly; rather than waste time recomputing it each time, make it a shared variable.

Once a variable is shared, any changes you make to it persist. For example, consider the following two test programs:

```
'CH8 \ P3.BAS
' A demonstration of local variables

DECLARE FUNCTION CountEses%(X$)

DEFINT A-Z
Count = 0
PRINT Count
Phrase$ = " Mississippi "
LenPhrase = LEN(Phrase$)

PRINT CountEses(Phrase$)
PRINT Count

END

FUNCTION CountEses%(X$)

   Shared LenPhrase

   FOR I = 1 TO LenPhrase
      IF MID$(X$,I,1) = "s" THEN Count = Count + 1
   NEXT I

   CountEses = Count

END FUNCTION
```

You'll see:

```
0
4
0
```

The first PRINT statement gives 0, because that's the current value of Count%. Next, it prints the number of times the letter *s* appears in the word *Mississippi*, which is 4. Finally, the value of Count% is displayed again. It still is 0, because I made Count% a local variable in the function. The variable Count% in the main module has nothing to do with the one in the function definition. Compare this to:

```
'CH8 \ P3a.BAS
' A demonstration of shared variables

DECLARE FUNCTION CountEses%(X$)
```

```
DEFINT A-Z

CLS
Count = 0
PRINT Count
Phrase$ = " Mississippi "
LenPhrase = LEN(Phrase$)

PRINT CountEses(Phrase$)
PRINT Count

END

Function CountEses(X$)

Shared LenPhrase, Count

FOR I = 1 TO LenPhrase
    IF MID$(X$,I,1) = "s" THEN Count = Count + 1
NEXT I

CountEses = Count

END FUNCTION
```

Here, I made Count a shared variable. Now, calling the function changes the value of Count. It now is 4. So, you'll see:

```
0
4
4
```

Note that, if you actually enter this program, the Smart Editor would insert another DEFINT A-Z as the first line of the window where the function is defined. This statement is inserted because DOS BASIC uses whatever definers are in effect at a given point for functions created at that point. To emphasize this point, the editor inserts the appropriate definer as the first line and makes the DECLARE statement that it automatically generates reflect this change.

At this point, these functions in QBasic are manipulating the values of variables. They massage the actual parameters; they don't change them. This process is called *passing by value*. In chapter 9, you'll see how to change the value of parameters. This procedure is called *passing by reference*.

In practice, you rarely should have to change the value of a shared variable. In some sense, a function should do one thing: it should manipulate values and perhaps make one new one. Changing a shared variable is best done by means of an assignment statement within the main body of the program. Your programs will be much easier to debug if you use shared variables only to communicate information to functions.

At this point, don't try to assign values to your formal parameters. Use them strictly as placeholders. We'll talk more about functions like:

```
FUNCTION INCR(X)
   X = X + 1
END FUNCTION
```

in chapter 9.

There's one final type of variable that you occasionally will use in a function: the static variable. This variable is local to the function, so it doesn't effect the rest of the program. However, its value is not reset each time the function is used, or called. A function using only STATIC variables will work a little faster, so QBasic allows you to *coerce*, or make, all variables in a function into static variables. This method is done by placing the key word *STATIC* on the end of the same line as the keyword *FUNCTION*, as follows:

```
FUNCTION ........ STATIC
```

I rarely use this method, however, because I regard it as a better programming practice to explicitly say which of my variables are static and which are shared. All the other variables within a function are local, but I also like to point out this fact in a remark statement.

I mainly use static variables as a debugging tool:

```
FUNCTION TestFunction
   STATIC   TimesCalled
      .

      .

      .

   TimesCalled = TimesCalled + 1
   PRINT "This function has been used"; TimesCalled
END FUNCTION
```

Making the variable TimesCalled a static variable means that it will keep track of the number of times I use the function, printing out the current value each time the function is called. If TimesCalled was a local variable, the value would be reset back to zero each time the function was called and you would lose the information it contains. Knowing how many times a function was called is often the key to diagnosing what's wrong with a program.

Finally, let me end this section by pointing out that you don't have to give every function a value. Sometimes, you are forced to exit it prematurely:

```
FUNCTION BailOut(X)
   IF X < 0 THEN
      EXIT FUNCTION
   ELSE
```

```
        .
        .
        .
    END IF
        .
        .
        .

    END FUNCTION
```

This function bails out if a negative value is sent to it. Now, calling the function with a negative value gives the function the default value of any numeric variable—zero. A string function that you bail out of would return the null string as its value.

I rarely use the EXIT FUNCTION command. I certainly don't use it as in the last example. I check out the information I want to send to a function before I call the function. I use the EXIT FUNCTION much like the EXIT DO: if it makes the program clearer. For example, some people would rewrite the find-separator function using an EXIT FUNCTION, because they thought it made the program clearer.

Some example programs

In this section, I want to develop three example programs in QBasic. They would be much more cumbersome in GW-BASIC. They will showcase the techniques of this chapter and chapter 7. These programs are a bit more complicated than the programs that you've seen to this point.

Dawkins' evolutionary demonstration program

Some people argue against evolution by saying it is as likely as a team of monkeys sitting down at a typewriter, randomly pecking keys, and the text of William Shakespeare's *Hamlet* popping out. How likely is this possibility? Just to get the title *Hamlet by William Shakespeare* requires about 100^{29} tries, because there are about 100 keys on a typewriter and 29 characters in the title. Assuming a monkey can type 500 characters a minute, it would take around 4×10^{46} years. (The quotient of $100^{29}/500$ gives the number of minutes. Dividing by the product of $60 \times 24 \times 365$ gives the number of years.) Because the maximum age scientists estimate that the universe has been around is only 25 trillion years (25×10^{12}), this argument, if it had any merit, certainly would cause evolutionists problems.

However, as Richard Dawkins points out in his superb book *The Blind Watchmaker* (Norton 1986)—from which I borrowed the ideas used in this discussion—this argument confuses what he calls *single-step change* with what he calls *cumulative change*. In single-step change (for example, the typing monkeys), the changes truly are random. There is no connection between the previous generation and the next generation. In cumulative change, the results of the previous generation is fed through some sort of sieve, which selects only those that have some desirable property to persist.

Here, again following Dawkins, is an outline for how the two types of change might be programmed:

Single step change

1. Start with a random string of the right length
2. Change one character randomly to obtain the child
3. Repeat the previous step
4. Continue until you get the phrase *Hamlet by William Shakespeare*.

Cumulative change

1. Start with a random string of the right length
2. Change one character randomly in the parent to obtain the child
3. Sieve out either the parent or child depending on some survival rule
4. Use the one that survived as the new parent and repeat the previous step
5. Continue until you get the phrase *Hamlet by William Shakespeare*

Because the program that follows is just a demonstration of the difference between the two types of change, it uses a nonevolutionary, teleogical (goal-directed) survival rule. The phrase that survives will be the one closest to the target phrase, *Hamlet by William Shakespeare.*

Again, Dawkins points out that this rule is not what happens in evolution. Here the sieving is done according to *the criterion of resemblance to a distant ideal target.* Evolution isn't like that; it has no long-term goal. Nonetheless, the speed at which it converges to the target phrase dramatically demonstrates the difference between the two types of change. On the average, it seems to take only around 11,000 generations.

Here's the program:

```
DECLARE FUNCTION DistToTarget%(A$, B$)
DECLARE FUNCTION Mutate$(A$)
DECLARE FUNCTION RndInt%(A%, B%)

' CH8 \ P4.BAS
' Dawkins' cumulative selection demo

CLS
DEFINT A-Z
RANDOMIZE TIMER
GenNumber = 0
Target$ = "Hamlet by William Shakespeare"
Parent$ = STRING$(29, "*")                          'A
```

```
LenTarget = LEN(Target$)

DO UNTIL Parent$ = Target$

   ParentDist = DistToTarget(Target$, Parent$)                    'B
   Child$ = Mutate$(Parent$)                                      'C
   ChildDist = DistToTarget(Target$, Child$)

   IF ChildDist < = ParentDist THEN Parent$ = Child$             'D
   GenNumber = GenNumber + 1
   IF GenNumber MOD 100 = 0 THEN                                  'E
      PRINT GenNumber, Parent$, ParentDist
   END IF

LOOP

PRINT "It took"; GenNumber; " generations to finish"

END

FUNCTION DistToTarget (A$, B$)

   ' has LOCAL variables CharDistance,TotalDistance,I

   SHARED LenTarget

   TotalDistance = 0
   FOR I = 1 TO LenTarget
      CharDistance = ASC(MID$(A$, I, 1)) - ASC(MID$(B$, I, 1))
      TotalDistance = TotalDistance + ABS(CharDistance)
   NEXT I

   DistToTarget = TotalDistance

END FUNCTION

FUNCTION Mutate$ (A$)

   ' has LOCAL variables RandomPos,RandomChar$,Temp$

   SHARED LenTarget

   Temp$ = A$
   RandomPos = RndInt(1, LenTarget)
   RandomChar$ = CHR$(RndInt(32, 126))

   MID$(Temp$, RandomPos) = RandomChar$

   Mutate$ = Temp$

END FUNCTION

FUNCTION RndInt (A, B)
```

```
RndInt = INT((B − A + 1) * RND(1)) + A
END FUNCTION
```

A   This statement is a convenient way to start off. It creates a string of length equal to the target phrase consisting only of asterisks.

B   This function will calculate the distance between two words. Character by character, it will add up:

```
ASC(MID$(X$,I,1)) − ASC(MID$(Y$,I,1)
```

(As I mentioned in chapter 7, this calculation is a common use of the ABS function.)

C   This line mutates a single character by randomly changing it, using the MID$ command because the size doesn't change.

D   This statement is the survival rule. The phrase that's closest to the target survives.

E   This statement lets you keep track of what's happening every 100 generations. (A number is 0 MOD of another number only when it's perfectly divisible by that number.) If you want to see every generation just use a PRINT statement here (but remember the 11,000 generations).

F   LenTarget is a perfect candidate for a shared, or global, variable.

If you run this program, you'll notice that the parent quickly mutates close to the target but takes a much longer time actually to reach the target. The reason is simple: once the program gets close to the goal, it's more likely that the mutations will be harmful.

Pig Latin generator

For the second programming example, I want to write a Pig Latin converter. Pig Latin is a well-known variant on English that children often use.

The rules are simple:

- All one-letter words stay the same.
- Words beginning with vowels get the suffix *way*.
- Words beginning with a string of consonants have the consonants shifted to the end and the suffix *ay* added.
- Any *q* moved because of the previous rule carries its *u* with it.
- *Y* is a consonant.

In its simplest form, an outline for a Pig Latin converter is:

- While there still are words, follow the rules given earlier to *pig latinize* the next word.

Here's a program to do this:

```
'CH8 \ P5.BAS
' A Pig Latin generator
' This program translates a phrase into
' Pig Latin. It modifies the 'find word'
' program by adding a 'latinize' function                        'A

DECLARE FUNCTION FindSeparator% (Phrase$, Position%)
DECLARE FUNCTION Latinfy$ (A$)
DECLARE FUNCTION ShiftCons$ (A$)

DEFINT A-Z
CONST True = - 1
CLS

DO
   PRINT "Please enter the phrase to parse."
   LINE INPUT "?"; Phrase$
   LenPhrase = LEN(Phrase$)
LOOP UNTIL LenPhrase > 0

BeforeSpace = 0
AfterSpace = FindSeparator%(Phrase$, BeforeSpace)

DO UNTIL AfterSpace = 0

   SizeOFWord = AfterSpace - BeforeSpace - 1
   NextWord$ = MID$(Phrase$, BeforeSpace + 1, SizeOFWord)
   IF SizeOFWord > 0 THEN
      PigWord$ = Latinfy$(NextWord$)                             'B
      PRINT PigWord$ + SPACE$(1);
   END IF

   BeforeSpace = AfterSpace
   AfterSpace = FindSeparator(Phrase$, BeforeSpace)

LOOP

FinalWord$ = MID$(Phrase$, BeforeSpace + 1)
PigWord$ = Latinfy(FinalWord$)
PRINT PigWord$ + SPACE$(1);

END

FUNCTION FindSeparator% (Phrase$, Position%)

   ' LOCAL variables are AfterSpace%, Answer%, LenString%, NxtChar$

   AfterSpace% = Position% + 1
```

```
        Answer% = 0
        LenString% = LEN(Phrase$)

        DO UNTIL Answer% < > 0 OR AfterSpace% > LenString%

          NxtChar$ = MID$(Phrase$, AfterSpace%, 1)

          SELECT CASE NxtChar$

            CASE CHR$(32), "!", "?"
              Answer% = AfterSpace%
            CASE ".", ";", ":"
              Answer% = AfterSpace%
            CASE ","
              Answer% = AfterSpace%
            CASE ELSE
              AfterSpace = AfterSpace% + 1

          END SELECT

        LOOP

        FindSeparator% = Answer%

      END FUNCTION

      FUNCTION Latinfy$ (A$)

        IF LEN(A$) = 1 THEN                                        'C
          Latinfy$ = A$
        ELSE
          FirstChar$ = UCASE$(LEFT$(A$, 1))

          SELECT CASE FirstChar$

            CASE "A", "E", "I", "O", "U"
              Latinfy$ = A$ + "way"
            CASE IS < "A"                                          'D
              Latinfy$ = A$
            CASE IS > "Z"
              Latinfy$ = A$
            CASE ELSE
              Latinfy$ = ShiftCons$(A$) + "ay"                     'E

          END SELECT

        END IF

      END FUNCTION

      FUNCTION ShiftCons$ (A$)
```

```
' LOCAL variables Count,NextChar$,Done

Count = 1
Done = 0
DO
    NextChar$ = UCASE$(MID$(A$, Count, 1))

    SELECT CASE NextChar$

        CASE "A", "E", "I", "O", "U"
            Done = True                                         'F
        CASE "Q"                                                'G
            Count = Count + 2
        CASE ELSE
            Count = Count + 1

    END SELECT

LOOP UNTIL Done

    ShiftCons$ = MID$(A$, Count) + LEFT$(A$, Count - 1)         'H

END FUNCTION
```

A   This program is a good demonstration of how long programs can be built up from building blocks. I'll have more to say about this in chapter 9.

B   As I mentioned earlier, all I had to do was change the find-next-word program to one that, instead of printing the next word, prints the converted form. I decided to strip out all punctuation and spaces along the way. I'll leave it to you to change the program so that the converted phrase retains the original punctuation.

C   This line translates the first rule: one-letter words remain the same.

D   This line translates the second rule: words with a leading vowel add *way*. The next case is to make sure numbers and other special characters are not transformed.

E   This statement calls the most complicated function—the one that shifts the consonants to the end.

F   I use a flag to detect when I finally hit a vowel.

G   By adding two to Count, I carry the *u* along with the *q*.

H   By starting with Count equal to 1 and incrementing Count every time a consonant shows up, when the loop ends, LEFT$(A$,Count – 1) must contain the leading consonants.

Infinite precision arithmetic

For the final example program in this chapter, I want to write an infinite precision adder. As you know, the limits that are on even long integers prevents you from adding really large numbers accurately. Sometimes, however, you'll want to add or multiply 100s of digits at a time. The easiest way to do this type of problem in QBasic is to first think of the large number as a string of digits. Now, do what you learned in elementary school:

1. Start from the right-most digit of each number
2. Add the digits
3. Compute the answer and the carry
4. Add the next two digits and the carry, if any
5. Compute the answer and the carry
6. Continue until there are no more digits.

Here's a function that takes two strings that consist only of digits and gives back a string that has the digits of the answer:

```
DEFINT A-Z
FUNCTION InfinAdd$ (A$, B$)

    ' This function takes two strings consisting only
    ' of digits with no leading or trailing spaces
    ' and returns a string which consist of the digits
    ' in the sum

    ' LOCAL variables are: LenA, DigInA, CurDigA and LenB, DigInB, CurDigB
    ' C$, CurDigC, dig, Answer, NextCarry, PreviousCarry

    LenA = LEN(A$)
    LenB = LEN(B$)
    DigInA = LEN(A$) - 1                                       'A
    DigInB = LEN(B$) - 1

    Dig = 0

    DO UNTIL Dig > DigInA AND Dig < DigInB

        IF Dig < = DigInA AND Dig < = DigInB THEN              'B
            CurDigA = VAL(MID$(A$, LenA - Dig, 1))
            CurDigB = VAL(MID$(B$, LenB - Dig, 1))
        ELSEIF Dig < = DigInA AND Dig > DigInB THEN
            CurDigA = VAL(MID$(A$, LenA - Dig, 1))
            CurDigB = 0
        ELSEIF Dig > DigInA AND Dig < = DigInB THEN
```

```
        CurDigA = 0
        CurDigB = VAL(MID$(B$, LenB - Dig, 1))
    END IF

    ANS = CurDigA + CurDigB + PreviousCarry                    'C
    NextCarry = ANS \ 10
    DigC = ANS MOD 10
    DigC$ = STR$(DigC): DigC$ = RIGHT$(DigC$, 1)               'D
    C$ = DigC$ + C$

    PreviousCarry = NextCarry
    Dig = Dig + 1

LOOP

IF NextCarry < > 0 THEN
    Last$ = STR$(NextCarry)
    C$ = RIGHT$(Last$, 1) + C$
END IF

    InfinAdd$ = C$

END FUNCTION
```

A   The number of digits in a number is one less than the length.

B   Because I chose not to pad the smaller number so that both numbers have the same number of digits by adding leading zeros, I needed this somewhat complicated block IF-THEN to take care of the three possibilities.

C   At any given moment, I need to keep track of the previous carry and the future carry. This line does exactly what you learned to do in elementary school.

D   Never forget the extra space that the STR$ command sticks on at the front of a converted number.

Now, to turn this into a usable infinite adder, you only need to add a function that accepts a string consisting of only digits. Moreover, because QBasic allows strings to have as many as 32,767 characters, you can add two rather large numbers together. This program is reasonably fast; it adds two 10,000 digit numbers in about 6 minutes on a basic PC.

A program that does infinite precision multiplication is similar and, if done naively, some what easier. You can imitate the elementary school method, calling the infinite adder function as needed.

Actually, there's a slightly faster way to do infinite precision multiplication, rather than blindly following the method you learned in elementary school. You do the partial adds as you go along. For example, to multiply 814 by 84, follow this outline:

1. Multiply 814 by 4, digit by digit, getting 3256.
2. Move in by one digit and start multiplying again. 8×4 gives a 2 with a carry of 3. Add the 2 to the 5 and the 3 to the 2. The total is now 3576. Now, multiply the 8 by the 1 and add it to the 5, getting 3 with a carry of 1. Add this to get 4376. Finally, multiply the 8 by the 8 to get 64. So, add 4 to the 4, getting 8, and carry the 6. The final answer is 68,376.

The tricky thing about programming this outline is keeping track of the various stages that tell you where you are in the process. I'll leave it to you. There are other methods that computer scientists have invented that are more complicated but, this one actually is one of the better ones. Besides saving time, this method also saves space.

9
CHAPTER

Procedures and subroutines

This chapter shows you how to use QBasic's SUB procedures, or *subprograms* as they often are called, and GW-BASIC's subroutines. A *SUB procedure* is a smaller helper program that you call as it is needed. Procedures generalize and extend the FUNCTION procedures of chapter 8. Unfortunately, they are not available in GW-BASIC, but I hope a GW-BASIC programmer will study this material. The flexibility that procedures give you over subroutines is an important reason to upgrade.

Procedures and/or subroutines are the last major addition to a DOS BASIC programmer's toolbox. When you master this material, in a very real sense, you will have finished learning how to program in DOS BASIC. From that point, it's just a matter of learning new commands and new ways of organizing your data.

Although, to this point, I've mostly avoided generalities on how to write programs, I don't think it's a good idea to continue doing so. As programs grow longer, the possibilities for mistakes—for bugs—probably grows even faster. Because you are close to mastering all the tools of a programmer, it's a good idea to see the methods that programmers have developed to make writing longer programs easier or at least less frustrating, which is why I'll begin the chapter with a section on structured programming.

Modular top-down programming

The method described here—modular, top-down structured program design—was developed from rules of thumb that programmers learned through experience. Don't take them as gospel. Ultimately, you will develop your own style for writing programs. What works for one person might not work for another. Still, just as artists benefit from knowing what techniques have worked in the past, programmers can learn from what programmers have done before them.

The first rule is *think first, code later*, which is sometimes expressed as *the sooner you start writing, the longer it takes*. You have some idea of what needs to be done, so you enter the View window and start writing code. When your first attempt doesn't work, you keep on modifying your program until it works or seems to work. This approach usually is referred to as *hacking away at the keyboard*.

Almost everyone occasionally will write programs with little or no preparation; that's one of the virtues of BASIC. Where do you draw the line? How long must a program be before it can benefit from some paper and pencil? Know your own limits. I find it hard to write a program longer than one screen (20 to 25 lines) without some sort of outline. Whenever I tried to do a longer program without an outline, even when I eventually got the program running, it ended up taking longer than if I had written an outline first.

Outlines don't have to be complicated. My complete outline for the Pig Latin program was:

1. While there are still words
   - Pig the next word
2. To pig a word
   - One letter words stay the same
   - Beginning vowels: add *way*
   - Beginning consonants (*y*, *qu* = *conson*): ROTATE and add *ay*
3. ROTATE
   - Find *conson*
   - Move *conson* to end

Perhaps, this outline might be a little hard for anyone but me to use; however, that's not the point of an outline. My outlines are for me; yours are for you. In particular, my outlines help me fix the concepts that I'll use in the program; yours should help you do the same. I find that a good rule is that, when it looks to me like a line in my outline will correspond to no more than 10 lines of code, I've done enough outlining and should start writing. However, only practice will let you see at a glance how long the coded version is likely to be.

Some people like to expand their outline to pseudocode. This process is especially common if you are developing a program with or for someone else. Pseudocode is an ill-defined cross between a programing language and English. While everyone seems to have their own idea of what pseudocode should look like, most programmers do agree that a pseudocode description, unlike an outline, should be sufficiently clear and detailed that any competent programmer can translate it into a running program.

Here's a pseudocode version of part of the previous outline:

```
Function(pig NEXT WORD)
   IF Length(NEXT WORD) = 1 THEN do nothing
   IF FirstLetter(NEXT WORD) = a, i, e, o, u THEN
      PIG(NEXT WORD) = NEXT WORD + way
   ELSE
   Find(leading consonants of NEXT WORD) '(qu is a consonant)
   PIG(NEXT WORD) = NEXT WORD − leading consonants + ay
```

The point is that, although, on the surface, a phrase like:

PIG(NEXT WORD) = NEXT WORD − leading consonants + *ay*

doesn't seem at all that close to QBasic, it is for an experienced programmer.

Think about writing a program this way. When you have something hard to do, you first divide it into several smaller jobs. Moreover, with most jobs the sub-tasks—the smaller jobs—have a natural order in which they should be done. You dig a hole for the foundation before you call the cement truck.

You should write programs from the general to the particular. Start with a conception of the big picture, then break it down in stages. This process lets you keep track of the forest even when there are a lot of trees. Your first outline lists the jobs that have to be done. Keep on refining your outline until the pieces to be coded are well within your limits. Stop massaging the problem when you can shut your eyes and see the code that does it.

Sometimes this step-wise refinement is described as *relentless massage*. Because programmers often say *massage a problem* when they mean *chew it over and analyze it*, the metaphor is striking and useful.

In a way, top-down design is like what high school teachers pushed at you as the right method to write papers: extensively outlining your term paper before you put pen to paper. The reasons are the same. There's a limit on the number of balls you can juggle; there's a limit on the number of ideas you can deal with at once.

Some people find a chart like the one in Fig. 9-1 to be helpful. The placement of the boxes indicate how the jobs relate. Each box usually will correspond to a SUB procedure, a user-defined FUNCTION procedure, or a subroutine. SUB procedures and FUNCTION procedures on a higher level use only the results of procedures and functions on the same or a lower level.

Programmers often call these building blocks *modules*. That's why what we're doing is called *modular programming*. Unfortunately, there's another more technical meaning of module when you upgrade to QuickBASIC.

Even if you can see how to program two completely separate jobs in one SUB or FUNCTION, it usually is better not to do so. Sticking to one job per procedure makes it easier to both debug the procedure and to optimize the code in it.

Most of a professional programmer's time is spent modifying programs writ-

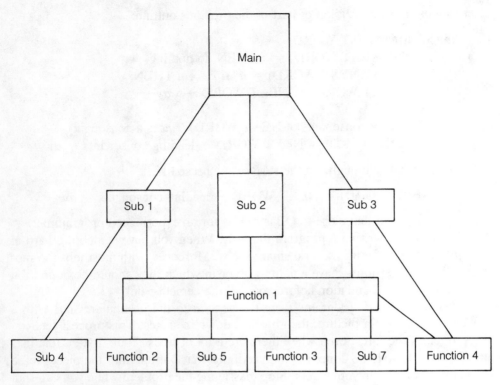

9-1 A programming diagram.

ten by other people. Imagine a big program that wasn't written top-down. No distinction was made between local and global variables; all variables are global. No attempt was made to write the program in digestible pieces with clear lines of communications between the pieces.

What happens? Because all variables are global, a little change you make could foul up the whole program. Because the pieces aren't digestible and the way they communicate is unclear, you can't be sure how they relate. Anything you do to one line might introduce side effects—possibly disastrous ones.

This kind of disaster was common until the late 1960s or early 1970s. Companies spent millions of dollars having programs modified. Then, they spent more money trying to anticipate the potential side effects the changes they just paid for might cause. After that, they hoped that more time and money would fix the side effects. No matter where they stopped, they never could be certain that the programs were free of bugs. Top-down design, when combined with programming languages that allow local and global variables, can stop side effects completely. Programs still have bugs, but these bugs don't cause epidemics. If you fix a small module in a giant top-down designed program, then you know how the changes effect everything.

Finally, it's worth pointing out that QBasic is a modern BASIC, so it was designed from the start to make modularizing a program possible and not all that difficult. GW-BASIC lacks local and global variables, as well as the multi-line function and subprograms that you need. For this reason alone, even if DOS 5.0 wasn't chock full of useful add-ons, I would have switched to QBasic.

Getting started with procedures in QBasic

You already have seen one method to modularize a program: a FUNCTION procedure. As you saw in chapter 8, a QBasic function can be made to do most anything, provided that what you want to do is get an answer, or value, out of it. As I mentioned there, although functions can make any kind of display that you want, it's not a good idea to do so unless the display is somehow related to what the function is designed to do. In any case, a function takes raw data, massages it, then returns a single value. In particular, although you can write a function that will work through a list as it's entered and find the smallest or largest value, it can't find both. A function can never order, or sort, a list. You'll see many ways to do this in chapters 10 and 11.

Suppose, for example, you wanted to print a song. One with many verses but only a single chorus. The outline is clear:

1. While there are verses left
   - Print verse
   - Print chorus
2. Loop

Unless you wrote a truly bizarre function, you could not easily translate this outline into QBasic using a function. To do this outline, you need a new structure: the procedure or subprogram.

The structure of the simplest kind of procedure, although one powerful enough to translate the outline, looks like:

```
SUB chorus

    many print statements

END SUB
```

The first line has the keyword SUB followed by the procedure's name. A procedure name can be up to 40 characters. Next, comes the statements that make up the procedure. Finally, there is the keyword END SUB to indicate the end of the procedure.

Just as for functions, QBasic keeps all your subprograms in separate windows. Also, you can cycle through them via Shift−F2.

Thinking of a program as a song with many choruses would be a good metaphor for a program and its procedures and functions, except that it misses one key point about using a procedure: each time you need the procedure, it's likely to be in a different situation. The procedure must change to meet new requirements. You need a way to transfer information between the main program and the procedure. You do this in much the same way as you did for functions: you give the procedure a parameter list. This parameter list is used to communicate between the main program and the procedure. For example, suppose you wanted to print the old song "100 bottles of beer on the wall."

100 bottles of beer on the wall,
100 bottles of beer,
If one of those bottles should happen to fall,
99 bottles of beer on the wall.

99 bottles of beer on the wall,
99 bottles of beer,
If one of those bottles should happen to fall,
98 bottles of beer on the wall.

98 bottles of beer on the wall,
98 bottles of beer,
If one of those bottles should happen to fall,
97 bottles of beer on the wall.

etc.

Here is a program to print the verses of this song using a procedure.

```
DECLARE SUB Chorus (X%)

'CH9 \ P1.BAS
'  A drinking song

DEFINT A-Z

FOR I = 100 TO 1 STEP  −1
   CALL Chorus(I)
NEXT I

END

SUB Chorus (X)

   PRINT
   PRINT X; "bottles of beer on the wall,"
   PRINT X; "bottles of beer,"
   PRINT "If one of those bottles should happen to fall,"
   PRINT X − 1; "bottles of beer on the wall."

END SUB
```

On each pass through the loop, the variable I is sent to the procedure, where it replaces the formal parameter X. Here the I also is called the *actual parameter*, as was the case for functions. Also just like with functions, the names you choose for your formal parameters are irrelevant. They just serve as placeholders. Note as well the DECLARE statement. Subprograms, like functions, require DECLARE statements to keep track of the type of parameters. As before, QBasic automatically generates the appropriate DECLARE statements when you save the program. Some people frequently save a program while developing it just to see what the DECLARE statements look like. This method can help you figure out what are the types of variables QBasic thinks it will handle, which is a good way to make sure that you haven't put in or left out a definer. Finally, note that you do not use a type identifier for a subprogram.

You might be thinking that this particular example seems a little forced. It's easy to rewrite the program using a FOR-NEXT loop. That's true, but writing the program using a procedure, or subprogram, changes the emphasis a little. It's a lot closer to my outline. Imagine a FOR-NEXT loop that had to surround 50 lines of code. In this situation, it's too easy to forget what the loop is doing. Most programmers prefer loops to be digestible. The whole loop better not involve more than a single screen of code in my case.

Subroutines

Subroutines are islands of codes that you can transfer to, yet DOS BASIC remembers from whence it came. A command like:

```
100 GOSUB 1000
```

transfers program control to the statement on line 1000. Processing continues until the BASIC interpreter encounters the command RETURN, at which point it picks up where it left off.

While less flexible than procedures, subroutines can serve many of the same functions. For example, to write the drinking song, you would use:

```
10  ' The drinking song
20  FOR I = 100 to 1 STEP −1
30  GOSUB 1000
40  NEXT I
50  END
999 '
1000  PRINT I;"bottles of beer on the wall"
1010  PRINT I;"bottles of beer"
1020  PRINT "If one of those bottles should happen to fall"
1030  PRINT I − 1;"bottles of beer on the wall"
1040  RETURN
```

The key here is the command RETURN. When DOS BASIC encounters this command, it returns to the statement following the GOSUB, which, in this case, is the NEXT command that cycles the loop one more time.

Perhaps you can see one of the problems. The I is being used for two places, making side effects possible. If I were to change the I inside the subroutine, it would foul up the loop's counter.

In complicated programs with GOSUBs, danger always lurks around the corner. Be careful about documenting what information is transferred and what changes are made to the variables in the main body of the program. You might want to consider using a convention, like always adding an *S*, to distinguish variables used locally in subroutines from those used globally in the main module.

Subroutines have another disadvantage: they are not islands of code—you inadvertently can fall into a subroutine. This statement means you must have an END command or some other barrier (STOP or GOTO) to separate the subroutines from the main body of the program.

Nonetheless, in GW-BASIC, you have little choice. You must use subroutines. They can clean up your programs to some extent. For example, rather than use multiple statements in an IF-THEN in GW-BASIC:

IF...THEN *statement 1:statement 2:statement 3...statement 10*

consider making the 10 statements into a subroutine:

IF...THEN GOSUB *location of the statements*

Similarly, for menu selections, there is a version of the GOSUB called the ON...GOSUB that you might find useful. The way this command works is that, when DOS BASIC encounters a statement like:

ON x GOSUB 1000,2000,3000,4000

it checks the current value of x. If it is 1, you GOSUB to the routine on line 1000; if 2, line 2000; etc.

In QBasic, you would just use a SELECT CASE.

Subroutines in QBasic

There are a couple of situations where you need subroutines in QBasic (see the section on event trapping at the end of this chapter); however, as you have probably grown to expect, QBasic is a bit more flexible. QBasic allows line numbers, so you can use the GOSUB as indicated earlier. You also can replace the line numbers with mnemonic labels.

A *label* is any legal QBasic variable name followed by a colon. The label must precede the line containing the statement. For example, here is the drinking song rewritten using a label:

```
' The drinking song
FOR I = 100 to 1 STEP -1
    GOSUB Chorus
NEXT I
END

CHORUS:
PRINT I;"bottles of beer on the wall"
PRINT I;"bottles of beer"
PRINT "If one of those bottles should happen to fall"
PRINT I-1;"bottles of beer on the wall"
RETURN
```

I must give you fair warning, though. Because subroutines do not allow parameters, communicating information to and from a subroutine always is messy. For example, consider the procedure SUB StripSpaces(X$) rewritten as a subroutine:

```
StripSpaces:

Temp$ = ""
FOR I = 1 TO LEN(X$)
    IF MID$(X$,I,1) < > CHR$(32) THEN Temp$ = Temp$ + MID$(X$,I,1)
NEXT I

RETURN
```

To strip the spaces off of the value of a variable, Phrase$, you need to say:

```
X$ = Phrase$
GOSUB StripSpace
Phrase$ = Temp$
```

The procedure is cleaner. You don't have to worry about unintentional side effects because of the variables I and Temp$. If you stick to procedures, you will know that side effects only come from parameters and shared variables.

More on QBasic procedures

For a more interesting program consider the frame builder, CH4 \ P18.BAS. A long program might want to put boxes around text in many different contexts. Here's that program rewritten and modified so that it's a procedure (I've eliminated the CLS screen commands because you might want to use this procedure to box existing text):

```
DECLARE SUB BoxDrawer (Rw%, Col%, Hsize%, Vsize%)

DEFINT A-Z
SUB BoxDrawer (Rw, Col, Hsize, Vsize)
```

```
'  CH9 \ P2.BAS
'  CH4 \ P18.BAS converted to a procedure

'  A rectangle drawer
'  this procedure accepts a row value
'  a column value and a horizontal and vertical size
'  it doesn't check the data.                              'A

'  LOCAL variables are: TopLftCor$, TopRtCor$,BotLftCor$,BotRtCor$
'  Start,VertFinish,EndCol                                 'B

TopLftCor$ = CHR$(218)                                     'C
TopRtCor$ = CHR$(191)

BotLftCor$ = CHR$(192)
BotRtCor$ = CHR$(217)

HorizLine$ = STRING$(Hsize − 2, 196)
VertLine$ = CHR$(179)

Top$ = TopLftCor$ + HorizLine$ + TopRtCor$
Bot$ = BotLftCor$ + HorizLine$ + BotRtCor$

LOCATE Rw, Col
PRINT Top$;

Start = Rw + 1
VertFinish = Rw + Vsize − 2
EndCol = Col + Hsize − 1

FOR I = Start TO VertFinish

    LOCATE I, Col
    PRINT VertLine$;
    LOCATE I, EndCol
    PRINT VertLine$;

NEXT I

LOCATE VertFinish + 1, Col
PRINT Bot$;

END SUB
```

A   Just like with a function, it's best to check the values that you send a procedure before you call the procedure. That's why I've eliminated the checks that were in the original program.

B   Again, just like with functions, you should initialize the local and shared variables before any executable statements.

C   Here you might prefer to allow double sided boxes. To make them, add
     another parameter (for example, Type) to the procedure and rewrite it
     as:

```
SUB BoxDrawer(Rw,Col,HSize,Vsize,Type)

SELECT CASE Type

  CASE 1

    TopLftCor$ = CHR$(218)
    TopRtCor$ = CHR$(191)
     .
     .
     .

  CASE ELSE

    TopLftCor$ = CHR$(201)
    TopRtCor$ = CHR$(187)
     .
     .
     .
```

Once the procedure is written and debugged, you can use it whenever you want in
whatever program needs it. For example, to box some text that you're about to
print on the screen, use the CSRLIN and POS(0) functions before and after you
print the text. For example, try the following:

```
'CH9 \ P2a.BAS
' A demo using the Box procedure

CLS
DEFINT A-Z

PRINT "Press any key to see the box procedure at work"
I$ = INPUT$(1)
LOCATE 12,21
TestString$ = "A Procedure a day keeps the bugs away"
PRINT TestString$

Row = CSRLIN - 2                                          'A
Column = 20
HorizSize = LEN(TestString$) + 2                          'B
VertSize = 3

CALL BoxDrawer(Row,Column,HorizSize,VertSize)

END
```

A   The CSRLIN function gives the current line the cursor is on, which is two lines down from where the box should start.

B   The box has to be two characters longer than the string.

When you start writing procedures in your programs is immaterial. My own preference is to do them after I've written all the *module-level code*, which is code that doesn't have it's own window. Presumably, in my outline, I've marked out what parameters they'll take, but QBasic doesn't mind. On the other hand, you can't run a program with a call to an unwritten procedure. For more on this subject, see the last section of this chapter.

As a final example for this section, I'll redo the bar graph program; only this time, I'll rewrite it as a group of procedure calls. I'll use separate procedures to draw the axes and to display an individual bar. Therefore, I easily can display as many bars as will fit on a single screen.

Here's the main module:

```
DECLARE SUB DrawAxes ( )
DECLARE SUB DrawBar (Where!, HowHigh!)
DECLARE FUNCTION GetValue ( )

'CH9 \ P3.BAS
' A bar graph program revisited

CLS
PRINT "This program draw up to a 25 bar, bar graph. You"
PRINT "can enter up to 25 numbers between 1 and 23."
PRINT
PRINT "Press any key to start."
I$ = INPUT$(1)
CLS

CALL DrawAxes

BARS = 1

Height = GetValue                                         'A

DO UNTIL Height = 0

   Location = 3 * BARS
   CALL DrawBar(Location, Height)                         'B

   BARS = BARS + 1
   IF BARS > 25 THEN EXIT DO                              'C

   Height = GetValue

LOOP
```

```
LOCATE 25, 1
PRINT SPACE$(79);
LOCATE 25, 1
PRINT "Press any key to clear screen";
I$ = INPUT$(1)
CLS
END
```

A   This function, which will accept the values for the heights of the bars, will need to be done carefully. After all, you don't want to disturb what already is displayed in the graph. The program also has to make sure the values are permissible.

B   The procedure to draw a bar obviously will use two parameters: Where to draw the bar and HowHigh to make it. Because I want to space the bars three spaces apart, I can use three times the number of the bar for the Where. HowHigh comes from the as-yet-unwritten function GetValue.

C   As I mentioned earlier, I use an EXIT LOOP only for abnormal methods of ending a loop. This situation qualifies because the natural way to end the program will be to enter a value of zero for the height of a bar.

That takes care of the main program. Notice how I've pushed most of the gritty details under the rug, which is quite common when using procedures. Your main programs will have a fairly clean look, containing directions and repeated procedure and function calls. Some people would even put the directions into procedure calls to make the main module into one long sequence of procedure and function calls. This arrangement also is a matter of taste. In any case, it's unlikely that the main module will need to be very long.

Here's the procedure to draw the axes:

```
SUB DrawAxes

    ' LOCAL variables are: TickMark$,BoxChar$,I

    TickMark$ = CHR$(95)
    BoxChar$ = CHR$(219)

    FOR I = 1 TO 22
        LOCATE I, 1
        PRINT BoxChar$ + TickMark$;
    NEXT I

    LOCATE 23, 1: PRINT BoxChar$;
    LOCATE 24, 1: PRINT STRING$(78, BoxChar$);

END SUB
```

Next, I will program the procedure to draw a bar. As mentioned previously, unlike the previous procedure, which didn't use any parameters (which is why the DECLARE statement used an empty set of parentheses), this procedure depends on two parameters: Where and HowHigh:

```
SUB DrawBar (Where, HowHigh)

    ' LOCAL Variables are: TopOfBar,BoxChar$,I

    BoxChar$ = CHR$(178)
    TopOfBar = 24 - HowHigh

    FOR I = TopOfBar TO 23
        LOCATE I, Where
        PRINT BoxChar$ + BoxChar$;
    NEXT I

END SUB
```

Finally, you need to write the function that gets the data. An input routine often is the most subtle part of a program; here is no exception. Bulletproofing input often requires more lines of code than seems necessary at first glance. For example, in what follows, I've decided to mask out all input except numbers. You can do this screening by accepting the number digit by digit, disregarding any other characters. As mentioned before, you can do this process by using the INPUT$(1) command. Once all the digits are in, you use the VAL command to convert them to a number. You saw a version of this kind of routine earlier.

This function is further complicated by the need to check that the values are not too big and by the requirement that the bars already on the screen are not disturbed. The easiest way to do the former is to use the 25th line of the screen for the data. You have to prevent the screen from scrolling. For the latter, you'll have to write the main part of the function as a loop that ends only when a number between 0 and 23 was entered.

Here's the function:

```
FUNCTION GetValue

    ' Draw axes
    ' modified from CH5 \ P19.BAS

    ' LOCAL variables are: Temp$, TempValue,Dig$

    DO                                                      'A

        LOCATE 25, 1                                        'B
        PRINT SPACE$(79);
        LOCATE 25, 1
        PRINT "Type a number between 1 and 23 (0 to end) and hit ";
```

```
          PRINT "enter when done.";
          LOCATE 25, 1

          Temp$ = ""
          Dig$ = INPUT$(1)
          PRINT SPACE$(79);                                          'C

          LOCATE 25, 1

          DO UNTIL Dig$ = CHR$(13)

             IF Dig$ < "0" OR Dig$ > "9" THEN
                BEEP
             ELSE
                PRINT Dig$;                                          'D
                Temp$ = Temp$ + Dig$
             END IF

             Dig$ = INPUT$(1)

          LOOP                                       'stops after enter key

          TempValue = VAL(Temp$)

       LOOP UNTIL TempValue > = 0 AND TempValue < = 23               'E

       GetValue = TempValue

    END FUNCTION
```

A   This loop will make sure that the number is acceptable.

B   I'll use the 25th line of the screen to accept data and give some simple
    directions. However, I have to be especially careful not to allow the
    screen to scroll. VIEW PRINT 25 TO 25 is another way to do this step.

C   This line erases the previous prompt.

D   I only print the digit if I'm sure that it is acceptable. In particular, the
    program never prints a carriage return, so the display never scrolls.

E   If you enter too large a number, the loop begins again. In particular, the
    string variable Temp$ is reinitialized.

You might be wondering why I used a function here. Why not a procedure, SUB
GetNumber, with a shared variable HowHigh? This choice is just a matter of taste.
As you probably have realized, a procedure can do anything a function can do, but
I feel it's a good idea to preserve the distinction. I use functions when I need to
massage values and/or make new ones. I use procedures in all other situations.
For me, functions massage and subprograms do.

    Finally, let me end this section by noting that, just as for functions, you can
use static variables in subprograms. Also just like for functions, static variables

mainly are used as debugging tools. Because procedures that use only static variables run faster, QBasic lets you force all variables to be static by writing:

SUB ....STATIC

Passing by reference or by value

Consider the following simple function:

```
FUNCTION INCR(X)
    X = X + 1
END FUNCTION
```

or

```
SUB ADD1(X)
    X = X + 1
END SUB
```

This situation is a new one for you. I've assigned a new value to the placeholder, or formal parameter. However, not only is there no reason not to make assignments to the placeholders in procedures and functions, but you also will never exploit fully the power of procedures until you become comfortable with what happens when you make assignments to the placeholders. When you assign to a formal parameter in a procedure or function, after you call the procedure or use the function, the value of the corresponding variable will change accordingly.

In particular, with the procedure given earlier, consider:

```
Number = 5
CALL ADD1(Number)
PRINT Number
PRINT ADD1(Number)
```

This fragment will display a 6 and a 7 on the screen.

Think about it this way: when you call a procedure or a function, QBasic replaces the placeholder with the variable, not with the value of the variable as it does with the older DEF FN functions. In the previous example, QBasic sends the variable Number to the procedure, where it replaces the placeholder X everywhere X occurred. (Actually, it sends the address in memory where the value of Number is stored.) Similarly, the second time QBasic sends the address of the variable, its current value is a 6, so it adds 1 and comes up with 7, which is now the current value of Number. In particular, calling the procedure with the statement CALL ADD1(Number) or using the function is the same as saying:

```
Number = Number + 1
```

because the variable Number substitutes for the placeholder X everywhere the variable X appeared.

As another example, suppose you needed to change a phrase by stripping out all the spaces of a phrase (i.e., a super version of the function LTRIM$). The outline is clear:

1. Find out where the spaces, CHR$(32), are and remove them.

You can use the MID$ command to extract the non-space characters in the string. The code that strips out the spaces is easy:

```
FOR Count = 1 TO LenPhrase
  IF MID$(Phrase$,Count,1) < > CHR$(32) THEN
    Temp$ = Temp$ + MID$(Phrase$,Count,1)
NEXT Count
```

When this loop ends, the value of Temp$ is the stripped phrase. Now, you have to decide whether you want to change the phrase or set up a new phrase. If you want the original phrase to change, incorporate the fragment given previously into a procedure:

```
SUB StripSpaces(X$)

  ' LOCAL variable is Count,LenPhrase$,Temp$

  LenPhrase = LEN(X$)

  FOR Count = 1 TO LenPhrase
    IF MID$(X$,Count,1) < > CHR$(32) THEN
      Temp$ = Temp$ + MID$(X$,Count,1)
  NEXT Count
  X$ = Temp$

END SUB
```

Now whenever you call the procedure:

```
CALL StripSpaces(Phrase$)
```

the original string Phrase$ changes. You could make a function out of it:

```
FUNCTION StripSpaces$(X$)

  ' LOCAL variable is Count,LenPhrase$,Temp$

  LenPhrase = LEN(X$)

  FOR Count = 1 TO LenPhrase
    IF MID$(X$,Count,1) < > CHR$(32) THEN
      Temp$ = Temp$ + MID$(X$,Count,1)
  NEXT Count
  StripSpaces$ = Temp$

END FUNCTION
```

The value of this function, StripSpaces$(Phrase$), is the stripped phrase, but the original Phrase$ still is intact. You also could add a line to the function to make it equivalent to the subprogram:

```
X$ = Temp$
```

Using a procedure or function with a variable is called passing by reference because the compiler sends the procedure the location in memory that the variables take up. Because the procedure or function now knows where the values of the variables are, it can change them. Obviously, this change can happen only if you make an assignment to a formal parameter within the function or procedure.

When you call an older DEF FN function, QBasic copies the values of the variables but doesn't send the location. Therefore, this type of function can't change anything.

Because procedures and functions can change the values of the variables used as actual parameters, anytime you call a procedure, you are, in a sense, defining a new group of shared variables—the variables you just sent as actual parameters.

How do you decide whether to make a variable shared or to send it as a parameter? Most programmers follow the convention that shared variables are for global information (like the value of π); therefore, you should not change the value of shared variables in a procedure. Procedures should change only the values of parameters. The reason for this convention stems from the methods you'll use to debug procedures (see the next section).

Occasionally, you'll want to send procedures the values of variables or even numeric expressions (numbers or calculations), in which case, they shouldn't change. This method is called *passing by value* and is exactly what happens with DEF FN functions. To pass information by value to a procedure, enclose the parameter in parentheses. For example, consider the following test program:

```
SUB ADDI(X)
   X = X + 1
END SUB

Number = 5

CALL ADD1((Number))              'NOTE THE EXTRA PARENTHESES!
PRINT Number

'compare this to

CALL ADD1(Number)
PRINT Number

END
```

What you'll see is:

```
5
6
```

You see a five then a six because, in the first call to the ADD1 procedure, you are passing the variable Number by value; the procedure doesn't, and can't, change the variable. In the second case, you're passing by reference; the procedure can, and does, change the value of Number: it makes it a 6. Essentially, the first call is a complicated way of saying:

```
CALL ADD1(5)
```

You also should be aware that, because procedures (in a sense) deal with variables (when you pass by reference) or with values (when you pass by value), the QBasic manual recommends that you do not pass the same variable by reference for more than one parameter. Don't say CALL BadExample(X,X), which leads to what is called *variable aliasing* and can lead to extremely subtle bugs. (Aliasing means two symbols are referring to the same place in memory.)

As a final example for this section, suppose you wanted to write a program to create and shuffle a deck of cards. You can think of a deck of cards as being a string variable:

```
DeckOfCard$ = "2♣3♣4♣5♣6♣7♣8♣9♣0♣J♣Q♣K♣A♣..."
```

I've used 0 for the 10 to keep all the cards the same length. Obviously, because this string variable will have 104 characters, you'll want the computer to do some of the work. You'll see a slightly awkward method now and a much better one in chapter 10.

In any case, because you want to change this variable when you shuffle the cards, you should write:

```
SUB Shuffle(X$)
```

as a procedure and not a function. This procedure will be similar to the Jumble program, CH7 \ P13.BAS. The only difference is that you have to move characters by twos, which is why I used a 0 for the 10. Here's the jumble program rewritten as a procedure to move two characters at a time:

```
DECLARE SUB Shuffle (Phrase$)
DECLARE FUNCTION Suit$ (X%)

'  a Jumble program (CH7 \ P13.BAS)
'  converted to a procedure
'  jumbles by twos

SUB Jumble (Phrase$)

   '  LOCAL variables are: LenPhrase,I

   RANDOMIZE TIMER
   LenPhrase = LEN(Phrase$) / 2                          'A
```

```
        FOR I = 1 TO LenPhrase

            INum = INT(LenPhrase * RND(1)) + 1
            NewChar$ = MID$(Phrase$, 2 * INum - 1, 2)              'B
            OldChar$ = MID$(Phrase$, 2 * I - 1, 2)

            MID$(Phrase$, 2 * I - 1, 2) = NewChar$                 'C
            MID$(Phrase$, 2 * INum - 1, 1) = OldChar$

        NEXT I

    END SUB
```

A   The number of cards is half the length of the phrase.

B   The cards are located starting in the first, third, fifth, etc. positions.

C   You need to move two characters at a time.

Next, you need to set up the deck of cards. By consulting, for example, the ASCII codes in the online help, you'll see that:

Clubs symbol (♣)	CHR$(5)
Diamonds symbol (♦)	CHR$(4)
Hearts symbol (♥)	CHR$(3)
Spades symbol (♠)	CHR$(6)

The easiest way to use this information is with a function. Here's a function that makes a suit of cards:

```
FUNCTION Suit$ (X%)

    'LOCAL variables I,Temp$

    Temp$ = ""

    FOR I = 2 TO 10
        Temp$ = Temp$ + RIGHT$( STR$(I), 1) + CHR$(X%)
    NEXT I

    HighCards$ = "J" + CHR$(X%) + "Q" + CHR$(X%) + "K" + CH- R$(X%) +
    "A"
        + CHR$(X%)
    Suit$ = Temp$ + HighCards$

END FUNCTION
```

Notice that if I equals 10, then RIGHT$(STR$(I),1) = "0". Now, you can call this function four times:

```
    DeckOfCards$ = Suit$(5) + Suit$(4) + Suit$(3) + Suit$(6)
```

Now that you've done all the preliminaries, here's a procedure that deals out and displays a bridge hand:

```
SUB Deal

    '  LOCAL variable is Cards

    SHARED DeckOfCards$

    CALL Shuffle(DeckOfCards$)

    For Cards = 1 TO 52
        PRINT MID$(DeckOfCards$,2*Cards$ – 1,2)                    'A
    NEXT Cards

END SUB
```

   A   Again, the cards start in the first, third, fifth, etc. positions.

Passing variables by reference versus passing them by value is a subtle concept. However, the distinction is important. Anyone doing structured programming needs to understand it. Knowing when to pass variables by value, as opposed to passing them by reference, is one of the marks of a master programmer. In chapter 13, you'll see a couple of more realistic examples of why this distinction is so important.

If you never make assignments to the parameters during the course of a procedure or function, there's no real difference other than memory use. Passing by value, because it involves copying the value of the variable, uses slightly more memory.

Testing and debugging programs

No matter how carefully you outline your program, after you write it you still will need to test it. Some people's idea of testing consists of running the program a few times, using slightly different inputs each time to see what happens. This method can work out well when you have a short program, but it's not effective or convincing for a long program, or even a short program that is in any way subtle.

For a sophisticated or long program, you should not only write the program top down, but you should also, as much as possible, test it from the top down. As you finish each procedure or function, combine it with the pieces you already have checked and test everything again. A higher-level procedure or function might need results from a piece that is not yet written. In this case, the best technique, which often is called *stub programming*, is to substitute constants, where necessary, for the results of unwritten procedures or functions. Define the SUB procedure or FUNCTION procedure but fill it with constants instead of having it do anything. The procedure calls still will work the same but they get only these constants—these test results—back from the test procedures or functions.

Testing programs is an art, not a science. There's no rule that always works. If your program is long and complicated, you can't test all the possibilities; you have to be content with reasonable ones.

The key is the word *reasonable*. The following story explains how subtle this concept can be:

A utility company had a complicated but, they thought, carefully checked program to send out bills and follow-up bills and to automatically cut off service if no response was received. One day, the story goes, someone went on vacation and shut off the electricity. The computer sent out a bill for $0.00, which understandably wasn't paid. After the requisite number of follow-up requests, the computer finally issued a termination notice, saying that, if this unfortunate person didn't pay $0.00 by Thursday, his electricity would be cut off automatically.

A frantic call (if he managed to get through to a real live person) might have succeeded in stopping the shut-off. The story doesn't say. If this story is true, then the programmer forgot to test what the program would do if the bill was $0.00. This event wasn't a reasonable possibility.

Finally, remember that regardless of how much you test, you can never be completely sure that your program won't crash. From experience, I know that, no matter how robust I try to make a program, it always seems that someone, somehow will find a way to crash it. However, my goal has always been to write programs that conform to a sign that I once saw. Slightly paraphrased it said:

Our goal is a program:
THAT SPUTTERS OUT AND DOESN'T BLOW UP!

The technical term for this is to *degrade gracefully*. A realistic goal is not a perfect program but one that is as robust as possible. Check the data you send to functions and procedures before you call them. Check what the user enters before the program uses it. Better yet, check the data while it's being entered.

Anyway, before you can bulletproof a program, you need one that at least seems to work. So, you've compiled the program and know there are no syntax errors, but you've tested the program and it doesn't work. There are bugs to isolate and eradicate. Don't be surprised or dismayed, bugs comes with the territory.

You have to find them and determine what kind they are. There actually are two kinds of bugs: logical and grammatical. The grammatical errors are things like a misspelled variable name leading to a default value that ruins the program. Surprisingly enough, they are often the most difficult kind of bug to detect. The best cure is a programmers tool called a *cross referencer*, or XREF, program. This kind of program works through the source code of a program and lists the names of all the variables that occur along with where they occur. You'll see how to write a version of an XREF program in chapter 13; however, a commercial version, like the one from Crescent Software (203-846-2500), can do much more.

To get rid of a more subtle logical bug, you have to isolate it. You need to find the part of the program that's causing the problem. If you've followed the modular approach, your life is a whole lot easier. If you've been top down testing the program as you develop it, then it's clear where the problem is.

Pinpointing the procedure or function that's causing the problem usually isn't hard if it's your program—mostly because you start off with a good idea of the logic of your program. If it's not your program or you waited until the program was finished, then you can use the following techniques to check the pieces one at a time. If the program wasn't modular, you're on your own. I don't know any way to check an unstructured program other than to work through it line by line. It often will be faster to rewrite it in a more structured fashion.

Let's assume that you've decided on the procedure or function that's causing the trouble. There are only three possibilities:

- The data going in is wrong—what you've fed to the procedure or function is confusing it.
- The data coming out is wrong—it's sending incorrect information to other parts of the program.
- There's something wrong inside the procedure or function. (For example, it doesn't clear the screen at the right time.)

In the first two cases, the fault is either in the parameters you send to the procedure or function, what you've assigned to the parameters, or the shared variables within the function or procedure.

How do you decide which? Well, it's hard to imagine a short, correctly written procedure or function where you couldn't analyze on a piece of paper what should happen in many cases. Work through the procedure or function by hand, playing computer. Don't make any assumptions other than what the computer would know at that point. Don't assume variables have certain values, unless you can convince yourself that they do.

Write a *driver program* using the Immediate window. A driver is a program fragment that calls a function or procedure with specific values. For example, suppose you know that when global variables var1 and var2 equal 10 and 20, respectively, the results of a procedure (using the global variable, global1) or a function have a value of 97. When you want to test how this procedure or function behaves at a particular place in a program, add a breakpoint and use the Immediate window to enter:

```
CALL WhateverYoureTesting(10,20)
PRINT "The value of the variable global1 is ";global1
```

See what happens. If the value of global1 isn't right, use the Debug menu to watch the important variables—the ones that affect global1. (However, you can watch variables within a procedure or function only if you've added them to the watch list from within that function or procedure.) There might be something wrong inside the procedure or function. If the value of global1 is right, then determine by hand what happens for some other values. Try the *boundary values*—the strange values, like the $0.00 that the programmer in the story forgot. If you always match up with what you expect, there probably is nothing wrong with the procedure or function. You now expect, and hope, that the problem comes from outside.

In practice, you have to make sure your driver fragment sends all the information needed by the procedure or function. That's not likely to be only two global variables. You might not want to use the Immediate window then. You might prefer to insert the code at the breakpoint.

Check each procedure that calls this procedure or function and apply the same techniques for them. Check what goes in and out of these procedures or functions. QBasic makes this process easy. Not only can you single step through a program you can step through a procedure or function. When you're debugging a program or using the stub programming method mentioned earlier, you can use F10 rather than F8 to single step. The important difference is that F10 treats a call to a function or subprogram as one step. This way you don't have to step through all the lines in all the functions and procedures in your program when you don't need to.

In every case then, you eventually wind your way down to a procedure or function that just doesn't work. You now know that you have an error internal to a procedure or function. To detect these errors, try these techniques:

- Add more variables to watch.
- Single step through the procedure using Restart, breakpoints, and the F8 or F10 key as needed. While you're doing this stepping, toggle back and forth to the output screen to see if what's there is what you expect.

Feeding a procedure or function specific numbers and using these techniques is not a cure-all. No technique can help unless you have a good grip on what the procedure or function should do. If you use an IF-THEN, are you testing for the right quantity? Should a $>=$ be a $>$? Watch the value of any Boolean relations that seem to be off. Check any loops that are inside the routine; loops are a common source of problems. Are counters initialized right? Do you have an off-by-one error? Are you testing your indeterminate loops at the top when you should do it at the bottom? All these conditions can be checked by watching the appropriate object.

Documentation, managing procedures, and program style

Although you can remember the logic of a complicated program for a while, you can't remember it forever. Good documentation is the key that can open the lock. Some people include the pseudocode or outline for the program as multiple remark statements. Along with meaningful variable names, this technique obviously is the best form of documentation. Try to avoid tricky code. If you need to do something extraordinarily clever, make sure it's extensively commented. (Most of the time, you'll find that the clever piece of code really wasn't needed.) Nothing is harder to change six months down the line than *cute code*. Cute code often comes from an attempt to get a program to run faster. While it is sometimes necessary, QBasic usually is fast enough so that cute coding is more often an ego thing. I'm reminded of a sign I once saw:

Rules for program optimization:
1. DON'T DO IT.
2. (For expert programmers only) *DON'T DO IT!*

The point is that, when you start thinking of tricks to speed up your programs, you easily can lose sight of the fundamental issue: making sure the programs run robustly in the first place.

Dramatic speedups usually come from shifts in the *algorithms* in the program, not from little tweaks. (An algorithm is the method you use to solve a problem.) For example, the second method of programming the infinite multiplier from chapter 8 is a better algorithm than the first, so a program using it would run much faster. Similarly, in problems that sort a list, it's the method that you choose that determines how fast the sort is. In chapters 10 and 11, you'll see how choosing the right sorting technique can speed up a program 1000 fold, which is more than any minor tweak can ever hope to accomplish. Discovering new and hopefully faster algorithms is one of the main tasks of computer scientists and mathematicians.

In any case, it's extremely difficult to modify or debug a program (even one that you, long ago, wrote yourself) that has few or no remark statements and little accompanying documentation and that has cute or some other kind of non-informative variable names. Because QBasic allows long variable names, don't make your programs a morass of variables named X, X13, X17, X39, etc.

Finally, as your QBasic programs become more sophisticated, they'll start using more and more procedures and functions—a program might have 15 subprograms and 12 functions. Obviously, this amount is too much to cycle through using Shift−F2. Instead, you can use a feature on the View menu. Open the View menu and hit S for *Subs* (the shortcut is F2). This option gives you a list of all the functions and procedures in your program. For example, Fig. 9-2 shows the list for the Pig Latin program. (Notice that the names of the functions are indented slightly from the name of the main module.) You can use this dialog box to start editing any of the procedures or the main module. All you have to do is move the highlighted bar to the piece you want to edit and hit Enter. That's what *edit in active* means.

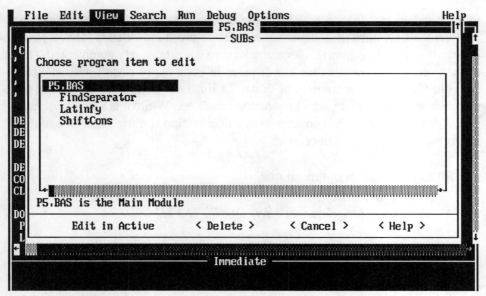

9-2 The subs dialog box.

Event trapping

Suppose you wanted to write a program that, much like QBasic itself, gives a user help when he or she presses the F1 key. The program must monitor the keyboard at all times. If the F1 key is pressed, the program must interrupt the normal flow of processing and jump to the help routine. You start the monitoring process, or *event trapping*, with the command:

    KEY(1) ON

After this command, between each statement that is processed, DOS BASIC checks whether the first function key was pressed. (To test the second function key use KEY(2) ON, etc.) The command:

    KEY(1) OFF

turns off the monitor. Obviously, this monitoring slows any program down. Therefore, when doing something that makes heavy use of the central processor, like sorting lists, you might want to turn event trapping off.

Having enabled event trapping, you have to tell the computer what to do. You can tell it with the statement:

    ON KEY(1) GOSUB ....

where the dots are for the label or line number of the subroutine that you want to transfer control to.

Nothing prevents you from GOSUBing to different places at different times in response to F1 or from trapping more than one function key at the same time. A new ON KEY(n) GOSUB overrides a previous one. Unfortunately, in the current version of QBasic, event trapping can direct flow only to a subroutine, not to a procedure.

Sometimes you want to turn off event trapping temporarily but have the compiler remember that the event happened. This technique is done with the command:

KEY(n) STOP

Once this command is processed, the compiler doesn't respond to the event, until you turn event trapping back on with the KEY(n) ON. At that point, it will do what it has to do. On the other hand, the command KEY(n) OFF mentioned before turns off event trapping and eliminates any memories. When DOS BASIC is inside a subroutine that was called by a KEY statement, DOS BASIC still keeps track of keystrokes. In effect, the GOSUB causes a KEY(n) stop to be executed as well.

You also can trap time or a joystick. For example, the command TIMER ON allows you to use:

ON TIMER(n) GOSUB ...

to transfer control to a subroutine every n seconds. Here, n is an integer from 1 to 86,400, which is the number of seconds in 24 hours. When you RETURN from the subroutine, the clock is reset back to 0. Similarly, TIMER OFF turns this type of event trapping off. TIMER STOP takes it off the hook temporarily; it keeps track of the time but doesn't do anything yet.

QBasic's extraordinary power even allows it to trap keys other than the function keys (unlike GW-BASIC). You can trap as many as 25 different keys at once. In addition to the 10 or 12 function keys, you can trap the four cursor keys, using the following commands:

KEY(11)	ON	Traps the up arrow
KEY(12)	ON	Traps the left arrow
KEY(13)	ON	Traps the right arrow
KEY(14)	ON	Traps the down arrow
KEY(30)	ON	Traps the F11 key
KEY(31)	ON	Traps the F12 key

Moreover, you can trap any other 11 keys or key combinations (like Ctrl−C) of your choice. Trapping these other keys is a bit tricky. The command:

KEY n, CHR$(state of keyboard) + CHR$(extended scan code)

tells QBasic to associate a certain key or combination of keys for future event trapping. The state of the keyboard is any combination of the following codes:

Right Shift	code 1	= &H1*
Left Shift	code 2	= &H2
Either Shift	code 3	= &H3**
Ctrl	code 4	= &H4
Alt	code 8	= &H8
Num Lock	code 32	= &H20
Caps Lock	code 64	= &H40

    * &H signifies hexadecimal notation. See chapter 10.

  ** QBasic treats all shift keys as the same. I view this condition as a bug.

You add these code numbers together to trap the combinations. For example, to trap both Ctrl and either shift use a 7 (4+3) inside the first CHR$.

The extended scan codes may be found in appendix E. For example, a C has scan code 46 (&H2E). So, the command:

```
KEY 18,CHR$(7) + CHR$(46)
```

when followed by a KEY(18) ON traps a Ctrl−C.

You also can prevent Ctrl−Break or even a system reset, Ctrl−Alt−Del, from interfering with a program by trapping them. For example, the extended code for the Break key is &H46, so:

```
KEY 15, CHR$(4) + CHR$(46)
```

sets up subroutine for Ctrl−Break.

10
CHAPTER

Error trapping and the GOTO

This short chapter explains error trapping. In trying to bulletproof your programs, especially if other people use them, assume people will do silly things: print without paper, save a file without inserting a disk, etc.

To use error trapping in DOS BASIC, you'll need a version of the GOTO statement. GOTOs should be used sparingly. This statement sends processing to a specific statement. It almost invariably confuses the issue. Rarely do you need this unconditional jump.

The last section of this chapter explains a bit about binary arithmetic, which occasionally is useful in error trapping.

Error trapping

The command that activates error trapping is ON ERROR GOTO . . . where the three dots are for the label or line number that define the error trap. This command, which can occur anywhere, stops DOS BASIC from bombing a program when an error occurs. Obviously, the ON ERROR command should transfer control to a piece of code that:

- Identifies the problem.
- Fixes it if possible.

For QBasic, the island of code that defines the error trap must be in the module level code and cannot be a function or subprogram.

If the error can be corrected, then the statement RESUME takes you back to the statement that caused the error in the first place. However, you can't correct an error if you don't know why it happened. You identify the problem by means of the ERR function. This function gives you an integer that you can assign to a variable. For example, by saying ErrorNumber = ERR, the value of the variable ErrorNumber can help you pick up the type of error. DOS BASIC can identify more than 40 run-time errors. Appendix F of this book gives you the most useful ones.

For example:

25   Device fault. (For example, trying to LPRINT when the printer is off.)
27   Out of paper.

The way you use this information is simple. Somewhere in the program, before the error can occur, place an ON ERROR GOTO statement. For example, in Q-Basic:

```
ON ERROR GOTO PrinterCheck
```

Now, write a module labeled by PrinterCheck to handle the errors.

```
PrinterCheck:

   ErrorNumber = ERR
   BEEP

   SELECT CASE ErrorNumber
     CASE 25
       PRINT "Your printer may not be on"
     CASE 27
       PRINT "You're probably out of paper"
     CASE ELSE
       PRINT "Please tell the operator ( = program author?) that"
       PRINT " error number ";ErrorNumber;"occurred."

   END SELECT

PRINT "If the error has been corrected press 'Y' otherwise "
PRINT "press any key to END"

Continue$ = INPUT$(1)

IF Continue$ = "Y" or Continue$ = "y" THEN RESUME ELSE END
```

The idea of this error trap is simple. The SELECT CASE statement is ideal. Each case tries to give some indication of where the problem is and, if possible, how to correct it. If the program reaches the CASE ELSE, then the error number has to be reported. In any case, the final block gives you the option of continuing or not.

In GW-BASIC, you'll need multiple IF-THEN statements. The ON ERROR must give the line number where the error trap starts.

Error trapping isn't a cure-all. Obviously, very little can be done if the hard disk had crashed or if the user doesn't have any paper around. Moreover, the PRINT statements in the error trap are likely to mess up the display, unless you save the screen or use a different video page to write the message. (See chapter 14 for information on this technique.)

The RESUME command is quite flexible because of two other variants that you can use:

RESUME NEXT   Sends processing to the statement following the one that caused the error.

RESUME *label or line number*   Sends processing to the statement identified by the label or line number.

ERRDEV$ occasionally is useful and is available in QBasic and in GW-BASIC (versions 3.0 and higher). This reserved variable gives you the name of the device that caused the error. It's values are given in Table 10-1.

Table 10-1   ERRDEV$ returns
the name of the device that caused an error.

A:	B:	C:	D:	E:	Disk drives
LPT1:	LPT2:	LPT3:	PRN:		The three printer ports and the generic printer
COM1:	COM2:				The two serial ports
CON	KYBD				Keyboard
SCRN					Video display
AUX					The auxiliary
CLOCK$					The clock

The lower nibble of the reserved variable ERRDEV also can give you some useful information, which mostly is useful for file handling programs. Use ERRDEV AND &HF to get these bits out. For example, if ERRDEV AND &HF equals 9, then the printer also is out of paper. For more information on what a nibble is, see the last section of this chapter.

There's one other error handling function, ERL, available in DOS BASIC. If your program has line numbers, then this will give you the line number for the error.

When developing a program, you might want to test how your error handler works. DOS BASIC includes the statement ERROR *errorcode number*, which, when processed, makes the compiler behave as if the error described by the given error number actually had occurred. This makes it easier to develop the trap.

If you are confident that you will no longer need an error trap, you can disable error trapping with the statement ON ERROR GOTO 0. Similarly, you can

change which error trap is in effect by using another ON ERROR GOTO statement. DOS BASIC uses the last statement ON ERROR STATEMENT that it processed to decide where to go.

The GOTO statement

DOS BASIC still allows certain commands that usually are best forgotten. In most
cases, they have long since been superseded. The most egregious offender is the
naked GOTO. This command sends processing to a statement indicated by a label
or line number. There is almost never any need to do this. You should always have
a reason for jumping to a different part of the program. Because QBasic has the
various forms of the EXIT command (EXIT DO and EXIT FOR), programs like:

```
FOR I = 1 TO 100
    PRINT I
    IF INKEY$ < > ""THEN GOTO Ych
NEXT I
Ych:
    PRINT "Abnormal exit!"
```

easily can be rewritten using the EXIT FOR. The only time that a GOTO is ever
needed in QBasic is when you're deep in a nested loop and want to get out because
of an abnormal condition.

GW-BASIC doesn't have the various forms of the EXIT statement; therefore,
you occasionally will use the GOTO inside a loop. This statement usually will
take the form:

IF *funny condition* THEN GOTO *somewhere*

The naked GOTO, or unconditional jump, was needed in early versions of BASIC
(AppleSoft for example) where there was neither a DO loop nor a WHILE loop.
Users were forced to mimic these useful statements by using the following kind of
ugly and confusing code:

```
10  IF X > 5 THEN GOTO 100
20  .
30  .
40  .

    .

    .
90 GOTO 10
100 END
```

Isn't it cleaner to say:

```
WHILE X < = 5
```

WEND

The reasons why the developers of modern programming techniques basically banned the GOTO is that it leads you down the path to *spaghetti programming*. This type of programming lead to programs with logic that was not apparent to anybody:

```
 10  GOTO 30
 20  GOTO 50
 30  GOTO 70
 40  PRINT "Does this statement print?"
 50  PRINT "Or this one?"
 60  GOTO 100
 70  PRINT "What about this one?"
 80  GOTO 20
 90  END
100  GOTO 90
```

You probably are thinking that no one ever wrote code this silly. If it was not quite this absurd, code that was written before the advent of structured programming techniques occasionally came close.

Bit twiddling

A computer ultimately is a giant collection of on-off switches; a disk is a collection of particles that can either be magnetized or not. Think of each memory location in your PC as being made up of eight on-off switches. This affects the internal representation of numbers inside a PC. For example, when you write 255, you mean two 100s, five 10s, and five 1s. The digits are arranged in positional notation, with each place holding numbers ten times as large as the one to the right (usually called *decimal notation*). Your computer would store this number in a single memory location as:

11111111

meaning one 128, one 64, one 32, one 16, one 8, one 4, one 2, and one 1. (One way to indicate that a number is a binary number in print is to use a subscript of 2.) Each of these switches is called a *bit* (for binary digit). When it stores a 1, the bit is said to be *on*. In binary notation, each place holds numbers twice as large as the one to the right. Eight bits form a *byte*, or one memory location; two bytes form a *word*; and half of a byte is called a *nibble*.

Table 10-2 shows you how to count to 15 in binary. In a single nibble, 15 is the largest number that can be stored. In a byte, 255 is the largest number that can be stored. Bits are numbered with the leftmost called the most significant; the rightmost bit is the least significant.

Binary	Decimal
0000	0
0001	1
0010	2
0011	3
0100	4
0101	5
0110	6
0111	7
1000	8
1001	9
1010	10
1011	11
1100	12
1101	13
1110	14
1111	15

Table 10-2 Counting to 15 in binary.

You might have thought that DOS BASIC using 0 for false was quite natural, but why -1 for its internal representation of true? To understand this, you first have to know that, ultimately, all the logical operators (NOT, AND, OR, XOR) work on the bit level. For each of the operators, QBasic looks at the bits one at a time and follows the following rules.

AND makes the binary digit 1 only if both bits are 1, otherwise the bit is 0. For example, if:

$$X = 12_{10} = 1100_2 \text{ and } Y = 7_{10} = 0111_2$$

then

$$X \text{ AND } Y = 4_{10} = 0100_2$$

because only in the third position are both bits 1. Because AND gives a 1 only if both X and Y have a 1 in that place, by ANDing with a number whose binary digit is a single 1 and all the rest of the bits are 0, you can isolate the binary digits of any number. This technique is called *masking*.

On the other hand, OR gives a 1 if either of the binary digits is 1. So, using the previous example, X OR Y = 15_{10} = 1111_2. Use OR to make sure that specific bytes of a variable are on. For example, X = X OR 64 makes sure that the fourth bit in X is on. X = X OR 96 turns on the third and fourth bit.

Remember that bits are numbered starting from 0. You can try all these in the Immediate window by entering, for example:

```
X = 12:Y = 7: PRINT X OR Y
```

One of the most interesting operators is XOR, which gives a one in a specific position if exactly one of the digits of X and Y in that position is 1. So, using the same example, X XOR Y = 11_{10} 1011_2. XOR has the useful property that XORing twice doesn't do anything:

(X XOR Y) XOR Y = X

There are two other operators, IMP and EQV. The former gives a 1 except when X has a 1 and Y has a 0. The latter gives a 1 when both X and Y are the same—both true or both false.

NOT works on a single number by reversing the bits. A 1 becomes a 0; a 0 becomes a 1. O.K. now why is -1 = TRUE? First off, QBasic stores each integer as a single word using only 15 bits. Therefore:

$0 = 000\ 0000\ 0000\ 0000_2$

(As you'll see, grouping by fours in binary is more useful than grouping by threes, as is done in decimals.)

$NOT\ 0 = 1111\ 1111\ 1111\ 1111_2$

You might expect this number, which is 65,535 in decimal, to be the largest integer expressible in 16 bits. However, because QuickBASIC uses only 15 bits for its integers, it uses the left most bit for the sign. A 1 in the leftmost bit means the number is negative. Moreover, it uses what is called *twos-compliment notation* for negative numbers. In twos-compliment notation, to represent a negative number, $-X$, you apply NOT to the 15 bits that give X, set the leftmost bit to 1, and add 1 to the result. So, for -1, you would take the bit pattern for 1:

000 0000 0000 0001

apply NOT:

111 1111 1111 1110

add a 1 to the leftmost bit:

1111 1111 1111 1110

and finally add 1. The result is:

1111 1111 1111 1111

which equals NOT 0 or -1.

Binary numbers obviously are a bit difficult for people to handle. It's much easier if you use *hexadecimal* numbers, or base 16. In this case, 10_{16} is 16 in decimal. Use A for decimal 10, B for decimal 11, C for decimal 12, D for decimal 13, E for decimal 14, and F for decimal 15. Each hexadecimal digit represents four binary digits, or one nibble. To convert binary numbers to *hex* (shorthand for hexadecimal), just group the digits from right to left in groups of four and convert. So, 1101 0111 is D7 in hex, because 1101 equals 13 in decimal, or D in hex, and 0111 is 7 in both decimal and hex. You can use hex numbers in QBasic by prefixing them with an &H. So, PRINT &HF + &HF would give a 30 on the screen (displays always are in decimal). Hex notation makes deciding on the numbers for line styles easy: change the pattern you want into 4 hexadecimal digits.

Moreover, DOS BASIC has built-in functions to convert a decimal number to a string containing the hexadecimal digits. The function is HEX$(*numeric expression*). So, HEX$(32767) equals "7FFF". (There's no built-in equivalent to VAL; you'll have to write one yourself.)

11
CHAPTER

Lists, arrays, and records

You've seen two methods of assigning values to variables: by using an LET assignment statement and by responding to various kinds of INPUT statements. In both these methods, the variables are named and their values assigned at essentially the same time. The methods in this chapter are different. You set aside space in the computer's memory that can be named and used in a systematic way, at any time during the course of the program. You also will see a more efficient method of building frequently used information inside a program. Finally, this chapter covers some of the many methods known to search and sort lists. Chapter 13 shows you more sophisticated methods.

Getting started with lists

Suppose you are writing a program that requires one variable with the value 1, a second with the value 2, a third with the value 3, and so on for 100 different variables. The outline for this kind of program cries out for a FOR-NEXT LOOP:

```
FOR I = 1 to 100
    Assign I to its variable
NEXT I
```

As another example, consider the graphing program, CH9 \ P2.BAS. This program used a user-defined function to accept the numbers. Moreover, I had to limit the function to accepting numbers smaller than 23 so that the bars would fit. Suppose, for example, that you wanted to allow values as large as 46. Then, you could keep the bars in proportion and still have them fit if you made each bar stand for two units. In general, to allow arbitrarily large or small values, find the largest value. Once you know that value, use it to scale the bars.

If the largest value was stored in a variable named Large, multiplying its value by 23/Large shrinks it to fit into 23 units. Now, multiply all the other values to be graphed by this scaling factor. Because you're assuming that Large contains the largest value, all the other variables will now fit into a 23 unit space as well.

Anyway, you already know how to find the largest value in a list and how to write the procedure to graph a bar. The only thing left is to see how to temporarily store the values while you're determining the scaling factor—the largest value. For example, suppose you wanted to do a bar graph for a 12-month period. You would like to say something like:

```
FOR I = 1 to 12
  INPUT MI
  IF MI > Large THEN Large = MI
NEXT I
```

If this loop were possible, the information just entered still would be available in the variables MI. Unfortunately, this statement is not quite correct. In DOS BASIC, MI is a perfectly good variable name for a single variable. DOS BASIC, however, cannot separate the I from the M.

After you see a systematic way to name variables, it's easy to take care of these problems. To understand this method, think about lists that you use in every day life. For example, suppose before going out on various errands, you made a list of where you must go. It might look like Table 11-1.

Errands	
1.	Dry cleaners
2.	Supermarket
3.	Drugstore
4.	Shoemaker
5.	Post office

Table 11-1 A list of errands.

If a copy of this list was left at home, when you call home, instead of saying *I'm at the drugstore*, you could say *I'm on my third errand*. The numbers point to the errands. The 3 indicates the third item on the list. Now, a company probably would come along and sell, for incredibly organized people, preprinted errand lists with perhaps twenty places or slots available on each page. Each day, someone could take out a new sheet and fill in the slots. These blank lines are exactly like the variables that can be filled with values inside a computer's memory.

To DOS BASIC, a list is just a collection of variables, each of which is identified by two things:

- The name of the list
- Its position in the list

The third errand on a list that mimics the preprinted errand forms might be called Errand$(3). The name of this list is Errand$ (notice the dollar sign that indicates that the variables on this list will hold words, or strings). The number in the parentheses usually is called a *subscript* or *pointer*. The term subscript comes from mathematics where the item M(5) is more likely to be written M_5. The term pointer is used because the 5 points to the row holding the information. To DOS BASIC, M5 is the name of a single variable, but M(5) is the name of the fifth element on a list called *M*.

Lists can't be open-ended in DOS BASIC. While the limits are quite large (in QBasic, you can have up to 32,768 items on certain kinds of lists), you must tell the interpreter how much memory to set aside for the list before you use it. Fortunately, it is never necessary to say exactly how long the list is. Just make sure that it is at least as long as the number of items that you want it to contain. The statement that gives the length of a list is called a *dimension statement*. The command is DIM. For example, if someone wanted to have an errand list that allowed 30 errands, they would have a statement like DIM ERRAND$(30). The dimension statement must come before you refer to any elements in the list. Values then can be assigned using a FOR-NEXT loop or, because you want to allow someone to stop before entering all 30 names, by a DO loop as in the following QBasic program:

```
' CH11 \ P1.BAS
' A simple list demo

CLS
DEFINT A-Z
DIM Errand$(30)
Index = 0

DO
    PRINT "You've entered";Index;"entries so far."
    INPUT "Enter the next errand − ZZZ when done"; Errand$          'A
    IF Errand$ < > "ZZZ" THEN                                        'B
        Index = Index + 1
        Errand$(Index) = Errand$
    END IF

LOOP UNTIL Index = 30 OR Errand$ = "ZZZ"

NumberOfItems = Index                                               'C
END
```

A   Notice that I set up a temporary variable Errand$. This variable keeps the flag off the list. It also shows that you can have a variable with the same name as a previously dimensioned list.

B   Once the program knows that the entry is acceptable, it first moves the pointer (adds 1 to Index) and only then fills in the entry. Do you see why the order is important? Notice as well that this IF-THEN is completely skipped when ZZZ is entered, which keeps the flag off the list. Enter a ZZZ and the program moves immediately to the loop test and leaves.

C   This line keeps track of the number of items on the list. In a program that will manipulate this list, in many ways, it's a good candidate for a shared, or global, variable.

(For GW-BASIC users, besides adding the appropriate line numbers, you'll need to use a WHILE/WEND statement.)

There are other ways, however. In DOS BASIC, all lists come with a zeroth entry. In the example, when you said DIM Errand$(30), DOS BASIC actually set aside 31 slots; the extra one being Errand$(0). This zeroth slot is useful for things like storing the number of significant items on the list. Rather than set up a new variable, what I probably would do is:

```
Errand$(0) = STR$(Index)
```

Now, to find the number of items (for example, to set up a FOR-NEXT loop), I can convert this entry back to a number using the VAL command.

Another, perhaps even more popular, alternative is to keep a flag (like the ZZZ) as the last item on a list. This flag let's you use an indeterminate loop to manipulate the list. All you would need to do would be to test for the flag. To do this test, modify the previous program as follows:

```
' CH11 \ P1a.BAS
' A simple list demo revisited and revised

CLS
DEFINT A-Z
DIM Errand$(30)
Index = 1

DO
   PRINT "You've entered";Index - 1;"entries so far."
   INPUT "Enter the next errand - ZZZ when done"; Errand$
   IF Errand$ = "ZZZ" THEN
      Errand$(Index) = "ZZZ"
   ELSE
      Errand$(Index) = Errand$
```

```
        Index = Index + 1
    END IF
LOOP UNTIL Index = 30 OR Errand$ = "ZZZ"

NumberOfItems = Index

END
```

Notice that here I've used the IF-THEN-ELSE to deal with the two possibilities: a real entry or the flag. Notice as well that the first entry could hold the flag.

Of the two methods, I find the idea of keeping the number of items currently used in the zeroth entry the most appealing possibility, but this matter is clearly a matter of taste. I find it comforting to always know how many entries are on a list. It makes debugging easier. Also, like most programmers, I find FOR-NEXT loops easier to use than DO (or WHILE/WEND) loops.

More on lists

Some people never use the zeroth entry of a list; they just find it confusing. If you are not going to use it in a program it certainly wastes space. For this reason, DOS BASIC has a command that eliminates the zeroth entry in all lists dimensioned from that point on. It is the OPTION BASE 1 statement. After this statement is processed, all new lists dimensioned begin with the first entry. After OPTION BASE 1, DIM Errand$(30) sets aside 30 spots, rather than 31.

However, QBasic goes GW-BASIC one step better. Suppose you wanted to write the input routine for a bar graph program for sales in the years 1981 through 1987. You could say something like:

```
DIM SalesInYear(7)
FOR I = 1 TO 7
    PRINT "Enter the sales in year"; 1980 + I
    INPUT SalesInYear(1980 + I)
NEXT I
```

However, this program requires 14 additions (two for each pass through the loop) and also is more complicated. This situation is so common that QBasic decided to enhance the language by allowing subscript ranges. Instead of saying:

```
DIM SalesInYear(7)
```

you now can say:

```
DIM SalesInYear(1981 TO 1987)
```

The keyword TO marks the range. You must put the smaller number first for this extension of the DIM command. Using this version of the DIM statement, you can rewrite the fragment above as:

```
DIM SalesInYear(1981 TO 1987)

FOR I = 1981 TO 1987
    PRINT "Enter the sales in year"; I
    INPUT SalesInYear(I)
NEXT I
```

Besides being much cleaner, this new fragment runs faster. In a large program with lists with thousands of entries, the savings can be substantial.

DOS BASIC makes it easy to use short lists. If a list has no more than 11 items, you don't need a dimension statement. As soon as the interpreter sees there is a subscript on a variable that has not previously been dimensioned, it assigns 11 places numbered from 0 to 10 for that item. If what the computer sees first is ITEM$(30) with no dimension statement before then, you'll get an error message. For this reason, if for no other, it's a good idea to dimension all lists, whether they are short or long.

Suppose a teacher wanted to write a program to start analyzing the data from a test or group of tests. Because both the number of students and the number of tests might vary from class to class, it would be better to enter the class size and number of tests before dimensioning. This step can be done by using a variable instead of a constant in the dimension statement. Using a variable to determine the length of the list is called *dynamic dimensioning*. For a single exam, you could use the following QBasic fragment:

```
INPUT "How many students in this class";StuNumber
DIM Grades(StuNumber),StuNames$(StuNumber)
```

or to allow more than one test:

```
INPUT "How many students in this class";StuNumber
INPUT "How many tests";NumOfTests
DIM Grades(StuNumber,NumOfTests),StuNames$(StuNumber)
```

Now, the list will hold a row for each student and a column for each exam. Notice that, in both these lists, the same row number marks the name of the student and his or her grade for the exam.

When you dynamically dimension a list or array, the interpreter sets aside space at that time. If the program is large, it's possible that you won't have enough room. If the program is too large, you'll get the dreaded Out of memory error. At this point, the only cure for this error is to refer to Table 11-2 first. The maximal number is theoretical. In practice, the limits are somewhat less. For GW-BASIC, they are dramatically less.

The total number of characters that can occur as values of string variables in a QBasic program is the same as the size of a file you can edit at one time. Both are limited to 64K, or 65,536 characters.

Table 11-2 Maximum number of entries and memory requirements for the various types of lists.

List type	Maximum number of entries per list	Memory requirement per entry
Integer	32,768	2 bytes
Long integer	16,384	4 bytes
Single precision	16,384	4 bytes
Double precision	8,192	8 bytes
String	16,384	4 bytes

To bulletproof a program that you think is getting close to the limits on memory, use the various forms of the FRE command in QBasic:

FRE(−1)   Gives the amount of room for arrays in QBasic

FRE(*"string"*)   Gives the amount of room for strings. (You can use any string expression here. This command can cause a delay as old strings space is reclaimed.)

For example, suppose the average name uses 20 characters. Then, you might use these commands in something like the following QBasic fragment:

```
DO
  CLS
  INPUT "Number of names";NumOfNames
  IF NumOfNames*20 > FRE("string") THEN                    'A
    PRINT "Not enough room for that many names."
    BEEP
  ELSE
    DIM Name$(NumOfNames)
    EXIT LOOP                                              'B
  END IF
LOOP
```

A   If each name takes up an average 20 characters or bytes, this line checks that there's enough room in string space for all the names. Notice that I didn't check the amount of list space, FRE(−1), as perhaps I should have. It's worth keeping in mind that the space set aside for a list doesn't contain the actual characters. It contains only the information on where the compiler will find them.

B   I chose to use the EXIT LOOP command rather than set up a flag variable and use a LOOP UNTIL. I think it gives a cleaner feel to the program.

As your programs grow longer, the possibility that you'll run out of space increases. This possibility is a particular problem in GW-BASIC. DOS BASIC allows you to reclaim the space used by a dynamically dimensioned array. This process is done with the ERASE command. For example:

```
ERASE ERRAND$
```

would erase the ERRAND$ array and free up the space it occupied.

If an array was not dimensioned dynamically in QBasic, the ERASE command simply resets all the entries back to zero for numeric lists and to the null string for string lists. Arrays that are not dimensioned dynamically are called *static lists*. Using the ERASE command on a static list gives a fast method to zero out the entries.

On the other hand, you occasionally might want to dimension an array dynamically so that you can reclaim the space if necessary. You can dimension an array this way, for example, by saying:

```
Size = 3000
DIM E(Size)
```

rather than:

```
DIM E(3000)
```

This method sets up a dynamic and erasable array with 3000 single-precision numeric entries. Remember that all lists that do not use variables in the dimension statement are static.

Another advantage of dynamic dimensioning in QBasic is that, with a little work, you can enlarge the dimensions if you goofed. The command REDIM *listname* sets aside a larger space for the list given by the name. Unfortunately, it also throws away all the information that was there to begin with. To get around this problem, you have to:

1. Set up a temporary list for the old information
2. Copy the information to the temporary list
3. REDIM the original list
4. Recopy the information from the temporary list back again.

Obviously, this method is a lot of bother and can take a fair amount of time, but dynamic dimensioning does give you this option. This technique often is needed in error traps (see chapter 15).

The type of list usually is given by an explicit type identifier: DIM E%(3000) is an integer list and DIM E#(3000) is a list for double-precision numbers. Just like for variables, the default is single-precision. However, also just like for variables, you can change the default by using a DEFINT, DEFDBL, etc. For example, if a DEFINT A-Z is in affect, DIM E(3000) sets up a list of integers.

I said earlier that DOS BASIC assumes arrays dimensioned with constants are static. You can change this assumption in QBasic if you want to by using a metacommand. You've not seen these yet, but these are statements that don't affect your program; instead, they affect how the interpreter treats your program. The one you need is $DYNAMIC. All metacommands must begin with REM or the apostrophe. They are not executable statements. Put:

```
REM $DYNAMIC
```

or

```
' $DYNAMIC
```

as the first line of a program and the compiler will assume that all lists are dynamic, except arrays that were implicitly defined without dimensioning. This assumption continues unless the compiler later encounters another metacommand: $STATIC. This metacommand restores the normal way DOS BASIC handles lists. So, if you place the $DYNAMIC metacommand before any lists are dimensioned, all the space used for a list can be reclaimed by a judicious use of the ERASE command.

Arrays

You also can have variables with more than one subscript. They're called *arrays*. Just as lists of data lead to a single subscript, tables of data lead to double subscripts. For example, suppose you wanted to store a multiplication table in memory as a table. You could create this table with the following fragment:

```
DIM MultTable(12, 12)

FOR I = 1 TO 12
  FOR J = 1 TO 12
    MultTable(I, J) = I*J
  NEXT J
NEXT I
```

To compute the number of items in an array, you multiply the number of entries. The dimension statement here sets aside either 144 (12*12) entries (if an OPTION BASE 1 has been processed previously) or 169 (13*13) entries (if an OPTION BASE 1 has not been processed).

So, in this example, there are either 12 rows and 12 columns or 13 rows and 13 columns. In general, the number of entries in an array is either the product of the numbers or the product of one more than the individual numbers used in the dimension statement.

The convention is to refer to the first entry as giving the number of rows and the second the number of columns. So, following this convention, I would describe this fragment as filling an entire row, column by column before moving to the next row.

As you can see, in arrays, the extra space taken up by the zeroth row and zeroth column can dramatically increase the space requirements for your arrays. The total number of entries cannot exceed the numbers given on the previous table. Thus, QBasic's range feature is even more welcome. A statement like:

```
DIM Salary(1 TO 50, 1980 TO 1987)
```

sets aside 50 rows (numbered 1 through 50) and 8 columns (numbered 1980 through 1987). So, this Salary array has 400 entries.

DOS BASIC allows you up to eight dimensions. In theory, you could use:

```
DIM LargeArray%(2, 2, 2, 2, 2, 2, 2, 2)
```

which would set aside either 2^8 (256) or 3^8 (6561) entries, depending on whether an OPTION BASE 1 statement has been processed. However, I've never used more than four dimensions in a program. Even a three dimensional array is uncommon.

For a more serious example of a program using arrays, consider the following program that constructs a *magic square*. A magic square is square where all the rows, columns, and long diagonals add up to the same number. They were once thought to have magical properties. The most famous one is probably:

```
16   3   2  13
 5  10  11   8
 9   6   7  12
 4  15  14   1
```

This square was shown in Albert Dürer's **famous print called** *Melancholy*, which was engraved in 1514.

Many people have devised rules for constructing magic squares. The one I'll use is called Loubère's rule and only works for *odd order magic squares*—those with an odd number of rows and columns. Here's the method:

1. Place a one in the center of the first row.
2. The numbers now go into the square in order by moving up on the diagonal to the right.
3. If you go off the top, wrap to the corresponding place in the bottom row.
4. If you go off to the right end, wrap around to the left column.
5. If a square already is filled or the upper right corner is reached, move down one row and continue applying these rules.

Here's a 5×5 magic square constructed with this rule:

```
17  24   1   8  15
23   5   7  14  16
 4   6  13  20  22
10  12  19  21   3
11  18  25   2   9
```

The following QBasic program is a bit more clumsy than necessary. Once I show you how to use arrays with procedures, it can be cleaned up considerably. Here's the program:

```
DECLARE FUNCTION NxtRow% (X%)
DECLARE FUNCTION NxtCol% (X%)

'  CH11 \ P2.BAS
' Magic squares by Loubère's rule

DEFINT A-Z

DO
  CLS                                                       'A
  PRINT "Number of dimensions - must be odd - maximum of 15";
  INPUT NumOfDim
LOOP UNTIL NumOfDim MOD 2 = 1 AND NumOfDim < 16

Row = 0                                                     'B
 Col = NumOfDim \ 2
Limit = NumOfDim - 1
DIM Magic(Limit, Limit)
SIZE = NumOfDim * NumOfDim
Magic(Row, Col) = 1

FOR I = 2 TO SIZE

  IF Row = 0 AND Col = Limit THEN                           'C
    NewRow = 1
    NewCol = Col
  ELSE
    NewRow = Row - 1
    NewCol = Col + 1
    NewRow = NxtRow(NewRow)                                 'D
    NewCol = NxtCol(NewCol)
  END IF

  ' find empty slot
  DO UNTIL Magic(NewRow, NewCol) = 0                        'E
    NewRow = Row + 1
    NewCol = Col
  LOOP

  Row = NewRow
  Col = NewCol
  Magic(Row, Col) = I
```

```
NEXT I

' print completed square
CLS                                                          'F
StartCol = 40 - (.5 * 5 * NumOfDim)
StartRow = 13 - (.5 * NumOfDim)
LOCATE StartRow, StartCol

FOR I = 0 TO Limit
  FOR J = 0 TO Limit
    PRINT USING "#####"; Magic(I, J);
  NEXT J

  StartRow = StartRow + 1
  LOCATE StartRow, StartCol
NEXT I

END

FUNCTION NxtCol (X)                                          'G

  SHARED NumOfDim, Limit

  IF X > Limit THEN
    NxtCol = X - NumOfDim
  ELSE
    NxtCol = X
  END IF

END FUNCTION

FUNCTION NxtRow (X)                                          'H

  SHARED NumOfDim

  IF X < 0 THEN
    NxtRow = X + NumOfDim
  ELSE
    NxtRow = X
  END IF

END FUNCTION
```

A   This loop continues until the user enters an odd number (that's what
    NumOfDim MOD 2 = 1 means).
B   This block initializes the various blocks. For example, the number of
    entries, Size, in a 7×7 magic square is 49.

C This statement corresponds to the special case of the right upper corner.

D This block is the first rule: up and to the right. This row might be off the square; the functions NxtRow and NxtCol take care of this possibility (see comments G and H).

E This loop stops when the program gets to an unoccupied square.

F This block prints the square.

G You wrap around by subtracting the number of columns (to move to the left most column).

H You wrap around by adding the number of rows (to move to the bottom row).

As I said before, once you see how to combine arrays with procedures, this program can be made much cleaner.

Reading data

Getting information, or *data*, into a computer is not one of life's great joys. In the good old days, about 15 or 20 years ago, hundreds of people sat in a room, each of them facing a large noisy machine that punched holes in cards. You took those cards and put them in another noisy machine that read the punch cards and sent the information into the computer, to be run a few hours or days later. With microcomputers, programmers have thankfully put the punch card, or batch job, era behind them. Nonetheless, typing in hundreds of LET or INPUT statements is not my idea of fun. If the data doesn't change much, it's silly to have to re-enter it each time the program is run. Using INPUT statements means you'll have to retype the information each time. Lots of assignment statements can make even a simple program too long.

The way around this inconvenience is to build the data into the program. The statement that does this is called the DATA statement. To grab information from a DATA list, use the READ statement. For example, here's a QBasic fragment that starts to print the old song, *The 12 days of Christmas*:

```
' Using the READ DATA combination

DIM Days$(12),Gifts$(12)

FOR I = 1 TO 12
   READ Days$(I),Gifts$(I)
NEXT I

DATA "first", "a partridge in a pear tree"
DATA "second", "two turtle doves and"
```

DATA "third", "three French hens"

.
.
.

As soon as DOS BASIC sees a READ statement, it looks for a DATA statement with something to READ. The READ command takes input from the DATA statements in order, much like an INPUT statement works. In this program, on the first pass through the loop, DOS BASIC reads the word *first* and assigns it to Days$(1). Because of the comma, the program stops before the phrase. Similarly, it reads the phrase *a partridge in a pear tree* and assigns it to Gifts$(1). On the second pass, it fills up Days$(2) and Gifts$(2), and so on. The nested loop combined with the READ-DATA combination replaces 24 assignments statements.

To display the song, finish creating the DATA statements and add the following fragment:

```
FOR I = 1 TO 12
   FOR J = I TO 1 STEP −1

      PRINT "On the ";Days$(I);" day of Christmas, my true love gave"
      PRINT " to me ";Gifts$(J)

   NEXT J
NEXT I
```

Here, J runs backwards starting from the correct day, as it does in the song.

In a DATA statement, each entry is separated from the next by a comma; however, no comma follows the last entry. You can put as many items in a single DATA statement as will fit comfortably on a line. It's a good idea to place quotes around strings (as I did), although the quotes are really necessary only if the string has a comma or carriage return inside of it, because DOS BASIC uses these as separators. If you put in more DATA than a program needs, the compiler reads only what it needs. On the other hand, if you ask for more data than is contained in the DATA statements, you'll get an Out of DATA error message.

Essentially, what DOS BASIC does is keep an invisible pointer at the last item it read. Each time it reads another item, it moves the pointer forward. The DATA statements are read in the order they appear in the source code. All items in the first DATA statement are read, then what's contained in the next data statement, and so on.

Occasionally, you need to reset this pointer yourself. You reset it with the RESTORE command. A bare RESTORE command sets the pointer back to the beginning of the first DATA statement—all the information in all the DATA statements is available again. This command is especially useful when you want to dynamically dimension a list according to the number of items in a DATA list.

Read through the list twice. On the first pass through the list, have the program count the number of items until it encounters a flag (something like 1E32 or ZZZZ). Now, dynamically dimension the list using this count. Next, use the RESTORE command to reset the pointer back to the start. Finally, have the program reread the DATA.

The RESTORE command is useful; however, sometimes, it's overkill to go all the way back to the first DATA statement. You might not want to go back to square one; you want to go back to a specific place—a specific DATA statement. To go to a specific DATA statement, you need to use a label (use a line number in GW-BASIC). For example:

```
Titles:
    DATA "Foundation","I Robot","Nightfall"
    DATA "Gulf","Misfit","Citizen of the Galaxy"
    DATA "Flandry","Vault of Ages"

Authors:
    DATA "Asimov","Heinlein","Anderson"
```

The statement RESTORE Authors sets the pointer at the first item in the DATA list following the Authors label (to Asimov in this case). The statement RESTORE Titles sets the pointer at the string Foundation.

Using lists and arrays with procedures in QBasic

QBasic has an extraordinary facility to use list and arrays in procedures and functions. As you'll soon see, unlike languages like Pascal, it's easy to send any size list or array to a procedure. One obvious way is to make the list or array a shared variable.

For example, suppose you want to make a list (called ExOfList) and an array (called ExOfArray) shared variables in a function. The syntax for doing this is:

```
FUNCTION Example
    SHARED ExOfList( ),ExOfArray( )
```

where the empty parentheses tell the compiler that the variable stands for a whole list or array. Similarly:

```
SUB Example
    SHARED ExOfList( ),ExOfArray( )
```

You also can create a list or array that is local or static within a procedure by dimensioning it within the function or procedure:

```
FUNCTION NextExample
    SHARED ExOfList( ),ExOfArray( )
    ' LOCAL lists will be LocalList( ),LocalArray( )
    DIM LocalList(10 TO 20),LocalArray(4,3)
```

or

```
SUB SimpleExample
    SHARED ExOfList( ),ExOfArray( )
    'LOCAL lists will be LocalList( ), LocalArray( )
    DIM LocalList(10 TO 20),LocalArray(4,3)
```

One way to turn this feature to your advantage is to send a procedure a parameter that controls the dimension of the list or array. For example:

```
CALL LessSimpleExample(SizeOfList,NumOfRows,NumOfCols)
    'LOCAL lists will be LocalList( ),LocalArray( )
    DIM LocalList(SizeOfList),LocalArray(NumOfRows,NumOfCols)
```

Space for a local list or array automatically is reclaimed when the procedure or function call is finished; space for a static list or array is not. This feature lets you call a procedure or function that uses local lists or arrays repeatedly, without quickly running out of space. Although you can only use it from within the procedure or function, it's invisible to the rest of the program.

Although you can begin to take advantage of QBasic's power by a judicious use of local, shared, and static lists, to take full advantage of QBasic's power, you'll want to send a list or array as a parameter to the procedure. The advantages of sending a list or array in this manner are the same as those for using normal parameters instead of shared variables: they increase flexibility. To send an array parameter to a procedure or function, put the name of the array followed by a set of empty parentheses in the parameter list. For example, assume that Array$ is a two-dimensional string array and BigArray% is a three-dimensional array of integers. Then:

```
SUB Example(List#( ),Array$( ),BigArray%( ),X%)
```

would allow the Example procedure to use and change a list of double-precision variables, an array of strings, a three-dimensional array of integers, and a final integer variable. Note that, just as with variables, list and array parameters are placeholders; they have no independent existence. To call the procedure, you might use a fragment like this:

```
DIM PopChange#(50),CityState$(3,10),TotalPop%(2,2,2)
```

Now, the statement:

```
CALL Example(PopChange#( ),CityState$( ),TotalPop%( ),X1#)
```

would call this procedure by sending it the current location (passing by reference) of the three arrays and the integer variable. Just as before, because the compiler knows where the variable, list, or array is located, it can change the contents.

Suppose you wanted to write a function procedure that would take a list of numbers and return the maximum entry. Because you might want to find the maximum entry for many different lists, you decide to write a procedure, FUNCTION FindMaximum(List( ),Max), that follows the following outline:

1. Start at the top of the list
2. Each time an entry is bigger than the current Max, swap it
3. Continue until you finish the list

This kind of outline obviously calls for a FOR-NEXT loop. The problem with translating this outline to a program is knowing where the lists starts or ends. You could arrange for every list to have a flag at the end, but then you would have trouble combining this procedure with QBasic's range feature. You could use the trick of reserving one entry in the list for the number of items in the list.

QBasic makes this process easier with the commands LBOUND and UBOUND that are not part of GW-BASIC. LBOUND gives the lowest possible index and UBOUND the highest in a list. For example, you easily can translate the outline to:

```
FUNCTION FindMax(A( ),Max)

   ' LOCAL variables Start%,Finish%,I

   Start% = LBOUND(A)
   Finish% = UBOUND(A)

   Max = A(Start%)

   FOR I = Start% TO Finish%
      IF A(I) > Max THEN Max = A(I)
   NEXT I

   END SUB
```

When this procedure is finished, the new value of Max would be the largest entry on the list.

In general, the command LBOUND(*NameOfArray, I*) gives the lower bound for the *I*th dimension. (For a list, the 1 is optional, like in the previous example.) So:

```
DIM Test%(1 TO 5,6 TO 10,7 TO 12)
PRINT LBOUND(Test%,2)
```

gives a 6 and

```
PRINT UBOUND(Test%(3))
```

gives a 12.

Suppose you wanted to write a general procedure to copy one two-dimensional string array to another. The LBOUND and UBOUND commands allow you to copy lists or arrays with different ranges, provided the total number of rows and columns are the same. Subtract the LBOUND from the UBOUND for each dimension and see if they match.

It's hard to stress enough the flexibility that QBasic's method for handling list and arrays within procedures gives, especially when combined with the LBOUND and UBOUND commands. For example, you might have learned about matrices in your math or engineering courses. It is close to impossible to write a general matrix package in standard Pascal; it's almost trivial in QBasic.

I should mention that you cannot pass an array by value to a procedure; you can only pass by value a specific entry in the array. To pass a specific entry, give the entry. For example:

```
CALL Example(A( ),B(10))
```

would send a procedure a list named A and the value of the 10th entry in another list named B.

You might be wondering why you can't pass lists and arrays by value. It's because, as I mentioned before, when QBasic passes by value, it makes a local copy of the variable. As you can well imagine, making local copies of a list with 200,000 entries would quickly run you out of memory.

One last point, the LBOUND and UBOUND are not a cure-all. If part of the list or array hasn't yet been filled, they might not help, which is why the trick mentioned in the first section of this chapter is sometimes useful. It was invented for earlier BASICs that didn't have UBOUND and LBOUND.

Searching

Suppose a long list of names is stored in the computer's memory. Now, you want to find out if a certain name is on the list. This task can be done easily. Just write a program to compare the name you want with all the names on the list. Because a modern computer works fairly rapidly, this method is quite effective for short lists. However, if the list had 5000 names and already was in alphabetical order, this method would be a silly waste of time. If you are looking in a telephone book for a name beginning with *K*, you don't start at page one. You split the book roughly in half and proceed from there.

When the information on the list you're searching already is ordered, you can speed things up by an extension of this method. Each time, the program will look at a list that is only half the size of the previous list. This technique speeds things up almost beyond belief.

Here's an outline for a program to search through a list that already is in alphabetical order.

1. Divide the list in half.
2. Determine whether the entry at the halfway mark is before or after the name you're looking for.

3. If you have gone too far, look at the first half; if not, look at the second half.

4. Go back to step 1 as long as there are names left to look at.

Suppose your list had 5000 names. After doing step 4, you go back to step 1 with a list of 2500 names. If you do it again, you have only 1250 names, the third time only 625, and so on. By the 12th time, there would be only two names to look for. What I just described is called doing a *binary search*.

An extraordinary feature of binary search is that this method is almost as fast for large lists as for small. In particular, suppose you are searching through the New York City telephone directory (with roughly 10,000,000 entries) and you had to find out if someone's name was there. Just by following this outline (and not doing any estimating of where the letters are), you would find out if the name was in the list of names in no more than 25 applications of step 4.

The procedure is a bit tricky, so it's worth spending a bit of time on. Here's a first attempt in QBasic (in GW-BASIC, you'd have to rewrite this as a subroutine and replace the SELECT CASE with the IF-THEN):

```
DECLARE SUB BinarySearch (A$( ), Target$)

SUB BinarySearch (X$( ), Target$)

    ' LOCAL variables are: Low, High, Middle
    SHARED TargetPosition

    TargetPosition = 0                              'A
    Low = LBOUND(X$)
    High = UBOUND(X$)                               'B
    DO
        Middle = (Low + High) \ 2                   'C

        SELECT CASE X$(Middle)                      'D

        CASE IS = Target$
            TargetPosition = Middle
        CASE IS > Target$
            High = Middle - 1                       'E
        CASE IS < Target$
            Low = Middle + 1

    END SELECT

    LOOP UNTIL TargetPosition < > 0
    PRINT TargetPosition

END SUB
```

A   This line initializes the shared variable TargetPosition. At the end of the procedure, it will contain the position of the target. (You also could set up another parameter for this information. An even better idea would be to turn the whole thing into a function whose value was the location of the target.)

B   I'm using the UBOUND/LBOUND method of finding the limits. The method described earlier to store the number of entries in the list as the zeroth entry is not needed here because I'm assuming the whole list is ordered.

C   I'm using the integer division operator—list indices are always integral.

D   Because there are three possibilities in the search, it's a perfect candidate for the SELECT CASE command. (You also can use the IF-THEN-ELSEIF.)

E   If the entry in the middle position is too large, I know that I should look at the first half of the list. Because it can't be the middle entry (I've eliminated that in the first CASE), I can move the high index down by one.

Now, you get to the problem in this preliminary version of binary search. The loop stops only if TargetPosition has a nonzero value—if the program has found the entry. Suppose the entry wasn't on the list. The loop would never stop. I've set up an infinite loop.

How can you fix this module so that it stops when there are no more entries left to check? As usual, a concrete example that you can play computer with helps. Suppose you are down to a list that consists of two names (for example, in the 42nd and 43rd positions). The 42nd entry is too small and the 43rd entry is too large. What does this procedure do? The first time you're in this situation, the value of Middle is set to $(42+43) \setminus 2$ or 42. Because you're assuming the value in the 42nd position is too small, the value of Low is set to one more than Middle (i.e, 43). The value of Low and High now are the same. What happens next? Because both Low and High are the same, the value of Middle also is the same. Now, the entry in the middle position is too large, so the value of High shrinks by one. Now, it's 42—less than the value of Low. This value gives you one way to end the loop. Change the loop to read:

```
LOOP UNTIL TargetPosition < > 0 OR High < Low
```

There's another way to write this loop that some people find easier to understand. It depends on realizing that something special happens for small lists (for example, when the difference between High and Low is 1). Arrange to leave the loop when the list has a size of one and add a few lines to take care of this special case:

```
IF (High − Low) < = 1 THEN
  IF A$(High) = Target$ THEN TargetPosition = High
```

```
    ELSE
      IF A$(Low) = Target$ Then TargetPosition = Low
    END IF
```

Notice that both these possibilities take care of the case when there is only one, or even no entries, left in the list. As I mentioned in chapter 10, it's the boundary cases that often cause the most subtle bugs.

While I'm on the subject of bugs, how do you write a test module for a binary search module? Obviously, you need a long, ordered list. One way to test the module is to have the list consist of all possible two-letter strings:

AA, AB, AC....BA, BB...ZZ

There are 26^2 or 676 two-letter combinations (using three letter combinations allows a list of 26^3 or 17,576 entries).

You can use the following fragment to create this list:

```
DEFINT A-Z

DIM A$(1 TO 676)
Index = 1

FOR I = 65 TO 90
  FOR J = 65 TO 90
    A$(Index) = CHR$(I) + CHR$(J)
    Index = Index + 1
  NEXT J
NEXT I
```

Now, you can try the binary search module with various possibilities (for example, a two-letter string that is on the list and one that is not) or test it with the first entry and the last.

Sorting

Programmers like ordered lists just as people prefer alphabetized lists for dictionaries and telephone books. In both cases, this preference is because approximations to binary search techniques work so fast. Ordering, or *sorting*, data is one of the most common demands placed on a computer. Unfortunately, sorting also is one of the most time-consuming tasks a computer can be asked to do. Because of the time factor, computer scientists have developed literally hundreds of different ways to sort lists. It's impossible to say which is best in all possible circumstances. In this section, you'll see four methods. The first two are useful only for short lists. The third is often the method of choice, even for lists having thousands of entries. The last one is called a *bubble sort*; I'll discuss it only to condemn it. Although it seems to be the one that is most commonly given in elementary books, it has few redeeming features and is best forgotten.

Chapter 13 discusses three more sorting methods. Those three usually are better than even the fastest sort presented in this section; unfortunately, they are much more difficult to program.

When you sit down to write a program, it always is a good idea to ask yourself if there's anything you do in real life that's analogous to what you want the computer to do. For sorting lists, what comes to my mind is ordering playing card hands. As far as I can tell, there are two types of people. First, there are those who pick up all the cards at once and sort their hands by first finding the smallest card, then the next smallest and so on. The other kind are those who pick up one card at a time, scan what they already have sorted, then immediately place the new card in the correct place. (For what it's worth, computer scientists have proved that these two methods take roughly the same amount of time, with the second method usually being a tiny bit faster.)

Each of these methods translates into a way to sort lists. The first usually is called a *ripple sort*. An outline for it is:

1. Start with the first entry
2. Look at the remaining entries one by one. Whenever you find a smaller entry, swap it with the first entry
3. Shrink the list: start with the second entry and look at the remaining entries
4. Continue until the list is sorted

Notice that, if, for example, the list had 50 entries, you only have to do steps 2 through 4 48 times. By the time this procedure works its way to the last entry, enough switching has happened so that the last entry has to be the largest entry.

Here's a QBasic procedure:

```
DECLARE SUB RippleSort (A$( ))

DEFINT A-Z

SUB RippleSort (A$( ))

  'LOCAL Variables are:NumOfEntries%,NumOfTimes%,I%,J%
  NumOfEntries% = UBOUND(A$)                                      'A
  NumOfTimes% = NumOfEntries% – 1

  FOR I% = 1 TO NumOfTimes%
    FOR J% = I% + 1 TO NumOfEntries%
      IF A$(J%) < A$(I%) THEN SWAP A$(J%), A$(I%)
    NEXT J%
  NEXT I%

END SUB
```

A   I'm assuming the list starts from zero. An even more elegant idea is to make this procedure depend on two more parameters (for example, Low and High) and use these parameters to establish the bounds on the loops.

How do you write a module to test a sort? Well, you need a way of creating random lists of strings. Here's one way:

```
DEFINT A-Z

DIM B$(100)
RANDOMIZE TIMER

FOR I = 1 TO 100
   RndInt = INT(26*RND(1)) + 1
   B$(I) = CHR$(RndInt+ 65)
NEXT I
```

Now, CALL RippleSort(B$( )). Print out the list to make sure it's been sorted:

```
FOR I = 1 TO 100
   PRINT B$(I)
NEXT I
```

The second method, usually called an *insertion sort*, is no harder to program. In this sort, at every stage, you'll have an already sorted list. Look through the list, from the first entry to the last, until you find something smaller than the new entry. Unfortunately, unlike the case with playing cards, you have to move all the entries down by one to make room for the new entry. This requirement leads to a slight tweak that can improve the performance considerably and is easier to program. Instead of moving forwards, move backwards. Now, each time the comparison fails, move the old entry down by one. If you use this method, you'll be moving a hole along with you as you move through the list. When the comparison finally fails, you drop the new entry into the hole.

Here's the QBasic procedure:

```
DECLARE SUB RippleSort (A$( ))

DEFINT A-Z

SUB RippleSort (A$( ))
   'LOCAL Variables are: NumOfEntries%,I%,J%, Temp$

   NumOfEntries% = UBOUND(A$)                          'A

   IF NumOfEntries% < = 1 THEN EXIT SUB                'B

   FOR I% = 2 TO NumOfEntries%

      Temp$ = A$(I%)
```

```
        FOR J% = I% – 1 TO 1 STEP – 1
            IF Temp$ > = A$(J%) THEN EXIT FOR                    'C
            A$(J% + 1) = A$(J%)
        NEXT J%

        A$(J% + 1) = Temp$                                       'D

    NEXT I%

END SUB
```

A   As before, you might want to make this procedure depend on a Low and High parameter.

B   It's easier to eliminate the special case of the list having one entry here.

C   This loop moves entries forward until conditions are ripe for the EXIT FOR. The program exits the loop when it has located the position of the hole.

D   This statement fills the hole.

Because these methods follow the playing card analogy closely, they were not hard to program. Moreover, for small lists, they are reasonably fast. Sorting 100 strings using the insertion sort or ripple sort takes about $2^1/2$ seconds on a basic PC. Unfortunately, sorting 200 entries takes about 10 seconds. Both these types of sorts have the unfortunate property that doubling the list quadruples the time. Sorting a list of 3200 names would take about $3/4$ of an hour.

You can see that these are not the methods to use for lists much longer than 100 or so entries. You need to turn to a faster method. Now, you can see why a binary search is so nice: doubling the list only adds one step.

The first of these faster sorts that I want to show you was discovered by Donald Shell around 30 years ago. It's unusual because, while the procedure is simple and short, understanding what makes it work is not. This fact is partially because there is nothing that you do in real life that's analogous to a Shell sort and partially because it's a really neat idea. Another problem is that, even after you understand why it works, it's unclear why it's so much faster than the previous two methods.

To understand the Shell sort, you should ask yourself what the advantages and disadvantages are of the two previous sorting methods. One obvious disadvantage of a ripple sort is that, most of the time, the comparisons in the various loops are wasted. The disadvantage of a insertion sort is that, most of the time, it moves objects inefficiently. Even when the list is mostly sorted, you still have to move the entries one by one to make the hole. The big advantage of a ripple sort is that it moves objects efficiently. Once the smallest object gets to the top, it stays there.

In a sense then, insertion and ripple sorts are opposites. Shell decided to improve the insertion sort by moving the keys long distances, as is done in a ripple sort. Consider the following list of numbers to sort:

57, 3, 12, 9, 1, 7, 8, 2, 5,4, 97, 6

Suppose that, instead of comparing the first entry to the second, you compare it with the seventh and, instead of comparing the second with the third, you compare it with the eighth. In short, you cut up the list into six different lists. Now, use an insertion sort on these six smaller lists. After these sorts are done, you have six lists, each of which is sorted (although the whole list still is likely to not be). Merge the smaller lists and break the large list into three new lists. Do an insertion sort on these three smaller lists and merge them again. Now, the resulting list is very close to being sorted. A final sort finishes up the process. (The insertion sort is very efficient when it doesn't have much work to do).

If the numbers already are stored in a list, you never have to break up the list into smaller lists. Instead, you shift your point of view by concentrating on the different sublists. Also, because on the earlier passes the entries moved fairly long distances, when you're down to the final step, not many more moves are needed.

Here's a version of Shell sort:

```
DEFINT A-Z
SUB ShellSort (A$( ))

    ' LOCAL variables are :NumOfEntries%,Increm%, J%, Temp$

    NumOfEntries% = UBOUND(A$)
    Increm% = NumOfEntries% \ 2

    DO UNTIL Increm% < 1                                    'A

        FOR I% = Increm% + 1 TO NumOfEntries%

            Temp$ = A$(I%)

            FOR J% = I% – Increm% TO 1 STEP – Increm%       'B
                IF Temp$ > = A$(J%) THEN EXIT FOR
                A$(J% + Increm%) = A$(J%)
            NEXT J%

            A$(J% + Increm%) = Temp$

        NEXT I%

        Increm% = Increm% \ 2

    LOOP

END SUB
```

A   This loop divides the lists into smaller lists.

B   This loop does the insertion sort on the smaller lists. Because each entry on the smaller list differs from the next by the number given in the loop from comment A, the STEP command provides a way of working with the smaller lists.

What's amazing about the Shell sort is that it's so much faster than the ripple or insertion sorts. Surprisingly, nobody yet knows how much faster it will be in general. In any case, to sort a list of 3600 names will take only about 95 seconds using a Shell sort on a basic PC.

The speed of a Shell sort depends somewhat on the numbers you use to split the list into smaller ones. These numbers usually are called the *increments* (the 6, 3, and 1 that I used in the previous example). They should be chosen with care. (Because the increments get smaller on each pass, the Shell sort is sometimes known as the *diminishing increment sort*.) The ones I used earlier (half of the current size of the list) were Shell's original choice. You can obtain slightly better results with other increments. One of the simpler choices that gives better results is:

1, 4, 13, 40, 121, 364, 1093, 3280, 9841, etc.

Each number is arrived at by multiplying the preceding number by 3 and adding 1. You start with the largest increment that's smaller than the size of your list. So, a list with 10,000 entries would start with an increment of 9841. In any case, no one yet knows the best choice of increments. Try other sequences and see if you get better results.

The best series of increments I've heard about was developed by Robert Sedgewick of Princeton. It's 1, 8, 23, 77, 281, 1073, 4193, 16577, etc. or $4^{j+1} + 3 \times 2^j + 1$. For small lists, however, it's not worth the extra trouble.

How do you write a realistic test module for a sorting routine? Obviously, you want to create a long list of random strings. This list is not very difficult to create, but it sometimes can take longer than the sort. Use the following fragment to create a list of random four-letter strings for a Shell sort:

```
DIM Test$(1 TO 3600)

FOR I% = 1 TO 3600
  FOR J% = 1 TO 4
    Cnumber = INT(26*RND(1))
    TEST$(I%) = TEST$(I%) + CHR$(Cnumber + 65)
  NEXT J%
NEXT I%
```

and call the various sort routines. (Actually, don't call anything except the Shell sort or the routines that will be discussed in chapter 12.) Finally, add a routine to print out the transformed list. If the result is an ordered list, you might want to add a routine to time the various sorts.

If you devise your own sort or want to test these, I suggest also testing the sorts on the two boundary cases. For a sorting routine these cases usually are thought of as when the list is either already ordered or completely in reverse order.

Finally, I want to end this section by saying something about the bubble sort that seems to be so prevalent. The idea of the bubble sort is that you constantly compare an entry with the one below it. This way the smallest one bubbles to the top. The code for this kind of sort is almost trivial:

```
FOR I = 2 TO N
  FOR J = N TO I STEP −1
    IF A$(J − 1) > A$(J) THEN SWAP A$(J − 1), A$(J)
  NEXT J
NEXT I
```

The problem is that the bubble sort is the slowest sort of all. Because it has no redeeming virtues that I'm aware of, it should be replaced, at the very least, by the ripple sort (which is just as easy to program) for small lists and one of the faster sorts, such as the Shell sort, for longer lists.

Case study: the eight queen problem

As a final example program, consider how you would represent a chessboard and the squares that a queen could control from a given square as entries in an array. The chessboard might be an 8×8 array of integers:

```
DIM ChessBoard%(8,8)
```

A queen controls all the squares on the two diagonals as well as the horizontal and vertical directions.

Suppose the queen was placed as shown in Fig. 11-1. In this representation, you might place a non-zero integer (for example, an 81, because CHR$(81) = Q) in the 5,4 position. The queen controls all squares with either a 5 in the first position (same row) or a 4 in the second position (same column). What about the diagonal squares it controls? Looking at the figure above you can see that the diagonal squares are:

1,8	2,1	2,7
3,2	3,6	4,3
4,5	6,3	6,5
7,2	7,6	8,1
8,7		

Essentially, you both add and subtract one from the original square until you get to the end of the board, either a one or an eight. Another way to think about it is that,

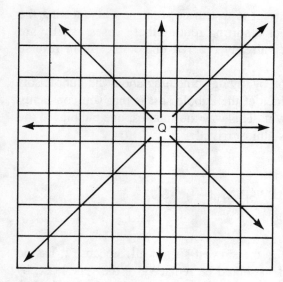

11-1 A queen controlling part of a board.

on the diagonals, either the sum of the numbers is 9 (5+4) or the difference is 1 (5−4).

The point of this discussion is that I want to show you a new method[1] for solving the classic eight queens problem. This method asks how you can place eight queens on a Chessboard so that no queen can take another. It usually is solved by a method called *backtracking*, which you'll see in the next chapter. Here, though, I want to present Undercoffer's method, which uses random numbers. His method is:

1. Choose a square at random and put a queen on it.
2. Mark all the squares controlled by the queen from step 1.
3. If there are any empty squares left (i.e., the number of squares marked is less than 64), repeat step 1.
4. If you have used up eight queens, print out a solution; otherwise, begin again from step 1.

Step 1 is easy. Use the random number generator and scale the results to get an integer between one and eight. For step 2, you can mark squares by starting with an array of zeros and replacing them with nonzero integers. Step 3 means keeping track of the number of queens and the total number of squares. Finally, step 4 means erasing the array and starting over again.

Here's the QBasic program:

```
' CH11 \ P3.BAS
' 8 Queens via random walk
```

---

[1]Undercoffer, Kurt J., *Pascal, Ada & Modula-2* 6, no. 2 (1987): 45-50.

```
DECLARE SUB FillBoard (X%, Y%)
DECLARE FUNCTION RandomInt% ( )

CLS
DEFINT A-Z
DIM ChessBoard(1 TO 8,1 TO 8)    ' or OPTION BASE 1

CONST Queen = 81              ' CHR$(82) = "Q"
CONST Star = 42              ' CHR$(42) = "*"
D = 1

RANDOMIZE TIMER

DO
    ERASE ChessBoard                                          'A
    SqCnt = 0
    QnCnt = 0

    DO WHILE SqCnt < 64                                       'B
        Row = RandomInt: C1 = RandomInt
        IF ChessBoard(Row, C1) = 0 THEN CALL FillBoard(Row, C1)
      LOOP

    LOCATE 25, 1: PRINT "Finished try#"; D;
    D = D + 1

LOOP UNTIL QnCnt = 8

' Print the chessboard

LOCATE 25, 1
BEEP
PRINT SPACE$(30); "Success on try#"; D – 1;

FOR I = 1 TO 8
    LOCATE (I + 7), 20
    FOR J = 1 TO 8
        PRINT CHR$(ChessBoard(I, J)); SPC(4);
    NEXT J
    PRINT
NEXT I

END

SUB FillBoard (X, Y)                                          'C

    SHARED ChessBoard( ), SqCnt, QnCnt

    ' Local variables are:Rw,C1,I,J
```

```
       FOR I = -1 TO 1
         FOR J = -1 TO 1

           Rw = X
           C1 = Y

           IF I < > 0 OR J < > 0 THEN

               DO WHILE Rw > 0 AND Rw < 9 AND C1 > 0 AND C1 < 9
                 IF ChessBoard(Rw, C1) = 0 THEN
                   ChessBoard(Rw, C1) = Star
                   SqCnt = SqCnt + 1
                 END IF

                 Rw = Rw + I
                 C1 = C1 + J
               LOOP

           END IF

         NEXT J
       NEXT I

       ChessBoard(X, Y) = Queen
       QnCnt = QnCnt + 1

   END SUB

   FUNCTION RandomInt
    RandomInt = INT(8 * RND(1)) + 1
   END FUNCTION
```

A   This large loop cycles until eight queens are placed. It starts with a
    fresh canvas for each attempt via the ERASE command and resets the
    count of the queens, QnCnt, and the squares, SqCnt.

B   This inner loop tries to place a single queen. First, it gets a random
    position on the board and places a queen there. If that square is not yet
    under the control of a previously placed queen (i.e., its value is 0), the
    loop calls the FillBoard procedure.

C   This procedure does the marking off of the squares. The work is done
    in the nested FOR-NEXT loops. Starting from the position of the
    queen (given by the parameters X and Y), it moves backwards and for-
    wards until it runs off the board. This task is the purpose of the DO-
    WHILE loop. The IF/THEN prevents writing over the queen's current
    position.

Records in QBasic

Remember one of the examples in this chapter using the teacher and the grades? I said:

DIM Grades(StuNumber,NumOfTests),StuNames$(StuNumber)

This statement is an example of a common phenomenon: parallel lists of numbers and strings with common row numbers to index related information.

Suppose you wanted to have a three-dimensional array for 100 employees in a company. The first column is to be for names, the second for salaries, and the third for social security numbers. This common situation can't be programmed except with a kludge (use the STR$ command). You probably would prefer to set up three parallel lists:

DIM Names$(100),SALARIES!(100),SocSec$(100)

One would be for the names, the second for salaries, and the third for social security numbers, which will be strings to include the dashes. Having set up the three list, you now would use the same pointer (i.e., the row number) to extract information from the three lists.

The way to avoid using multiple list in this example is to use a new structure called a *record*. Records are new to BASIC, although they are common in programming languages such as C or Pascal. Essentially, a record is a type of mixed variable that you create. It usually mixes different kinds of numbers and strings.

Before I can show you what a record is, I need to introduce a new type of string variable: strings of fixed length. These are set up with a variant on the DIM command. For example:

DIM ShortString AS STRING*10

This statement sets up a string variable even though it does not use the dollar sign identifier. However, this variable can only hold strings with a length of 10 characters or less. If you assign a longer string to ShortString (for example, ShortString = "antidisestablishment"), what you get is ShortString = "antidisest" (i.e., the string is truncated on the right). Similarly, if you assign a shorter string to ShortString (for example, ShortString = "a"), you still get a string of length 10. Fixed length strings are right-padded if necessary.

Now, back to records. While QBasic 4.5 will let you avoid maintaining parallel structures (like the employee list given earlier), there are costs. The major cost is that you must decide how long a name might be in the worst case. If you turn out to be wrong, the extra letters will be lost, because you can use only fixed length strings in records. A minor cost is that you might end up wasting a lot of space in memory if, for example, one name had a length of 39 characters and all the others were less than 20. QBasic would have to set aside space as if all the names were 39 characters long.

However, here's the first step, enter:

```
TYPE VitalInfo
    Name AS STRING * 50
    Salary AS LONG
    SocSecNumber AS STRING * 11
END TYPE
```

This fragment defines the type. From this point on, in the program, it's just as good a variable type for variables as single-precision or double-precision.

Now to set up a single variable of type VitalInfo say:

```
DIM YourName AS VitalInfo
```

This variant on the DIM command sets up a single mixed variable. Usually, you would say that YourName is a record variable of type VitalInfo. Now, you use a period to isolate the parts of this record:

```
YourName.Name = "Howard"
YourName.Salary = 100000
YourName.SocSecNumber = "036-78-9987"
```

You also can set up an array of these record variables:

```
DIM CompanyRecord(1 TO 75) AS VitalInfo
```

This statement sets up a list capable of holding 75 of these records. Now, you can fill this array with a loop:

```
FOR I = 1 TO 75
    PRINT "Name of";I;"'th employee"
    INPUT CompanyRecord(I).Name
    INPUT "Salary";CompanyRecord(I).Salary
    INPUT "Social security number";CompanyName.SocSecNumber
NEXT I
```

Note the periods for each component, or element, of the record.

You can even have a component of a record be a record itself. For example, you could make up a RecordOfSalary type to keep track of monthly earnings along with the previous year's salary:

```
TYPE RecordOfSalary
    SalInJan AS INTEGER
    SalInFeb AS INTEGER
    SalInMar AS INTEGER
    SalInApr AS INTEGER
    SalInMay AS INTEGER
    SalInJun AS INTEGER
```

```
        SalnJul AS INTEGER
        SalnAug AS INTEGER
        SalnSep AS INTEGER
        SalnOct AS INTEGER
        SalnNov AS INTEGER
        SalnDec AS INTEGER
        SalnPrevYear AS LONG
    END TYPE
```

Now, you can set up a record of records:

```
    TYPE    ExpandedVitalInfo
        Name AS STRING * 50
        Salary AS RecordOfSalary
        SocSecNumber AS STRING * 11
    END TYPE
```

Filling out all the information needed for a single record now is that much harder. Filling in the record RecordOfSalary for a single employee requires at least 13 lines of code, so filling in a record of type ExpandedVitalInfo requires at least 15. It also gets a little messy to refer to the information in ExpandedVitalInfo. You thread your way down by using more periods. After the following statement

```
    DIM GaryStats AS ExpandedVitalInfo
```

set up a variable of this new type. Use a statement like:

```
    PRINT GaryStats.Salary.SalnPrevYrSal
```

to display the information on the previous year's salary.

I should point out that your life is made a little bit easier because you can swap one record with another or assign one record to another if they are both of the same type. They need to have been dimensioned in exactly the same way. You cannot swap or assign a variable of type VitalInfo with or to a variable of type ExpandedVitalInfo.

You can have records as one of the parameters in functions or subprograms:

```
    SUB AnalyzeSalary(X AS ExpandedVitalInfo)
```

would be the first line of a procedure that allows and requires parameters of type ExpandedVitalInfo to be passed to it. Now, you can call it:

```
    CALL AnalyzeSalary(GaryStats)
```

to massage the salary information. You also can pass individual components of a record whenever they match the type of the parameter.

You're probably wondering why the fuss about records. After all, parallel lists are not that difficult to manage. They can even be an advantage, because you're not restricted to fixed length strings when using them. The short answer to this is that records are amazingly useful when dealing with random access files (see chapter 15).

The other reason is that new versions of QBasic will undoubtedly go further with records. Languages such as C and Pascal have shown that records can be the most important *data structure* in a program. A data structure is a way of organizing information. QBasic 2.0 might eliminate many of the hassles and problems involved in programming with records. In this hypothetical version of QBasic, records would be vital to good programming.

Finally, let me mention that you can use the DIM-AS to set up other variables. For example:

```
DIM A(1 TO 10) AS INTEGER
DIM A AS INTEGER
```

sets up an integer array A with a range of 1 to 10 and an integer variable A. This method is less confining then:

```
DEFINT A
DIM A(1 TO 10))
```

One peculiarity of using this form to specify the type of variables is that you now also must use the AS clause whenever you share the variable in a procedure or function. You must say:

```
SHARED A( ) AS INTEGER
```

rather than

```
SHARED A( )
```

Don't worry if you forget, the QBasic Smart Editor will remind you.

12
CHAPTER

Sight and SOUND

Most of this chapter is about graphics—picture drawing by a computer. With suitable hardware, the graphics power of PCs (as released by your programs) is astounding. Figure 12-1 is an example of what you can draw with a short (24 line) program from chapter 14. Admittedly, the program will be a bit subtle, but it still is only 24 lines.

I should mention that, although graphics usually are distinguished from text, this distinction isn't absolute. As you saw in chapter 3, you can combine the LOCATE command with the CHR$ command to draw primitive kinds of pictures. In any case, the graphics statements in this chapter are far more powerful. Assuming you have suitable hardware, they allow you to control each dot (usually called a *pixel* or *picture element*) that appears on the screen. If you take a magnifying glass to the screen, you can see that each character is made up of many of these pixels. Now, you potentially can control each one.

With certain expensive combinations of hardware and monitors, you can divide the screen into 307,200 dots and can color them with any one of 16 colors chosen from more than 200,000 possible colors.

You should be aware that the online help files for the graphics commands are particularly good. If you are using QBasic, it's worth consulting them.

Computer graphics is a subject where advanced mathematics must inevitably rear its head. However, this chapter uses almost none. Chapter 14, on the other hand, will use advanced mathematics. I do not go beyond trigonometry in any of the examples. If you wish, you can just skip the math and use the programs; the results are pretty spectacular.

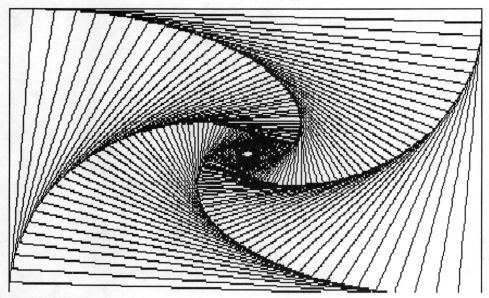

12-1 Nested squares.

Finally, I end this chapter with a short section on sound. Unfortunately, while DOS BASIC's commands for sounds effects, in theory, are quite powerful, in practice they are limited by the tinny speaker that most PCs have. For this reason, I don't think it's worth spending much time on them.

Getting started

You can use DOS BASIC's graphics statements only if you have the appropriate hardware, which usually is called a *graphics board*. All but the earliest versions of DOS BASIC allow you to control either a CGA (color graphics adapter), an EGA (enhanced graphics adaptor), or VGA. QBasic also supports the Hercules graphic card and ATT's proprietary graphics card. Unlike the CGA, EGA, and VGA, both of these graphics cards allow you to draw in only two colors—usually green and white. If you have a Hercules card, you have to run a program called HERC.COM before running QBasic. The setup program would detect whether this step is necessary.

Having the right kind of board is not enough, you also need the appropriate monitor. There are four kinds of monitors you can use: the monochrome monitors, which in spite of the name use two colors, and three kinds of color monitors. To get graphics from a monochrome monitor you usually use a Hercules or Hercules-compatible board; however, they will work with EGA and VGA boards as well. As for color monitors, the most primitive and the cheapest are called composite monitors. These usually are attached to a color graphics adaptor. (TV sets equipped with an RF modulator work like composite monitors.) Next up on the scale is the RGB monitor, which can be attached to all three types of boards. However, to take full advantage of a VGA card, you need a special analog monitor. These monitors are priced starting at around $300; the price quickly escalates from there. A 19-inch analog color monitor that can take full advantage of a 386SX VGA's graphics probably will cost more than the computer. (A good way to think about an analog monitor is that, with one, you can easily adjust the exact amount of red, blue, or green in the signal.)

Because the commands that control a color graphics adaptor will work with any color card, I'll use them to illustrate most of the ideas in this chapter. The results might be slightly different with the varying combinations of different hardware. EGA and VGA boards recognize some specialized commands that I'll describe in the section in this chapter on other screen modes.

I should point out that it's possible to write a program that determines what kind of graphics board a computer has and adjusts itself accordingly.

The two graphics modes that work with all graphic boards usually are called *medium resolution* and *high resolution*. Medium resolution allows up to four colors on the screen; high resolution allows only two. The tradeoff is that the pixels are much larger in medium resolution than in high-resolution mode. The pictures are much finer in the latter.

Medium resolution divides the screen into 64,000 tiny rectangles, which you can control individually. After the command SCREEN 1, which clears the screen and enables medium-resolution graphics, DOS BASIC sets aside a grid that's 320 columns across and 200 rows down. If you have a composite monitor, it's better to say SCREEN 1,0. (If you don't have a graphics adaptor, you'll get an error message.) You identify each of the blocks by means of its coordinates. Unlike with text (the LOCATE command), you place the column first, then the row. Moreover, both indices start with 0, so the columns are numbered from 0 to 319 and the rows from 0 to 199. For example:

(0,0)	is the top left corner
(319,0)	is the top right corner
(0,199)	is the bottom left corner
(319,199)	is the bottom right corner
(160,100)	is roughly in the center

If two points have the same first coordinate, they're on the same vertical line. If they have the same second coordinate, they're on the same horizontal line.

The next step is to decide what colors you want. Colors are selected via the COLOR command, which takes two integer arguments:

COLOR x,y

The first position specifies the background color. Here, you have the most leeway.

You can choose any one of 16 colors for the background. The colors are the same as for the text graphics described in chapter 4. If you have an EGA or VGA, the section in this chapter on other screen modes will show you how to change these colors.

Table 12-1 is a list of the colors and their corresponding arguments. See chapter 3, your manual, or QBasic's the online help for information on how these arguments are interpreted on monochrome monitors.

Table 12-1 Colors and their corresponding arguments.

0	Black	5	Magenta	10	Light green
1	Blue	6	Brown	11	Light cyan
2	Green	7	White	12	Light red
3	Cyan	8	Gray	13	Light magenta
4	Red	9	Light blue	14	Yellow
				15	High intensity white

Issuing a COLOR command blanks the screen and switches the background color, as the following fragment demonstrates:

```
SCREEN 1
LOCATE 1,1
PRINT "PRESS ANY KEY FOR THE NEXT COLOR"

FOR CNumber = 0 TO 15
    LOCATE 12,1
    PRINT "This is color #";CNumber
    COLOR CNumber,0
    SLEEP
NEXT CNumber
```

The second entry in the COLOR command is a bit less powerful. This argument controls what usually is called the *palette*. Just like an artist's palette holds the colors he or she has available, this second entry controls what colors you have available for the foreground. Also, because the COLOR command blanks the screen, you can't use this command to change colors in midstream, which is possible only when you have an EGA or VGA board (see the section on other screen modes). Moreover, unless you have an EGA or VGA card, you're stuck with the standard colors. The colors for Palette 0 (COLOR *bkgrnd*,1) are green, red, and brown. The colors for palette 1 (COLOR *bkgrnd*,2) are cyan, magenta, and white.

For example, the command COLOR 5,0 means that you have a magenta background and that green, red, and brown are the available foreground colors. Similarly, the command COLOR 14,1 gives you yellow background and cyan, magenta, and white are the foreground colors. The colors contained in a palette usually are called the *attributes* of that palette. Think of them as the tubes of color that you have available for that particular palette.

In summary, to get started in medium-resolution graphics, issue two commands:

```
SCREEN 1,0
COLOR background,palette number
```

Even integers in the second entry give palette zero; odd numbers give palette one.

When you are in medium-resolution mode (screen 1), you easily can mix text and graphics, although you normally do not have the higher-order ASCII characters available. However, versions of DOS after 3.1 have a means of accessing them—check the DOS manual. As before, you use the LOCATE command to position the text, but you have to convert the text rows and columns in the LOCATE command to pixel coordinates to figure out where the text will appear. To calculate in which graphics rows and columns the letters will appear, multiply the text row and column by 8 and reverse the positions. For example:

```
SCREEN 1
COLOR 3,0
LOCATE 5,9
PRINT "Hello world!"
```

This fragment puts you in medium resolution, turns the background color to cyan, and prints the message in brown letters starting at position (72,40). Text always appears in the third color of the current palette.

One important difference worth noting is that after a SCREEN 1 command, text appears twice as wide—40 characters to a line instead of 80. These wide characters also can be used in text mode by issuing the command WIDTH 40. The command WIDTH 80 brings things back to normal. Both WIDTH commands erase the screen, so you can't combine the two sizes.

The command SCREEN 0, which erases the screen and seems to bring you back to normal TEXT mode, doesn't quite return you to the normal text mode. It keeps the width at 40, so the number of characters is 40 per line. To completely return to normal, you need to issue two commands:

```
SCREEN 0
WIDTH 80
```

High-resolution graphics are turned on by the command SCREEN 2. This command erases the screen and sets up a grid 640 pixels across and 200 down. The row positions remain at 0 to 199; the column positions now are numbered 0 to 639. (If you have a Hercules card, screen 3 gives you a 720×348 grid; however, for simplicity, I'll assume your resolution is 640×200). Therefore:

(0,0)   remains the top left corner
(320,100)   is roughly the center
(639,199)   is the bottom right corner

In screens 2 and 3, you have only two colors available and text appears in its normal (WIDTH 80) size.

Notice that 80 (640/8) and 40 (320/8) are the widths in the two modes. This fact isn't a coincidence. In both cases, text is made by filling in pixels in an 8×8 grid—only the size of the pixels changes. The number of vertical pixels always is eight, so you don't double the 25 rows for text allowed per character (because the vertical resolution is 200 pixels in both modes).

Pixel control

Now, you know how the screen is divided in the two basic graphics modes. You turn a pixel on by using the following command:

PSET(x,y)

All you need to do is fill in the two entries: the first with the column and the second with the row. After DOS BASIC processes this statement, the pixel defined by that point lights up. Obviously, where that point is depends on whether you previously issued a SCREEN 1 or SCREEN 2 command. So, after a SCREEN 1 command:

PSET(319,0)

would turn on the top right corner pixel; however, after a SCREEN 2 command, the lit pixel would be in the center of the first row. The command:

PRESET(x,y)

turns off the point.

It's possible to PSET outside the limits of the screen. For example, you can issue PSET(2000,1000) and no error message will result. This command is an example of *clipping*, which more generally refers to DOS BASIC cutting off any part of an object that is off the screen. For example, the following simple QBasic program uses PSET to draw a straight line in medium-resolution mode down the center of the screen with a small amount of clipping:

```
'  CH12 \ P1.BAS
'  line via PSET with a bit of "clipping"

SCREEN 1
COLOR 1,0
```

```
FOR I = 0 TO 250
   PSET (160,I)
NEXT I

END
```

When this program ends, you still are in graphics mode. To leave it and return to normal text mode, issue the SCREEN 0: WIDTH 80 combination using the Immediate window or direct mode.

The color used by PSET usually is the one with the highest number in the current palette. (In high resolution, 0 is the background and 1 is the foreground.) You can change this setting in screen 1. For example, in the previous fragment, the command COLOR 0,1 means that you used blue as the background and the zeroth palette for the foreground colors. Thus, because yellow has the highest number in that palette, you'll get a yellow line. You choose among the colors in the current palette by a modification of the PSET command. For example, if you wanted to get a red line (color 2 of the current palette), use PSET(160,I),2 in the fragment. Color 1 would match the background color, so it would be invisible.

In general the PSET command looks like:

PSET(*column,row*),*color code*

Suppose you wanted to erase every other dot in this line. Although there are many ways to erase the dots, at this point, the simplest way is to notice that redrawing a point in the background color obviously erases the first line:

```
FOR I = 0 TO 199 STEP 2
   PSET (160,I), 0
NEXT I
```

Another possibility is a variant on the PSET command. PRESET(*x,y*) turns off the color of the pixel given in the parentheses.

Obviously, if you had to draw everything by plotting individual points, graphics programming would be too time-consuming. Instead, DOS BASIC comes with a rich supply of graphics commands, or *graphics primitives*, that allow you to plot such geometric figures as lines, boxes, circles, ellipses, or wedges with a single statement.

For example, the statement:

LINE (160,0) − (160,199)

draws the line given in the first fragment given earlier. More generally, the statement:

LINE (*StartColumn,StartRow*) − (*EndCol,EndRow*), *ColorCode*

gives you a line connecting the two points with the given coordinates, using the color specified by *ColorCode*. For example, the following QBasic program gives you a starburst by drawing random lines in random colors from the center of the screen:

```
'  CH12 \ P2.BAS
'  random lines in random colors

RANDOMIZE TIMER
SCREEN 1,0

FOR I = 1 TO 100
   Col = INT(320*RND(1))
   Row = INT(200*RND(1))
   CCode = 1 + INT(3*RND(1))
   LINE (160,100) - (Col,Row) , CCode
NEXT I

LOCATE 24,1
PRINT "Press any key to erase screen";
A$ = INPUT$(1)
SCREEN 0
WIDTH 80

END
```

The body of the FOR-NEXT loop calculates a random point and color code on each pass. Next, it draws a line from the center of the screen to that point. The block following the loop lets you get back to normal or use the SLEEP command. I usually have a block like this one at the end of any QBasic graphics program that I'm developing, because the ubiquitous Press any key to continue that appears when a DOS BASIC program finishes often wipes out a portion of the painted screen.

Suppose you wanted to draw a rocket ship as shown in Fig. 12-2. Because you can read off the coordinates from the diagram, it's easy, if a bit tedious, to write the program:

```
'  CH12 \ P3.BAS
'  A rocket ship

SCREEN 1

LINE (120, 199) – (200, 199)
LINE – (180, 179)
LINE – (180, 49)
LINE – (160, 19)
```

```
LINE – (140, 49)
LINE – (140, 179)
LINE – (120, 199)

SLEEP
END
```

Although it's possible to draw almost anything by outlining it using graph paper, obviously, as the object becomes more complicated, this method becomes less and less practical. One of the reasons why mathematics is needed for computer

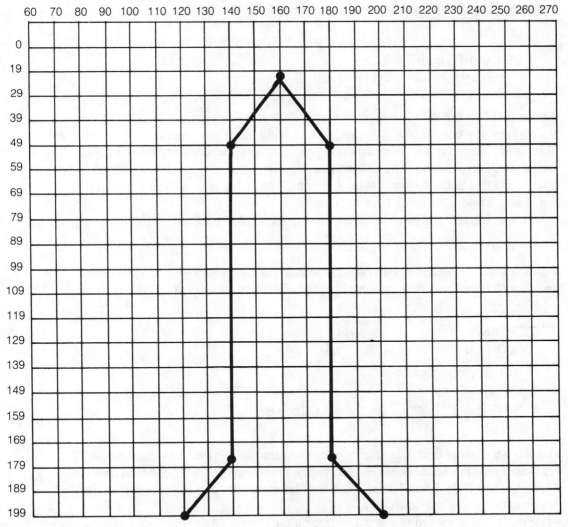

12-2 A rocket ship.

graphics is to give formulas for various complicated objects. The formulas then shorten the length of the program because they themselves incorporate an enormous amount of information. This method makes it practical to write the program, whereas writing a few thousand PSET statements obviously is not.

A modification of the LINE command lets you draw a rectangle. The statement:

```
LINE (FirstCol,FirstRow) – (SecCol,SecRow),CCode,B
```

draws a rectangle in the given color code (*CCode*) whose opposite corners are given by (*FirstCol,FirstRow*) and (*SecCol,SecRow*). For example, the following fragment gives you nested boxes on the high-resolution screen:

```
SCREEN 2

FOR I = 1 TO 65 STEP 5
   LINE (5*I,I) – (639 – 5*I,199 – I),,B
NEXT I
```

Notice that I've left off the color code but still kept the comma to separate out the B. Without this comma, DOS BASIC would think the B was the name of a variable rather than the box command. If you leave out the comma, DOS BASIC would think your asking for a line connecting (5*I,I) and (639 – 5*I,199 – I) with a color code that is the current value of B, which probably is 0, so you'd get nothing. I also could have put a 1 for the color code.

If you used BF rather than B, you would get a filled box, so:

```
LINE (FirstCol,FirstRow) – (SecCol,SecRow),CCode,BF
```

yields a solid rectangle whose opposite corners are given by (*FirstCol,FirstRow*) and (*SecCol,SecRow*). For example, change the fragment to read:

```
DEFINT A-Z
SCREEN 1
COLOR 0,0

FOR I = 1 TO 32 STEP 3
   CCode = I MOD 4
   LINE (5*I,I) – (320 – 5*I,199 – I),CCode,BF
NEXT I
```

and you get a rather dramatic nesting of colored frames. You get this result for two reasons. First, the MOD function lets you cycle through the color codes in order. Second, when DOS BASIC draws each smaller rectangle, it overdraws part of the previous one using the new color.

Suppose you wanted to place a square on the screen. Your first instinct might be to use 3.2 columns for each row in high resolution mode, because there are 640 columns and only 200 rows. This technique might work, but it probably won't because monitor screens are rarely square. You are likely to run into what usually is called the problem of aspect ratio. *Aspect ratio* is simply the ratio of the distance between two pixels in adjacent rows and columns. If the distance between each column is exactly the same as the distance between each row, the aspect ratio is one and you have the ideal situation. It's easy to draw a square because the fudge factor will be 3.2 columns per row in screen 2 and 1.6 in screen 1. If not, you have to calculate the fudge factor. The best way to do this calculation is to check your monitor with a little test program that I'll show you next.

A good bet on most monitors, however, is that the height of the screen is $3/4$ of the width. So, use 2.4 ($3.2 \times 3/4$) columns for each row in high resolution and 1.2 columns per row in medium resolution to get close to a perfect square.

Here's the QBasic version of the test program. Run it and keep track of when the rectangle appears squarest—that's the number of columns to use per row in high resolution. Use half that number in medium resolution.

```
'  CH12 \ P4.BAS
'  aspect ratio test

SCREEN 2

Aspect = 1.5

LOCATE 1,5
PRINT "This program demonstrates aspect ratios for the high";
PRINT " resolution"
PRINT "screen. It starts at 1.5 columns/row and moves by .1";
PRINT " increments"
PRINT "to 3 columns/row."

PRINT:PRINT "Press X to end, any other key to continue."
A$ = INPUT$(1)
CLS

DO Until Aspect > = 3 OR A$ = "X"
    LINE(150,50) − (150 + 100*Aspect,150),,BF
    LOCATE 24,1
    PRINT USING "This is aspect ratio #.#";Aspect;
    PRINT ". Press X to end, any other key to continue.";
    A$ = INPUT$(1)
    Aspect = Aspect + 0.1
LOOP

END
```

Although QBasic has many powerful tools to do animation, you now have the tools to simulate one kind of animation: a so-called drunkard's walk (or a random walk, as it's more technically called). All this term means is an object whose movements over time can be plotted. If it seems to move randomly, you have a random walk. To simulate a random walk, I'll put a tiny square in the middle of the screen and move it around, erasing the previous square each time. However, instead of moving the square a fixed amount, I'll have it move up and down and left and right randomly. As you'll see, the square will spend most of it's time in a narrow range around the center. Here's the QBasic version of this program:

```
'  CH12 \ P5.BAS
'  moving squares to imitate a 'random walk'

RANDOMIZE TIMER
SCREEN 1
COLOR 0
DEFINT A-Z
X = 160: Y = 100

FOR I = 0 TO 500

    XMove = 6*RND(1)
    YMove = 5*RND(1)

    IF RND(1) < .5 THEN X = X + XMOVE ELSE X = X – XMOVE          'A
    IF RND(1) < .5 THEN Y = Y + YMOVE ELSE Y = Y – YMOVE

    IF X < 0 OR X > 293 OR Y < 0 OR Y > 194 THEN
        '  DO NOTHING
    ELSE
        LINE (X,Y) – (X + 6,Y + 5),2,BF
        LINE (X,Y) – (X + 6,Y + 5),0,BF                          'B
    END IF

NEXT I

LOCATE 24,1
PRINT "Press any key to return to text mode";
A$ = INPUT$(1)
SCREEN 0
WIDTH 80

END
```

A   This line gives the random motion. The box moves up or down and left or right depending on whether the random number generator delivers a number less than 0.5 or not.

B   By redrawing the rectangle in the background color, it's erased, giving the animation. If you remove this line, the animation is lost, but it's replaced by a visible trace of where the box has been. Change the ELSE clause to read:

```
CCode = 1 + 3*RND(1)
LINE (X,Y) – (X + 6,Y + 5),CCode,BF
```

and the results usually are a quite attractive random pattern.

DOS BASIC keeps track of where it stopped plotting. This feature usually is called the *last point referenced* (LPR). If you are continuing a line from the last point referenced, DOS BASIC allows you to omit it in the LINE command. For example:

```
LINE – (160,90)
```

draws a line from the last point referenced to the point with coordinates 160,90. When you start any graphics mode with a SCREEN command, the last point referenced is the center of the screen. Moreover, the screen clears and the default color is white. After a LINE command, the last point referenced is the endpoint of the line—the second coordinate pair.

Up to now, I've been using *absolute coordinates*. Each point is associated with a unique row and column. It occasionally is useful to use *relative coordinates*, where each point is defined by how far it is away from the last point referenced. For example, if you say PSET(12,100) or PRESET(12,100) (which makes 12,100 the last point referenced), you can say:

```
PSET STEP(50,10)
```

and you will have turned on the point in column 62 (50+12) and row 110 (10+100). In general, when DOS BASIC sees the command STEP (x,y) in a graphics command, it uses the point whose coordinates are x units to the right or left and y units up or down from the last point referenced, depending on whether x and y are positive or not.

Circles, ellipses, and pie charts

Normally, to describe a circle in DOS BASIC, you give its center and radius. For example, after a SCREEN 1 command:

```
CIRCLE (160,100), 60
```

draws a circle of radius 60 in the third color of the current palette. The last point referenced after a CIRCLE command is always the center of the circle, or (160,100) in this example. On the other hand:

```
CIRCLE (160,100),60,CCode
```

would draw a circle of radius 60 in the color code indicated here by the variable CCode. Here's a QBasic sample program that shows off this version of the circle command:

```
'  CH12 \ P6.BAS
'  nested circles

DEFINT A-Z
SCREEN 1
COLOR 1,1

FOR I = 59 TO 259 STEP 4
    CCode = 1 + (I MOD 3)
    CIRCLE (I,100),60,CCode
NEXT I

SLEEP
SCREEN 0
WIDTH 80
END
```

These circles are a bit jagged because the resolution in screen 1 is minimal. If you don't mind the loss of color, you can smooth them up considerably by using high-resolution (screen 2) graphics.

You might be wondering what the radius is exactly. Is it 60 columns or 60 rows or both 60 columns and 60 rows as a mathematical radius would be? It turns out that the CIRCLE command usually counts pixels by columns to determine the radius. It then scales the number of rows by dividing by 1.2. So, a circle of width 60 would take 60 columns and only 50 rows in medium resolution mode. In high resolution, the computer divides the number of columns by 2.4 to get the number of rows. So, the CIRCLE commands in this program had DOS BASIC plot what it hopes will be a circle by assuming that your monitor has the 4:3 width to height ratio discussed earlier. Obviously, if you have a monitor that has a different aspect ratio, you must override DOS BASIC's assumption. You can override this assumption by using a variant on the CIRCLE command that you'll see shortly.

You might have seen pie charts used to display data. DOS BASIC sets up a pie chart with a modification of the circle command. First, you need some terminology. A *sector* is a pie-shaped region of a circle; an *arc* is the outer boundary of a sector (see Fig. 12-3).

To draw a sector or arc, you have to tell DOS BASIC what angle to start at and at which angle to finish. This information is given in radian measure, which you might have seen in school and is used in the trigonometric functions in DOS BASIC. Radian measure isn't very difficult. It measures angles by what percentage of the circumference of a circle with a radius of one that it gives. All the way around the circle is 2π radians, because 2π is the length of the circumference of

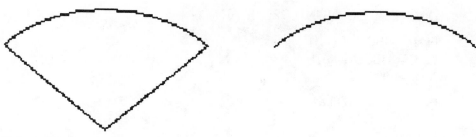

12-3 A sector versus an arc.

this circle. So, 360° is approximately 6.29 radians; ¹/2 a circle is π radians, or 180°; ¹/4 circle is π/2 radians, or 90°; and so on. To go from degrees to radians, multiply by π/180; to go back, multiply by ¹⁸⁰/π. In any case, the statement:

```
CIRCLE (XRad,Yrad),radius,CCode,StartAngle,EndAngle
```

draws an arc of the circle starting at the angle indicated in radians by *StartAngle* and ending at *EndAngle*. To get a sector, use negative signs. So, assuming that you've set up a variable called Pie, which is equal to 3.14159, then:

```
CIRCLE (160,100),60,,Pie/4,Pie/2
```

gives you an arc. The following command:

```
CIRCLE (160,100),60,, – Pie/4, – Pie/2
```

gives you a sector.

There are a few peculiarities of these commands that I should mention. First, although mathematics allows negative angles, DOS BASIC does not. The negative sign only serves to indicate that the program should draw a sector rather than an arc. Second, if you want your arc to start with a vertical line pointed due east (i.e., 0° or 0 radians), you shouldn't use – 0 for the *StartAngle* or *EndAngle*. Instead, use –2π. The final peculiarity is that angles in the CIRCLE command can have only values between –2π and 2π.

Suppose you wanted to write a general pie-making program. By that, I mean a program that takes a bunch of numbers that are stored in an array and sets up a pie chart using the numbers. Essentially, what you need to do is to determine what percentage of the total each positive number is and set up an arc using that percentage. Here's the QBasic procedure:

```
SUB MakePie( A(),SizeOfCircle)
    ' This procedure takes an array of positive entries and
    ' creates a pie chart using proportions determined by the
    ' array.
    ' LOCAL variables: I,First,Last,Total,StartAngle,EndAngle

    SHARED TwoPie          'TwoPie should be 6.28...
```

```
DIM I, First, Last AS INTEGER '8*ATN(1)

First = LBOUND(A,1)
Last = UBOUND(A,1)
Total = 0

FOR I = First TO Last
   Total = Total + A(I)
NEXT I

SCREEN 2

StartAngle = - TwoPie

FOR I = First TO Last
   EndAngle = ((A(I)/Total)*TwoPie) + StartAngle                    'A
   CIRCLE (320,100),SizeOfCircle,1,StartAngle,EndAngle
   StartAngle = EndAngle
NEXT I

END SUB
```

A   This line is the key. A(I)/Total gives what fraction of the total that a par-
    ticular entry is. Multiplying by TwoPie gives the radian equivalent.
    Because StartAngle is -2π, adding this angle gives the necessary neg-
    ative number for the size of the sector, starting due east and going
    counterclockwise.

You can test this procedure by simply creating some random arrays of random
sizes with random positive entries and call the procedure. (This procedure is a
little hard to convert to GW-BASIC. What you have to do is write a subroutine and
somehow keep track of the size of the list by using the zeroth entry.)

The CIRCLE command allows you to adjust the aspect ratio by adding one
more option:

```
CIRCLE [STEP] (XCenter,YCenter),radius,,,,aspect
```

The four commas must be there even if you are not using the color code and angle
options that you saw earlier. STEP is optional. This version of the CIRCLE command lets you change the default ratio of columns to rows. It really is an ellipse
command.

If the aspect ratio is less than one, the radius is taken in the column direction
and the ellipse is stretched in the horizontal direction. If the aspect ratio is greater
than one, the radius is taken in the row direction and the ellipse is stretched in the
vertical. Here's a QBasic program that demonstrates this principle:

```
' CH12 \ P7.BAS
' Aspect ratio test for ellipses
```

```
SCREEN 2
PRINT "Press any key to continue"
SLEEP

FOR I = 0.1 TO 2 STEP 0.1
    CIRCLE (320, 100),75,,,,I
    LOCATE 24, 10
    PRINT "This is aspect ratio"; I;
    PRINT " Press any key to continue";
    SLEEP
    CLS
NEXT I

SLEEP

END
```

Although this program stops when the aspect ratio reaches 2, you could continue making it bigger. As the aspect ratio gets larger, the ellipses get closer and closer to a vertical line.

You also can fill in enclosed areas using the PAINT command. The command:

PAINT [STEP] x,y,color,bordercolor

begins filling in the area and stops whenever it gets to a pixel of the color given by *bordercolor*. If you leave this parameter out, DOS BASIC stops painting when it encounters a pixel whose color is that of the paint command itself (the third entry).

How the paint command actually will work in practice is a bit subtle, but a good analogy to keep in mind is a spreading paint slick. A slick will stop whenever it hits a boundary point. On the other hand, it could continue forever if there's a hole in the boundary, not matter how small. The following two fragments show this principle. First, you can paint a circle:

```
SCREEN 1
CIRCLE (160,100),75
PAINT (160,100)
```

This fragment gives you a white circle. Now, insert a PRESET command to turn one pixel off:

```
SCREEN 1
CIRCLE (160,100),75
PRESET (235,100)
PAINT (160,100)
```

and rerun the fragment. What you'll see is the whole screen gradually turning white. The moral is to make sure your boundaries are solid.

I should point out that the whole concept of a boundary is a subtle one in mathematics as is finding an inside point. In this case, the only points on the boundary that are easy to calculate are the ones on the horizontal.

The DRAW command

The rocket ship program was short but tedious. The DRAW command gives you a much more powerful way to create any graphics figure that you can sketch. Essentially, the DRAW command gives you control of a pen that you move and lift as needed. Like using a pen, it's hard to draw curves. Moreover, once an object is drawn, you can store it, rotate it, scale it, or move it with a single command.

For example, the command DRAW "U10" draws a 10 pixel line directly up from the last point referenced. In general, the DRAW command uses certain combinations of command strings and numerals. Here are a few more of these command strings:

U   Up
D   Down
L   Left
R   Right
E   Diagonally up and to the right
H   Diagonally up and to the left
F   Diagonally down and to the right
G   Diagonally down and to the left

These commands alone are enough to let you imitate the famous Etch-A-Sketch toy.

For another example, the following fragment redraws the rocket ship given before. First, make (120,199) the last point referenced:

PSET (120,199)

There are other ways to do that part. Now, enter:

DRAW "R80 H20 U100 H20 G20 D100 G20"

This command moves the pen 80 pixels to the right, up to the left 20 pixels, straight up 100 pixels, etc. Here, as in any DRAW statement, the spaces are there to improve readability; DOS BASIC doesn't care.

However, you can do much more. Set up a string:

RocketShip$ = "R80 H20 U100 H20 G20 D100 G20"

Now, to have two rocket ships on the screen, use the following fragment:

```
PSET (50,199)              'set LPR
Draw RocketShip$
PSET (200,199)             'reset LPR
Draw RocketShip$
```

Most of the power of the DRAW command comes after you've set up string variables that will draw the figures that you're interested in. You can add commands before you issue a DRAW command (or add them inside a DRAW command) that scale, rotate, change color, or paint the object. For example:

```
DRAW "Snumber"
```

Enlarges the object by a factor given by the value of *number* divided by four.

A command like DRAW "S4" gives you the size indicated in the original string. The number must be between 1 and 255. Later you will see a way to incorporate a numeric variable.

Scaling easily can lead to clipping your image. A command like DRAW "S64" enlarges your figure by a factor of 16. Few figures will fit on the screen at this scale.

For an example of scaling, try the following fragment:

```
SCREEN 1
PSET (20,199)
DRAW "S1"
Draw Rocket$
```

Now, try the following QBasic program:

```
'  CH12 \ P8.BAS
'  An armada

CLS
Rocket$ = "R80 H20 U100 H20 G20 D100 G20"
SCREEN 1

LOCATE 1, 10
PRINT "Buck Rogers redeux"

FOR I = 1 TO 4

    SCALE$ = "S" + STR$(I)                                    'A
    DRAW SCALE$
    NewPos = NewPos + 5 + (20 * I)                            'B
    PSET (NewPos, 199)
    DRAW Rocket$

NEXT I

SLEEP

END
```

A   This statement is the most interesting line. Although there are other ways to incorporate numeric variables into a DRAW command, this way is by far the simplest. Just change the numeric variable using STR$ and concatenate with a plus sign.

B   The position of the next rocket has to take into account the size of the rocket. Because scale 1 is one-quarter size, S2 half size, etc., the rockets would be 20, 40, 60, and 80 pixels across.

Now, let's go back to the analogy of a pen plotting. The prefix command B lifts the pen. So, a command like:

```
DRAW "BU10"
```

moves the last point referenced 10 points up but does no plotting. The command:

```
DRAW "M x,y"
```

moves to the point x,y. If the pen is down, this command has the same effect as LINE − (x,y). For example, when the pen is down, the command DRAW "M +x,+y" would work like LINE − STEP (x,y) A plus or minus sign in the M command means to use relative coordinates.

On the other hand, DRAW "BM x,y" is a rapid way to move the last point referenced without plotting the point x,y. For example, you could use it to remove the PSET commands from the previous program.

The prefix N allows you to plot without changing the last point referenced. DRAW "ND10" draws a line 10 pixels long but doesn't change the LPR.

Suppose you wanted to make the rocket ship move. One way to animate it would be to:

1. Draw Rocket$
2. Change to the background color and wait a bit
3. Draw Rocket$ again
4. Change the LPR
5. Redraw the rocket

The command string to set the drawing color is C. Here's a QBasic program that moves the rocket (the conversion of the outline is complicated by the fact that a statement like SLEEP.1 isn't possible yet in QBasic):

```
'  CH12 \ P9.BAS
'  another way to animate

DECLARE SUB Delay (x!)

SCREEN 1
Rocket$ = "R80 H20 U100 H20 G20 D100 G20"

FOR I = 199 TO 50 STEP − 10
```

```
        Row$ = STR$(I)
        DRAW "S1"
        DRAW "BM" + "140" + "," + Row$                          'A
        DRAW Rocket$
        CALL Delay(0.1)
        DRAW "C0"
        DRAW Rocket$
        DRAW "C3"
    NEXT I

SUB Delay (x!)

    StartTime = TIMER

    DO UNTIL TIMER – StartTime > = x
    LOOP

END SUB
```

A   This line again creates a string using concatenation.

The DRAW command also lets you rotate a figure a certain number of degrees (not radians). The prefix TA followed by the number of degrees rotates the figure to be plotted. For example:

```
DRAW "BM 100,160"
DRAW "TA 45"
DRAW Rocket$
```

gives you the original sized rocket at a 45° angle (counterclockwise).

Finally, the command DRAW "P x,y" works exactly like the command PAINT (x,y), using whatever color has been set by the previous C command.

Other screen modes:
some powers of EGA and VGA cards

EGA and VGA cards give you enormous powers. The help files that explain how to control them are about 20 pages long, so they're a bit intimidating. What I want to do in this section is to give you an introduction. Hopefully, after reading the section the help files won't be quite so intimidating.

So far, you've seen SCREENS 1 and 2. As I mentioned, SCREEN 3 for Hercules cards works like SCREEN 2, except the resolution is higher. The following sections briefly explain what the other screen modes can do.

SCREEN 4   The command is available on ATT and Olivetti computers and Q-Basic only. It is given in the help file (I haven't got one of those machines to check out what follows). In this mode, you have a 640×400 graphics; text is 80 characters per line. You can access 16 colors through the COLOR statement; however, background is always black.

SCREEN 7 This command requires EGA or VGA graphics. It supports 320×200 graphics. Text is 40 characters per line, with 25 lines. You can choose from 16 foreground colors (any of 16 attributes) in a single palette with 16 background colors.

SCREEN 8 This command requires EGA or VGA graphics. It supports 640×200 graphics. Text is 80 characters per line, with 25 lines. You can choose 16 colors for any of 16 attributes in a single palette with 16 background colors.

SCREEN 9 This command requires EGA or VGA graphics. It supports 640×350 graphics. Text is 80 characters per line for either 25 or 43 lines. Depending on the memory on your graphics card, you can choose either 4 or 16 colors from 64 different colors for the foreground and 64 colors for the background.

SCREEN 10 This command requires EGA or VGA graphics and is for use with a monochrome monitor only. It supports 640×350 graphics. Text is 80 characters per line for either 25 or 43 lines.

SCREEN 11 This command requires VGA graphics or PS2/25s and 30s with MCGA (the semi-VGA). It supports 640×480 and 80 characters per line for either 30 or 60 lines. Two foreground colors can be chosen from among 262,144 (256K) colors.

SCREEN 12 This command works only on VGA graphics. It supports 640×480 graphics, with 80 characters per line for either 30 or 60 lines. This time, there will be 16 foreground colors chosen from the same 262,144 colors as in screen 11.

SCREEN 13 This command requires VGA graphics or the semi-VGA of a PS2/ 30. It supports 320×200 resolution. Text is 40 characters for only 25 lines. This screen allows up to 256 foreground colors to be chosen from the same 262,144 colors.

Whenever you are allowed more than 25 lines, the command WIDTH is used to change the number of lines. For example, WIDTH ,43 sets the number of lines to 43 after a SCREEN 10 command.

Suppose for a second that you are in SCREEN 1. Recall that in SCREEN 1, you had two palettes each with four fixed colors. As I said earlier, these colors usually are called *attributes*. Therefore, the numbers used in coloring pixels via any graphics command are called *attribute numbers*.

Now, suppose you have an EGA or VGA card and QBasic or version 3.2 or later of GW-BASIC. Then, you can change these previously fixed colors—change the colors assigned to the different attribute numbers. For example, the command:

PALETTE 1,14

would change the color in attribute one to the color with code 14, which happens to be yellow. The 16 colors that you can use to replace the default ones are exactly those for the background colors that were given in Table 12-1. A PALETTE command with no other entries restores the default colors.

In general, the PALETTE command chooses the colors for any of these modes by assigning a color to an attribute. The number of attributes depends on the screen mode. Then, attributes are used in commands (like DRAW "Cx", LINE, and CIRCLE) to draw objects. For example, the command:

LINE (x1,y1) − (x2,y2),attribute,[B[F]]

would give you a line, box, or filled box in the color specified by the current value of *attribute*.

Moreover, the PALETTE command will change the screen instantaneously. For example, if a part of the screen appears in attribute 2 and you were allowed 64 colors, the command PALETTE 2,53 would recolor that part of the screen in the 53rd color. Because there are 15 attributes possible in text mode when you have an EGA or VGA card, you also can use the PALETTE command to change the colors for text (screen 0) as well.

One place to show off the PALETTE command is in screen 9. In this mode, if you have enough memory on your graphics board, you can have 16 colors on the screen at any one time—chosen from the 64 background colors.

For the following QBasic example program, recall that text appears in the highest color in a given palette and the background is in the lowest color of the palette. Here's a program that shows off changing the text colors using the PAL ETTE command:

```
'  CH12 \ P10.BAS
'  A demonstration of the PALETTE command in SCREEN 9

DEFINT A-Z
SCREEN 9
FOR ColorNumber = 0 TO 63
    PALETTE 0, ColorNumber                                    'A
    CLS
    TextColor = (ColorNumber + 1) MOD 64
    PALETTE 15, TextColor                                     'B

    LOCATE 1, 1
    PRINT "The background color is"; ColorNumber;
    PRINT "while the text appears in color number"; TextColor
    SLEEP 2
NEXT ColorNumber

END
```

A   Because the PALETTE command works instantaneously, this line changes the background color on each pass.

B   As I mentioned, text appears in the highest color of the palette. The program is always using the next highest numbered color. (The MOD command is just to wrap around when the program gets to 64.)

A more dramatic demonstration would be to change all the colors in a palette simultaneously. This action is done using the PALETTE USING statement. The command:

PALETTE USING *array*

(where *array* is an array of integers or long integers) changes the colors in the palette by using the integers or long integers stored in the array for the color attributes. You must dimension the array to have at least as many entries as there are attributes. For example, suppose you have:

```
DIM A%(0 TO 31)
A%(0) = 12
A%(1) = 15
A%(2) = 37
    .
    .
```

PALETTE USING A would change the first attribute to color number 12, the second to color number 15, and so on. If an entry in the array is −1, the attribute stays its original color. Any other negative entry in A, or one that is too large, would give an error message.

I dimensioned this list at 31, or 32 entries, to show off an optional feature of PALETTE USING. For example, you could say:

PALETTE USING A(16)

Now, the colors would be taken starting from the 16th entry and going to the 31st entry. The general form is:

PALETTE USING *arrayname(index)*

where *index* determines where to start. You must have dimensioned the array so that there's enough room starting from the index to fill all the attributes.

Here's a QBasic program that changes all 16 colors in screen 9's palette simultaneously. Because you can only displace 16 colors at any one time, it shows them off in four groups of 16 colors each:

```
DECLARE SUB Demo (A%(), I%)

' CH12 \ P11.BAS
' A demonstration of the PALETTE USING command in SCREEN 9
```

```
DEFINT A-Z
DIM Attrib(0 TO 63)

SCREEN 9

FOR I = 0 TO 3

    FOR J = 0 TO 15
        Attrib((16 * I) + J) = (16 * I) + J                          'A
    NEXT J

    CALL Demo(Attrib(), I)

NEXT I

END

' This SUB demonstrates the PALETTE USING command

SUB Demo (A(), J)

    ' LOCAL Variable Count

    CLS

    PALETTE USING A(16 * J)                                          'B

    FOR Count = 0 TO 14                                              'C
        LINE (0, 22 * Count) - (640, (22 * Count) + 21), Count, BF
    NEXT Count

    LINE (0, 330) - (640, 350), 15, BF

    LOCATE 1, 10
    PRINT "This shows off colors "; 16 * J; " to"; (16 * J) + 15;
    PRINT " Press any key to continue.";
    I$ = INPUT$(1)

END SUB
```

A   This loop fills an array with the integers from 0 to 63 in groups of four (indexed by I). I can the use the counter I in the call to the subprogram.

B   This line moves the starting index along for the PALETTE command. On the first call, it starts with 0; at the second, with 16; and so on.

C   This loop draws colored boxes 22 lines wide (except for the last box, which is only twenty lines wide).

Because the PALETTE USING A() command works instantaneously, I really didn't need to write the program this way. Do you see how it might be changed?

I mentioned that you might need a long integer array for the PALETTE USING command because, in screens 11 through 13, the color numbers can be as large as 4,144,959. For the analog monitors that are needed in these modes, colors are determined by explicitly setting the intensity of the blue, green, and red signal according to the formula:

(65536×blue intensity)+(256×green intensity)+red intensity

where the intensity for all the colors is a number between 0 (turn off that color component) and 63 (maximize that color component). A color code of:

(65536*63)

gives the bluest color possible. (256*63) is the greenest; 63 the reddest. 4144959 gives the one closest to white; 0 is closest to black. By combining the amount of blue, green, and red intensity, you can customize colors to your heart's content.

Sound

Sound is measured in Hertz (Hz is the abbreviation). 1 Hz would be one cycle per second. Ideally, humans can hear sounds between 20 Hz and 20,000 Hz. The BEEP command gives a sound at 800 Hz for about one quarter of a second. Theoretically, the SOUND command lets you play a given pure tone for a given amount of time. It's used as follows:

SOUND *frequency in Hz, duration*

The duration is measured in clock ticks, which are about $1/18$ of a second ($10/182$ to be precise). So, the command:

SOUND 800,18

is like BEEPing four times. The command SOUND 523,18 would play a sound close to a middle C (the frequency of middle C is 523.25 Hz, but frequencies in DOS BASIC must be integers).

Combining the SOUND command with a FOR-NEXT loop gives you an easy way to incorporate sound effects into your programs. For example:

```
FOR I = 100 TO 5000 STEP 10
   SOUND I,1
NEXT I
```

Sounds beyond 5000 Hz are unlikely to be audible on a PC's speaker.

DOS BASIC also can use the PLAY command to generate music. To use this facility, you have to know how music is scored. If you do, the online help for the PLAY command is quite detailed and those who are interested might want to look there.

It's possible to write a program that can automate the process of entering notes. Anyone who reads the Help file and knows enough about music shouldn't have much of a problem writing a program to make the computer enter the notes. In all honesty, however, IBM PC's are not known for their musical abilities.

As a sampling of what you have to do, here is how to play something that sounds like the first few notes of *Auld Lang Syne*:

```
PLAY "O3 C8 F8. F4 A4 G4. F4 G4 A4 F4. F4 A4"
```

13
CHAPTER

Recursion

Recursion is a general method of solving problems by reducing them to simpler problems of a similar type. For the experienced programmer, it presents a unique perspective on certain problems, often leading to particularly elegant solutions and, therefore, to equally elegant programs.

Unfortunately, recursion essentially is impossible in GW-BASIC, so not much in this chapter will be useful—until you upgrade. I hope this chapter provides yet another reason to upgrade.

Sometimes, recursion is thought of as a mysterious, even mystical, process; however, this reputation is undeserved. (For example, see the Pulitzer prize winning book *Gödel, Escher, Bach* by Douglas Hofstadter, a book some people swear by and others swear at. I oscillate between the extremes.)

One typical example of recursive problem solving seems innate—at least with children. I have never met a three-year-old who does not know intuitively how to solve the following problem:

Problem: How do I deal with my parents?
Solution: Deal with father first, then deal with mother.

This method of solving a problem is called *divide and conquer* and clearly has a long history.

For a more serious example of divide and conquer, consider the following old problem. You have seven balls and a balance scale. One ball is heavier than the other six. Find the heaviest ball in just two weighings. To solve this problem, first try to solve a simpler case: three balls. Notice that, if you try to balance two balls, there are only two possibilities:

- They balance (in which case, the remaining ball is the heaviest).
- They don't (in which case, the heaviest one is obvious).

Now, to do the seven balls problem, divide the balls into two groups of three with one left over. If they balance, the heaviest one is the one left over. If they don't, whichever side is heavier also is obvious. You've reduced the problem to the previous case. Similarly, you can do 15 balls in 3 weighings, 31 in four, and so forth.

As a final example of divide and conquer, here's an outline of a recursive method for sorting, which is called a merge sort. It follows this outline:

1. If a list has one entry, stop
2. If it has more than one entry:
   - Sort the first half
   - Sort the second half
   - Combine, or merge, the two lists

As long as the operation of combining the two lists takes substantially less time than the sorting process, you have a viable method of sorting. As you'll soon see, it does and you do.

Not all examples of recursion are examples of divide and conquer. You can have recursive definitions. For example, your descendants are either your children or a descendent of one of your children.

It's recursive because it uses itself. It might even seem circular. However, it's not circular because the circle returns to a different place: I defined a descendent of yours using descendants of your children.

As another example, a counting number is either one or a number that is one more than a counting number. So, two is a counting number because it's one more than one, three is because it's one more than two, and so on.

Similarly, the old proverb of:

A journey of a thousand miles must begin with a single step.

is a recursive solution to the following *Journey* problem:

1. To Journey (1000 miles)
   - Journey 1 mile
   - Journey (999 miles)

It's worth pointing out that a recursive solution to a problem will always follow the following outline:

1. If the problem is trivial, do the obvious
2. Otherwise:
   - Simplify the problem
   - Solve recursively (break the problem into several simpler problems)
   - Combine the solutions to the simpler problems into a solution to the original problem.

A recursive procedure constantly calls itself. Each time it calls itself in a simpler situation, until it gets to the trivial case, at which point it stops. (There also is *indirect recursion*, where a function calls itself via an intermediary: function A calls function B, which in turn calls function C, which calls function A.) So, I should have written the outline for the *Journey* problem as:

1. To Journey (How many miles)
   - Journey one mile
   - If done stop and rest
   - Else Journey (one fewer miles)

Recursive functions

You know that a function can call another function—*nested function calls*. Recursion occurs when the function eventually calls itself. Before I get to recursion, stop and think for a second what the computer must do when one function calls another. Obviously, it has to communicate the current value of all parameter variables to the new function. What it does is copy the values or the locations of the variables to a reserved area in its memory, which is called the *stack*. Now, suppose this second function needs the results from a third function. This function call requires yet another copying of the values of the variables, and so on. However, this copying can take place regardless of the nature of the other functions. It is this ability that makes recursion possible.

I'll give you an example. In chapter 1, I introduced the notion of the factorial of a positive integer. You'll recall that it's the product of the numbers from 1 up to the integer and that the custom is to use an exclamation point to symbolize it. For example:

$$2! = 2 \times 1 = 2$$
$$3! = 3 \times 2 \times 1 = 6$$
$$4! = 4 \times 3 \times 2 \times 1 = 24$$

The following fragment is a recursive version of a definition of the factorial:

```
DECLARE FUNCTION Factorial& (N&)
DEFLNG A-Z

FUNCTION Factorial (N)

   IF N < = 1 THEN
      Factorial = 1
   ELSE
      Factorial = N * Factorial(N – 1)        'note the call to itself
   END IF                                     'in a simpler situation

END FUNCTION
```

Suppose I now say PRINT Factorial(4). The compiler will do the following:

- It calls the function, with N equal to 4. The first statement processed is the IF-THEN test. Because the IF clause is false, it processes the ELSE clause.
- It computes 4∗Factorial(3).
- It tries to compute Factorial(3). So, it now has to start building up its stack. The stack will hold partial results—those obtained to date. What gets pushed onto the stack can be thought of as a little card containing the status and values of all the variables, as well as what still is left up in the air. In this case, the card would say:

  N = 3. Need to compute $4 \times$Factorial(3)

- Now, it repeats the process, calling the factorial function with a variable now having the value 3. So, another card gets pushed onto the stack:

  N = 2. Need to compute $3 \times$Factorial(2)

- It repeats the process again, so the stack contains three cards.
- Now, it does one final call with the variable N having the value 1 and sets up a fourth card.

At this point, the process can stop. The top card no longer contains an unknown quantity. By the first clause, Factorial(1) is 1, so you can start popping the stack. The results of the top card feed into the second card. Now, you can figure out what the second card stands for (the number 2), so you can pop the stack one more time and feed the information accumulated to the third card (the number 6). Finally, you feed the results to the bottom card and come out with 24, or 4!. Because the stack is empty, this number is the answer.

The explanation of the process takes much longer than the actual solution via QBasic. QBasic keeps track of the partial results of any operation in its stack—you need not be aware of the stack most of the time. The only time you do become aware of the stack is when it overflows and your program crashes or behaves erratically. To prevent this error, you can increase the room QBasic sets aside for the stack by using the CLEAR command in the form of:

    CLEAR ,, *StackSize*

Obviously, it's not a good idea to wait until your program behaves strangely to increase the size of the stack. Especially when you're developing a program, it's a good idea to monitor the amount of stack space. Have the computer notify you when the stack is getting tight. The way to do this check is to use a variant of the FRE command that was discussed in chapter 11. FRE(−2) tells you the amount of room left on the stack:

    IF FRE(−2) < 100 THEN PRINT "Help! tight stack."

More generally, you can insert breakpoints and single step through your program so that you can monitor the stack via PRINT FRE(−2) commands from the Immediate window.

Unfortunately, this information can't be used immediately. A statement like:

```
IF FRE(−2) < 100 THEN CLEAR ,, 5000
```

has the unfortunate side effect of resetting all your variables back to zero or the null string. The moral is that you should make the stack increaser the first executable statement in your program. Another moral is monitor the stack while you're developing the program and make sure there's enough room before making the program stand alone.

There are many other examples of recursive functions. For example, the Fibonacci numbers are defined as follows:

- The first Fibonacci number is 1 (in symbols: Fib(1) = 0)
- The second one also is 1 (in symbols: FIB(2) = 1)
- From that point on, the next Fibonacci number is the sum of the two preceding ones (in symbols FIB(n) = FIB(n−1)+FIB(n−2)).

For example:

$$FIB(3) = FIB(2)+FIB(1) \ (1+1 = 2)$$
$$FIB(4) = FIB(3)+FIB(2) \ (2+1 = 3)$$
$$FIB(5) = FIB(4)+FIB(3) \ (3+2 = 5)$$

The recursive definition of the Fibonacci numbers is almost trivial:

```
DECLARE FUNCTION Fib% (N%)
DEFINT A-Z

FUNCTION Fib (N)

    IF N < = 2 THEN
        Fib = 1
    ELSE
        Fib = Fib(N − 1)+Fib(N − 2)
    END IF

END FUNCTION
```

Note the pattern. The simple case is taken care of first. This simple step is followed by statements that reduce the calculation to a simpler case. Finally, the program combines the results of the simpler cases to finish the definition.

I should point out that, however elegant this program might seem, it turns out to be an incredibly inefficient way to calculate these numbers. See the last section in this chapter for more on this topic. (I also arbitrarily defined the Fibonacci numbers at negative N to be one.)

Some people, called Elliot wave theorists, claim the stock market follows patterns generated by Fibonacci numbers—a claim that is on a par with fear of the number 13. In any case, Fibonacci numbers arose when an early mathematician, Leonardo of Pisa, tried to model the following problem:

> A man has one pair of rabbits at a certain place entirely surrounded by a wall. We wish to know how many pairs can be bred from it in one year, if the nature of these rabbits is that they breed every month one other pair and begin to breed in the second month after their birth.[1]

As a final example of a recursive function, consider the calculation of the greatest common divisor (GCD) of two numbers. For those who have forgotten their high school mathematics, a *greatest common divisor* is defined as the largest number that divides evenly into both of a pair of numbers. So, the GCD of 4 and 6 is 2, because 2 is the largest number that divides both 4 and 6.

Around 2000 years ago, Euclid gave the following method of computing the GCD of two numbers a and b:

If b divides a, then the GCD is b. Otherwise, the $GCD(a,b) = GCD(b,a$ MOD $b)$

This method usually is called the *Euclidian Algorithm*. Algorithms are what programing is ultimately about. More precisely, an *algorithm* is a method of solving a problem that is both precise and finite—the method must not go on forever. In the case of the Euclidian algorithm, because the MOD operation shrinks the number each time, the process must stop.

You will recall that the MOD function gives the remainder you get from dividing b into a; it obviously is less than b. If a MOD b is 0, b divides a. The following fragment is this recursive outline translated into a QBasic function:

```
DECLARE FUNCTION GCD% (P%, Q%)
DEFINT A-Z

FUNCTION GCD (P, Q)

   IF Q MOD P = 0 THEN
      GCD = P
   ELSE
      GCD = GCD(Q, P MOD Q)
   END IF

END FUNCTION
```

Here, the pattern is a trivial case followed by a reduction to a simpler case. There is no need to combine results. Also, because the MOD function is not restricted to

---

[1]*A source book in mathematics*, ed. D.J. Struik (Harvard University Press, 1969) p 2-3.

short integers, it's easy enough to change the function to work with long integers as well.

Simple recursive procedures

Just as you can have recursive functions, through the magic of the stack, you can have recursive procedures. A good example of this feature is a rewritten version of the binary search method for looking through an ordered list:

```
If list has length one
    then check directly (the simple case)
Else
    look at the middle of the list
If the middle entry is too big then
    search the first half
Else
    search the second half.
```

Note that this outline for a recursive solution is quite close to a person's intuitive notion of how to search.

The following fragment is this outline translated to a procedure:

```
DECLARE SUB RecursiveBinSearch (X$, A$(), low%, high%)

SUB RecursiveBinSearch (X$, A$(), low, high)

    ' LOCAL variable is: Mid

    IF low > high THEN                                          'A
        PRINT "Target not found"
        EXIT SUB
    END IF

    mid = (low + high) \ 2

    IF A$(mid) = X$ THEN
        PRINT "Target found at the"; mid; "entry"              'B
    ELSE IF A$(mid) > X$ THEN
        t = mid - 1
        CALL RecursiveBinSearch(X$, A$(), low, mid - 1)        'C
    ELSE
        CALL RecursiveBinSearch(X$, A$(), mid + 1, high)
    END IF

END SUB
```

A   If the list is empty, there's nothing to do.

B   If the program has found the entry, there's nothing to do.

C   Again, the essence of recursion is doing the same thing in a simple case.

You test this procedure by writing the appropriate module-level code to set up an ordered list:

```
DEFINT A-Z

DIM B$(255)
FOR i = 1 TO 255
   B$(i) = CHR$(i)
NEXT

B$(105) = "it"
```

Now, try something like:

```
CALL RecursiveBinSearch("it", B$(), 1, 255)
```

and

```
CALL RecursiveBinSearch("itt", B$(), 1, 255)
```

Note that I didn't bother enlarging the stack. A binary recursive search can't possibly use up much of the stack.

Whenever you're trying to understand a recursive program, it's a good idea to think about what is in the stack and what happens when the stack finally is popped. In this case, each card on the stack contains:

- The address of the array A$(). Arrays are always passed by reference.
- The current values of the variables Low and High and a new copy of the local variable Mid.

This information also is the key when debugging a recursive procedure. After all, watching variables on the stack is useless if you don't know what they're supposed to do.

By now, you might be thinking that recursion is just a fancy way of avoiding loops. There's some truth to this statement, but there are many problems for which it would be hard to find the loop equivalent. The simplest example of this idea is the famous Tower of Hanoi problem. (As the following quote indicates, it originally was called the Tower of Brahma). Here's the problem:

In the great temple at Benares, says he, beneath the dome which marks the center of the world, rests a brass plate in which are fixed three diamond needles, each a cubit high and as thick as the body of a bee. On one of these needles, at the creation, God placed sixty-four discs of pure gold, the largest disc resting on the brass plate, and the others getting smaller and smaller up to the top one. This is the Tower of Brahma. Day and night unceasingly the priests transfer the discs from one diamond needle to another according to the fixed and immutable laws of Brahma, which require that the priest on duty must not move more than one disc at a time and that he must place this disc on a needle so that there is no smaller disc below it. When the sixty-four discs shall have been thus transferred from the needle on which at the creation God placed them to one of the other needles, tower, temple and Brahmins alike will crumble into dust, and with a thunderclap the world will vanish.[2]

I'll continue to use 64 discs in the explanation that follows, but solving this problem with this many discs would take the priests, or a super computer for that matter, more time than scientists say the universe has been around or is likely to be around. For n disks, the solution takes 2^{n-1} steps. For 64 disks, this number has 19 digits—approximately $1.844674E+19$, according to QBasic.

Anyway, to solve this problem recursively, you need to decide on the trivial case. (It's when the tower is down to one disc, or height one.) Next, you have to find a way to simplify the problem while retaining the same form and making sure that this process eventually does lead to the trivial case. The key is to note that the bottom disc is irrelevant when you move the first 63 discs from the first tower to any other tower. Because it's larger than any disc, you can just as well regard a peg with it alone as being empty when it comes to moving discs around. Next, note that you can change the destination temporarily if it helps simplify the problem. Given all this information, here's an outline of a solution to the Tower of Hanoi:

1. Move the top 63 discs to tower 2 using tower 3 (the simpler case)
2. Move the bottom disc to its destination (tower 3).
3. Move the top 62 discs to tower 1 using tower 3

To move 62 disks is a problem of smaller size. Just as before, the bottom disk will be irrelevant.

Here's the procedure with some module-level code that implements this outline:

```
DECLARE SUB SolveTowerOfHanoi(Hght!, FromTowr!, ToTowr!, UsingTowr!)
CLEAR , , 10000          ' Needs a lot of stack room!
CLS
INPUT "How many discs - don't try too many!"; NumberOfDiscs
CALL SolveTowerOfHanoi(NumberOfDiscs, 1, 2, 3)
END

SUB SolveTowerOfHanoi (Height, FromTower, ToTower, UsingTower)

   IF Height = 1 THEN
      PRINT "Move a disc from tower #"; FromTower; "to tower#"; ToTower
```

---

[2] W.W. Rouse Ball and H.S.M. Coxeter. *Mathematical recreations and essays* (Dover 1987) p 317.

```
    ELSE
        CALL SolveTowerOfHanoi(Height – 1, FromTower, UsingTower, ToTower)
        PRINT "Move a disc from tower #"; FromTower; "to tower #"; ToTower
        CALL SolveTowerOfHanoi(Height – 1, UsingTower, ToTower, FromTower)
    END IF

    END SUB
```

As mentioned in the outline, the key to this solution is the switch in the destinations between:

```
CALL SolveTowerOfHanoi(Height – 1,FromTower,UsingTower,ToTower)
```

and

```
CALL SolveTowerOfHanoi(Height – 1,UsingTower,ToTower,FromTower)
```

This program might be confusing. If so, I suggest analyzing the stack for the simple case of three discs by playing computer. (The watch window can act as a crib if necessary.)

Two more complicated recursions

Suppose you're stuck in a maze. At any point, you can go in one of four directions (north, east, south, and west); however, some of these directions might be blocked at some places in the maze. How do you find your way out? Obviously, you'd try to analyze your way out. A computer program doesn't have this option, but it does work quickly—quickly enough that sophisticated trial and error can lead to a way out. Given the speed of QBasic, there's an easy recursive solution to getting out of any maze:

1. Mark the square you're on
2. If you can go north, do so and mark that square
3. If not, go east and mark that square

    .   .

    .   .

By marking the squares, you've made the problem simpler. There's one less square to worry about. Because you eventually either find a way out or get stuck, this outline fulfills the pattern for a recursive solution.

In the following procedure, I've assumed that the maze is stored as an array of characters with the barrier being marked with a string variable called Barrier$, the empty squares marked with a character I'll call NotUsed$, and the goal marked with an exclamation point. (For a large maze, you might need to store it as an array of integers to save space.)

The following fragment is the procedure:

```
SUB FindExit (Row, Col)
   SHARED Maze$(), Finished, Barrier$, NotUsed$
   STATIC CharNum                                                    'A

   CALL PrintMaze
   CharNum = CharNum + 1                                             'B
   IF CharNum = 89 THEN CharNum = 0

   MarkChar$ = CHR$(33 + CharNum)
   Maze$(Row, Col) = MarkChar$

   ' these blocks do the recursion 4 blocks = 4 ways to travel
   IF NOT Finished THEN                                              'C
      SELECT CASE Maze$(Row, Col - 1)
         CASE NotUsed$
            CALL FindExit(Row, Col - 1)                         'try to go west
         CASE "!"
            Finished = True
      END SELECT
   END IF

   IF NOT Finished THEN
      SELECT CASE Maze$(Row - 1, Col)
         CASE NotUsed$
            CALL FindExit(Row - 1, Col)
         CASE "!"
            Finished = True
      END SELECT
   END IF                                                           'North

   IF NOT Finished THEN
      SELECT CASE Maze$(Row, Col + 1)
         CASE NotUsed$
            CALL FindExit(Row, Col + 1)
         CASE "!"
            Finished = True
      END SELECT
   END IF

   IF NOT Finished THEN
      SELECT CASE Maze$(Row + 1, Col)
         CASE NotUsed$
```

```
          CALL FindExit(Row + 1, Col)
        CASE "!"
          Finished = True
      END SELECT
    END IF

END SUB
```

A   I mark each square with a different ASCII character. By making
    CharNum a static variable, I ensure that, on each recursive pass, a dif-
    ferent marker is used. Moreover, because, at each call, I'm going to
    print the current status of the maze (with a call to SUB that has not
    been written yet), using successive ASCII characters as markers makes
    my progress from step to step clearer.

B   I don't want to go to the higher ASCII characters, especially because
    I'm using CHR$(219) as the boundary marker.

C   This block and it's three sibling blocks are the key to the recursion. I
    use a shared flag variable (Finished) to mark when I've succeeded.
    Because it's shared, any changes I make remain as QBasic pops the
    stack. (A local variable would not work. Would a STATIC variable
    work?) If you still are confused as to what this block is doing, imagine
    that you are a mouse sitting at a square. You look to your left. If that
    square hasn't been marked, you move to it, checking whether it's your
    goal. If it's not, you start over. If going to your left doesn't work, you
    try going up, and so forth.

The main module for this procedure might look like the following fragment:

```
DECLARE SUB Initialize (Size%)
DECLARE SUB FindExit (Row%, Col%)
DECLARE SUB PrintMaze ()
CLEAR , , 32000                          'needs maximal stack size

DEFINT A-Z                               ' integers speed things up

CONST True = -1
CONST False = 0
NotUsed$ = ""
Barrier$ = CHR$(219)
Finished = False
CLS

INPUT "How big is the maze";Size
DIM SHARED Maze$(Size,Size)                              'A
CALL Initialize(Size)                                    'B
```

```
CLS
PRINT "Enter starting row and column"
INPUT "row"; StartRow
INPUT "column"; StartCol CALL PrintMaze                              'C

CALL FindExit(StartRow, StartCol)                     ' where to start

IF Finished THEN                                                     'D
  CALL PrintMaze
ELSE                                    'gets here if all squares used up
  BEEP
  CLS
  PRINT "No way Out!"
END IF
```

A   This statement is another variant on the DIM command. It indicates
    that the Maze$ array will be a shared, or global, variable for all the
    procedures in this program.

B   This subprogram will set up the maze.

C   Printing the maze is an obvious candidate for a SUB.

D   Again, because Finished is a shared variable, I know its value reflects
    whether FindExit worked or not.

Now, to the Initialize SUB. The most elegant way to set up the maze is to use a
variant on the curser mover program from chapter 6; however, for illustration purposes, I've set it up using a simple 10×10 maze, which was created with a loop:

```
SUB Initialize(Size)

    SHARED Maze$(), Barrier$

    Size = 10

    FOR I = 0 TO Size
       Maze$(0, I) = Barrier$
       Maze$(Size, I) = Barrier$
       Maze$(5, I) = Barrier$
       Maze$(I, 0) = Barrier$
       Maze$(I, Size) = Barrier$
    NEXT I

    Maze$(9, 5) = "!"
    Maze$(5, 2) = NotUsed$                      'need to leave a way out!
END SUB

'  SUB to print the Maze
```

```
SUB PrintMaze

    CLS

    SHARED Maze$(),Size

    FOR I = 0 TO Size
        FOR J = 0 TO Size
            PRINT USING " \ \ "; Maze$(I, J);
        NEXT J
        PRINT
    NEXT I

END SUB
```

One way to understand this procedure is to imagine a tree; it is sometimes called a *decision tree*. From any given square, you have multiple branches. The branches continue blossoming out until the procedure gets stuck. Then, it backtracks to where it started and goes west. More precisely, starting from any square, the procedure systematically exhausts all the possible squares it can get to by first going west, leaving a trail of used squares. If one of these possibilities leads to an exit, the procedure ends and the flag given by the shared variable Finished flips to true. Otherwise, the procedure backtracks all the way back to the starting square and tries to go north. It can do this only if the square directly north of the starting square is not marked already. Similarly, if it hasn't found an exit going north, it tries east and south. If none of these directions are possible, the maze has no exit and the procedure ends.

As you can well imagine this process can take time. You might want to experiment with larger mazes, but be prepared to change Maze$ to an array of integers. Note that each square searched can add a card to the stack.

If you run the program with a large maze, why not monitor the changing free stack space? In general, the cards on the stack contain the current value of the row and column and the address of the array. Each call to the procedure makes a permanent change to the array. Without making the array a shared variable, there would be no way to keep track of where the computer's been.

The final example I want to give in this section is much shorter, but it's very tricky. Before I do, recall that, each time you run the jumble program, you probably will get a different rearrangement of the original string. Suppose, however that you wanted to generate all possible jumbles. (The technical term for a jumble is a *permutation*. For a string of length n, there are n! different permutations.) The key to writing this program is to note that, to obtain all the permutations of a string (for example, *abcd*), you only need follow the outline:

1. List *a* concatenated to all permutations of *bcd*
2. List *b* concatenated to all permutations of *acd*

3. List *c* concatenated to all permutations of *abd*
4. List *d* concatenated to all permutations of *abc*

Now, to get the permutations of any of the three letter combinations, repeat the process:

- *b* together with all the permutations of *cd*
- *c* with the permutations of *bd*
- *d* with the permutation of *bc*

Stop when you are working with a string of length one.

The problem with following this outline is that it's easier to do on paper than on a computer. Somehow you have to keep track of which characters you've switched. Each time you call the procedure, you need a different version of the string variable you're permuting. You want the procedure to play with a different value on each card in the stack. On the other hand, you need to preserve the identity of the original string, if only to move the letters in it around. All this means is that you want to pass by value rather than by reference. Next, you need to keep track of which letters you've switched so you will know when to stop. The best way to keep track of them is to make the procedure depend on two parameters, with the second parameter—an integer—giving the current position within the string.

The following fragment contains the procedure:

```
SUB Permute(A$,n)

    'LOCAL variables LenA,Temp$,First$,I

    LenA = LEN(A$)

    IF n = LenA THEN
        PRINT A$                          'A
    ELSE
        FOR I = n TO LenA
            CALL Switch(A$,n,I)           'B
            CALL Permute((A$),n + 1)      'C
        NEXT I
    END IF

END SUB
```

A   When n is the length of A, there's nothing left to do.

B   This procedure interchanges two characters. It's pretty easy:

```
        SUB Switch(A$,I,J)

            ' LOCAL variable T$
```

```
            T$ = MID$(A$,I,1)
            MID$(A$,I,1) = MID$(A$,J,1)
            MID$(A$,J,1) = T$

        END SUB
```

However, note that, because I want the changes to persist, I passed by reference here. I made it a separate procedure because I prefer to keep procedures to single tasks.

C   Here, on the other hand, I want the stack to contain a new copy of the variable each time it is called, so I passed by value. I want to switch the letters only in the new value of the variable. Here again, it's a good idea to draw a tree that shows what follows what and what the values of the various variables are.

To use this procedure, you only have to enter:

```
CALL Permute(X$,1)
```

Recursive sorts

So far, you've seen three useful methods for sorting: insertion, ripple, and Shell sorts. Insertion and ripple sorts are good for short lists; the Shell sort is good for moderate-sized lists. The sorts you'll see in this section are among the fastest known. They are the ones of choice for large lists.

The first one, merge sort, has the easiest outline. You saw it in the introduction:

1. If a list has one entry, stop
2. If it has more than one entry:
   • Sort the first half
   • Sort the second half
   • Combine, merge, the two

Once you write the merge, the procedure to sort a list procedure is almost trivial:

```
SUB MergeSort (a$(), Start, Finish)

    'LOCAL Variable is Mid

    IF Start < Finish THEN
        Mid = (Start + Finish) \ 2
        CALL MergeSort(a$(), Start, Mid)
        CALL MergeSort(a$(), Mid + 1, Finish)
        CALL Merge(a$(), Start, Mid, Finish)
    END IF

END SUB
```

This procedure keeps on splitting the list. When it gets to n lists of size one, the Merge procedure will combine them into $n/2$ ordered lists of size two, $n/4$ ordered lists of size four, $n/8$ ordered lists of size eight, and so on. At this point, I really have swept the details under the rug by moving them to the Merge procedure, which has not yet been written.

Merging two ordered files or ordered parts of the same file is intuitively obvious but a bit tricky to program. What you have to do is set up a temporary array and work your way slowly through the lists, filling up the temporary array with the appropriate entry from one of the two lists. When you're done, you have to write the temporary array back to the original array.

The following fragment is the QBasic code for the Merge procedure:

```
SUB Merge (a$(), Start, Mid, Finish)

    'LOCAL variables are:
    'Temp$(),Begin1,End1,Begin2,End2,TempLocation,I

    DIM Temp$(Start TO Finish)

    Begin1 = Start
    End1 = Mid
    Begin2 = End1 + 1
    End2 = Finish

    TempLocation = Start

    DO WHILE Begin1 < = End1 AND Begin2 < = End2               'A
        IF a$(Begin1) < = a$(Begin2) THEN
            Temp$(TempLocation) = a$(Begin1)
            TempLocation = TempLocation + 1
            Begin1 = Begin1 + 1
        ELSE
            Temp$(TempLocation) = a$(Begin2)
            TempLocation = TempLocation + 1
            Begin2 = Begin2 + 1
        END IF
    LOOP

    IF Begin1 < = End1 THEN                                     'B
        FOR I = Begin1 TO End1
            Temp$(TempLocation) = a$(I)
            TempLocation = TempLocation + 1
        NEXT I
    ELSEIF Begin2 < = End2 THEN
        FOR I = Begin2 TO End2
            Temp$(TempLocation) = a$(I)
```

```
      TempLocation = TempLocation + 1
   NEXT I
END IF

FOR I = Start TO Finish                                   'C
   a$(I) = Temp$(I)
NEXT I

END SUB
```

A   This loop runs through the list. It systematically compares entries in both and moves the smaller one to the temporary list. After every move, it shifts a pointer (TempLocation) that moves one step forward within the temporary list. Similarly, it moves a pointer within a given sublist (either Begin1 or Begin2) whenever it does a swap. The loop constantly checks the status of these pointers to avoid going past the boundaries of the individual sublists.

B   The program gets to here when one of the sublists is used up. This block copies the remainder of the other list to the temporary array.

C   This loop copies the temporary array back to the original array. Without doing this loop, the recursion would fail.

Although merge sort theoretically is one of the fastest sorts, in practice, the naive formulation given previously is too slow. Sorting a list of 1000 random four-letter strings takes about 6 1/4 minutes (436.71 seconds on a basic PC), which is even slower than an insertion sort, which takes about 4 minutes (234.09 seconds). It is far slower than Shell sort, which takes about 17 seconds to work through this problem. However, unlike insertion sorts, doubling the size of the list no longer quadruples the time; it slightly more than doubles it. So, even this naive formulation of a merge sort will be much faster than an insertion sort for a list of 2000 items. The Shell sort, however, still remains much faster; it takes 41 seconds.

One problem is that copying the temporary array back to the original list takes too much time. Unfortunately, there's little you can do about it. (Wouldn't it be nice to have a built-in SWAP for lists?)

On the other hand, the procedure also spends too much time and stack space on the trivial cases of lists of sizes one and two. You can dramatically speed up a merge sort and save a lot of stack space by modifying what the procedure regards as the trivial case. For example, suppose you directly sort all lists of length one or two by swapping entries as needed. Change the original procedure to the following fragment:

```
SUB MergeSort(A$(1),Start,Finish)

   'LOCAL variable is Mid
```

```
IF Finish – Start < = 1 THEN
    IF A$(Finish) < A$(Start) THEN SWAP A$(Finish),A$(Start)
ELSE
    MID = (Start + Finish) \ 2
    CALL MergeSort(A$(),Start,Mid)
    CALL MergeSort(A$(),Mid + 1,Finish)
    CALL Merge(A$(),Start,Mid,Finish)
END IF

END SUB
```

Now, the program is directly swapping the entries when the lists are tiny. The savings are dramatic. Sorting 1000 random four-letter combinations now only takes about 3³/4 minutes (229.37 seconds) on a basic PC—about half as much time as it took before. Now, it's slightly faster than insertion sort. Even more dramatic savings result by modifying the trivial case even further. Recall that an insertion or a ripple sort is fast for small lists (for example, lists of size 64 or less). If you add an insertion sort procedure to a program containing a merge sort and rewrite the fundamental procedure to match the following fragment:

```
IF Finish – Start < = 63 THEN
    CALL InsertSort(A$(),Start,Finish)
ELSE
    MID = (Start + Finish) \ 2
    CALL MergeSort(A$(),Start,Mid)
    CALL MergeSort(A$(),Mid + 1,Finish)
    CALL Merge(A$(),Start,Mid,Finish)
END IF

END SUB
```

the improvements are incredible. Sorting a list of 1000 four-letter strings now takes less than 1/2 a minute (26.75 seconds) on a basic PC. Sorting a list of 2000 strings takes less than 1 minute (56.61 seconds). (I decided to use 64 items as the trivial case by experimenting; it gave the best results.)

This modified merge now is almost as fast as a Shell sort and is faster than a Shell sort once the list has more than, say, 3000 entries and is roughly the same for lists of size 2200 through 3000. Thus, combining an insertion sort with a merge sort gives you a fast sort for large lists. In theory, you could modify a merge sort to be even faster by using a Shell sort for lists of moderate size, but I won't bother presenting that version here.

In any case, all these tweaks preserve the essential advantage of the original merge sort: doubling the list still only slightly more than doubles the time needed. Unfortunately, all the versions of the merge sort do have one big disadvantage.

Ironically, this disadvantage shows up only for the very large lists on which the merge sort should shine. You need twice as much space as is needed for a Shell sort, because of the temporary array used in the merge procedure. You're likely to run out of space for very large lists. So, the merge sort is of more theoretical than practical interest in most situations.

As many people have remarked, finding a better general purpose sort is the better mousetrap of computer science. Unfortunately, the best general purpose sort currently known, which usually is called a *quick sort*, is unlike the various modifications of the merge sort in that it is not guaranteed to work fast. In very unlikely situations, it can be the slowest sort of all.

If the merge sort is a divide and conquer recursion, then the quick sort can be thought of as a conquer by dividing recursion. To see what I mean, consider the following list of numbers:

5, 12, 4, 9, 17, 21, 19, 41, 39

The number 17 is in an enviable place: all the numbers to the left of it are smaller than it and all the numbers to the right of it are greater than it. This fact means that 17 is in the correct position when this list is sorted. It partitions the list and will not have to be moved by any sort. The idea of a quick sort is to create these splitters artificially on smaller and smaller lists. Here's the basic outline:

1. Take the middle entry of a list
2. By swapping elements within the list, make this element into a splitter. (Note that this element might need to move. This step obviously is the most difficult part to program.)
3. Divide the list into two smaller lists at the splitter and repeat steps 1 and 2.
4. Continue until both the lists created by making a splitter have, at most, a size of one.

The following fragment translates this outline into a procedure (all numeric variables are assumed to be integers):

```
SUB QuickSort (A$(), start, finish)

    'Local variable PosOfSplitter

    IF finish > start THEN
        CALL Partition(A$(), start, finish, PosOfSplitter)
        CALL QuickSort(A$(), start, PosOfSplitter – 1)
        CALL QuickSort(A$(), PosOfSplitter + 1, finish)
    END IF

END SUB
```

Now, you need to write the procedure that forces the splitter. This procedure is

subtle and makes a quick sort harder to program than a merge sort. Luckily, there are many ways to program this sort. The one I'll show you here is inspired by the insertion sort. You move the splitter out of the way first. Next, you start from the left end of the list and look for any entries that are smaller than the splitter. Whenever you find one, move it, keeping track of how many elements you've moved. When you get to the end of the list, this marker will tell you where to put back the splitter. The following fragment is this procedure:

```
SUB Partition (A$(), start, finish, LocOfSplitter)

    ' LOCAL variables are:SplitPos,NewStart,I,Splitter$

   SplitPos = (start + finish) \ 2
   Splitter$ = A$(SplitPos)

   SWAP A$(SplitPos), A$(start)                    'get it out of the way

   LeftPos = start

   FOR i = start + 1 TO finish
      IF A$(i) < Splitter$ THEN
         LeftPos = LeftPos + 1
         SWAP A$(LeftPos), A$(i)
      END IF
   NEXT i

   SWAP A$(start), A$(LeftPos)                     ' LeftPos marks the hole

   LocOfSplitter = LeftPos                         ' This gets passed to the
                                                   ' original procedure.

END SUB
```

A quick sort usually is quite fast. To sort a list of 2000 random four-letter strings takes around 17.3 seconds. However, how fast a quick sort works depends completely on how much the splitter splits. The ideal is when it splits the list in two. If each time you sort the smaller list and the element you are trying to make into a splitter is the smallest or the largest in the list then, in one of the recursive calls, too little work is done (in the other, too much is done). This imbalance makes the quick sort slow down. For all practical purposes, it becomes a complicated version of the insertion sort. If this horrible situation should come to pass, you might end up waiting a long time to sort a list of 2000 entries. Luckily, this worst case is quite unlikely, but it can happen. To prevent this computer scientists suggest that you:

1. Use an insertion or ripple sort for small lists, much like I did in the tweaked version of a merge sort. (My tests show that this sort works best when you use an insertion or ripple sort on lists of size eight or less.) This

sort speeds up the program considerably. Sorting a list of 2000 random four-letter strings now takes around 15 seconds—around a 15% improvement! It also saves stack space.

2. Most important, to eliminate the chance of the worst case happening, don't use the middle element as the potential splitter. One idea is to use the random number generator to find a random element on the list. Change the lines:

```
SplitPos = (Start + Finish) \ 2
Splitter$ = A$(SplitPos)
```

to be:

```
SplitPos = Start + INT((Finish − Start + 1)*RND(1))
```

Step 2 makes it almost inconceivable that you'll end up in the worst case. The problem is that using the random number generator takes time. While it makes the worst case almost inconceivable, according to my tests, it does slow the average case down by around 25% (23.8 seconds versus 17.3 seconds). On the other hand, if you use this idea in the tweaked version described earlier, the deterioration is much less. My tests show that this combination takes around 16.5 seconds. This time is only a 10% reduction and still is faster than the original version of the quick sort. Far fewer calls to the random number generator are necessary because you're not dealing with small lists. This sort is my personal favorite version of the quick sort and is the sort I use in consulting. Again, all times were done on my basic 4.77 MHz PC.

Another possibility that many people prefer is to keep on using an insertion or ripple sort for small lists; however, instead of calling the random number generator to find a candidate for the splitter, use the median of the start of the list, the middle term, and the end of the list. The code for finding the median of three items is almost trivial and doesn't take much time either.

Finally, I discussed so many sorts because they illustrate the techniques so well, but there's a more serious reason as well. Although the quick sort and the Shell sort are fast, they do have one disadvantage that insertion, ripple, and merge sorts do not have. They are not stable. To understand what stability means, suppose you have a list of names and addresses that already is ordered alphabetically by name. Suppose, now, that you want to resort the list by city and state. Obviously, you want the list to be ordered alphabetically by name within each state. Unfortunately, if you use a quick or Shell sort, the alphabetical order of the names will disappear. With a merge sort, you can preserve the old order within the new.

Binary trees

In many cases, you don't really need to sort a list, rather you sort the list so that you can easily search through the list using a binary search. Suppose you have a person entering random names and you want to be able to prevent duplicates. If the list were ordered, this check would be easy; however, a new entry would require resorting the list. (If you choose this option, use an insertion sort. It obviously is the best way to insert a new item.) Finally, you might know that, at some point in the future, you frequently will need to search through the list, possibly ordering the list as well. Stopping and resorting the list each time the user enters a new name obviously is not the method of choice if the final ordering happens in the far future.

It should come as no surprise that programmers have long searched for methods of accepting information for a list so that you still can search through the list as fast as through an ordered list (i.e, as fast as binary search) and hopefully, at some future time, sort it quickly as well. All this should take place without having to stop and constantly resort.

You can't expect to get something for nothing. The methods that programmers invented require more sophisticated programs and use a lot more space. Moreover, unless you use very sophisticated methods, which are not described here, this method works only if the names are entered in a random order. If someone applies these methods when entering an ordered list, the results will be horrible.

To understand this method, which is called *binary trees*, suppose you have a list of names:

Joan, Susan, Gary, Karie, Ted, Saul, David, Al, Harry, Hal

Start by putting the first name on the top of a piece of paper:

Joan

Because the name Susan comes after Joan alphabetically, draw an arrow pointing to the right (this arrow sometimes is called an *after* or *right arrow*):

Gary comes before Joan, so draw a left arrow—a *before arrow*:

Karie comes after Joan but before Susan, so the picture looks like:

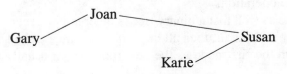

Ted comes after Joan and after Susan, so the picture now looks like:

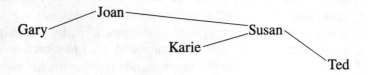

The idea is that, when you insert a new name, follow the branches in the right order. Saul comes after Joan, before Sue, and after Karie. At the next step, the picture looks like:

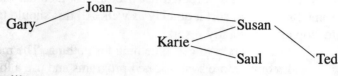

Finally, the picture looks like:

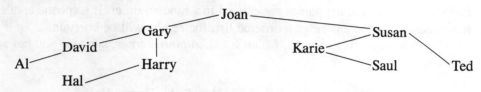

Naturally enough, programmers call the resulting diagram a *binary tree*. It's called binary because there's never more than two branches and tree because the picture resembles an upside down tree.

It's a good idea to learn some of the terminology that computer scientists use to describe binary trees. For example, they say that each of the names form a *node* on the binary tree. The top node is called the *root* of the tree. The node directly above another node is called the *parent* of that node. So, Karie is the parent node for Saul and Gary is the parent node for Al and Harry. Every parent in a tree can have either no children, a younger (left) child, an older (right) child, or both. A node that has no children is said to be a *leaf*.

When you enter names and form a binary tree by following the previous procedure, you are said to have *loaded the tree*. Adding a new name to a loaded tree is fairly quick, almost as fast as just sticking the name on at the end of an ordinary list. Although, now, instead of merely sticking it on at the end, you follow the correct branch of the tree until you can go no further. At that point, stick the new name where the hole is. Note that searching a tree and loading a tree are basically the same operation.

Note as well that a binary tree is inherently a recursive object. After all, start from any node at all, then all the nodes that are attached to it form a binary tree as well with the first node as the new root, which usually is called a *sub-tree*. The left child of a parent forms the *left sub-tree* and the right child of a parent forms the *right sub-tree*. It is this recursive property that will make most of the operations on a binary tree simple.

A recursive version of loading a tree will be a procedure that depends on the contents of the current position in the tree, as well as the sub-tree. An outline in something close to pseudocode might look like:

```
Procedure LoadATree(Tree,NodeIntree,ThingToAdd)
   IF the current node is empty, add the word there
   ELSE
      IF the word precedes the contents of the node
         CALL LoadATree(Left Tree, LeftChild, ThingToAdd)
      ELSE
         CALL LoadATree(Right tree, RightChild, ThingToAdd)
```

To write a program that implements this pseudocode, you have to decide on how you're going to represent the arrows and the holes. This representation usually is called the *data structure*. The ideal situation would be to use a three-column array. Each row on the array would use the first column for the contents of the node, the second column for the row the left child is on, and the third column for the row the right child is pointing to.

The trouble with this structure is that, if you use a string array, you can't use numbers for the entries in the second and third columns (the rows of the children). So, you might turn to a list of records of type:

```
TYPE ContentsOfTree
   NodeContents AS STRING*?
   RowOFLftChil AS INTEGER
   RowOfRtChild AS INTEGER
END TYPE
```

The problem with this type is indicated by the question mark. How much room should you allow for the NodeContents?

So, you go back to thinking about using the string equivalent of the row numbers, converting them back and forth via VAL and STR$. In the example, the 10×3 array would look like Table 13-1.

So, for example, the third row of the array that will represent the tree would contain three strings—one in each column:

```
"Gary"    "7"    "9"
```

Note that the first column has the entries in the order they were entered; it's the other two columns that give the extra information needed to quickly search through the tree.

However, I prefer to use the idea of parallel lists that I talked about in chapter

Table 13-1
The array describing the binary tree.

Node Number	Contents of Node	Left child	Right child
1	Joan	3	2
2	Susan	4	5
3	Gary	7	9
4	Karie	− 1*	6
5	Ted	− 1*	− 1*
6	Mike	− 1*	− 1*
7	David	8	9
8	Al	− 1*	− 1*
9	Harry	10	− 1*
10	Hal	− 1*	− 1*

*The −1 means that there is nothing to point to.

12 (among other reasons, because it saves space; however, it ultimately is a matter of taste).

So, the first list will hold the contents of the nodes. It will be a string array. I'll use a two-column integer array for the pointers to the left and right children.

The following fragment is the procedure to load a tree:

```
SUB LoadAtree (nodes$(), arrows%(), item$, CurrentPos%)          'A

  ' LOCAL variables are:Items%,WhereToGo%,Direction$

  Items% = VAL(nodes$(0))

  IF Items% = 0 THEN                                             'B
    nodes$(0) = "1"
    nodes$(1) = item$
    arrows%(1, 0) = − 1
    arrows%(1, 1) = − 1
    EXIT SUB
  END IF

  IF item$ < nodes$(CurrentPos%) THEN
    WhereToGo% = arrows%(CurrentPos%, 0)
    Direction$ = "left"
  ELSE
    WhereToGo% = arrows%(CurrentPos%, 1)
    Direction$ = "right"
  END IF

  IF WhereToGo% = − 1 THEN                                       'C
```

```
        Items% = Items% + 1
        nodes$(Items%) = item$
        arrows%(Items%, 0) = -1
        arrows%(Items%, 1) = -1
        nodes$(0) = STR$(Items%)

        ' Now change pointers on parent node

        SELECT CASE Direction$
          CASE "left"
            arrows%(CurrentPos%, 0) = Items%
          CASE "right"
            arrows%(CurrentPos%, 1) = Items%
        END SELECT
      ELSE
        CALL LoadAtree(nodes$(), arrows%(), item$, WhereToGo%)        'D
      END IF

    END SUB
```

A   As mentioned earlier, the contents of the nodes are stored in a string
    array indicated by the parameter array Nodes$(x), with Nodes$(0)
    being the string equivalent of the number of items. The arrows are
    stored in an array Arrows%(x,y). The parameter Item$ is for the item to
    be loaded. The parameter CurrentPos% is used to indicate where the
    program is in the tree. (To load the tree, call this procedure with Cur-
    rentPos% = 1.)

B   You need a special case when you're setting up the tree. Note that I'll
    use the zeroth position of the nodes to keep track of the number of
    items. This information is necessary for two reasons. First, you have to
    know in what row of the array you'll add the next entry. Second, when
    using this procedure, you have to have dimensioned the arrays previ-
    ously. A robust program would constantly monitor this number.

C   This statement provides a way out of the recursion. When the arrow is
    pointing to a hole, it's time to place the entry.

D   This statement starts the recursion.

In a more serious example, you would have to increase the dimension of the arrays
to allow enough room. In any case, you can use the following fragment to print
out the table:

```
SUB PrintaTree (Tree$(), arrows%())

    ' LOCAL variable is NumberOfItems
    CLS
```

```
PRINT "Row            Contents      Row 'before'    Row 'after'"
PRINT "Number         of Node       arrow points    arrow points"
PRINT "( = node                     to              to"
PRINT "number)"

PRINT : PRINT

NumberOfItems = VAL(Tree$(0))

FOR I = 1 TO NumberOfItems
    PRINT I, Tree$(I), arrows%(I, 0), arrows%(I, 1)
NEXT I

END SUB
```

You might want to slow this procedure down with some empty INPUT$(1) or SLEEP statements.

Modifying the LoadATree to SearchATree is almost trivial and I'll leave that to you. In any case, you should be aware that the efficiency of SearchATree depends on the shape of the tree. The best situation, which usually is called a *complete* or *balanced tree*, occurs when the tree is as bushy as possible. In this case, it works as fast as an ordinary binary search. The worst case is when someone gives you an ordered list. In this case, the tree is as narrow as possible. If you use SearchATree, you'll end up searching the list one item at a time (see Fig. 13-1).

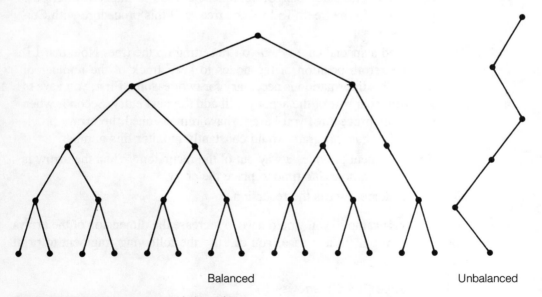

Balanced   Unbalanced

13-1 A balanced tree versus an unbalanced tree.

One of the nicest features of trees is that you can sort the items in the tree quite fast—about as quickly as a quick sort. To rapidly sort the items, you have to *traverse* (move through) nodes cleverly. Here's an outline of how this sort is done (it usually is called an *in order traversal*):

1. Go left as far as you can. Print the node.
2. Print the parent of the node from step 1.
3. From the parent, go right if you can. If you can, go right and repeat step 1. If you can't, move up to the grandparent from step 1 and repeat step 3.

This outline obviously describes a recursive procedure. The following fragment is one version that implements this outline:

```
SUB TreeSort (Nodes$(), Arrows%(), CurrentPos%)

  ' LOCAL variable is: WhereToGo%

  IF Arrows%(CurrentPos%, 0) < > − 1 THEN
     WhereToGo% = Arrows%(CurrentPos%, 0)
     CALL TreeSort(Nodes$(), Arrows%(), WhereToGo%)
  END IF

  PRINT Nodes$(CurrentPos%)

  IF Arrows%(CurrentPos%, 1) < > − 1 THEN
     WhereToGo% = Arrows%(CurrentPos%, 1)
     CALL TreeSort(Nodes$(), Arrows%(), WhereToGo%)
  END IF

END SUB
```

To use this procedure in the example above:

```
CALL TreeSort(Tree$(),Arrows%(),1)
```

The only problem with using this method to sort a list is that, just like using SearchATree, its efficiency completely depends on the shape of the tree. The closer the tree is to being complete (maximum bushiness) the faster this sort works. On the other hand, if the tree degenerates because the names entered already were ordered, TreeSort degenerates does as well.

Consult an advanced book on algorithms to learn how to make sure your trees stay balanced. Keeping a tree balanced requires carefully monitoring of the shape of the tree and making some rather complicated switches.

Trees do have one other problem, especially when you're using arrays to represent the contents of the nodes and the pointers. It's quite painful to delete a node. It's almost never worth the trouble to try to reclaim the space. The best method I know to delete a node is to follow the following outline (I'll leave the details to you):

1. If the node has no children, simply delete it.
2. If the node has one child, attach the parent of the node to be deleted to the lone child.
3. If the node to be deleted has two children, go to its left child, then as far right as possible. This node is the entry that, alphabetically, comes right in front of the entry being deleted. Swap it with the entry that is to be deleted.

In spite of the occasional problems, binary trees are an extremely useful technique. Most of the time, they are the best way to build an index. As you'll see in chapter 15, they are the key to writing an XREF program to cross reference your programs.

When not to use recursion

Many of the example programs I showed you could have been solved by *iteration*—writing a loop. To quote Niklaus Wirth, the inventor of Pascal, ". . . the lesson to be drawn is to avoid the use of recursion when there is an *obvious* solution by iteration."[3]

The reason is that, although a recursive procedure often is shorter to write, it almost inevitably takes longer and uses much more memory to run. You might counter that memory is cheap; however, no matter what you do in QBasic, the stack is no larger than 32K.

As Wirth and others have pointed out, what should be the standard examples of when not to use recursion also are the examples most commonly given of recursion: the factorial and the Fibonacci numbers. (I plead guilty to showing them to you; however, for example, Microsoft gives only the factorial in its manuals.)

Both the factorial and recursion can be computed easier and faster and use much less memory using a loop. The factorial is obvious, the Fibonacci numbers only slightly less so. You need to keep track of the previous two Fibonacci numbers, as shown in the following fragment:

```
DECLARE FUNCTION Fib% (n%)

FUNCTION Fib% (n)

    ' LOCAL variables are: I,First,Second,CurrentFib

    IF n < = 1 THEN
        Fib% = n
        EXIT FUNCTION
```

---

[3]Wirth, Niklaus. *Algorithms + Data Structures = Programs*. (Prentice-Hall) p 130 (italics in the original).

```
    ELSE
        First = 0
        Second = 1
        FOR I = 2 TO n
            CurrentFib = First + Second
            First = Second
            Second = CurrentFib
        NEXT I
        Fib% = CurrentFib
    END IF

END FUNCTION
```

Although you can use the TIMER command to demonstrate the difference between the two versions, a more graphic demonstration is achieved by drawing a diagram (Fig. 13-2) of how much wasted effort there is in the recursive version of Fibonacci.

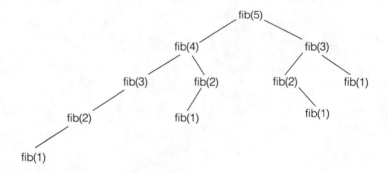

13-2 The calls needed for a recursive fib.

Note that, to compute FIB(4) recursively, a program has to compute FIB(3) twice, compute FIB(2) three times, and get to the trivial case 5 times. It never saves the information it laboriously computes—it just recomputes it constantly.

Another example of where you can replace recursion are the procedures to LoadATree and SearchATree. Because the recursive call happens only at the end when a hole has not yet been detected, you can rewrite that part of the procedure in LoadATree, for example, as in the following fragment:

```
DO UNTIL WhereToGo% = −1

    IF Item$ < Nodes$(CurrentPos%) THEN
        WhereToGo% = Arrows%(CurrentPos%,0)
        Direction$ = "left"
    ELSE
```

```
        WhereToGo% = Arrows%(CurrentPos%,1)
        Direction$ = "right"
    END IF

    LOOP
```

For those who are interested, the reason it's easy to change the original version to a non-recursive, iterative version is that LoadATree is a *tail recursive program*. When you make the recursive call, nothing is left to be done on the stack; it doesn't need to remember anything. Any tail recursive program can be changed to a loop that is controlled by the trivial case—exactly as was done in the previous fragment. On the other hand, TreeSort is not tail recursive because the stack contains many requests to print a node.

One other point that might be of interest to you is that you can theoretically translate any recursive procedure (tail recursive or not) into an iterative version. The trouble is that you do it by setting up a stack and keeping track of everything—work best done by the computer.

14
CHAPTER

Graphics:
curves and fractals

Here's where the math starts. The first section uses the *X-Y*, or Cartesian, plane and a tiny bit of analytic geometry. The remaining sections use polar coordinates and some trigonometry. I thought it only right to give you fair warning.

Figuring out the math, however, is worth it. The last section of this chapter introduces you to *fractals*. Fractals are amazing objects whose study continues to be at the forefront of current research in computer graphics. Figures 14-1 and 14-2 are examples of what the programs described in that section can draw. To understand the fractals section, you'll need to have read chapter 13 on recursion (and also have QBasic).

As you can see, Fig. 14-2 is a reasonable portrait of what a coast line (two-dimensional landscape) looks like. Even more sophisticated three-dimensional fractals are used by such film makers as George Lucas (of Star Wars fame) for special effects within their movies. The genesis sequence in *Star Trek II: Wrath of Khan* was done using them.

Finally, I still will be using SCREEN 1 or SCREEN 2 for the example programs in this chapter. If you have better graphics hardware, you now know how to use it.

The WINDOW command, some simple math, and some pretty pictures

The screen normally is numbered with (0,0) being the top left corner. This arrangement obviously is inconvenient for doing mathematics. Mathematicians

14-1 The Koch snowflake.

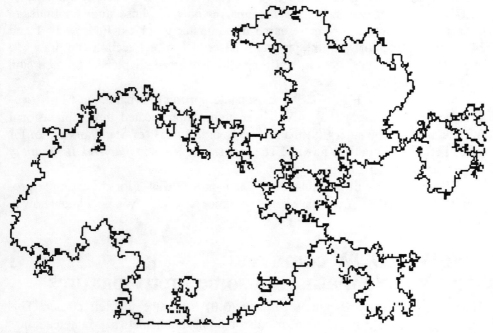

14-2 A fractal coastline.

330 *Graphics: curves and fractals*

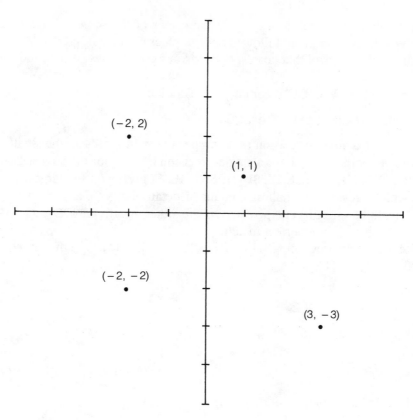

14-3 The Cartesian plane.

use an X-Y system, with X measuring how far horizontally you are from a central point, the *origin*, and Y measuring how far from the center you are vertically. For example, Fig. 14-3 plots a few points on the plane.

The command WINDOW sets up new coordinates, which you can use in any of the graphics commands, that mimics the coordinates in the plane. For example:

```
WINDOW (-320,100)-(320,-100)
```

sets up a new coordinate system with the coordinates of the top left corner being $(-320,100)$ and the bottom right corner being $(320,-100)$. After this command:

```
PSET (-320,100)
PSET (320,100)
PSET (320,-100)
PSET (-320,-100)
PSET (0,0)
```

would illuminate the four corners in a clockwise order starting from the top left, then it illuminates the point at roughly the center of the screen. Whenever you issue a WINDOW command followed by a graphics command, DOS BASIC automatically finds the pixel that corresponds to your coordinates, rounding if necessary.

In general the WINDOW command looks like:

WINDOW (*LeftX, TopY*) – (*RightX, BottomY*)

where *LeftX* is a single-precision real number that will represent the smallest, or left most, *X* coordinate, *TopY* is a single-precision number for the largest *Y* coordinate, etc. WINDOW (– E38,1E38) – (1E38, – 1E38) gives you the largest possible scale, which means the smallest amount of detail. Large *X* and *Y* changes are needed to light up adjacent pixels. On the other hand, WINDOW (– 319,99)-(320, – 100) gives you a perfect match.

The following program, CH14 ∖ P1.BAS, is a QBasic program that sets up an *X-Y* axis in SCREEN 2:

```
'  CH14 ∖ P1.BAS

SCREEN 2
WINDOW (– 5,5) – (5, – 5)

LINE (– 5,0) – (5,0)                                        'X Axis
LINE (0,5) – (0, – 5)                                       'Y Axis

'  Now to label the axes add:

LOCATE 12,1: PRINT "X Axis";
FOR I = 1 TO 6
   LOCATE I,42
   PRINT MID$("Y Axis",I ,1);
NEXT I

END
```

I locate the cursor on the 12th text line and 42nd column to be a bit away from the center. Finally, you might want to add little lines as tick marks:

```
FOR I =  – 5 TO 5
   IF I < > 0 THEN
       LINE (I,0.2) – (I, – 0.2)
       LINE (– 0.1,I) – (0.1,I)
   END IF
NEXT I
```

This fragment actually is the most interesting. It takes into account that, with this WINDOW setting, a horizontal line as long as a vertical one needs roughly twice the vertical distance.

Labeling objects after a WINDOW command is made easier with two commands: PMAP and POINT. After a WINDOW command, PMAP(X,0) gives the ordinary pixel column coordinate for the point X. PMAP(Y,1) gives you the ordinary row coordinate corresponding to Y.

As you can imagine, these commands make captioning graphics easier. If you want to mark a specific place on the screen after a WINDOW command, go to the Immediate window, issue two PMAP commands to find its ordinary coordinates, and convert these coordinates to text rows and columns by dividing by the appropriate number (divide by 8 for rows and by 8 or 16 for columns). Finally, use LOCATE to put the text where you want it.

Similarly, you can do this process in the reverse order. PMAP(Column,3) gives you the *X* coordinate in your WINDOW and PMAP(RowCord,4) gives you the *Y* coordinate in the WINDOW for points given in their ordinary coordinates.

POINT works with the last point referenced, or LPR. POINT(0) gives you ordinary column coordinate of the LPR; POINT(1) the ordinary row coordinate. On the other hand, after a WINDOW command, POINT(2) gives you the *X* coordinate and POINT(3) gives the *Y* coordinate using the window's *X-Y* coordinates.

The WINDOW command makes graphing any mathematical function trivial. The only problems come in deciding the maximum and minimum values to use for the WINDOW statement, which often requires using calculus. However, as before, QBasic will clip any figure that is off the axis, so no problems result with setting the wrong scale. (A sophisticated graphics program would let you zoom in or out by allowing the WINDOW command to change and regraphing as necessary.)

Program CH14 \ P2.BAS is a program for a Cosine graph:

```
' CH14 \ P2.BAS
DEFSNG A – Z
TwoPie! = 8*ATN(1)
SCREEN 2
WINDOW ( – TwoPie,1) – (TwoPie, – 1)

For I = – TwoPie! TO TwoPie! STEP 0.01
    PSET (I,COS(I))
NEXT I

END
```

I'll leave it to you to put in the axes and mark them. I also will leave it to you to experiment with other functions—ones that you might need for school or work.

Now that you know about the WINDOW command, you now can get to some serious picture drawing. The first method I want to show you depends on the following simple idea. Imagine two points in the plane chasing each other. As the second point moves, draw the line connecting the first point's old position to the

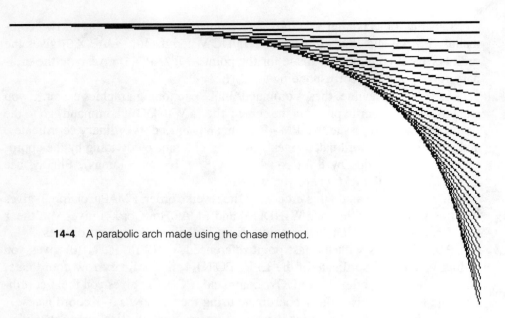

14-4 A parabolic arch made using the chase method.

new position of the second point. Now move the first point down this line a little bit (for example, 10% of the way). Continue the process. Figure 14-4 shows what you get if the second point moves directly down 5 units and the first point always moves 10% of the way.

   To implement this idea, you need a formula that calculates the new coordinate. Suppose that you want the point halfway down on the line connecting (50,100) to (100,200). It's pretty obvious that it has to be at (75,150). However, suppose you wanted a point that was only 10% of the way along this line. This point turns out to be at (55,110), because, in some sense, you have 50 X units to move and 100 Y units to move. In general, the formula to move on a line connecting $(x1,y1)$ to $(x2,y2)$ is:

   $(1-t) \times x1 + t \times x2$

for the new X coordinate and:

   $(1-t) \times y1 + t \times y2$

for the new Y coordinate. Here t is the percent moved expressed as a decimal.

   Given this formula, CH14 \ P3.BAS is the QBasic program that draws the parabolic arch described previously:

```
'CH14 \ P3.BAS
'  a parabolic arch

DEFSNG A – Z
SCREEN 2
WINDOW ( – 300, 100) – (300, – 100)
```

```
x1 = -300: x2 = 300
y1 = 100: y2 = 100

PerCent = 0.1

DO UNTIL y2 < -100
    y2 = y2-5                                    ' down five units
    LINE (x1, y1)-(x2, y2)                       ' connect the points

    x1 = (1-PerCent)*x1+(PerCent*x2)             'move down the line
    y1 = (1-PerCent)*y1+(PerCent*y2)

LOOP                                'change to WHILE/WEND for GW-BASIC

END
```

Although not a bad start, you really don't start getting results until you add more points. Imagine the four points start at the corners of a square. The first chases the second, the second chases the third, the third the fourth, and the fourth chases the first. Figure 14-5 shows you what you get after only two moves.

Obviously, what is happening is that each square is both rotating and shrinking. Before I give you the program, however, I need to remind you of one more formula: the so called *distance formula*. This formula states that the distance between two points *(x1,y1)* and *(x2,y2)* in the plane is:

$$\sqrt{(x2-x1)^2+(y2-y1)^2}$$

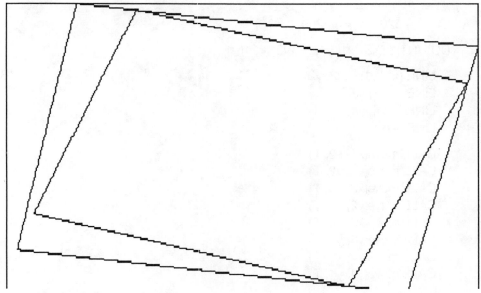

14-5 Rotating squares.

In QBasic, you could use the following fragment:

```
FUNCTION Dist(x1,y1,x2,y2)

A = (x2 − x1)*(x2 − x1)
B = (y2 − y1)*(y2 − y1)

Dist = SQR(A + B)

END FUNCTION
```

The purpose of having a distance function is to know when to stop.

CH14 \ P4.BAS is the program that drew Fig. 12-1. It needs the DIST function given above:

```
DECLARE SUB move (a!, B!, T!)
DECLARE FUNCTION DIST! (x1!, y1!, x2!, y2!)

' CH14 \ P4.BAS
' Nested (rotated) squares

DEFSNG A − Z
SCREEN 2
WINDOW (− 320, 200) − (320, − 200)

T = 0.05                                        'Percentage moved if 5%
x1 = − 320: y1 = 200
x2 = 320: y2 = 200
x3 = 320: y3 = − 200
x4 = − 320: y4 = − 200

DO UNTIL DIST(x1, y1, x2, y2) < 10              'A

   LINE (x1, y1) − (x2, y2)                     'B
   LINE − (x3, y3)
   LINE − (x4, y4)
   LINE − (x1, y1)

   CALL move(x1, x2, T)                         'C
   CALL move(y1, y2, T)
   CALL move(x2, x3, T)
   CALL move(y2, y3, T)
   CALL move(x3, x4, T)
   CALL move(y3, y4, T)
   CALL move(x4, x1, T)
   CALL move(y4, y1, T)

LOOP
```

```
SLEEP

END

FUNCTION DIST (x1, y1, x2, y2)

    a = (x2 − x1)*(x2 − x1)
    B = (y2 − y1)*(y2 − y1)

    DIST = SQR(a + B)

END FUNCTION

SUB move (a, B, T)
    a = (1 − T)*a + T*B
END SUB
```

A   This line stops the process when the points get close enough.

B   I can't use the box command because the square is rotated.

C   This block finds the new coordinates for each of the four points. By adding more parameters, I could have made the move subprogram make the changes one point at a time, instead of one coordinate at a time.

If you imagine the points are moving independently along curves, the kind of pictures can be even more dramatic. Figure 14-6 is one of the simplest ones. In this picture, you should imagine one point is constantly moving around a circle around the origin while the other point chases it by moving along a line of sight.

To write a program to do this chase or to construct one whose results are even more dramatic (chases along more complicated curves), you'll need formulas for

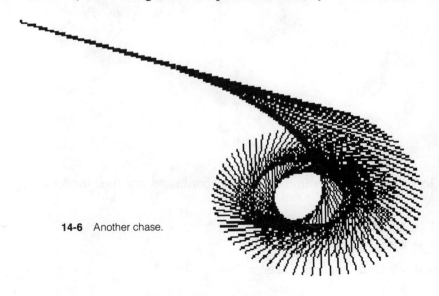

14-6 Another chase.

the curves, which is the subject of the next section. After reading that section, you'll have no trouble writing a program to draw these chases.

Polar coordinates

Most complicated mathematical curves are described more easily using *polar coordinates*. With polar coordinates, you describe the position of a point by saying how far it is from the origin and at what angle a line connecting the origin to the point makes with the positive X axis. Figure 14-7 shows an example of polar coordinates.

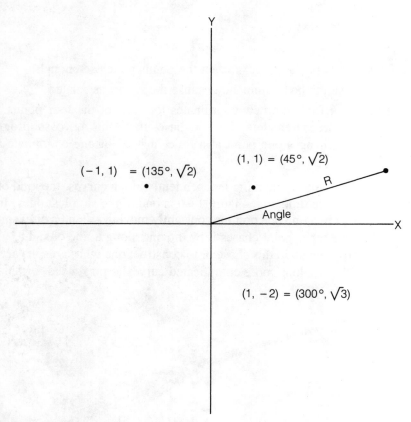

14-7 Polar coordinates.

To go from polar coordinates to X-Y coordinates one uses the following formulas:

$X = R \times \text{COS}(\textit{Angle})$
$Y = R \times \text{SIN}(\textit{Angle})$

where *Angle* is the angle indicated in Fig. 14-7.

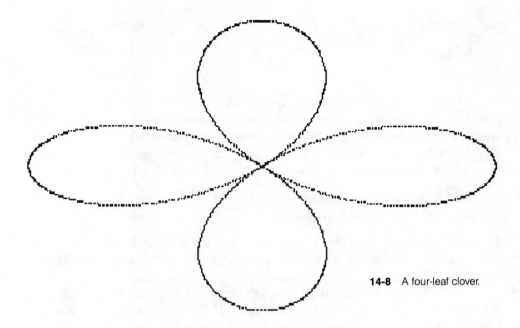

14-8 A four-leaf clover.

To go from *X-Y* coordinates to polar coordinates, use:

$$R = \sqrt{X^2 + Y^2}$$

The angle is ATN(Y/X), unless X is zero.

The point of polar coordinates for you is that the equation of a curve might have a much simpler formula in polar coordinates than in rectangular *X-Y* coordinates. For example, the equation of a circle of radius 10 around the origin is simply *R = 10*, instead of $X^2 + Y^2 = 100$. As a more interesting example, you easily can draw objects like a four leaf clover (Fig. 14-8). The formula for this object is R = COS(2*Angle), as the angle runs from 0 to 2π (0° to 360°). If you combine this formula with the conversion formulas for *X* and *Y* given previously, you have the following simple program that draws a four leaf clover:

```
'CH14 \ P5.BAS
DEFSNG A – Z

TwoPie = 8 * ATN(1)
SCREEN 2
WINDOW (– 2, 2) – (2, – 2)

FOR I = 0 TO TwoPie STEP 0.01

    R = COS(2 * I)
    X = R * COS(I)
    Y = R * SIN(I)
```

```
    PSET (x, y)

NEXT I

END
```

Don't be surprised if this program takes a bit of time to run. After all, it requires a few thousand sine and cosine computations. For that reason, there's a common way to speed up polar graphs. Instead of going from 0 to 2π, use the symmetry in the sine and cosine function. You really only have to compute sines and cosines from 0 to π if you add a PSET$(-x, -y)$. This trick works because:

```
SIN(180 + Angle)  =  - SIN(Angle)
COS(180 + Angle)  =  - COS(Angle)
```

In general, you have to know the formula for the object in question. Over the years, people have figured out a lot of this information and it's readily available in libraries.

The following demonstration program collects a large number of examples through the use of a random number generator. It also uses the following observation: if you slightly twist the conversion formulas from $X = R*COS(Angle)$ to $X = R*COS(RandomInteger*Angle)$, then the pictures are even more dramatic.

The following program is long, but nothing in it is very difficult. The most important is the following fragment that chooses the function to be graphed:

```
FUNCTION RofTheta (Theta, Curv%)

SHARED FFActr() AS INTEGER                                        'A
SELECT CASE Curv%

    CASE 1                                                       'B
       RofTheta = 1 + (2*COS(2*Theta))
    CASE 2
       RofTheta = COS(4*Theta)
    CASE 3
       RofTheta = Theta/2
    CASE 4
       RofTheta = (2*SIN(FFActr(3)*Theta)) - (2*COS(FFActr(4)*Theta))
    CASE 5
       RofTheta = 3*COS(FFActr(1)*Theta)
    CASE 6
       RofTheta = 1 + (FFActr(1)*COS(FFActr(2)*FFActr(3)*Theta))
    CASE 7
       RofTheta = 1 + (FFActr(1)*COS(FFActr(2)*Theta))
    CASE 8
       RofTheta = (FFActr(1)*SIN(Theta))/(2 + COS(Theta))
```

```
    CASE ELSE
        A = (FFActr(1)*COS(FFActr(3)*Theta))
        B = (FFActr(2)*SIN(FFActr(4)*Theta))
        RofTheta = A + B

END SELECT

END FUNCTION
```

A This array stores the various fudge factors—random integers that I set up elsewhere.

B The first three cases set up three unfudged curves: a loop-the-loop, a four-leaf clover, and a spiral. The other cases are affected by the random integers used as fudge factors.

Now, to graph the curves, just modify the normal polar graphing module to allow twisted coordinates. The parameter Tf% acts as a switch to determine whether to twist the coordinates or not.

```
SUB PolarPlot (Curve%, Tf%)

SHARED Pie, limit%, FFActr( ) AS INTEGER

    ' This procedure plots the graph using either normal or twisted
    ' polar coordinates

    CLS
    FOR I = 0 TO Pie STEP 0.005
        IF Tf% = TRUE THEN                                    'Fudge it
            X = RofTheta(I, Curve%) * COS(FFActr(5) * I)
            y = RofTheta(I, Curve%) * SIN(FFActr(6) * I)
        ELSE                                                  'reg polar
            X = RofTheta(I, Curve%) * COS(I)                  'coord
            y = RofTheta(I, Curve%) * SIN(I)
        END IF
        IF X > limit% OR y > limit% THEN STOP
        PSET (X, y): PSET (-X, -y)
    NEXT I

END SUB
```

Here's the rest of the program:

```
DECLARE SUB PolarPlot (Curve%, I%)
DECLARE FUNCTION AskIfComplicated% ( )
DECLARE SUB MakeFudgeFactors (A%( ))
DECLARE FUNCTION MaxSize% (C%)
DECLARE FUNCTION RofTheta! (Theta!, C%)
```

```
'  CH14 \ P6.BAS
'  A polar coordinate demo

DIM FFActr(1 TO 7) AS INTEGER       'stores 8 random integers

CONST TRUE  =  - 1
CONST FALSE  =  NOT TRUE

Pie  =  4 * ATN(1)

SCREEN 2

PRINT "Press X to eXit any other key to continue.";
YN$  =  INPUT$(1)

DO UNTIL YN$  =  "X"

   CLS
   Complicated%  =  AskIfComplicated%

   '  Now CALL a procedure that gets 7 random integers
   CALL MakeFudgeFactors(FFActr( ))

   "  This block sizes the window depending on the chosen curve
   CurveNumber%  =  FFActr(7)
   limit%  =  MaxSize%(CurveNumber%)
   WINDOW ( - limit%, limit%) - (limit%,  - limit%)

   CALL PolarPlot(CurveNumber%, Complicated%)
   LOCATE 1, 1: PRINT "Press any key to continue  -  X to eXit.";
   YN$  =  INPUT$(1)

LOOP
CLS

END

FUNCTION AskIfComplicated%

   CLS
   PRINT "If you want the picture to be really complicated ";
   PRINT "press Y."
   YN$  =  INPUT$(1)

   IF UCASE$(YN$)  =  "Y" THEN
      AskIfComplicated%  =  TRUE
   ELSE
      AskIfComplicated%  =  FALSE
   END IF
   CLS
```

```
END FUNCTION

SUB MakeFudgeFactors (A%())

    ' This sub creates an array of 7 random integers between 1 and 9
    ' local variables X,N%

    CLS

    INPUT "Enter a positive integer as 'seed'"; N%
    RANDOMIZE N%

    FOR I = 1 TO 7
       A%(I) = 1 + (8 * RND(1))
    NEXT I

END SUB

FUNCTION MaxSize% (C%)

    ' This function determines the sizes of the curve
    ' and uses that 'COS and SIN are both at most 1

    SHARED FFActr( ) AS INTEGER

    SELECT CASE C%
       CASE 1 TO 5
          MaxSize% = 4
       CASE 6 TO 8
          MaxSize% = 1 + FFActr(1)
       CASE ELSE
          MaxSize% = FFActr(1) + FFActr(2)
    END SELECT

END FUNCTION
```

Figure 14-9 is an example of what you can get out of this program.

Multiple screen pages

Occasionally, you'll want to temporarily overwrite or erase the screen. Up until now, however, you haven't seen a good way to get the screen back to its original form. For example, error trapping occasionally will involve writing messages on the screen asking you to correct the error so that you can continue. After you correct the error, how do you get back to the original screen?

The easiest way is to use the multiple screen pages that your PC provides in text mode. For example, you can write on one text screen while displaying the other, then switch back and forth between them. This swapping is done by a modification of the SCREEN command.

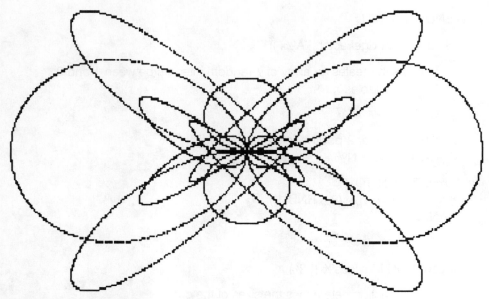

14-9 A twisted polar graph.

The full form of the SCREEN command takes four options:

SCREEN *x1, x2, x3, x4*

You already have seen the first two options. Recall that the first slot is for the screen mode and the second is not zero when you want color to be displayed on a composite monitor. The last two slots are the ones that concern you now. The third slot holds the number of the page that you're currently writing to; the fourth holds the page that's currently visible. In 80-column text mode (SCREEN 0:WIDTH 80), you have four pages, numbered 0 to 3, for these slots. A fragment like:

```
SCREEN 0,, 1, 0
CALL WriteMessage
SCREEN 0, , 1, 1
```

will call a procedure to write a message on the next text page, while keeping the original text screen intact.

```
SCREEN 0,, 1,1
```

will display the new message. Finally, you can use:

```
SCREEN 0,, 0, 0
```

to go back to displaying and writing on the original screen.

DOS BASIC also makes it easy to copy the contents of one screen page to another. The command:

PCOPY *frompage, topage*

copies the entire contents of one screen page to another. One common use of PCOPY is when you want to preserve the original page intact but still use part of it in the second page.

Fractals

Besides some trigonometry this section depends on understanding recursion. So the programs will work only in QBasic.

Benoit Mandelbrot of IBM, who coined the term *fractal*, is doing much to show how useful the idea is. He says that fractals are most often *identical at all scales*. This description is the simplest way to get at many fractals. They are objects that remain essentially the same, no matter how powerful the magnifying glass. The large scale structure is repeated ad infinitum in the small.

One of Mandelbrot's standard examples is a coastline. From an airplane, from the ground, or using a magnifying glass, you get the same pattern on an even smaller scale.

An outline description of a general fractal is:

1. Draw the object in the large
2. Replace pieces of the large object with smaller versions of itself.

This outline obviously is a description of a recursive process.

Before you get to any of the classic fractals look at Fig. 14-10. As you can see, this figure consists of squares, the corners of which are replaced by still smaller squares. The pseudocode for this program might be something like:

SUB Draw A Square
    At each corner of the square, draw a square of smaller size
    CALL Draw A Square unless the squares are already too small
END SUB

CH14 \ P7.BAS is a program that implements this outline:

```
' CH14 \ P7.BAS
' recursive squares

DECLARE SUB square (x%, y%, size%)
DEFINT A – Z

SCREEN 2
WINDOW ( – 2000, 2000) – (2000, – 2000)

CALL Square( – 1000, 1000, 2000)
```

14-10 An incomplete recursive shrinking square.

```
END

SUB Square (x, y, Size)                                              'A

    IF Size < 50 THEN EXIT SUB

    LINE (x, y) – (x + Size, y – Size), , B                         'B

    CALL Square(x – Size/4, y + Size/4, Size/2)                     'C
    CALL Square(x + Size – Size/4, y + Size/4, Size/2)
    CALL Square(x – Size/4, y – Size + Size/4, Size/2)
    CALL Square(x + Size – Size/4, y – Size + Size/4, Size/2)

END SUB
```

A   This line gives a way to terminate the recursion.

B   This line draws the large square.

C   This line is the recursive call. There are four new corners, each one is
    moved 1/4 of the size of the previous in or out from the previous one
    and is 1/2 as big.

Figure 14-11 is a screen dump of the start of one of the first fractals to be discovered. It's the beginning of a fractal called the *Koch snowflake*, which you saw in the first figure in this chapter.

As you can see, this figure consists of a Star of David repeated on an ever-smaller scale. The key to programming this object is to notice that, if, for exam-

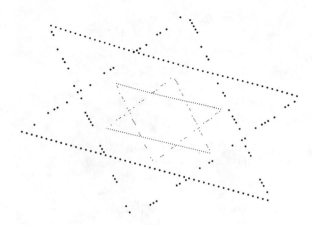

14-11 The start of a Koch snowflake.

ple, you start from the center of the Star of David of size eight, then each vertex has either a one-, two-, or four-unit shift in the *X* or *Y* level.

Once you understand this technique, then writing the program only requires setting up an array that, on each call, holds the current values for the 12 vertices. CH14 \ P8.BAS is the program:

```
' CH14 \ P8.BAS
' The Koch snowflake

DECLARE SUB Koch (x%, y%, size%)

CLEAR ,,10000

DEFINT A – Z
SCREEN 1
COLOR 0, 2
WINDOW ( – 100, 100) – (100, – 100)
CALL Koch(0, 0, 120)

END

SUB Koch (x, y, size)

    'local variables are X( ), Y( ), shift, i, colnum
    DIM x(12), y(12)

    IF Size < 5 THEN EXIT SUB
    shift = size/8
    x(1) = x: y(1) = y + 4 * shift
    x(2) = x + shift: y(2) = y + 2 * shift
    x(3) = x + 3 * shift: y(3) = y(2)
    x(4) = x + 2 * shift: y(4) = y
    x(5) = x(3): y(5) = y – 2 * shift
```

```
x(6) = x(2): y(6) = y(5)
x(7) = x: y(7) = y - 4 * shift
x(8) = x - shift: y(8) = y(5)
x(9) = x - 3 * shift: y(9) = y(5)
x(10) = x - 2 * shift: y(10) = y
x(11) = x(9): y(11) = y(2)
x(12) = x(8): y(12) = y(2)

LINE (x(1), y(1)) - (x(5), y(5))                              'A
LINE - (x(9), y(9))
LINE - (x(1), y(1))

LINE (x(3), y(3)) - (x(7), y(7))                              'B
LINE - (x(11), y(11))
LINE - (x(3), y(3))

CALL Koch(x, y, 2 * shift)                                    'C
FOR i = 1 TO 12
    CALL Koch(x(i), y(i), 3 * shift)                          'D
NEXT i

END SUB
```

A   This block draws part of the star.

B   This block draws the rest of the star.

C   This line creates ever-smaller stars in the middle of each star.

D   This line creates a star at each of the twelve vertices.

To understand the remaining fractal curves, observe that there's another way to think of the Koch snowflake. What the program is doing is replacing each straight line segment by a line segment that looks like Fig. 14-12.

This idea of continually replacing a straight line with a bent line is the key to the next two curves. In the first, which usually is called a *C-curve*, you replace each straight line by a bend, as in Fig. 14-13. This process eventually yields a figure that looks like Fig. 14-14.

For the next fractal, called the *Dragon curve*, modify the C-Curve by putting the bends on opposite sides. The replacement parts alternately go out and in. Figure 14-15 shows a picture of what you get.

The pseudocode for both these programs is the same:

```
SUB DrawAFractal with MakeABend
    If the line isn't too small, replace the line with the bent one
    CALL SUB for the smaller line
```

The only point remaining is to describe mathematically how to make a bend. This point is where trigonometry comes in. What you need is a formula that, given a

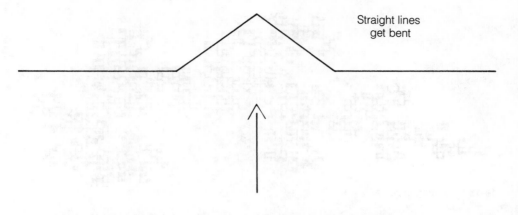

Straight lines
get bent

14-12 The twist for the Koch curve.

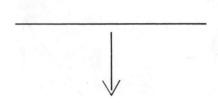

14-13 The building block for the C-curve.

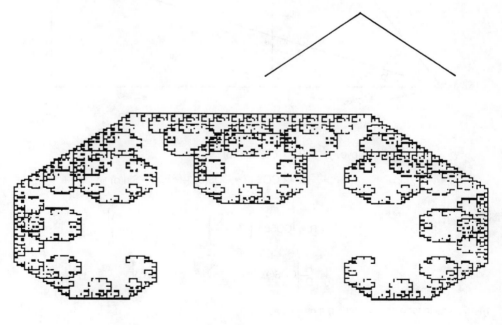

14-14 A C-curve.

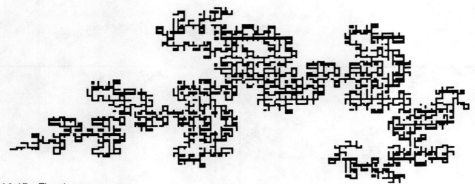

14-15 The dragon curve.

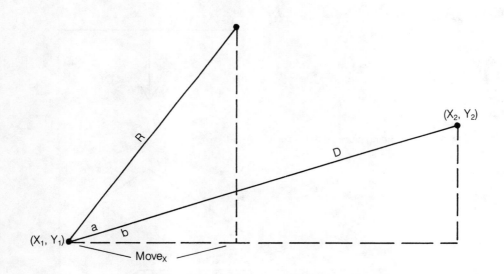

$$\text{Move}_X = R \bullet COS\,(a + b)$$

$$= R \bullet \left[COS(a) \bullet COS(b) - \sin(a) \bullet Sin(b) \right]$$

$$= R \bullet \left[COS(a) \left(\frac{X_2 - X_1}{D} \right) - \sin(a) \left(\frac{Y_2 - Y_1}{D} \right) \right]$$

$$= \frac{R}{D} \left[COS(a)(X_2 - X_1) - \sin(a)\,(Y_2 - Y_1) \right]$$

14-16 The trigonometry of finding a new point.

line connecting any two points and angle, finds the coordinate of the new point. Look at Fig. 14-16. Notice that if the angle is 45°, as it is in the C and Dragon curves, then the size of the spike is:

COS(45°)∗D = (SQR(2)/2)∗D

because the triangle is a 45°-45°-90° right triangle. Using this formula, the keys to a program for the C-curve are the following MoveX and MoveY functions:

```
FUNCTION MoveX! (X1!, y1!, x2!, Y2!)

    ' local variables: Angle(in radians), D, XShift, YShift

    Angle = Radians!(45)

    D = Dist(X1, x2, y1, Y2)
    R = (SQR(2) / 2) ∗ D

    XShift = COS(Angle) ∗ (x2 − X1)
    YShift = SIN(Angle) ∗ (Y2 − y1)

    MoveX = R / D ∗ (XShift − YShift)
END FUNCTION

FUNCTION MoveY! (X1!, y1!, x2!, Y2!)

    ' local variables: Angle(in radians), D, XShift, YShift

    Angle = Radians(45)

    D = Dist(X1, x2, y1, Y2)
    R = (SQR(2) / 2) ∗ D

    XShift = SIN(Angle) ∗ (x2 − X1)
    YShift = COS(Angle) ∗ (Y2 − y1)

    MoveY! = R / D ∗ (XShift + YShift)
END FUNCTION

' This block is the main recursive SUB:

SUB Curve (X1, y1, x2, Y2)
    DEFSNG A − Z
    DistPt = Dist(X1, y1, x2, Y2)

    IF DistPt < 10 THEN
        EXIT SUB
    END IF

    nx1 = X1 + MoveX(X1, y1, x2, Y2)                    'find the coord
```

```
    ny1 = y1 + MoveY(X1, y1, x2, Y2)              'for the spike
    LINE (X1, y1) – (x2, Y2), 0          'erase the previous line
    LINE (X1, y1) – (nx1, ny1)              ' make the spike
    LINE – (x2, Y2)

    CALL Curve(X1, y1, nx1, ny1)         'now recurse on the
    CALL Curve(nx1, ny1, x2, Y2)                   'spikes
END SUB
```

Here's the rest of the program for the C-curve:

```
'CH14 \ P9.BAS
'A C-Curve

DECLARE FUNCTION Radians! (X!)
DECLARE FUNCTION MoveY! (X1!, y1!, x2!, Y2!)
DECLARE FUNCTION MoveX! (X1!, y1!, x2!, Y2!)
DECLARE FUNCTION Dist! (X1!, y1!, x2!, Y2!)
DECLARE SUB Curve (X1!, y1!, x2!, Y2!)

DEFSNG A – Z

CLEAR ,,12000                            'more stack space
SCREEN 2

CONST PI = 3.14159

WINDOW (– 500!, 500!) – (500!, – 500!)

X1 = – 250: y1 = – 200
x2 = 250: Y2 = – 200

CALL Curve(X1, y1, x2, Y2)

SLEEP
END

FUNCTION Dist (X1, y1, x2, Y2)
  ' finds the distance between points
  ' local variables are: x,y

    X = (x2 – X1) * (x2 – X1)
    y = (Y2 – y1) * (Y2 – y1)
    Dist = SQR(X + y)

END FUNCTION

FUNCTION Radians! (X!)
  'converts degrees to radians
```

```
        Radians! = X! * PI / 180
    END FUNCTION
```

The nice thing about these kinds of fractals is that all you ever have to do is change the MoveX and MoveY functions. For the dragon curve, you need to modify them so that they alternate sides each time—a perfect situation for static variables. For example, the following fragment is the modification of the MoveX! function (the MoveY! function is similar):

```
FUNCTION MoveX! (X1!, y1!, x2!, Y2!)
    ' modified mover for Dragon curve
    ' local variables: Angle(in radians), D, XShift, YShift
    STATIC J
    J = J + 1

    Angle = Radians!(45)
    IF J MOD 2 = 0 THEN Angle = -Angle            'alternate on each call!

    D = Dist(X1, x2, y1, Y2)
    R = (SQR(2) / 2) * D

    XShift = COS(Angle) * (x2 - X1)
    YShift = SIN(Angle) * (Y2 - y1)

    MoveX = R / D * (XShift - YShift)

END FUNCTION
```

Finally, it's time to show you the coastline program that drew Fig. 14-2. Again, the only difference between this figure and the two preceding curves is that, this time, the angle is to be random, as is the size of each spike. To do this modification, you have to change the move functions by incorporating a random factor for the angle (instead of 45°) and for the size of the spike (instead of COS(45°)*D). For example, in the following fragment, the lines by comments A and B do this modification:

```
FUNCTION MoveX! (x1!, y1!, x2!, y2!)
    ' local variables: Angle(in radians), D, XShift, YShift

    Angle = Radians!(15 + 60 * RND(1))                          'A

    IF RND(1) > 0.5 THEN Angle = -Angle

    D = Dist(x1, x2, y1, y2)
    R = (0.15 + (.6 * RND(1))) * D                              'B

    XShift = COS(Angle) * (x2 - x1)
    YShift = SIN(Angle) * (y2 - y1)
```

```
    MoveX = (R / D) * (XShift - YShift)

END FUNCTION
```

Instead of one call that acts recursively on a single line, this time, the program will build the shoreline out of three recursive calls to three lines that form a triangle. The following fragment will do this fractal:

```
WINDOW (-500!, 500!)-(500!, -500!)

x1 = -250: y1 = 200
x2 = 250: y2 = 200

CALL Curve(x1, y1, x2, y2)
CALL Curve(x2, y2, 0, -y2)
CALL Curve(0, -y2, x1, y1)
```

Obviously, I have sampled only some of the richness available in the study of fractals.

15
CHAPTER

Working
with files

This chapter shows you how to handle disks and disk files within DOS BASIC. The first section explains the built-in file handling commands and the SHELL command, which lets you invoke DOS commands, such as COPY or FORMAT, from within DOS BASIC programs. The next four sections explain sequential files. Then, I will turn to random access files, which are much simpler to handle in QBasic than in GW-BASIC because of records (see chapter 11). Finally, I will end the chapter with a short discussion of *cryptography*—how to make the information in files secure from a casual probe.

SHELL: interacting with DOS

DOS BASIC has six commands that mimic customary DOS commands:

MKDIR	Make a directory
CHDIR	Change directory
RMDIR	Remove an empty directory
FILES	List files in the current directory
KILL	Delete a file
NAME *file1* AS *file2*	Rename *file1* as *file2*

You use these commands by following them with a string or string variable. For example, MKDIR "TestDir" would add a subdirectory called TestDir to the current directory. MKDIR "C:\TestDir" adds it to the root of the C: drive.

The three commands that handle files also accept the normal DOS wild cards. For example, FILES "*.BAS" would give a listing of the files in the current directory with a BAS extension. KILL "*.*" deletes all the files in the current directory. NAME actually can do a bit more than the DOS REN command. NAME can copy from one directory in the current drive to another. To do this command, give the full pathname. The command:

NAME "C: \ QB \ Test.BAS" AS "C: \ Examples \ Test"

moves the Test program from the QB directory to the Examples directory of your hard drive.

Although a few of DOS's utility programs are built into DOS BASIC (usually with slightly different names, such as FILES for a variant on DIR/W and KILL for DEL), most of them are not built into DOS BASIC. The SHELL command, which is not available in versions of GW-BASIC before 3.0, lets you run any COM, EXE, or BAT file from within a DOS BASIC program. For example, if you wanted to display a directory in the form most people are accustomed to see it, use:

SHELL "DIR"

or

SHELL "DIR/P"

The general form is:

SHELL *string*

where *string* contains the name of the stand-alone program or batch file that you want to execute.

The SHELL command has to be used with care, especially while you're developing the program from within QBasic. You must have enough memory to keep QBasic, the current program, a new copy of DOS, and the program you're SHELLing to in memory simultaneously. In addition, you must have set DOS's PATH command or have a disk containing the program that you are SHELLing to in the current drive.

If you know DOS well, then the SHELL command, when combined with pipes and filters, which are discussed briefly in chapter 16, gives you an extraordinary powerful addition to DOS BASIC.

Sequential files

Using sequential files in DOS BASIC is analogous to recording information on a cassette tape. It turns out that the analogy is quite close, so a particularly useful one to keep in mind. For example, the operations on sequential files that are analogous to easy tasks for a cassette recorder, such as recording an album on a blank tape, will be easy. Those operations analogous to harder tasks, such as splicing tapes together or making a change within a tape, will be harder.

More precisely, a sequential file is best when you know that you will:

- Rarely make changes within the file.
- Process the information it contains from start to finish, not needing to constantly jump around.
- Any information that you intend to add to the file can safely be tucked away at the end.

It's not that you can't do these things with sequential files; it's just that they're a bit painful and time consuming.

Using a sequential text file called SONG in the currently active directory, the command OPEN "SONG" FOR INPUT AS #1 is analogous to pressing Play on a cassette player then putting it on Pause. OPEN "SONG" FOR OUTPUT AS #1 is similar to pressing Record and Pause on a cassette player. CLOSE #1 is like taking the tape out of the cassette player.

Each time DOS BASIC sees the OPEN command, it gets ready to send information into or take information out of the file. It sets up a *channel* to communicate with the file. What follows the OPEN command is the name of the file you are working with. It must be surrounded by quotes. Unless it is in the current directory, you have to give its full hierarchical pathname. You also can use a string variable if its current value is a legal filename. The rules for filenames are the rules that DOS imposes: at most eight characters, followed by an optional period, followed by an optional three-character extension. The characters you can use are the letters *A* through *Z*, the numbers 0 through 9, and the following special non-alphanumeric characters:

( ) { } @ # $ % & ^ ! – _ ' /

Lowercase letters are automatically converted to uppercase.

Finally, DOS BASIC needs a *file identifier*, which is a number (preceded by the pound sign) that you will use to identify the file. Although you can't change this number until you close the file, the next time you need the file, you can open it with a different identifier number. The number of possible files you can have open at once is limited by DOS to eight files unless you change your CONFIG.SYS file (see any book on DOS to learn how to change your CONFIG.SYS file).

When DOS BASIC processes an OPEN command, it also reserves a file buffer in the computer's memory. Without a buffer, each piece of information sent to or from the disk would be recorded or played back separately. Because mechanical operations, like writing to a disk, are much slower than writing to RAM, reading from or writing to a disk would waste a lot of time. Instead, when a file buffer fills up, DOS BASIC tells DOS to activate the appropriate drive and a whole packet of information is sent in a continuous stream to the disk. The number of buffers also can be changed from your CONFIG.SYS file.

The CLOSE command empties the buffer and tells DOS to update the FAT (file allocation table). For this reason, a sudden power outage when you have a file OPEN almost inevitably leads to lost information, occasionally even to a corrupted disk. (The CHKDSK/f command often is necessary when this event happens.)

The PRINT command usually sends information to the screen. A variant, the PRINT # command, is one way to send information to a file. CH15 \ P1.BAS is an example of a QBasic program that sends one piece of information to a file named SONG.

```
'  CH15 \ P1.BAS
'  Writing to a file

OPEN "SONG" FOR OUTPUT AS #1
PRINT #1, "TESTING, 1 2 3"

CLOSE #1

END
```

After the usual remark statements, the first executable statement tells QBasic that you are going to set up a file named SONG, having file identifier #1. Note that, if a file already exists in the current directory with the name SONG, the existing file is erased by this statement. Opening a file for output starts a file anew; the contents of a previous file with the same name are lost.

Next is the statement that actually sends the information to the file. The comma is necessary, but what follows the comma can be anything that might occur in an ordinary PRINT statement. What appears in the file is a mirror image of what would have occurred on the screen. For example, the file does not contain quotation marks. More precisely, the file will contain the word TESTING followed by a comma, the numeral 1, a space, the numeral 2, a space, and the numeral 3. Although you might not have thought of it at first, the program then adds on the characters that define a carriage return/line feed combination: CHR$(13) (carriage return) and CHR$(10) (line feed).

It is extremely important that you keep in mind that the PRINT # command works exactly like the PRINT command. By now, you are well aware of the automatic carriage return/line feed combination that follows an ordinary PRINT statement. More precisely, if I had changed the line to read:

```
PRINT #1, "TESTING, 1 2 3";
```

the file would contain two fewer characters. The CHR$(13) and CHR$(10) would no longer be there because the semicolon suppresses the carriage return/line feed combination, just like for an ordinary PRINT statement.

I am harping on this idea because the cardinal rule of file handling is that you must know the exact structure of a file if you want to be able to efficiently re-use the information that it contains.

As a third example, suppose I change the line to read:

```
PRINT #1, "TESTING",1,2,3
```

Now, the file contains many spaces, CHR$(32), that were not there before. To see why this fact must be true, just recall that a comma in a PRINT statement moves the cursor to the next print zone by inserting spaces. If you use a comma in a PRINT # statement, the same spaces are placed in your file.

Finally, the command CLOSE, followed by a file identifier, moves whatever is in the appropriate file buffer to the disk. The computer *flushes* the buffer to the disk. The command CLOSE without a file identifier flushes all open buffers; it closes all open files.

Once a file is open, DOS BASIC has a command LOF(*string*) to tell you how large a file is. To use this command, place the appropriate file identifier number within the parentheses. To see this command at work (and to confirm what I said about the sizes of the various versions of the SONG file described above), try the following program:

```
'  CH15 \ P2.BAS
'  a file tester
'  demonstrates the 'mirror' image property of PRINT #

OPEN "TEST1" FOR OUTPUT AS #1
OPEN "TEST2" FOR OUTPUT AS #2
OPEN "TEST3" FOR OUTPUT AS #3

PRINT #1, "TESTING, 1,2,3"
PRINT #2, "TESTING, 1,2,3";
PRINT #3, "TESTING, ,1,2,3"

PRINT LOF(1)
PRINT LOF(2)
PRINT LOF(3)

CLOSE
END
```

If you run this program, what you'll see is:

```
16
14
47
```

As you can see, the first file does contain two more characters than the second, which accounts for the carriage return/line feed combination. The third file contains far more than the 14 characters in the phrase TESTING, 1 2 3. The extra characters, as you'll soon see, are indeed spaces.

Reading back information from a file

To read information back from a file, you must open the file for input using its name and must give it a file identifier that currently is not being used within the program. It doesn't have to be the same identifier that it was set up with originally. In QBasic, the easiest way to find an unused file identifier is with the command FREEFILE. The value of FREEFILE is always the next unused file identifier number. Therefore, you merely have to have a statement like:

```
FreeFileNumber = FREEFILE
```

at the appropriate point in your program followed by:

```
OPEN "filename" FOR INPUT AS #FreeFileNumber
```

In GW-BASIC, you have to keep track of this information yourself.

Next, choose a variant on the INPUT command to retrieve the information. For example, suppose you wanted to read back the file TEST1. This file contains the word *TESTING* followed by a comma, which is followed by the numbers. It ends with the carriage return/line feed combination. To decide on the easiest way to read this information back from this file, pretend for a second that you were going to enter this information into the computer via the keyboard. You could not simply say INPUT A$, because that would pick up only the word *TESTING*. The INPUT command would read information only up to the first comma. So, you would likely use LINE INPUT A$, because, as you know, the LINE INPUT command disregards any spaces or commas that might have been typed. It accepts all the information typed until the Enter key was hit. The carriage return/line feed combination corresponds to the Enter key.

CH15 \ P3.BAS is a QBasic program to read back and print out the contents of the file named TEST1:

```
'CH15 \ P3.BAS
' Reading back a file

OPEN "TEST1" FOR INPUT AS #1

LINE INPUT #1, A$
PRINT A$

CLOSE #1
END
```

As an alternative you could have used CH15 \ P4.BAS:

```
'CH15 \ P4.BAS

OPEN "TEST1" FOR INPUT AS #1

INPUT #1,A$,B$,C$,D$
PRINT A$;" ";B$;" ";C$;" ";D$

CLOSE #1
END
```
or CH15 \ P5:
```
'CH15 \ P5.BAS

OPEN "TEST1" FOR INPUT AS #1

INPUT #1,A$,B,C,D
PRINT A$;B;C;D

CLOSE #1
END
```

Both of these programs seem rather clumsy. The last program has recovered the numbers as numbers, rather than as strings of numerals. If you have stored numbers in a file, then this program is one method to retrieve them; it avoids the use of the VAL function.

If you know how many entries there are in a file, then a FOR-NEXT loop often is the easiest way to read the information back. For example, suppose you're a teacher with a class of 25 students. You know the currently active disk contains a file called GRADES. The file contains information about the class in the following form:

Student's Name (First, Last)
First exam grade
Second exam grade
Third exam grade
Fourth exam grade

One useful piece of terminology for discussing this situation is that of *fields* and *records*. Think of this file as being made up of 25 records and each record consisting of 5 fields. Usually, a program that manipulates this file will read back the information by records, or five fields at a time. Each field can be picked up by a single INPUT #, rather than needing the LINE INPUT command. The similarity with user-defined records (see chapter 11) is not a coincidence. You often will find yourself filling in the components of a record from a file.

If you are using QBasic, then knowing the exact format of this file means that you easily can write a procedure that will retrieve this information. First, set up a record type:

```
TYPE StudentRecord
    NAME AS STRING * 50
    FirstExam AS INTEGER
    SecondExam AS INTEGER
    ThirdExam AS INTEGER
    FourthExam AS INTEGER
END TYPE
```

Now, make up an array of 25 StudentRecords:

```
DIM Grades(1 TO 25) AS StudentRecord
```

Then, use the following fragment:

```
SUB RetrieveGrade

    SHARED Grades( )
    FileNum = FREEFILE
    OPEN "GRADES" FOR INPUT AS #FileNum
    DIM I AS INTEGER

    FOR I = 1 TO 25
        INPUT #FileNum, Grade(I).NAME
        INPUT #FileNum, Grade(I).FirstExam
        INPUT #FileNum, Grade(I).SecondExam
        INPUT #FileNum, Grade(I).ThirdExam
        INPUT #FileNum, Grade(I).FourthExam
    NEXT I

    CLOSE FileNum

END SUB
```

Now, each row of the array Grades contains a record with the name and grades of a student. You easily could incorporate this type of SUB into a program that analyzes the grades. (For a GW-BASIC program, you could use parallel lists and a subroutine.)

Regardless of which version of BASIC you are using, it's worth noting that this file had a simple structure, because the cardinal rule remains: you can't do anything with a file until you bring the information you need from it into memory.

The more complicated the structure of the file, the harder it will be to bring the information into memory. If you can keep the structure of your files simple, filling up an array often is the method of choice. The reason is that, once the information contained in the file is stored in an array, massaging the information is easy, usually requiring only a few FOR-NEXT loops to run through the array.

For example, suppose I want to write a procedure or subroutine that can return the average grade and number absent on each exam. As always, when dealing with an array of records, you could have chosen to store this information in two parallel arrays or one string array. In this case, if I had chosen to store this information in an array of strings rather than as in the array of records given earlier, I could write a SUB that would take a parameter for the exam number, as in the following fragment:

```
SUB AnalysisOfExams(ExamNumber)

  SHARED Grades$( )

  NumAbsent = 0
  Total = 0

  FOR I = 1 TO 25

    IF Grades(I,ExamNumber) = "absent" THEN
      NumAbsent = NumAbsent + 1
    ELSE
      Total = Total + VAL(Grades$(I,ExamNumber))
    END IF

  NEXT I

  PRINT  "The number absent was";NumAbsent
  PRINT  "The class average was";Total \ (25 − NumAbsent)

END SUB
```

This procedure is straightforward. The parameter tells the procedure what exam number (what column of the array) to look at and the FOR-NEXT loop runs through each row. The VAL command is needed because the exam grades are stored in a string array.

Adding to an existing file

The GRADE file contained the student's name followed by a list of his or her grades. This order is a bit unnatural. A different, more natural kind of file structure would occur if the teacher enters everything in steps: the student's names, then, after a while, the results of the first exam, and so on. To write a program to allow the teacher to add more information later, you need a command that lets you add information to the end of an existing file. The command is APPEND.

The statement OPEN *filename* FOR APPEND AS #*n* does three things at once:

- It opens the file and sets up the appropriate buffer. If the file doesn't exist, DOS BASIC creates it.
- It locates the end of the file on the disk.
- It prepares to OUTPUT to the file at its end.

Recall that, if you open an existing file for output, you erase it. Only by using the APPEND command can you add to an existing file.

If I was writing this program for myself, for a single class' records, I probably would update this file using a short program that reads the students' names and stores them in an array before the appending. CH15 \ P6.BAS is a QBasic program that shows how:

```
'CH15 \ P6.BAS
DIM StudentNames$(25)
OPEN "Grades" FOR INPUT AS # 1                              'A

FOR I = 1 TO 25
   INPUT #1, StudentNames$(I)
NEXT I

CLOSE #1                                                    'B

OPEN "Grades" FOR APPEND AS #1

FOR I = 1 TO 25
   PRINT "The grade for ";StudentNames$(I);" is ";
   INPUT Grade$
   PRINT #1, Grade$
NEXT I

CLOSE
END
```

A   I'm assuming the file already was created and contains the names of the students.

B   To change a file's status, it has to be closed. Once this command is processed, the next command lets you add to it.

You probably will find yourself writing lots of these quick-and-dirty programs as you become more familiar with file handling techniques. Although they're never very robust, they do get the job done. You need special techniques to make file handling programs robust (see the next section of this chapter).

Suppose, however, that you were teaching five classes, each with a different number of students. Then, I'm sure that the quick-and-dirty approach is not worthwhile. It's possible to get the classes mixed up, which could lead to an error message or even losing a student's grades. To prevent this kind of mishap, write a header to all your files. Use this header to put standard information about the file at the beginning of the file.

To write a usable grade book program, I'd use the first few entries in the file for the name of the class, the semester, the number of exams, and the number of students. This kind of information isn't likely to change. (If you do want to change it, then binary file techniques are best. These techniques are available only in QBasic.) The heading has the added advantage that you can use it to set up the bounds on the loops that will read and process the information contained in the file. The following fragment is a QBasic procedure that you might use to set up a grade book on a disk in the currently active directory:

```
SUB SetUpGrade
    'LOCAL variables are: ' FileName$, FileNum, ClassName$, ExamNum,
StuNum

    CLS

    INPUT "What is the name of the file for this class"; FileName$
    INPUT "What is the name of the class";ClassName$

    FileNum = FREEFILE OPEN FileName$ FOR OUTPUT AS #FileNum
    PRINT #FileNum,ClassName$
    INPUT "How many exams";ExamNum
    PRINT #FileNum,ExamNum
    INPUT "How many students";StuNum
    PRINT #FileNum,StuNum

    CLOSE #FileNum
END SUB
```

Getting serious with sequential files

While FOR-NEXT loops are a convenient way to read back information contained in a file, there obviously are times when they are not practical. There might be too much information in the file or you might not know what limits to use. You need a way to implement the following outline:

1. While there's information left in the file
   - Get next piece of INFO
   - Process it
2. LOOP

To implement this outline, you need a way to test when you're at the end of the file. The statement in DOS BASIC that lets you check for the end of the file is reasonably mnemonic. It's called EOF(n), for end of file, where the parentheses hold the file identifier number. Using this statement, a quite general QBasic program to read back the information contained in a file set up with PRINT # statements might look like:

```
FileNum = FREEFILE
OPEN filename FOR INPUT AS #FileNum
```

```
LINE INPUT #FileNum, A$

DO UNTIL EOF(FileNum)
    '   process line - this would probably be a procedure call or
    '   function call
    LINE INPUT #FileNum, A$
LOOP
CLOSE #FileNum
```

You should use a loop at the top to take into account the unlikely possibility that the file exists but doesn't contain any information (i.e., it was opened for output, but nothing was actually sent to the file). This fragment is a more or less direct translation of the outline. It picks up a line of data (i.e., all the data up to a carriage return/line feed pair). It continues reading lines of data until it gets to the end of the file.

In GW-BASIC, you would have to write the loop as:

```
WHILE NOT EOF(1) ...
```

and keep track of an available file number, which always seems unnatural to me.

This kind of fragment is the key to writing a simple print formatter for text files (like the README.DOC or PACKING.LST that come with many programs). All you need to know is that you can LINE INPUT each line—that they're not too long or too short.

One common use of the EOF(n) statement is to read back the information contained in a file character-by-character. The analogy to keep in mind again is that one reads a file as if it were input from the keyboard. Recall that you pick up individual characters from the keyboard with INPUT$($n$). It should come as no surprise then that you pick up individual characters from a file with the statement:

```
INPUT$(x, #y)
```

where the first entry holds the number of characters and the second holds the file identifier. So:

```
SixChar$ = INPUT$(6,#2)
```

picks up six characters from a file opened for input with file identifier #2 and assigns the string to a string variable named SixChar$. Just like with the ordinary INPUT$ command, you combine INPUT$($x$, #$y$) with an assignment statement.

The following program is a QBasic program that reads back the contents of a file character-by-character, and prints both the ASCII code and the character on the same line:

```
'CH15 \ P7.BAS
'  A 'semi' master file reader
```

```
INPUT "What is the name of the file";FileName$

FileNum = FREEFILE
OPEN FileName$ FOR INPUT AS #FileNum

A$ = INPUT$(1,#FileNum)

DO UNTIL EOF(FileNum)
   PRINT A$,ASC(A$)
   A$ = INPUT$(1,#FileNum)
LOOP

CLOSE FileNum
END
```

If you use this program on the files TEST1, TEST2, and TEST3, which were created earlier in this chapter, you easily can check that the spaces and carriage return/line feed combinations that I claimed the various form of the PRINT # sends to a file are there.

Although the INPUT$(x, #y) statement lets you examine the structure of many files character-by-character, it shouldn't be overused. Unfortunately, it's possible that files created by commercial programs will not to be readable with this method. It turns out that what DOS BASIC really is doing when it tests for the end of a file with EOF(n) is that it is searching for a Ctrl−Z, CHR$(26). You can see this by trying to use the previous program to read back a file created with the following test program:

```
'CH15 \ P8.BAS
'demonstrates Ctrl − Z ( = ^Z = CHR$(26) as EOF

FileNum = FREEFILE
OPEN "TEST" FOR OUTPUT AS #FileNum
PRINT #FileNum, CHR$(26)

FOR I = 1 TO 10
   PRINT #FileNum, "The previous program can't ever read this"
NEXT I

CLOSE #FileNum

END
```

Because it can be very important to massage non-ASCII files (LOTUS 1-2-3, dBase, etc.), QBasic has added another method of reading back files that, among its other powers, gets around this Ctrl−Z problem. (See the section on binary file techniques in this chapter; GW-BASIC users are out of luck.)

In any case, even if a file is readable by this method, it usually is better to think of a file as being made up of fields, which possibly are grouped into records.

Each field is separated from the next by a *delimiter*—a comma or carriage return/ line feed combination. The delimiter is what lets you use a single INPUT # to pick up the field. This method is much faster than doing it character-by-character.

The WRITE # and PRINT # USING commands

Because you send information to files as though they were the screen, you again have to solve the problems of:

- How to send special characters, like quotation marks, to the screen.
- How to nicely format a file.

As the section heading indicates, you solve both these problems with commands analogous to the ones that solved them for the screen. For example, as I briefly mentioned in chapter 3, the WRITE command sends information to the screen surrounded by quotation marks:

    WRITE "Testing 1, 2, 3"

displays:

    "Testing 1, 2, 3"

on the screen. Similarly:

    WRITE #3, "Testing 1,2, 3"

sends an exact copy of this string, including the quotes and the commas, to the output or append file with identifier number 3. This statement is a less cumbersome way of saying:

    PRINT #3,CHR$(34);
    PRINT #3,"Testing 1, 2, 3";
    PRINT #3,CHR$(34)

Note the two semicolons that prevent inadvertent carriage return/line feed combinations.

As long as you send individual pieces of information to a file, the PRINT # and WRITE # command can be used interchangeably:

    PRINT #FileNum,"Hello"

and

    WRITE #FileNum,"Hello"

Both of these statements put a single piece of information into a file. In either case, you can read back the information using the INPUT # command. However, the files won't be the same size. The WRITE command adds two quotation marks, CHR$(34), to the file. It's only when you send more than one piece of information at a time that the differences really emerge. For example, to send three numbers to a file, using:

```
PRINT #FileNum, 1, 2, 3
```

sends a rather large number of superfluous spaces. The command:

```
WRITE #FileNum, 1,2,3
```

sends the appropriate commas to the file, saving space and making it easier to read back the information. It's equivalent to the cumbersome:

```
PRINT #FileNum,1;",";2;",";3
```

Simply put, use WRITE # together with INPUT and PRINT # with LINE INPUT.

The PRINT # USING is used rarely. Most people prefer to format the file after the information is read back. However, if you do want to experiment with it, it will send information to the file using the same spacing or formatting characters it would send to the screen.

To summarize, when you work with a sequential file, output as if it were the screen and input as if it were the keyboard.

Error trapping: making a file program robust

Usually, when you're testing a program, you don't care if you get a run-time error and your program crashes. When an open file already exists, however, after a crash, strange things might get written onto your files or information you need might never get there. Even if you've thoroughly debugged the program, someone might try to send information to a full disk or try to access a file that doesn't exist. To solve these problems, you must stop the program when, for example, it faces a full disk. The command that activates error trapping is, as you saw in chapter 10:

```
ON ERROR GOTO ...
```

where the three dots are for the label or line number that defines the error trap. Now, you need to transfer control to a module that:

- Identifies the problem.
- Fixes the problem if possible.

If the error can be corrected, you can use RESUME to continue processing.

You can't correct an error if you don't know why it happened. Table 15-1 gives the error codes that are most common to file handling programs. You use this information just as was outlined in chapter 10. For example, somewhere in the program, before the error can occur, place the QBasic statement:

```
ON ERROR GOTO DiskCheck
```

Now, write a module that is similar to the following fragment. It can be labeled

Table 15-1 The DOS BASIC error codes,
with the error messages and possible causes and remedies.

25	Device fault: for example, trying to LPRINT when the printer is off.
53	File not found: probably a typo.
55	File already opened: you obviously can't open what already is opened.
57	Device I/O error: your hardware is acting up (I/O stands for Input/Output, but check the disk drive anyway).
61	Disk full: not enough room to do what you want (one way to prevent this error is to check the amount of free space available on a disk before you start massive file I/O. Unfortunately, the only way this check can be done in DOS BASIC is cumbersome).
62	Input past end: you put the test for EOF in the wrong place.
64	Bad filename: you didn't follow the DOS naming conventions for a filename.
70	Permission denied: the disk you're writing to has the write-protect notch covered.
71	Drive not ready: the door is opened or there isn't a disk in the drive.
72	Disk media error: time to throw out the floppy or start thinking about the state of your hard disk.
76	Path not found: probably a typo—you asked to open a file on a non-existent path.

DiskCheck or whatever name or line number you chose:

```
DiskCheck:

    ErrorNumber = ERR
    BEEP

    SELECT CASE ErrorNumber

        CASE 53
            PRINT "Your file was not found. Please check on the "
            PRINT "spelling or call your operator for assistance."

        CASE 61
            PRINT "The disk is full. Please replace with a slightly"
            PRINT "less used model " 'could SHELL to FORMAT.COM here

        CASE 71
            PRINT "I think the drive door is open - please check"

        CASE 72
            PRINT "Possibly big problems on your hard disk. You'd"
            PRINT "better pray that a low level re-format can help - "
            PRINT "definitely time to call your operator for assistance"
```

```
CASE 57
    PRINT "Possibly big problems on your hardware. You"
    PRINT "definitely should call your operator for assistance"

CASE ELSE
    PRINT "Please tell the operator ( = program author?) that"
    PRINT " error number ";ErrorNumber;"occurred."

END SELECT

PRINT "If the error has been corrected press 'Y' otherwise"
PRINT "press any other key to END"

Continue$ = INPUT$(1)

IF Continue$ = "Y" or Continue$ = "y" THEN RESUME ELSE
END
```

The idea of this error trap is simple; the SELECT CASE statement is ideal. (GW-BASIC users need multiple IF-THENs.) Each case tries to give some indication of where the problem is and, if possible, how to correct it. If you reach the CASE ELSE, the error number has to be reported. In any case, the final block gives you the option of continuing or not.

Error trapping isn't a cure-all. Obviously, little can be done about a hard disk crash. On the other hand, if you can shell to the FORMAT command (see the first section of this chapter), not having a formatted floppy around is not irreparable.

As always, the PRINT statements in the error trap are likely to mess up the display, unless special precautions are taken (see chapter 14). A very complete DiskCheck module is your best bet at making a file handling program robust. I usually start with the same module containing this kind of error trap when writing a serious file handling program. Writing a file handling program without an error trap is an awful idea.

Using devices: some final notes on sequential files

The information inside a sequential file is packed tight and is hard to change, but that doesn't mean you can't do it. If the changes you're making don't alter the size of the file and you're using QBasic, the section on binary files is your best bet. This section will explain some other ways to change sequential files that do not use these techniques.

The APPEND command lets you add information to the end of a sequential file. Suppose now you want to add information to the beginning of a file. First, copy the information to a temporary file. The best way is to use the SHELL and COPY commands to append one file to another.

However, suppose you weren't sure the information was to go at the beginning or that you wanted to remove or replace information already in the file. Imagine what you might do if these modifications were to be done to a cassette tape. First, you'd record the words to be added on a separate tape with a little bit of *leader*—some blank tape so that you can cut and paste. Then, you'd find where on the tape the new information is to go and *splice*, or cut, the tapes. For example, to place information at the beginning of an old file, you can:

1. Set up a temporary file to hold the new information.
2. Append everything in the old file to the temporary file.

Now, the temporary file contains everything you want. Delete, or kill, the old file and rename the temporary file.

Next, suppose you want to make changes within a file. If the size of the file doesn't change, binary file techniques are always the best. If it's necessary to change the size of the file, you need to complete the following steps.

Suppose, for example, you want to change all occurrences of the words Turbo Pascal in a file to DOS BASIC or, more generally, to write your own search and replace function. Then:

1. Read the information in the file into a temporary file, stopping whenever you get to the string Turbo Pascal.
2. Print "DOS BASIC"; into the temporary file,
3. Move past the occurrence of the word Turbo Pascal and continue repeating the first two steps until you reach the end of the file.
4. Now, kill the original file and rename the temporary file back to the original file's name.

Because you have to read the information back character-by-character, a program that implements this outline can run for quite a bit of time. The program will run a lot faster and is much simpler if you know that each occurrence of the string you're searching for was in a separate field. If this situation occurred, you could use a loop that, in pseudocode, is:

```
OPEN ORIGINAL FILE
OPEN TEMP FILE

INPUT Field from original file
   DO UNTIL EOF(ORIGINAL)
      IF field < > "Turbo Pascal" THEN
         WRITE IT TO TEMP
      ELSE
         WRITE "DOS BASIC" to TEMP
      INPUT nextfield
   LOOP
```

```
KILL ORIGINAL
NAME TEMP as ORIGINAL
```

The idea of extracting words from a file occurs frequently. Suppose you want to index a file. Usually, an index throws away the common words and keeps track of the rest. As mentioned in chapter 13, a binary tree is perfect for building an index. More precisely, here's an outline of how to write a useful indexing program in QBasic:

1. Find a list of the most common words. Incorporate this list into an ordered array of CommonWords(x).
2. Extract each word. You saw how to do this process in chapter 5.
3. Check to see if the word is on the list of common words—binary search.
4. If the word is not on the list, add it to the tree.
5. Use the tree sort from chapter 13 to print out the index.

When the end of file is reached the binary tree contains all the information. (By making the nodes of the tree more complicated you can keep track of where the words occurred and how many times they occurred.)

You can use this idea to write your own programmer's cross referencer (XREF). Take the source code of a program and index everything except numbers and DOS BASIC's reserved words.

Table 15-2 is a list of the devices that DOS BASIC allows you to communicate with. Although they are not sequential files, DOS BASIC handles communicating with devices as if they were. For example, after:

```
OPEN "LPT2:" FOR OUTPUT AS #3
```

the statement PRINT #3,A$ would send information to the device—presumably a printer of some type—that is attached to the second parallel port. If you don't have

Table 15-2 The devices that DOS BASIC allows you to communicate with.

Name	Description	Input/ Output
COM1:	First serial port	Both
COM2:	Second serial port	Both
CONS:	The screen	Output
KYBD:	The keyboard	Input
LPT1:	First parallel port	Output
LPT2:	Second parallel port	Output
LPT3:	Third parallel port	Output
SCRN:	The screen	Output

a second parallel port or the printer isn't online, you'll get an error message. Because LPRINT only sends information to LPT1:, you need the PRINT # command to send information out if you have printers attached to more than one port on your machine.

The commands that open COM1: or COM2: both accept certain parameters controlling baud rate, stop bits, and the like. For more on what these terms mean, consult any book on serial communications. For the full syntax of these commands, consult the online help files or your manual.

Getting started with random access files

Suppose you were tired of having to search through entire cassettes for certain songs. To avoid this inconvenience, you decide to put those songs that you want instant access to on individual cassettes. The advantages are obvious, but there are disadvantages as well. First, to gain more or less instant access to an individual song, you're going to waste a considerable amount of blank tape on each cassette. If, to prevent this, you decide to create a standard size tape, one that holds, say, four minutes, you're sure to have at least a couple of songs that run more than four minutes. It's clear that, no matter what you do, you'll either waste space or have a few songs that won't fit. Also, if you single out too many songs for separate tapes, then you increase the number of cassettes you have to store. If you have hundreds of tapes, each containing an individual song, you're almost back where you started. It can't possibly be easy to find an individual song if you have to search through a hundred tapes. At this point, you would probably choose to alphabetize the tapes by some key feature (singer, title, etc.), set up an index, or both.

Random access files are stored on a disk in such a way that they have much the same advantages and disadvantages as the song collector's tapes. You gain instant access to individual pieces of information, but only at some cost. You must standardize the packets of information involved, so some things might not fit or the space will not be used efficiently. If the file grows to big—with too many pieces of information—you'll have to set up another file to index the first.

When setting up a sequential file, it occasionally is useful to think of a group of fields as forming a single record. For example, grouping the fields by fives gives a logical and convenient way to read back the information contained in the grade book program. It's worth stressing that this particular grouping was not intrinsic to the file; it's only the way I look at the file. The only intrinsic divisions within a sequential file are those created by the delimiters. When you read back information, you read it field by field, with the delimiters acting as barriers. In a random access file, however, the notion of the record is built in. A random file is a special disk file that is arranged by records, which lets you immediately move to the 15th record without having to pass through the 14th. This shortcut can and does save a considerable amount of time.

When you first set up a random access file, you specify the maximum length for each record. When you go to fill up an individual record, you can put in less information than this preset limit, but you can never put in more. So, just like the song collector, you might need to prepare for the worst possible situation.

The command that sets up a random access file is analogous to the one for opening a sequential file. For example:

```
OPEN "SAMPLE.RND" AS #5 LEN = 100
```

opens a random access file called SAMPLE.RND on the current directory with file identifier of 5. Each record can hold 100 bytes, or characters. Opening a sequential file as a random access file with LEN = 1 is one way to get a handle on each byte of a file; however, for QBasic users, binary file techniques are better.

Note that, unlike the situation for sequential files, you don't have to specify whether you're opening the file for input, output, or append. As you'll soon see, this distinction is taken care of in the commands that manipulate a random access file. An open random access file can be read from and written to essentially simultaneously. You can have any mixture of random access and sequential files open at the same time; the only restrictions are set by DOS (the FILES command in your CONFIG.SYS file). To prevent confusion between file types, I try (as in the previous example) to use an extension like RND for all my random access files.

Similarly, you close a file opened for random access with the CLOSE command followed by the file identifier number. As before, the command CLOSE alone closes all open files. This fact is especially useful because a sophisticated program for random files often has many files open simultaneously—both sequential and random.

Suppose you wanted to write a random access file that would keep track of someone's library. You start by designing the form. You decide on five categories:

Author
Title
Subject
Publisher
Miscellaneous

After looking over your library, you decide to use the size limits shown in Table 15-3 for the categories. So, the total for each record is 98 characters. A random access file to fit this form is set up via:

```
OPEN "MYLIB.RND" AS FileNum LEN = 98
```

where FileNum = FREEFILE.

Just as each file has an identifier number, each record within a random access file has a record number. A single random access file can hold from 1 to

Category	Size
AUTHOR	20
TITLE	30
SUBJECT	15
PUBLISHER	20
MISCELLANEOUS	13

Table 15-3 Size limitations for each of the categories in the library file.

16,777,216 records. Moreover, you don't have to fill the records in order. As you'll see, you can place information in the 15th record without ever having touched the first 14. The disadvantage of using random access files, however, is that DOS BASIC automatically would set aside enough space for the first 14 records on the disk, even if nothing was in them.

Random access files in QBasic

I've been using the word record incessantly; this repetition is no coincidence. One of the main reasons QBasic implemented record types was to simplify working with random access files. First, set up a type:

```
TYPE BOOKINFO
    Author AS STRING*20
    Title AS STRING*30
    Subject AS STRING*15
    Publisher AS STRING*20
    Miscellaneous AS STRING*13
END TYPE
```

Next, suppose ExampleOfBook was previously dimensioned as being of type BOOKINFO. Then, the command:

```
GET filenum,10,ExampleOfBook
```

would transfer the contents of the 10th record from the random access file into the record variable ExampleOfBook, automatically filling in the correct components of ExampleOfBook.

The command:

```
PUT filenum,37,ExampleOfBook
```

would send the components of ExampleOfBook to the 37th record of file #2.

This method of sending information to a random access file is unique to Q-Basic, but it's a very valuable improvement. QBasic also allows you to use an older and much clumsier method, which needs what are called field variables.

Random access files in GW-BASIC

As I mentioned before, to speed disk operations up, DOS-BASIC buffers information. Information is taken from a disk in chunks, rather than a bit at a time. Usually, this process is transparent to the user; however, for random access files in GW- BASIC (and QBasic, if you choose this method) this transparency no longer exists.

It's best to think of the buffer as holding the information in at least one record. The command:

```
GET # 1,10
```

would transfer the contents of the 10th record from the random access file that previously was opened with identifier number 1 to the buffer. The command:

```
PUT #2,37
```

would send the contents of the buffer set up for the random access file that was opened with identifier number 2 to record number 37. As mentioned before, you can do this operation without having sent any information to the first 36 records at all.

Using the PUT or GET commands for random access file is just the first of two steps. You need other commands to get the information out of or to the buffer. Moreover, the communication can be done only through intermediaries called *field variables*, which sometimes are called *buffer variables*. For example, to set up the field variables for the library file:

```
FIELD #1,  20  AS Author$,
           30  AS Title$,
           15  AS Subject$,
           20  AS Publisher$,
           13  AS Miscellaneous$,
```

In general the FIELD command takes the form:

```
FIELD #id, size AS string variable [,size AS string variable]
```

where the brackets allow you to add more field variables as needed. Each field variable must be preceded by the size of that field, followed by the keyword AS, and separated from the next field variable by a comma.

You cannot use the FIELD command until you've opened the file. Also, the total lengths can't add up to more than the length at which the random access file was opened. On the other hand, you can have more than one FIELD command for the same file. This ability allows you to borrow from one field if another field threatened to overflow by setting up other field variables with different names. For example, you might have set up a second FIELD statement in a special exception handling subroutine, or procedure:

```
FIELD #1  20  AS Author$,
          40  AS LargeTitle$,
          15  AS Subject$,
          20  AS Publisher$,
           3  AS SmallMisc$,
```

The field variable Author$ still refers to the first 20 characters in the buffer, but the new field variable LargeTitle$ would refer to the next 40 characters. Having many FIELD statements can, with substantial extra programming, give you a way around some of the limitations of your first FIELD command. The problem is determining which records have which shape.

Only strings can be sent to or taken from a random access file. Numbers have to be changed to strings. When you use records, this change happens automatically.

To summarize, here are the two steps needed to get information from a random access file using field variables:

1. Get the record containing the information.
2. Use the appropriate field variable to pick up its piece of the buffer.

For example, the commands:

```
GET #1, 100
   CurrentAuthor$ = Author$
   CurrentTitle$ = Title$
   CurrentPub$ = Publisher$
```

fills the buffer with the contents of the 100th record in your library file. Next, it assigns the contents of the Author$ field to a variable named CurrentAuthor$, the contents of the Title$ field to a variable CurrentTitle$, and the contents of the Publisher$ field to the variable CurrentPub$. Note that you do not have to empty all the fields of the buffer nor empty them in any particular order. Field variables know which part of the buffer they refer to.

On the other hand, you might be tempted to send information to the buffer by assigning strings to the FIELD variables. Although quite natural, it unfortunately does not work this way. You must never assign to a FIELD variable. Any attempt to do so by an ordinary assignment statement like:

```
Author$ = "Gary Cornell"
```
or an INPUT statement like:
```
INPUT Author$
```

automatically eliminates Author$ as a way to communicate with the random access file. Only processing another FIELD command can reconnect it. Forgetting this fact leads to programs that behave strangely; it's a hard bug to find once it's introduced. So, field variables might seem like ordinary string variables, but they're not.

If you can't use assignment statements to send information to the buffer, how do you do it? The answer is: by using two new commands LSET and RSET. For example:

```
LSET Author$ = "Gary Cornell"
```

fills up the field variable with my name and pads it with 8 spaces on the right, or at the end of the string, to use up the assigned space for this field variable. It *left justifies* the string. The command:

```
RSET Author$ = "Gary Cornell"
```

fills up the field variable with my name and pads it with 8 spaces on the left to fill up the assigned space for this field variable. It *right justifies* the string.

Obviously, LSET and RSET work differently only if the length of the string is less than that specified when setting up the field variable. One command pads from the left; the other does it from the right. If you consistently use LSET, when you read back the strings, they will be left aligned. If you consistently use RSET, they will be right aligned. (As you'll soon see, this feature makes RSET useful when sending numeric information to a random access file.) Note, however, that, if the string you want to assign to the field variable has too many characters, both these commands throw away enough characters from the end of the string so that it will fit.

Nothing prevents you from mixing LSET and RSET commands when filling the buffer. Mixing them, however, makes it harder to neatly display the information the random access file contains.

The following statements complete the assignments to the field variables:

```
LSET Title$ = "Complete DOS BASIC"
LSET Author$ = "Gary Cornell"
LSET Subject$ = "Computer Programming"
LSET Publisher$ = "TAB McGraw-Hill"
LSET Miscellaneous$ = "no comment"
```

Note that, because the field variable Subject$ was set up to hold only 15 characters, this field variable only contains the substring Computer Progra. Also, note that all the other fields are left justified by adding spaces, CHR$(32), to the end of them. Now that you've filled up the buffer—sent enough information to fill up a whole record—the command:

```
PUT #1,2
```

sends this information to the second record on the disk. You need not assign to all the buffer variables and fill the buffer before you PUT information to the file; however, not doing so occasionally leads to problems. The problems arise because DOS BASIC reserves space on the disk for the right number of characters for each record without overwriting the characters that might have been there already. The best way to be sure that your random access file doesn't contain left over junk from previously deleted files is to completely fill the buffer for each record before PUTing it. If you want that field to be blank, use:

LSET *field variable* = *" "*

In any case, I sent this information to the second record because I'm a strong believer in using the first record for a header. I'd use the header to keep information like the number of records currently stored, the names of the fields, and when the file was last updated.

Suppose I wanted to use the first record to contain information like the names of the fields and the number of records. Sending the names of the fields is easy, LSET (or RSET) the appropriate FIELD variables. Finding the best way to send the number of records (= number of books stored) is a bit more difficult—although obviously during the course of the program I'll have kept track of this.

Numbers in random access files

As I mentioned before, you can send only strings to a random access file. Your first instinct might be to use the STR$ command to change the records containing numbers to a string, then send them to the buffer as before. Although workable, this natural method turns out to be second best. The problem is that the STR$ command uses one character for each digit in the number, which wastes space. Instead, DOS BASIC provides commands that change all numbers of the same type (integer, single-precision, etc.) into strings of the same size. For example, 1137 will take the same amount of space as -32768. The savings are substantial:

- Integers take two characters.
- Long integers take four characters.
- Single-precision numbers also take four characters.
- Double-precision numbers take eight characters.

The commands needed to make these conversions are:

MKI$	Integers or variables
MKL$	Long integer or variables
MKS$	Single-precision numbers or variables
MKD$	Double-precision numbers or variables

For example:

NumberOfBook$ = MKI$(NumberOfBooks%)

assigns a special string form, of the integer variable NumberOfBooks% to the string variable NumberOfBooks$. This string form is suitable only for sending to a random access file. Note, however, if you now say:

```
PRINT NumberOfBooks$
```

all you'll see is garbage. The MKI$ and its cousins, unlike the STR$ command, transform numbers so that the information is hidden. You can no longer display the information without converting it back. However, like any string, you can send this information to the random access buffer via LSET and RSET or you can then PUT it away.

To recover the information you have to fill the buffer via the appropriate GET command and assignment to the field variables; however, after that, an extra step is needed to reconvert things back to normal. The following commands are used to convert these special strings:

CVI   Back to an integer
CVL   Back to a long integer
CVS   Back to a single-precision number
CVD   Back to a double-precision number

For example:

```
PreviousNumOfBooks% = CVI(NumberOfBooks$)
```

Note that, just as you can't use STR$ to convert a number into this special string form, you can't use VAL to convert it back.

It occasionally is said that one advantage of random access files over sequential files is that numbers take up so much less room. I've never understood this reasoning, because nothing prevents you from using these conversion functions in your sequential files. The only disadvantage is that you no longer can see the contents of the file via the DOS TYPE command and that the programs to manipulate files with these transformed numbers obviously are more complicated. Nonetheless, as you'll see in the last section of this chapter, using these for a string is occasionally useful.

Finally, there is one problem that can arise when you use QBasic in reading older random access files, or vice versa. Microsoft has switched to a new format—the IEEE standard—for its internal representation of numbers. This change only causes conversion problems in dealing with random access files. The solution is to use two new commands: MKSMBF$ and MKDMBF$. The former stands for *make single-precision number in Microsoft binary format*; the latter stands for *make double-precision number in Microsoft binary format*. Microsoft binary format is the name given to the original GW-BASIC format for numbers. Use these functions in QBasic when you want to read back a random access file created by the older method.

Indices

The record types you create determine the size of the random access file. Because records can hold numbers as well as strings, it's a bit messy to compute the length of a record variable of a given record type. You have to remember that an integer takes two bytes, a long integer takes four, etc. QBasic makes it trivial, however, because the LEN command not only gives the length of a string, but it also gives you the length of a record as well. Take any variable of the given type. For example, you've entered DIM ExampleOfRecord AS ThisType. Set LenOfRecord = LEN(ExampleOfRecord) and use this value to set the length for the OPEN command used to create the random access file.

If you have the information that you want to transfer to a newly created random access file stored in an array of records, you can use a loop to send the information there. The loop counter determines where to put the record. Usually, however, you set up a variable whose value is the number of the next record you want to read from or write to.

Similarly, you could read back all the information in a random access file using the EOF flag:

```
DO UNTIL EOF(filenum)
   I = I + 1
   GET filenum, VariableOfrecordType(I)
LOOP
```

There are many problems with doing this loop naively. For one, you're unlikely to want all the information contained in the file at once. It might not fit anyway; suppose you have 1,000,000 records. Also, go back to square one. How do you even know what length to use to open the random access file? While there are many ways to determine this size, I prefer to set up another file that contains this and other vital information about the random access file. At the very least, it will contain information about the sizes and types of the fields and possibly names for the fields and the number of records stored to date. It might even contain an index of certain keys and the numbers of the records that contain that key.

Indices are vital to a random access file. A data base manager is nothing more than a more or less elaborate program to manage random access files. It's speed depends on how the program finds the record containing keyed information. This search can be done effectively only through indices. (The alternative is to examine the relevant component of each record.)

An index can be as simple as a sequential file containing a list of keys followed by a record number or be a more elaborate ordered one. However, for all but the smallest random access files, indices are best created using binary trees (see chapter 13). Recall that you had an array of integers (called arrows%) that pointed to the left and right children of a given node. Imagine the contents of the node as the key. Now, you're trying to find the record number that contains this key. The solution is simple: add another column to this array, arrows%, to hold the record number containing the information keyed by the contents of the node.

In all cases, however, you're likely to read the index into an array or arrays. If you don't like binary trees or are using GW-BASIC, the next best alternative is to quick or Shell sort it on the keys once they get there. Now, you can work with the contents of only a few records at a time.

Using binary files in QBasic: some simple file utilities

Binary files are not a new type of file but a new way of manipulating any kind of file. Binary file techniques let you read or change any byte of a file. Among other features, binary file techniques do not care about any embedded EOFs, Ctrl−Z or CHR$(26), that the file might have. (Recall that it was impossible to read back the file created in CH15 \ P6.BAS using sequential file techniques.) The command:

```
OPEN filename FOR BINARY AS filenum
```

sets up a file to be read with these techniques.

Just as with random access files, you can now both read and write to the file. For example, one way to pick up the information from a file open in binary file mode is with the INPUT$(x, #y) command that you saw in section, "Getting serious with sequential files." It works the same way. The first slot still holds the number of characters; the second holds the file identifier number. For example, the following fragment prints the contents of any file, regardless of any embedded control characters:

```
SUB PrintAFile(A$)
    ' example of binary input

    FileNum = FREEFILE                              ' get free file i.d.
    OPEN A$ FOR BINARY AS #FileNum

    FOR I = 1 TO LOF(FileNum)
        Char$ = INPUT$(1,#FileNum)
        PRINT Char$;
    NEXT I

END SUB
```

More often than not, however, you'll want to modify this module by adding some filtering lines. For example, making it strip out the control characters or those with ASCII codes greater than 127. Once you strip such a file, it can, for example, be displayed with the DOS type command or more easily sent by a modem.

For example, the WordStar word processing program (from which the QBasic editor gets some of its editing commands) normally stores a file in such a way that, when you use the DOS TYPE command, you would have trouble reading the file. Similarly, someone who had a different word processing program might have trouble using it.

Here's a somewhat simplified description of what WordStar does:

- It uses certain control codes inside the file, such as Ctrl−B for bold.
- The end of each line has the high-order bit set. If the word processing program had to word wrap a line, the ASCII code of the last character is increased by 128.
- It uses the carriage return/line feed combination, CHR$(10)+CHR$(13), for hard returns—when someone has hit the Enter key, rather than the program doing a word wrap.

It's easy to modify the module given above to strip out all control codes and to shift the high-order bit back. For those who do use WordStar, the program will not strip out dot commands. I'll leave the changes needed for that to you.

The following fragment shows how to strip out the control codes and to shift the high-order bit:

```
SUB StripAFile(A$)
    ' example of binary input

    FileNum = FREEFILE                          ' get free file i.d.
    OPEN A$ FOR BINARY AS #FileNum
    FOR I = 1 TO LOF(FileNum)

        Char$ = INPUT$(1,#FileNum)

        SELECT CASE Char$;
          CASE IS < CHR$(32)
            CHAR$ = ""
          CASE IS > CHR$(128)
            CharCode = ASC(Char$)
            CHAR$ = CHR$(CharCode − 128)
        END SELECT

        PRINT Char$;

    NEXT I

END SUB
```

In a more general program, you probably would want to do something more than print the character.

QBasic maintains a file pointer within a file opened for BINARY. Each time you use INPUT$, the file pointer moves one position further within the file. The command SEEK is a fast-forward and a rewind command combined into one. More precisely:

SEEK *filenum, position number*

moves the file pointer for the file with the identifier *filenum* directly to the byte in that position. Any INPUT$(*x, y*) would start picking up characters from this location.

SEEK has another use. SEEK(*filenum*) tells you the position number for the last byte read for either a binary or sequential file. You also can use the SEEK function with random access files. Now, it will return the record number of the next record.

To place information within a file opened for binary, you use a modification of the PUT command. For example:

PUT #1,100,A$

would place the contents of the string value directly into the file with file identifier 1, starting at the 100th byte. The number of characters sent to this file is given by LEN(A$). The PUT command will overwrite whatever was there. If you leave a space for the byte position but don't specify it in the PUT command:

PUT #1, , A$

the information is placed wherever the file pointer is currently located.

The GET command also will work with a binary file. Here though, you are best off dimensioning the variable as a fixed length string, because the command:

GET *file#, position*, A$

picks up only as many characters as is the current length of A$. You could use a normal string variable if you are careful to initialize it to have the correct length.

Now that you know the commands for working on the byte level for a file, you're in a position to write any file utility you might like. You also now can use the information contained in a book like *File Formats for Popular PC Software* by Jeff Walden (Wiley 1986). Hopefully, the manual to your favorite program contains this information as well.

Now, you can massage the output of any application program. A good example of this technique can be found in the December 13, 1988 issue of *PC Magazine*. This issue had a very useful article about using QuickBASIC binary mode to massage LOTUS 1-2-3 files. The technique would work in QBasic as well.

Ciphers

Now, you know that a simple utility program using binary file techniques can read back the information contained in any file. So, the data contained in your files is readily available to anyone with a compatible computer, a little programming skill, and a copy of your disk. In the next few sections, you'll see how to encode a file so that only people having the right key can read your file easily. The methods I show you aren't perfect; however, considering how easy they are to implement, they are surprisingly secure. Along the way, you'll see how your computer can help you break some of the most common codes. The computer will do the dirty work, but you'll have to supply the insight.

Cryptographers distinguish between a code and a cipher. To *encode*, for the professional, means to change whole words. For example, a company will refer to a product being developed by a code name until it's released. The code name for the IBM PC Jr. was supposed to be *peanut*. To *encipher*, on the other hand, means to have rules for changing the individual letters that make up a word. What I'm going to show you here are, to professionals, cipher methods. Like the dictionary, however, I occasionally will use the terms interchangeably.

First, I need to give you a little history. All the earliest ciphers that are known about use simple substitutions. For example, Julius Caesar kept his messages secret by taking each letter in the message and replacing it with the one three letters further on. So, the letter *A* would be replaced by *D*, *B* by *E*, and so on until you got to the letters after *X*. Because *X* is the 24th letter of the alphabet, you have to wrap around back to the beginning of the alphabet. *X* becomes *A*, *Y* becomes *B*, and *Z* becomes *C*.

Here's a normal alphabet with a complete Caesar alphabet below it:

ABCDEFGHIJKLMNOPQRSTUVWXYZ
DEFGHIJKLMNOPQRSTUVWXYZABC

(Actually, in Caesar's time, the alphabet had fewer letters—23 instead of 26. For example, *U* and *V* developed out of *V* around 1000 years ago. *J* came around 500 years after that.)

For example, the sentence:

Can you read this

becomes:

Fdq brx uhdg wklv

Shift ciphers go back further than Caesar; one occurs in the Bible. In Jeremiah 25 and 26, the prophet conceals his prophecy by changing the name of Babylon using a cipher that splits the Hebrew alphabet in half and replaces the first letter with the middle letter, the second with the letter to the right of the middle, and so on.

The following fragment is a function that shifts any character by any number of characters, wrapping around if necessary:

```
SUB CaesarShift(A$,Shift%)

    CharNum = ASC(A$) + Shift

    DO UNTIL CharNum > = 0 AND CharNum < = 255          'A
```

```
        IF CharNum < 0 THEN
            CharNum = CharNum + 256
        ELSE
            CharNum = CharNum – 256
        END IF
    LOOP

    A$ = CHR$(CharNum)

END SUB
```

A   This little loop wraps around until the shifted character code will give an ASCII character.

It wouldn't be hard to incorporate this procedure into a file encryptor. Just pass the contents of the file character-by-character to the procedure. The trouble is that a shift cipher is easy to break; you can even do it by hand. Look at the coded message and run back down the alphabet by steps, shifting the letters back step-by-step. After no more than 25 steps, you're done. Here's what you get at each step in the example:

Fdq brx uhdg wklv
Ecp aqw tgcf vjku
Dbo zpv sfbe uijt
Can you read this

Note that it's better to work with the whole message rather than individual words because, occasionally, English words, or clear text, will show up by mistake. For example, the word *HTQI* backs up to the word *FROG* on the second try and to the word *COLD* on the fifth.

Decoding a Caesar cipher, simple as it is, stresses the usefulness of the computer and its limitations. It can do the drudgery, but you have to recognize when to stop. For the more complicated ciphers described later in this chapter, this division of labor is essential.

More complicated ciphers

Because a shift cipher provides virtually no security, the next step is to change the letters in a more random manner. Write down the alphabet and write all the letters in some crazy order below it:

ABCDEFGHIJKLMNOPQRSTUVWXYZ
QAZXSWEDCVFRBGTYHNUJMIKOPL

Now, every time you see an *A* in your original message, replace it with a *Q*. All *B*s become *A*s, *C*s become *Z*s, and so on. This cipher can't be broken by the techniques used for shift ciphers, but it's extremely hard to remember the random alphabet used for the code. So, around 1600, in an attempt to combine the virtues of this method with the ease shift codes, people began to use a *key word cipher*. The idea is to replace the letters of the alphabet by the letters in the key words, using the order they occur there. For example, suppose my key is *THE RAY GUN ZAPPED ME QUICKLY*. Now, look at the following:

ABCDEFGHIJKLMNOPQRSTUVWXYZ

and

THERAYGUNZPDMQICKLBFJOSVWX

I've taken the individual letters from the key phrase, avoiding duplicates as needed, and placed them below the normal alphabet. Because my key phrase contains only 18 different letters, I've placed the unused letters at the end. To encipher a message using this code, replace the letters in the original message with the ones directly below them—*A* with *T*, *B* with *H*, and so on.

Here's one possible outline for a procedure that takes a key phrase and creates the code:

1. Get key phrase
2. Run through each letter in key phrase
3. Check if the letter already is used
4. If not used:
    * Store in next place in cipher list
    * Mark that letter as used
5. Continue until no more letters are left in the key phrase
6. Now, store unused letters from normal alphabet into key

This outline, however, turns out not to be quite the best way of proceeding. To find the best way, you should imagine that what really is going on is a swapping between two alphabets—an encoding one and a decoding one. Suppose you wanted to decipher a message enciphered this way. If you see an *A* in the coded message, the original letter must have been an *E* because an *A* is below an *E* in the alphabets given earlier.

To set up the lists, start with two ordinary alphabets. Now, because *T* replaces *A*, you swap the *A* in the first alphabet with the *T* in the second. Next, you swap the *B* and the *H*.

How can you tell if a letter already is used? Just look at that letter's position in the second alphabet. If the letter still is there, that letter has not been used. When you are done with the letters in the key phrase, any remaining letters should be swapped out of the first alphabet into the second one.

To actually write this program, you should set up two lists. To make life easier, use two arrays of integers that are dimensioned to run from 65 to 90 (the ASCII codes for A-Z).

The following fragment dimensions the arrays and loads values into them:

```
DIM EncodeAlph(65 TO 90),DecodeAlph(65 TO 90)
'Now call:

SUB Initialize

  SHARED EncodeAlph( ),DecodeAlph( )

  FOR I = 65 TO 90
    EncodeAlph(I) = I
    DecodeAlph(I) = I
  NEXT I

END SUB
```

Now, you can write the SUB that makes both lists by translating the preceding outline. To do that, you need to keep track of where you are in the original alphabet, because that determines where the letter will go. Call that variable PosOfLet. Each time you use a letter from the key, swap out the letter determined by this position number with it's counterpart in the other alphabet determined from the key and increase PosOfLet by one. The tricky part comes when you've used up all the letters in the key. Now, you have to decide where to put the remaining letters from the first alphabet. The problems come because there is no convenient pointer to the unused letters in the second alphabet. To take care of this problem, set the used letters to the negative of their ASCII values. For example, if *X*, *Y*, and *Z* were the only letters not used in the key, they would be the only ones that still were positive in the decode alphabet.

The following fragment will correct this problem:

```
SUB Makelists (Key$)

  SHARED EncodeAlph( ), DecodeAlph( )

  LenKey = LEN(Key$)
  PosOfLetUsed = 65                                      'start with ASC("A")

  FOR I = 1 TO LenKey

    A$ = MID$(Key$, I, 1): A$ = UCASE$(A$)

    SELECT CASE A$
      CASE "A" TO "Z"
        A = ASC(A$)
        IF DecodeAlph(A) = A THEN                        'character not yet used
          EncodeAlph(PosOfLetUsed) = A
          DecodeAlph(A) = -PosOfLetUsed
          'swap the encode/decode and flag a used char
          PosOfLetUsed = PosOfLetUsed + 1
        END IF
```

```
        CASE ELSE
        '  if the character is not a letter
        '  you can do something with these
      END SELECT
    NEXT I

    '  Now throw in unused letters
    '  This loop should end if either I've used up all 26 letters or
    '  I can't find any new letters to swap - the X,Y,Z case

    FOR I = 65 TO 90                         '  start looking in 2nd alphabet here
      IF DecodeAlph(I) = I THEN
        EncodeAlph(PosOfLetUsed) = I
        DecodeAlph(I) = – PosOfLetUsed        'swap the encode/decode
        PosOfLetUsed = PosOfLetUsed + 1
      END IF

    NEXT I

  END SUB
```

Now, to encode or decode a letter is almost trivial. Suppose you wanted to encode a *C*, CHR$(67), you have to look at the value of Encode(67) to find the ASCII for the coded version. Similarly, to decode a *C*, you just have to look at the absolute value of the entry in Decode(67). Thus, you can pass the appropriate array as a parameter and use the following fragment:

```
  SUB EncodeDecode(A( ),X$)

    X = ASC(UCASE$(X$))
    X$ = CHR$(A(ABS(X)))

  END SUB
```

Breaking substitution ciphers

Having spent all of the previous section on a fairly subtle program to create a keyword ciphers, you might expect it to be secure, or at least difficult to break. Unfortunately, any substitution cipher can be broken, given enough text. Assuming the encoded text originally was written in standard, everyday English, it's pretty easy if you have even one thousand words of encoded text.

This section explains how, given enough text, you can break any substitution cipher. All it will require is patience, some paper, and perhaps a program or two that you might want to write. Along the way, you'll learn how to recognize, with some degree of certainty, whether the person used a substitution cipher.

After reading this section, you probably don't want to use a keyword cipher, so I end this chapter with a different ciphering method that is much harder to break. I'd venture to say that most people would find it impossible.

The key to breaking a substitution code is to remember that letters do not exist in isolation. *E* is almost certainly the most common letter. *T* is likely to be the next most common. The frequency of *A*s is likely to be third highest. Over the years, cryptographers have examined thousands of pages of text to determine the frequency of letters in standard English. Table 15-4 shows some of what they found (in order of occurrence in large samples).

Table 15-4
A frequency table of letter usage in English text.

I over 10%	II 5−10%	III 2−4.9%	IV 1−1.9%	V Under 1%
E(13%)	A(8.1%)	L(4%)	G	V
T(10%)	O(7.9%)	D(3.8%)	P	K
	N(7%)	F(3%)	Y	X
	I(7%)	C(3%)	W	J
	S(6.5%)	M(2.5%)	B	Q
	R(6.3%)	U(2.4%)		Z
	H(5.4%)			

Some lists reverse a few of the letters. They put *H* before *R* and *D* before *L* for example. Also, the percentages are only approximate. What's important is that, only in extraordinary circumstances, do letters wander out of these groups. For example, somebody once wrote a novel without using the letter *E*.

If you have an enciphered text and it has symbols, which might or might not be letters, and the various symbols occur in approximately these proportions, you quite likely have a substitution cipher at work.

Here is some more information on substitution ciphers:

- A single letter word is *A*, *I*, or very rarely *O*
- The most common two-letter words are *OF*, *TO*, *IN*, *IT*, *BE*, *AS*, *AT*, *SO*, *WE*, *HE*
- The most common three-letter words are *THE*, *AND*, *FOR*, *WAS*, *HIS*, *BUT*, *YOU*, *ARE*
- Four-letter words are *THAT*, *HAVE*, *FROM*, *THIS*, *WILL*, *YOUR*
- Initial letters of words are *T*, *A*, *O*, *S*, *W*, *I*, *H*, *C*, *B*
- Final letters are *E*, *S*, *D*, *T*, *N*, *Y*, *F*, *R*

To prevent a cryptographer from using this extremely useful information, it's quite common to eliminate spaces between words and punctuation and to use only uppercase letters. After all, YOUCANREADTHISCANTYOU?

Since the invention of the telegraph, the custom was to send coded messages in groups of five (for example, *IXLPD EXPUT FQDUA*), but these groups would rarely correspond to words.

To replace this lost information, cryptographers have investigated the most common two and three letter combinations, which are called *bigrams* and *trigrams*. The most common bigrams are:

TH, HE, AN, RE, IN, AT, ON, ER, ND, ED, OF, EA, ST, TI, and *EN*

The most common trigrams are:

THE, AND, ING, ENT, TIO, ION, FOR, NDE, HAS, and *NCE*

The average vowel count is 40%. Two vowels almost never occur together; however, when they do, they're likely to be in order: *AI, IE*, or *EI*.

To decipher text encoded with a substitution cipher, find the frequencies of the letters or symbols. Then, substitute the letters using the frequency tables. If your text is long enough, you probably are done at this point—you should be able to read the raw text. For example, even if a few letters are wrong you'll get something like:

TOYEORNOTTOYETHATIDTHEKZEDTION

but you can understand this phrase. The process you unconsciously use to understand this fractured text is part of the active area of computer science called artificial intelligence. Here, any program you write will only get you to this point, then your intuition must take over.

If the text isn't long enough, some of the frequencies will be off; you'll have to try to make changes. Usually, you'll be able to keep within the groups.

At the least any program you write needs procedures to:

- Analyze the frequency of the letters
- Analyze the frequency of the bigrams
- Display the best guess for the text
- At any point, allow you to enter changes and to redisplay the text using this modified key
- Display the current key

I'll leave the actual program up to you.

A semi-practical cipher

The problem with a simple substitution cipher is that, by always replacing a letter by the same symbol, someone can break it using frequency analysis. One way to avoid this method of breaking a code is to change the substitution. For example, instead of always replacing an *E* with the letter *T*, use a *T* the first time and a *Z* the next. So, each time an *E* occurs, the program replaces it with another letter. This method is called a *multi-alphabet substitution cipher*. It's much more difficult to break this cipher, but it also is much more difficult to set up. After all, you have to devise a way of getting these multiple alphabets.

I'll use the built-in random number generator in DOS BASIC to generate my alphabets. Recall that the command:

```
X = RND(1)
```

gives you a different random number between 0 and 1. This statement is the key to breaking the cipher that I'm going to show you. However, given enough data, a professional cryptographer or a good amateur can find out the next number in the sequence. A cryptographer would say the random number generator in DOS BASIC isn't *cryptographically secure*. Finding and proving that you have a cryptographically secure random number generator is probably the most important problem in cryptography. The random number generators that cryptographers think are best rely on the fact that, with current knowledge, it's very difficult to factor large numbers. However, even these have not been proved to be secure. All that has been proven is that, if factoring is hard, then they are secure. So, they ultimately depend on nobody ever discovering a fast method for factoring. Most mathematicians, including myself, believe this assumption will hold, but that belief is a far cry from proving it.

Anyway, the idea behind the following cipher is that you scale the number generated by the computer and use it to determine the Caesar shift. Now, instead of using the same shift for the next letter, use the random number generator to get a different shift for each letter. Each time you encode a letter, it's transformed differently.

Unfortunately, this method won't quite work. Because the patterns obviously don't repeat (that's what is meant by *random*), there isn't any reasonable method of decoding the message. You would never know what to shift back by. You have to modify this idea slightly. Recall that DOS BASIC has a built-in debugging tool for dealing with programs that use random numbers. If you use:

```
RANDOMIZE Seed
```

then DOS BASIC always gives you the same sequence of random numbers. Each seed gives a different, repeatable sequence of random numbers. Ask the person for a key (for example, a four-digit number). Use this key to reseed the random number generator:

```
RANDOMIZE Key
```

Now, you can generate a list of shifts, one for each character in the file:

```
NextShift = INT(256*RND(1))
```

Use these shifts just like a Caesar cipher. Call this shift generator for each letter in the message.

The whole point of repeatability is that if you process the command RANDOMIZE *Key* again, when you generate Caesar shifts, you get the same series of numbers you did before. Just as before, if you know what the original shift was, you can reverse it just as easily.

Unfortunately, this technique doesn't quite work in the current version of QBasic. The RANDOMIZE *Key* doesn't work as announced. Instead, you have to say X = RND(*negative number*) to get the repeatable sequence.

In any case, I'll leave it up to you to implement this method, because there's a much more elegant way of proceeding. Recall that, in the bit twiddling section from chapter 14, the XOR command has the nice property that, if B = A XOR Shift and C = B XOR Shift, then the value of C is the value of A. Thus, by XORing twice, you get back to where you started. You can use the same module to both encode and decode. The following fragment is a QBasic version of the SUB to implement this technique:

```
SUB EncodeDecode (filename$, keyvalue)

    DIM SingleChar AS STRING *1                      'for use in GET and PUT
    X = RND( - keyvalue)
    FileNum = FREEFILE
    OPEN filename$ FOR BINARY AS #FileNum

    FOR I = 1 TO LOF(FileNum)
       GET #FileNum, I, SingleChar
       CharNum = ASC(SingleChar)
       RandomInteger = INT(256 * RND(1))
       CharNum = CharNum XOR RandomInteger           'this is it
       SingleChar = CHR$(CharNum)
       PUT #FileNum, I, SingleChar
    NEXT I
    CLOSE #FileNum

END SUB
```

<big><big>**16**</big></big>

CHAPTER

Finishing up

This chapter shows the rudiments of batch file programming, as well as giving you some hints on where to go from here. The language used for batch files can be thought of as an extremely primitive form of BASIC. It lacks most of the features that make programming easy, but enough was left in so that you occasionally will find it useful to use these techniques.

Batch files basics: the AUTOEXEC.BAT file

Often you want your computer to initialize itself when you turn it on. For example, instead of being greeted by the infamous A> prompt (or C> if you have a hard disk) you might prefer something like the date, the time, the full pathname, and a pleasant message:

```
Mon 1-1-89
9:46:01
Current path is: C:\QBBOOK\CH1
May I help you?
>
```

Customizing your system is done from a file called AUTOEXEC.BAT, which must be in the root directory of your boot disk—the disk or drive from which DOS loads. After DOS is loaded, it immediately looks for a file called AUTOEXEC-.BAT and executes any of the DOS commands that it finds there.

The DOS command that changes the prompt is called PROMPT. Here are some of the options for this command:

PROMPT $D   Gives the date
PROMPT $P   Gives the current pathname

```
PROMPT $T     Gives the current time
PROMPT $_     Gives a new line
PROMPT $G     Gives the > prompt
```

You can combine these options. PROMPT D__$P gives the date on one line and the path on a new line. Finally, to get a message, enter the message after a dollar sign. The PROMPT command that gives the example shown earlier is:

```
PROMPT $D$__$T$__$P$__$ May I help you?$__$G
```

You can try various combinations of the PROMPT command. They go into effect immediately. The PROMPT command alone goes back to a > prompt.

Other commands that you are likely to want in your AUTOEXEC.BAT file include the PATH command, which tells DOS where to find programs.

In general, any file with the extension BAT is used to hold groups of DOS commands that are meant to be executed at one shot. For example, I have a file called QBPROG.BAT in the BATCH directory of my hard disk that contains the following two commands:

```
CD \ QBPROG
QBASIC
```

Now, when I'm anywhere at all, I enter QBPROG and DOS looks in the BATCH directory, which is included in my path, and executes both these commands. Thus, I end up in the QBPROG directory running QBasic. Batch files make navigating the vast expanses of modern hard disks possible.

To create a batch file, you need to write the text, or ASCII, file containing the commands. If you are using DOS 5.0, you have a full screen editor called EDIT, which is similar to the QBasic editor and is ideal for writing batch files. If you are using an earlier version of DOS, you need to use EDLIN or the text, or document, mode of your word processor to create them.

The commands available for batch programming

If you press the Ctrl−C combination, any batch files stops and displays:

```
Terminate Batch Job (Y/N)?
```

If you hit Y or y, then DOS ends the batch program. On the other hand, if you hit an N or n, then DOS moves on to the next command in the batch file, even if the original command had more to do.

The command PAUSE, which usually is followed by a message, temporarily stops executing the batch file. For example, if DOS processes the command:

```
PAUSE "Please insert a disk in drive A"
```

then you would see:

Please insert a disk in Drive A
Press any key to continue ...

and the batch file would wait until you pressed a key before it would execute the next command.

DOS usually displays the commands it is executing during a batch file. If you don't want DOS to display the commands, use the command ECHO OFF. Then, until DOS processes the command ECHO ON, the batch file executes silently.

Versions of DOS after 3.3 are more flexible. You can use an at sign (@) in front of any batch command to prevent it from being echoed; you don't need to do it wholesale.

The REM command works just like it does in BASIC: it turns any statement into a comment. Judicious use of them make your batch files easier to understand.

Parameters

Whenever you give DOS a command, DOS divides what you enter into a command and its parameters—the options that the command works with. For example, in COPY *.BAS A:, the DOS command is COPY and the two command line parameters are *.BAS and A:

Suppose you want to write a simple batch file that, in a situation like the one given previously, first prompts you to put a disk in the A drive and then does the copy. Here's what the batch file would look like:

```
PAUSE "Place a disk in the A: drive"
COPY %1 A:
```

Suppose you call this file COPYA.BAT. To use the file, all you have to do is enter:

```
COPYA.BAT *.BAS
```

As you might guess, DOS uses the %1 to hold the first command line parameter. Whenever DOS sees a %1 in a batch file, it systematically replaces all occurrences of it with the first command line parameter.

You can have up to nine parameters, labeled %1 through %9. %0 is reserved for the command itself.

IF EXIST, the GOTO, and IF STRING1 == STRING 2

Suppose you want to copy a file only if it exists. For this condition, you need one of the two primitive IF statements available to batch file programmers. It's:

```
IF EXISTS filename DOS command
```

Notice that there's no THEN.

For example, suppose you wanted to write a little batch file that would start up whatever version of BASIC was found in the \ DOS directory. The first line of the batch file might look like this:

```
IF EXISTS C: \ DOS \ QBasic.EXE QBasic
```

Unfortunately, this file won't quite work unless you work at it. For example, suppose you followed this model and made the second line:

```
IF EXISTS C: \ DOS \ GWBASIC.EXE
```

Now, suppose you had both versions of BASIC. Because batch files remember where they left off, after the file left QBasic, it immediately would be plopped into GW-BASIC, which probably is not what you wanted.

This situation is one where you need an IF-THEN-ELSE, but batch files don't have an ELSE. You need to improvise using the GOTO statement.

The way this statement works in batch file programming is that you put a label in your batch file by using a colon followed by the label, which is the exact opposite of QBasic. For example, :FINISHED is a label.

Here's one way to write a batch file program that starts up only one version of BASIC:

```
IF EXISTS    C: \ DOS \ QBASIC.EXE     GOTO BestBASIC
IF EXISTS    C: \ DOS \ BASICA.EXE     GOTO IBMBASIC
IF EXISTS    C: \ DOS \ GWBASIC.EXE  GOTO CLONE
REM
:BESTBASIC
   C: \ DOS \ QBASIC.EXE
   GOTO FINISHED
REM
:IBMBASIC
   C: \ DOS \ BASICA.EXE
   GOTO FINISHED
REM
:CLONE
   C: \ DOS \ GWBASIC.EXE
   GOTO FINISHED
REM
:FINISHED
```

You occasionally might want to use the keyword NOT. This word takes the form of IF NOT EXISTS ....

The other form of the IF available to batch file programs tests for string equality. Usually, you combine this form with the named parameters discussed above. For example:

```
IF %1 = = TEST
```

tests whether the first command parameter is the string TEST. Note the two equals signs and the lack of quotes around the string. You can use the NOT here as well.

There are a couple of other features in batch programming that are used less frequently. To learn about those features, as well as to go further in batch file programming, try reading *Enhanced MS-DOS Batch File Programming* by Dan Gookin. The book is available from TAB/McGraw-Hill.

Pipes and filters

There are two more features of DOS that I want to introduce: pipes and filters. These are commands that redirect the results of a DOS command somewhere else. For example, suppose you want to get a printed copy of a directory. If the directory filled only one screen, you could use Print Screen key; however, if it was any larger, you'd be in trouble. The command:

```
DIR > LPT1:
```

redirects the result of the DIR command to LPT1: (the printer that's hopefully attached to the first parallel port). More generally, the greater than sign is used to send the result of a DOS command, which ordinarily would be displayed on the screen, somewhere else. For example:

```
TYPE PACKING.LST > COM1:
```

sends the contents of the file PACKING.LST to the first serial port and:

```
TYPE PACKING.LST > LPT1:
```

is a more complicated version of COPY PACKING.LST LPT1:. Similarly:

```
DIR > "A:DIRFILE"
```

sets up a file containing the contents of the current directory.

Another useful feature is *filtering*. A filter, which usually is a small program, takes information, processes it in some way, and sends the result somewhere else. One of the most useful filters is the MORE filter. MORE changes the way the display works with long files. Now, after every 23 lines, the display stops scrolling and waits for you to press a key before continuing—much like the DIR/P command. For example:

```
TYPE README.DOC | MORE
```

lets you examine the README file one screen at a time, without having to constantly fight with Ctrl−Num Lock. The ¦ symbol usually is located above the backslash key; it's not a colon.

For this filter to work, DOS has to know where the MORE program is; it usually is found in the same place as DOS itself. Make sure that the PATH includes the location of any filters you use. Other filters let you SORT a file or FIND a file that contains a piece of information. Consult any book on DOS for more information on these filters.

Recommended sources for further study

The first thing you should do is think seriously about upgrading to QuickBASIC. This program is a more sophisticated version of QBasic, with superior debugging capabilities and the ability to develop stand-alone programs. Because the syntax is the same as for QBasic, the transition after reading this book will be painless.

If you get interested in Microsoft Windows, then a product that you must have is Visual Basic. This package is a revolutionary product that makes windows programming easy and fun. (I've written a book on Visual Basic, which is available from the Osborne division of McGraw-Hill.)

If you like the power of batch languages and would like to go further with them, Mansfield Software (1-203-429-8402) sells a full-featured batch language called REXX that I like a lot. If you want to transform a GW-BASIC program into a QBasic program, then David Schneider, who wrote two very good reference books for BASIC programmers, sells a disk of utilities that includes a useful conversion program. The address is:

David's Utilities
P.O. Box 728
College Park, Maryland 20740

His two handbooks are *The Handbook of BASIC* for GW-BASIC users and *The Handbook of QuickBASIC* for QBasic users (both are from Brady).

Serious BASIC programmers should be aware of the magazine *BasicPro*, which started in 1991. It seems to be developing into an incredibly useful forum for BASIC programmers.

One place that I turn to for ideas for fun and interesting programs is A. K. Dewdney's *Computer Recreations* column in *Scientific American*. Many of the earlier columns were collected in *The Armchair Universe* (Freeman, 1988) and the *Magic Mountain* (Freeman, 1990). If you want to find out more about graphics or need other ideas on interesting programs, then this column is a good place to start.

If you want to use the methods described in chapter 14 and need to look up the formulas for various curves, try *A Catalog of Special Plane Curves* by J. Lawrence (Dover, 1978). To learn more about fractals, go on to *The Science of*

Fractal Images, which was edited by H. O. Peitgen and D. Saupe (Springer-Verlag, 1988). Be prepared for the mathematics, however.

A book on IBM graphics, which uses relatively little math, is *The Art of Graphics for the IBM PC* by J. McGregor and A. Watt (Addison-Wesley, 1986). Unfortunately, all the programs are written in interpreted BASIC, which doesn't allow recursion. Hence, the programs occasionally are very hard to read. The text, however, is clear.

To understand the most modern ciphers, those devised within the last 20 years, also requires a fair amount of mathematics. However, you can start with D. Kahn's massive book, *The Code-Breakers* (Macmillan, 1967). This book is a lot of fun to read from cover to cover or to dip into occasionally. Next, try F. Higenbottom's *Codes and Ciphers* (David MacKay, 1973). Finally, for those who don't mind a bit of math, try *Elementary Cryptoanalysis* by A. Sinkov (Mathematical Association of America, 1968) or *Elementary Cryptoanalysis* by H. Gaines (Dover, 1956).

For more on algorithms, the standard textbook is R. Sedgewick's *Algorithms* (Addison-Wesley, 1988).

I hope you will move on to QuickBASIC. Even if you do, you might consider learning a bit about assembly language. Programming in assembler is tedious and you have to buy an assembler, but it can give you incredible power. If you rewrite a crucial part of a QuickBASIC program as a CALL to an assembly language program, the speedups sometimes seem miraculous. My favorite book on assembler is R. Lafore's *Assembly Language Primer* (New American Library, 1984). Be warned that, at present, all assemblers are unpleasant; none have an integrated environment like QBasic.

There are three other computer languages that are popular for microcomputers. Pascal is the main instructional language of the universities, although it's far from being my favorite language. Because QBasic borrowed—and often improved—many of the best features of Pascal, you won't find the transition very difficult, however. The best Pascal compiler is Borland International's Turbo Pascal. (If you are a student, then call Borland to find out if their special student price still is available.) There are literally 100s of books on Turbo Pascal available. To be quite honest, I don't know them well enough to have a favorite. I do have a favorite book on Pascal; it's my favorite book on programming. I've learned a lot from it and it's influenced how I explained structured programming in this book and in my classes. It's *Oh Pascal* by Doug Cooper and Michael Clancy (Norton, 1985). Unfortunately, there's only a small add-in book for Turbo Pascal.

The language of professional programmers seems, more and more, to be C. This language was invented at Bell Labs to write operating systems, so it is much closer to assembly language than any other popular language. Because it's close to assembly language, it's fast. However, for the very same reason, it's cryptic. It's been described as a write-only language. I don't particularly like C, but I do find myself using it more often than assembly language. I suggest that before you go out and buy a C compiler (a QBasic programmer will find Microsoft's Quick C the easiest to get used to and it comes with an excellent tutorial) that you look at *The Art of C Programming* by Robin Jones and Ian Stewart (Springer Verlag, 1987). It's well written. After you finish reading it, you should be able to decide if you want to program in C at all.

APPENDIX

GW-BASIC versus QBasic

This appendix summarizes the differences between GW-BASIC and QBasic. It briefly explains the commands new to QBasic and the differences between commands that have the same names but work differently.

The first thing you must do in converting a BASIC, BASICA, or GW-BASIC program to QBasic is to make sure that the file has been saved in ASCII form using the SAVE *"fname"*, A option.

The following statements in interpreted BASIC are editing commands or commands concerned with running a program. Their counterparts in QBasic are done from one of the menus. In particular, the editing facilities of QBasic are far superior.

AUTO   (Line numbers aren't needed in QBasic anyway.)

CONT   Is done from the Run menu or via the F5 shortcut. It usually is done after the Restart command or a break: Ctrl−Break or a debugging break.

DELETE   Select the block and then hit the DEL key or use Cut option from the Edit menu to move it to the clipboard.

EDIT   Move the cursor to the appropriate line, then edit to your heart's content.

LIST   Makes the View window active and scroll.

LLIST   Use PRINT on the File menu to print the active window.

LOAD   Is done from the File menu.

MERGE

NEW	Is done from the File menu.
RENUM	(QBasic doesn't need line numbers.)
RUN	Shift−F5 or Start on the Run menu.
SAVE	Done from the File menu.

The MOTOR command has no counterpart in QBasic. The following commands have been superseded:

DEF USR	These commands set up a machine language routine in interpreted BASIC.
USR	

The following statements work a bit differently:

BLOAD, BSAVE	These statements theoretically work the same; however, what they might do can be different. QBasic and GW-BASIC use different memory locations for similar functions.
CALL	Calls a subprogram, not an assembly language routine.
CHAIN	QBasic does not support the ALL, DELETE, or MERGE commands or using a line number.
CLEAR	The first position is used in interpreted BASIC for the DATA segment. This isn't used in QBasic (that's why you need a comma to set the stack size).
COMMON	When used to pass values of variables via CHAIN, it must appear before any executable statement.
DEFINT, DEFSNG, etc.	In QBasic, these commands must appear on a physical line before any variables that you want to effect. (In interpreted BASIC, the order can be affected by branches.)
DEF FN	Order as for a definer
DIM	Order as for a definer or DEF FN
PEEK and POKE	Be very careful with any program that PEEKs or POKEs. The locations used by QBasic might be different.
RESUME	If an error occurs in using a DEF FN function, QBasic continues execution at the line that defines the function.
SYSTEM	In QBasic, this command ends a program and takes you back to DOS or the QBasic environment, depending on whether the program is stand-alone or not.
RUN	The ,R option that keeps files open isn't supported.

The following commands are new to QBasic. The commands are listed with summaries of what they do:

$DYNAMIC	A metacommand; after processing this command, Q Basic makes all arrays dynamic.
$STATIC	Arrays will be static from that point on.
CALL	Calls a subprogram and allows passing by value or by reference.
CLNG	Converts to the long integer data type, which is new to QBasic.
CONST	Lets you set up named constants.
CVSMBF, CVDMBF	Is needed to convert random access files in GW-BASIC to QBasic. See the on-line help.
DECLARE	Performs the bookkeeping for function procedures and subprograms. The interpreter automatically places this command when you save a program.
DEF FN/END DEF	Allows multi-line function definitions (it is better to use function procedures).
DEFLNG	Specifies a range of variables as being of the long integer type.
DO/LOOP	Flexible form for indeterminate loops.
EXIT	Allows abnormal termination of loops, functions, and subprograms.
FREEFILE	Gives you the next available number for file access.
FUNCTION	Allows sophisticated user-defined functions with parameter passing.
IF-THEN ELSE/ELSEIF	Allows multi-line, multi-branch IF-THEN statements.
LBOUND/UBOUND	Gives the lower or upper subscript value. These commands are useful because of QBasic's ability to dimension arrays from any starting to ending point.
LCASE$/UCASE$	Converts a string to lower or uppercase.
LTRIM$/RTRIM$	Removes all spaces from the left or right of a string.
MKL$	Converts long integers into strings of length four.
MKSMBF$, MKDMBF$	Converts single- or double-precision numbers to strings. These commands are needed when converting QBasic random access files to GW-BASIC form.
OPEN fname FOR BINARY	Allows file access as a string of bits.

REDIM	Allows you to change the size of a previously dimensioned array.
SEEK	Used in binary access to files.
SELECT CASE	Used for handling multiple branches based on the value of an expression.
SUB/END SUB	Used for defining subprograms.
TYPE/END TYPE	Used for defining user-defined record types. Strings must have a fixed length.
VIEW PRINT	Defines a text viewport.

B
APPENDIX

Options on starting QBasic

The following options can be used when you are starting up, or loading, QBasic on your computer. Most of these options can be combined, where they are not mutually exclusive.

QBASIC /B
: Use this option when you have a monochrome monitor attached to a color graphics (CGA) card. The option can be combined with /NOHI for laptops.

QBASIC /filename
: This option loads the file named in the *filename* parameter.

QBASIC /G
: This option also is useful only with a CGA. It allows faster screen updating at the risk of some snow.

QBASIC / H
: This option gives the highest resolution possible.

QBASIC /MBF
: Use this option when working with a program that uses Microsoft's previous format for numbers.

QBASIC / NOHI
: This option lets you use a monochrome monitor that doesn't support high intensity. It is used mostly laptops (see QBASIC /B).

QBASIC /RUN *program*
: This option loads QBasic and runs the program named in the parameter *program*.

C
APPENDIX

QBasic's shortcut keys and editing commands

Most of this information is available online. You can find it under Contents in the Help menu.

F1   Used when the cursor is on a specific keyword. It gives help on that command.

Shift−F1   Ranges from Help on Help to help on any menu item.

Alt−F1   Lets you move backwards to previous help screens.

F2   Opens a window listing modules with their associated SUBs and function procedures. It allows you to edit a specific procedure or function.

Shift−F2   Moves to the main module, a function, or a procedure (alphabetically). It places the module in the active view window.

Ctrl−F2   Moves backwards. It is the opposite of Shift−F2.

F3   Repeats last find (Edit menu).

F4   Switches back and forth from the output screen to the development environment.

F5   Continue command. It is used after a break or restart (Run menu).

Shift—F5   Starts program execution (Start on Run menu).

F6   Makes the next window active.

Shift—F6   Makes the previous window active.

F7   Executes the program up to current cursor position.

F8   Single steps through program.

F9   Toggles breakpoints on and off (Debug menu).

F10   Single steps but treats procedures and functions as single objects (steps through).

The following keystrokes are QBasic window functions:

Ctrl—F10   Switch active window between original size and full screen.
Alt—+   Enlarges active window one line.
Alt——   Shrinks active window one line.

The following table describes the editing keys. The last column gives the WordStar equivalent, which QBasic also supports. (Notice the WordStar commands form a diamond on the left-hand side of the keyboard.)

Character left	Left arrow	Ctrl—S
Character right	Right arrow	Ctrl—D
Line up	Up arrow	Ctrl—E
Line down	Down arrow	Ctrl—X
First indentation level	Home	
Beginning of line		Ctrl—Q—S
End of line	End	Ctrl—Q—D
Beginning of next line	Ctrl—Enter	Ctrl—J
Page Up	PgUp	Ctrl—R
Page down	PgDn	Ctrl—C
Top of window		Ctrl—Q—E
Bottom of window		Ctrl—Q—X
Top of document	Ctrl—Home	Ctrl—Q—R
End of document	Ctrl—End	Ctrl—Q—C
Word left	Ctrl—Left arrow	Ctrl—A
Word right	Ctrl—Right arrow	Ctrl—F
Screen left	Ctrl—PgUp	
Screen right	Ctrl—PgDn	

The insert mode is toggled on and off by the Ins key or Ctrl—V. The cursor will change from an underscore character to a solid rectangle. You can insert a line below the current line with the End—Enter combination or insert a line above the current line with the Home—Ctrl—N combination.

The Tab key inserts spaces; the number of spaces is determined via the Display option on the Options menu.

The following keystrokes can be used for simple deletions:

Character at cursor	Del or Ctrl−G
Character before cursor	Backspace or Ctrl−H
Word	Ctrl−T
The whole line	Ctrl−Y
To end of line	Ctrl−Q−Y

The last two keystrokes actually place the deleted text in the clipboard. The clipboard is used to cut, copy, and paste. Once text has been placed there, you can paste it by moving the cursor and hitting Shift−Ins or by using Paste on the Edit menu.

All the other ways to place text in the clipboard require selecting the text by holding down the Shift key while using any of the cursor movement keys given earlier. As you move the cursor, you select more or less text. Selected text is either highlighted or appears in reverse video, depending on your monitor. Once text is selected you can:

Completely delete it	Del key
Indent it	Tab
Cut it to the clipboard	Shift−Del or use the Edit menu
Copy it to the clipboard	Ctrl−Ins or use the Edit menu

Because text remains in the clipboard until it is replaced by another operation, you can even paste multiple copies. To deselect text, hit any arrow key. Deselecting the text is essential because, while text is selected, any key you press will replace the selected text. As you can imagine, this is extremely frustrating—lean on the keyboard and all the selected text is gone.

Finally, you can scroll the text in the active window by using the following keystrokes:

Up one line	Ctrl−Up arrow	Ctrl−W
Down a line	Ctrl−Down arrow	Ctrl−Z
Page up	PgUp	Ctrl−R
Page down	PgDn	Ctrl−C
Window left	Ctrl−PgUp	
Window right	Ctrl−PgDn	

D
APPENDIX

Using mice
with QBasic

First, I need to give you some terminology. The *mouse cursor* is a block that moves as you move the mouse. *To click* means to press a mouse button once. *To double click* means press the same button twice in quick succession. *To drag* means to hold down the left mouse button and move the mouse. Using this terminology, here are the mouse equivalents for many of the commands:

Choose a menu item Move the mouse cursor to the menu and click the left button. Move the mouse cursor to an item and click again.

Close a menu Move the mouse cursor off the menu and click the left button.

Make a window active Move the mouse cursor inside the window and click the left button.

Scroll text For a single line or character, click the left button with the mouse cursor at the appropriate scroll arrow. Otherwise, drag the scroll box to roughly the position on scroll bar. To scroll one page, move the mouse cursor to the scroll bar and click the left button.

Load a program or file Move the mouse cursor to the filename (as revealed in a dialog box) and double click on it. You also can click once and hit Enter.

The right mouse button gives context sensitive help.

E

Reserved words and scan codes

The following list contains the reserved words used in QBasic and GW-BASIC. Words followed by one asterisk apply to QBasic only. Words followed by two asterisks apply to GW-BASIC only.

ABS	CHAIN	CVS
ACCESS	CHDIR	CVSMBF
ALIAS	CHR$	DATA
AND	CINT	DATE$
ANY	CIRCLE	DECLARE*
APPEND	CLEAR	DEF
AS	CLNG*	DEFDBL
ASC	CLOSE	DEFINT
ATN	CLS	DEFLNG*
AUTO**	COLOR	DEFSNG
BASE	COM	DEFSTR
BEEP	COMMON	DIM
BINARY	CONST	DO*
BLOAD	CONT**	DRAW
BSAVE	COS	EDIT**
BYVAL	CSNG	ELSE
CALL	CSRLIN	ELSEIF*
CALLS*	CVD	END
CASE*	CVDMBF	ENDIF
CDBL	CVI	ENVIRON
CDECL	CVL	ENVIRON$

EOF	LIST**	PEN
EQV	LLIST**	PLAY
ERASE	LOAD	PMAP
ERDEV	LOC*	POINT
ERDEV$	LOCAL	POKE
ERL	LOCATE	POS
ERR	LOCK	PRESET
ERROR	LOF	PRINT
EXIT*	LOG	PSET
EXP	LONG	PUT
FIELD	LOOP*	RANDOM
FILEATTR*	LPOS	RANDOMIZE
FILES	LPRINT	READ
FIX	LSET	REDIM*
FOR	LTRIM$*	REM
FRE	MERGE**	RENUM**
FREEFILE*	MID$	RESTORE
FUNCTION*	MKD	RESUME
GET	MKDIR	RETURN
GOSUB	MKDMBF$*	RIGHT$
GOTO	MKI$	RMDIR
HEX$	MKL$*	RND
IF	MKS$	RSET
IMP	MKSMBF$*	RTRIM$*
INKEY$	MOD	RUN
INP	MOTOR**	SADD*
INPUT	NAME	SAVE**
INPUT$	NEW**	SCREEN
INSTR	NEXT	SEEK*
INT	NOT	SEG
INTEGER	OCT$	SELECT*
IOCTL	OFF	SETMEM*
IOCTL$	ON	SGN
IS	OPEN	SHARED*
KEY	OPTION	SHELL
KILL	OR	SIGNAL
LBOUND*	OUT	SIN
LCASE$*	OUTPUT	SINGLE
LEFT$	PAINT	SLEEP
LEN	PALETTE	SOUND
LET	PCOPY	SPACE$
LINE	PEEK	SPC

SQRP	THEN	USR**
STATIC*	TIME$	VARPTR
STEP	TIMER	VARPTR$
STICK	TO	VIEW
STOP	TROFF	WAIT
STR$	TRON	WEND
STRIG	TYPE*	WHILE
STRING	UBOUND*	WIDTH
STRING$	UCASE$*	WINDOW
SUB*	UEVENT	WRITE
SYSTEM	UNLOCK	XOR
TAB	UNTIL	
TAN	USING	

The following list contains the scan codes for all of the keys on your keyboard.

Esc	1	A	30	Caps Lock	58
! or 1	2	S	31	F1	59
@ or 2	3	D	32	F2	60
# or 3	4	F	33	F3	61
$ or 4	5	G	34	F4	62
% or 5	6	H	35	F5	63
^ or 6	7	J	36	F6	64
& or 7	8	K	37	F7	65
* or 8	9	L	38	F8	66
(or 9	10	: or ;	39	F9	67
) or 0	11	" or '	40	F10	68
_ or −	12	~ or '	41	F11	133
+ or =	13	Left Shift	42	F12	134
Bksp	14	| or \	43	Num Lock	69
Tab	15	Z	44	Scroll Lock	70
Q	16	X	45	Home or 7	71
W	17	C	46	Up arrow or 8	72
E	18	V	47	PgUp or 9	73
R	19	B	48	Keypad −	74
T	20	N	49	Left arrow or 4	75
Y	21	M	50	Center or 5	76
U	22	< or ,	51	Right arrow or 6	77
I	23	> or .	52	Keypad +	78
O	24	? or /	53	End or 1	79
P	25	Right Shift	54	Down arrow or 2	80
{ or [	26	Prt Sc or *	55	PgDn or 3	81
} or]	27	Alt	56	Ins or 0	82
Enter	28	Spacebar	57	Del or .	83
Ctrl	29				

F
APPENDIX

Error messages

This appendix is a list of run-time error messages that you might need to trap.

Error number	Description of error	Possible cause/solution
11	Division by zero	
24	Device timeout	Printer not online.
25	Device fault	General hardware problem.
27	Out of paper	
52	Bad filename	Form of filename not allowed.
53	File not found	Check the full pathname.
54	Bad file mode	
55	File already open	Close the file.
57	Device I/O error	Problems with the disk.
58	File already exists	You can't rename it the way you want.
61	Disk full	If you're lucky, you can SHELL to FORMAT-.COM.
67	Too many files	A directory or subdirectory has limits on the number of files it allows—112 and 255 respectively.
68	Device unavailable	Turn it on.
69	COM buffer overflow	Empty it more often or use the QB /C option when starting QBasic to enlarge it.
70	Permission denied	A write-protect tab might be on.
71	Disk not ready	Put the disk in and make sure the drive door is closed.
72	Disk media error	The disk is corrupted; replace the disk.
75	Path/File access error	Check the full pathname.
76	Path not found	Check the full pathname.

Index

GW-BASIC programming (*cont.*)
 debugging, 43-44
 delete lines, DELETE command, 30
 editing keys, 22
 erase program, NEW command, 29
 function keys, soft function keys, 21
 indeterminate loops, 112-113
 line numbers, 27-30
 loading programs, LOAD command, 29
 opening screen, 21
 printout of program text, LIST and LLIST, 28, 30
 QBasic vs., 403-406
 random-file file management, 377-380
 remarks (REM statements), 28-29
 reserved words, 415-417
 resume execution, CONT command, 44, 79
 running programs, RUN command, 28-29
 saving programs: tokenized vs. ASCII forms, 29
 scan codes, 415, 417
 variables, 35

H
help, 8-12
 environment help, 9
 exiting help, Esc key, 8-9
 hyperlinks, 9-11
 indexed topics, 9-10
 keys and commands, 11
 printout of help screens, 12-14
 reserved-word list, 42
 "survival guide," QBasic, 6-7
HEX$( ), convert decimal to hex number, 234
hexidecimal numbers, 233-234
high-order ASCII code, 91
Hofstadter, Douglas, 297
hyperlink, help, 9-11

I
identifiers, numeric, DEFINT, DEFLNG, DEFSNG, DEFDBL, DEFSTR, 63

IF EXIST, 397-398
IF-THEN statements, 5, 115-123, 206, 228, 371
 alphabetize a list, 116-118
 AND, OR, NOT use, 118-120
 average calculation, 118-120, 125-126
 block IF-THEN in QBasic, 124-126
 ELSEIF clause, 132-134
 eureka loops, 120-123
 EXIT DO command, 121-122
 sort numerical list, 116-118
IF-THEN-ELSE statements, 123-124, 140
Immediate window, 6, 32, 131
indentation, programming text indentations, 73, 107
indeterminate loops (*see also* loops), 99-113
indexed help topics, 9-10
indices, random-access file management, 382-383
infinite loops, 78-79
infinite precision arithmetic program, 195-197
initializing variables, 40
INKEY$, 108-109, 144
input focus, dialog boxes, 14
INPUT statement, 34-35, 235, 247, 360
INPUT$, 52-53, 76, 144, 212, 383-385
Insert mode, 18
insertion sorts, 257-258, 317-318
INSTR( ), 147-149, 152, 176
INT( ), integer-only, 161
integers, 61
intermediate overflow, 62, 169
interpilers, 4
interpreters, 3-4
invariants, loop invariants, 80

J
jumble program, 161-163, 217-219, 310-312

K
Kemeny, John, 3
KEY OFF/ON commands, 58, 224-226
key word ciphers, 387-390

keyboards
 event trapping, 224-226
 keypress test, INKEY$, 108-109, 144
KILL command, 355, 356
Koch snowflake, fractals, 330, 346-348
Kurtz, Thomas, 3

L
labels, subroutines, 206
language development, 2-5
LBOUND command, 251-252
LCASE$, 117
leaf node, binary tree, 320
LEFT$( ), leftmost character in string, 143-144, 176
LEN( ), length of string, 139-140
LET statement, 34-38, 235, 247
LINE command, 275-278, 281
line drawing, 275-278, 281, 333-334
line feeds, 54
line functions, 5
LINE INPUT command, 39, 140, 360
line numbers, programming in GW-BASIC automatic generation, AUTO command, 29
 GW-BASIC use, 27-28
 QBasic use, 24
 renumber, RENUM command, 29-30
line spacing, printing, 56
linking, 3
list boxes, dialog box, 17
LIST command, 28, 30
lists, 235-268
 $DYNAMIC metacommand, 243
 $STATIC metacommand, 243
 character limits, variables, FRE command, 240-242
 dynamic dimensioning, 240-243
 flagging lists, loops, 238-239
 length of list, dimension statements, DIM, 237-240
 metacommands, 242-243
 number of entries in list, VAL command, 238

BASICs for DOS

If you are intrigued with the possibilities of the programs included in *BASICs for DOS* (TAB Book No. 3769), you should definitely consider having the ready-to-run disk containing the examples. These files are guaranteed free of manufacturer's defects. (If you have any problems, return the disk within 30 days, and we'll send you a new one.) Not only will you save the time and effort of typing the data, but also the disk eliminates the possibility of errors in the data. Interested?

Available on either 5$1/4$″ or 3$1/2$″ disk requiring QBasic or QuickBASIC at $24.95, plus $2.50 shipping and handling.